"A true treasure trove! This volume brings to print the previously recorded but unpublished theology-of-mission lectures of John Howard Yoder. Yoder was a man of his times in terms of the issues he engaged. But he was a remarkable theologian who in these chapters brings timeless missiological insights to bear, from a believers church perspective, on the church's continuing engagement in mission."

Craig Van Gelder, professor of congregational mission, Luther Seminary

JOHN HOWARD YODER

THEOLOGY
of MISSION

A Believers Church Perspective

EDITED BY
GAYLE GERBER KOONTZ
AND ANDY ALEXIS-BAKER

IVP Academic

An imprint of InterVarsity Press
Downers Grove, Illinois

InterVarsity Press
P.O. Box 1400, Downers Grove, IL 60515-1426
World Wide Web: www.ivpress.com
Email: email@ivpress.com

©2014 by Gayle Gerber Koontz and Andy Alexis-Baker

InterVarsity Press® is the book-publishing division of InterVarsity Christian Fellowship/USA®, a movement of students and faculty active on campus at hundreds of universities, colleges and schools of nursing in the United States of America, and a member movement of the International Fellowship of Evangelical Students. For information about local and regional activities, write Public Relations Dept., InterVarsity Christian Fellowship/USA, 6400 Schroeder Rd., P.O. Box 7895, Madison, WI 53707-7895, or visit the IVCF website at www.intervarsity.org.

Scripture quotations, unless otherwise noted, are from the New Revised Standard Version of the Bible, copyright 1989 by the Division of Christian Education of the National Council of the Churches of Christ in the USA. Used by permission. All rights reserved.

The Afterword, "As You Go," by John Howard Yoder was originally published by Herald Press, ©1961. Used by permission.

Cover design: David Fassett
Interior design: Beth Hagenberg
Images: abstract painting: Ordered by Ron Waddams. Private Collection, The Bridgeman Art Library.
    Vintage labels: © aleksandar velasevic/iStockphoto

ISBN 978-0-8308-4033-5 (print)
ISBN 978-0-8308-7193-3 (digital)

Printed in the United States of America ∞

Library of Congress Cataloging-in-Publication Data
A catalog record for this book is available from the Library of Congress.

P	19	18	17	16	15	14	13	12	11	10	9	8	7	6	5	4	3	2	1
Y	30	29	28	27	26	25	24	23	22	21	20	19	18	17	16	15	14			

Contents

EDITORS' PREFACE 7
by Gayle Gerber Koontz and Andy Alexis-Baker

INTRODUCTION 13
John Howard Yoder's Mission Theology
Context and Contribution, by Wilbert R. Shenk

YODER'S INTRODUCTION TO THE TOPIC 35

1. The Prophets 49
Israel and the Nations

2. Jesus' Public Ministry and the Nations 62

3. The Great Commission and Acts. 75

4. The Ministry of Paul in Salvation History 91

5. Other Texts and the New Testament's Theology of Mission . 115

6. Mission and Systematic Theology 129

7. Church Types and Mission 145
A Radical Reformation Perspective

8. Pietist Perspective on Mission 161

9. The Church as Missionary 182

10. The Church as Responsible 193

11. The Church as Local. 211

12. The Church as Laity 228

13. Ministry in a Missionary Context 240

14. People Movements and the Free Church 251

15. Salvation Is Historical 265

16. Salvation Is for the World 289

17. Message and Medium 310
    Presence

18. Message and Medium 322
    Servanthood

19. Theology of Religions 338
    Particularity and Universalism

20. Radical Reformation Perspectives on Religion 352

21. Christianity and Other Faiths 362

22. The Missionary Challenge of Non-Non-Christian Faiths . . . 375

23. Judaism as a Non-Non-Christian Faith 386

AFTERWORD: AS YOU GO 399

APPENDIX 423

SUBJECT INDEX 427

NAME INDEX 431

SCRIPTURE INDEX 432

EDITORS' PREFACE

In the past half century many Christians have become skeptical about Christian missionary efforts. Western missionary organizations are struggling more than ever to meet their budgets as donations wane. Missiology programs have a hard time attracting North American students. Ask people what first comes to mind when they think of missions, and one is likely to hear words such as *colonialism*, *violence* and *disrespect*. All of this is understandable. For many years Christian mission was intertwined with the march of Western empires across the rest of the world. Missionaries were sometimes the first wave of a long process that undermined other cultures and peoples. Scholarly books document this process.[1] Popular fiction, such as Chinua Achebe's *Things Fall Apart*, vividly narrates the way Christian missionaries bulldozed their way through non-Western cultures and environments to bring people their Western understanding of God and the church. The good news was too often intertwined with the violent machines of conquest.

Anyone concerned about peace and justice has to wrestle with the legacy of missions in the long advance of Western imperialism. No ethicist or theologian from the Mennonite tradition can avoid it. Although John Howard Yoder is best known for his work on issues of war and peace, the topic of this book—theology of mission—preoccupied him

---

[1]For example, see Luis Rivera, *A Violent Evangelism: The Political and Religious Conquest of the Americas* (Louisville: Westminster John Knox, 1992) and Richard Fletcher, *The Barbarian Conversion: From Paganism to Christianity* (New York: Henry Holt, 1997).

as a scholar, teacher, missionary and ecumenical dialogue partner for most of his life. He sought to articulate a theological basis for a free church or believers church approach to Christian mission in which sharing the gospel message, disentangled from Western industry and militarism, could become a profound practice of Christian peacemaking, a vessel for God's saving work.

ABOUT THIS BOOK

From 1964 to 1983, Yoder taught a course on theology of mission at Associated Mennonite Biblical Seminaries (AMBS).[2] In 1973, the course sessions were recorded onto reel-to-reel audiocassettes, and then recorded again in 1976; however, we could find only nine lectures from the 1976 course. Yoder planned to have the lectures transcribed, printed and used for course material as he did with his lectures for the course "Christian Attitudes to War, Peace, and Revolution."[3] As Yoder said in a memo to Wilbert Shenk in February 1983: "We already have a taped transcription from the last time the course was offered six years ago. It is proposed that this be typed off and reproduced so the students can read it prior to class session. This would enable the same class format which I have used in two other subjects for years and would also facilitate the preparation of an informal publication such as had been done with two of my other courses."[4]

Like the war, peace and revolution lectures, Yoder thought that the theology of mission lectures might someday be edited for publication as a book. In one memo he wrote in 1973, Yoder hinted that he might want to revise the lectures for publication at a future date, saying an informal transcription would be "a separate question from whether a more polished version should be created which would be visible for commercial

---

[2]The seminary was renamed Anabaptist Mennonite Biblical Seminary in 2012. Yoder's course was titled "Theology of Mission," not "Theology of Missions." This reflected the shift in terminology beginning to be accepted in response to the conceptual development from the 1950s of *missio Dei* as the true source of missionary action. Yoder, however, neither refers to this term nor discusses the concept.

[3]Posthumously edited and published as John Howard Yoder, *Christian Attitudes to War, Peace and Revolution*, ed. Andy Alexis-Baker and Ted Koontz (Grand Rapids: Brazos Press, 2009).

[4]John H. Yoder to Wilbert Shenk, 4 February, 1983, John Howard Yoder Collection, Hist. Mss. 1–48, Box 181, Mennonite Church USA Archives, Goshen, IN.

publication either as a unit or in small segments."[5] He went on to indicate that if he could get a sabbatical from teaching he would be willing to work on writing a book on mission based on the lectures.

In 1984, Yoder left AMBS and began teaching full time at Notre Dame, where he no longer had the opportunity to teach about mission. The tapes were stored away in a cellar at AMBS and forgotten. In 2006 Gayle began teaching a course on Yoder's theological legacy. Several years later, when Wilbert Shenk was invited to class to reflect on Yoder's contributions to mission theology and practice, Shenk mentioned that some former students had told him how formative Yoder's course on theology of mission had been in their lives and ministry. Shenk thought there might be tapes of the lectures somewhere. After a number of months of fruitless searching, the director of the AMBS library finally discovered the "lost" tapes in a box in the basement of the seminary.

Immediately after finding the recordings, Andy set to work transcribing the lectures so the two of us could see whether they were worth publishing in book format. At the same time we contacted the Yoder family representative and the AMBS Institute of Mennonite Studies; both encouraged us to proceed with the project. Once we had transcripts in hand, we consulted with several missiologists and mission staff persons and were encouraged by the enthusiastic response we received. We set to work editing the chapters.

What We Have Done to the Text

We have edited the course lectures significantly. The transcriptions were, obviously, a replica of the spoken form in which Yoder delivered the lectures. Although we wanted to preserve the more informal, oral quality of Yoder's voice in the final manuscript, we repaired awkward or unclear syntax, changed passive to active voice where possible, attended to consistency in verb tense, and reorganized for clarity some of the material that we believe Yoder himself would have done in preparing a manuscript for publication. We also added a number of transitional sentences or phrases where we thought such things were needed in a written

---

[5]Ibid.

manuscript. Finally, we reduced the length of these lectures by carefully removing repetitious or unnecessary paragraphs, sentences, phrases or words and by removing most of the class discussion material that followed the lectures.

Because these chapters were delivered as lectures over several days, Yoder usually summarized the previous day's lecture to remind students what they had heard. If these summaries were done well, we sometimes used them in place of something he said in his lecture. Usually, however, these summaries were not needed and interrupted the flow of the written text; these we deleted. In addition, Yoder began many class sessions with prayer. We removed the prayers because in his course notes he clearly stated that he believed prayers should be spoken rather than written.

Since these were class lectures, we developed all the footnotes. Some of the footnotes emerged from questions in which a student wanted Yoder to clarify something he spoke about in a lecture. In general, when we felt material from class discussion should be included, we either added a footnote or incorporated the comments into the lecture itself. Occasionally Yoder included references or other side comments in his course lecture notes. We included most of those notations in footnotes at the appropriate places as well. When we thought it was needed, we added supplemental editorial footnotes.

We also added headings. Sometimes the course notes already had headings, so we simply added them to the text. Other times, we created them for ease of reading, based on Yoder's own wording in the lecture or something he wrote in his notes. Wherever possible we used his own words.

AUDIENCE

We envision several audiences for this book. Seminary students and professors who are studying the theology of Christian mission may find that this book gives a particularly helpful perspective on an Anabaptist view of mission from one of the leading ethicists of the twentieth century. This book could serve as a textbook in missiology or ecclesiology. In addition, those who have followed Yoder's work over the years will find this book to be some of his most striking unpublished material since *The Politics of Jesus*. Yoder is simply not as well-known as a missiologist as he is as an ethicist. This book demonstrates how Yoder's concerns for attentiveness to the biblical texts and their witness to God's work in Jesus, for believers church ecclesiology, for historical memory and particularity, for ecumenical relationships, and for faithful Christian discipleship that includes nonviolence as an ethical commitment, intersect and coalesce in his theology of mission. Yoder taught some version of this course for over twenty years, and as Wilbert Shenk shows in his introduction to this volume, Yoder had a long-term interest and involvement in mission work and theology.

ACKNOWLEDGEMENTS

Wilbert Shenk not only first mentioned the possible existence of the lecture tapes but later agreed to write the introduction to this book—a time-consuming research and writing project. He also helped facilitate discussions and coordinate our work with that of several other scholars anticipating work on Yoder and missions, including James Krabill, Neal Blough and Joon-Sik Park who are exploring how they might further contribute to thinking about Yoder as a missionary and mission theologian. We are especially grateful to Eileen Saner, director of library services at Anabaptist Mennonite Biblical Seminary, who did not give up until she found the 1973 reel-to-reel tapes that first set things in motion. Colleen McFadden at the Mennonite Church USA Archives in Goshen, Indiana, patiently pulled box after box from Yoder's collection and beyond that helped us search for lost material. Without her help we would not have found the nine uncataloged tapes from the 1976 course. Martha Yoder Maust, representative for the Yoder family concerning posthumous publications of John Howard Yoder's work, and the Institute of Mennonite Studies generously gave their blessing to this work. Finally, we want to honor the editors at InterVarsity Press who respectfully and competently shepherded us and this project through to completion.

We recognize that John Howard Yoder is a complex, controversial figure in theological scholarship. He is remembered as a brilliant theologian who helped many to engage the Christian gospel in fresh ways. In troubling contrast, he is remembered also for his long-term sexual harassment of women.

We recognize the tensions involved in presenting the past work of someone who so passionately called Christians to reconciling lives and yet used his position of power to abuse others. At the time of this publication, a new effort is underway in Yoder's ecclesial and teaching institutions to understand and speak truthfully about what happened while he was a part of these communities, with a view to bringing healing to those who still suffer from the consequences of his actions.

It is our hope that those in the academy and others studying Yoder's work will not dismiss the complexity of these issues but continue to evaluate, appropriate and criticize Yoder's work in the full context of his scholarly, ecclesial and personal legacy.

In this project we have tried to honestly and faithfully preserve the various nuances of Yoder's perspective on Christian mission, hoping that, as he might have said, it will point readers beyond himself toward the astonishing, reconciling mission of God through Jesus Christ.

Gayle Gerber Koontz
Andy Alexis-Baker
Elkhart, Indiana, May 2013

INTRODUCTION

John Howard Yoder's Mission Theology

Context and Contribution
by Wilbert R. Shenk

John Howard Yoder's missional engagements represent an important dimension of his personal commitment and public ministry, yet scholars have largely overlooked his contribution to mission thought and practice. His Anabaptist heritage, European theological education and practical engagements in mission leadership permitted him to develop a believers church understanding of mission that uniquely integrated biblical insights, historical perspectives, and commitment to Jesus' way of peace, ecclesiology and ethics.[1] His ideas often pointed to later developments in mission theology and continue to resonate strongly today.

During the years 1949–1969 Yoder was directly involved in mission program leadership. After 1969 he took on increased academic administrative and teaching duties, but he continued to contribute in both practical and theoretical ways through consulting with mission agencies and personnel, participating in conferences, and writing.

---

[1]Yoder began using "believers church" in the mid-1960s, likely to indicate a deeper ecclesiology than communicated by the traditional "free church" nomenclature, which tended to be tied primarily to the church/state relationship.

1949–1957: PROGRAM ADMINISTRATOR, MENNONITE CENTRAL COMMITTEE, EUROPE

Yoder left for Europe the spring of 1949. During World War II the Mennonite Central Committee (MCC) began sending volunteers to help war sufferers and refugees.[2] This effort grew greatly following the war's end. As part of this expanded program, Yoder was assigned to a children's home in Alsace, Eastern France. The other part of his commission was to promote Christian witness to peace, "a new sort of missionary work, one in which little has as yet been done, but which offers great opportunity for creative work."[3] Harold S. Bender, assistant secretary of MCC, defined Yoder's assignment in the context of urgent spiritual questions that Europeans were raising. How can people have hope when they have experienced two devastating wars resulting in widespread destruction and displacement all within the space of thirty years? The foundations of Western civilization were crumbling, and it was insufficient to be concerned only about physical and material needs.[4] The loss of hope had taken a heavy toll across Europe.

Yoder was soon introduced to the International Mennonite Peace Committee and later the Puiduix Theological Conference, an ecumenical group that met regularly to study "The Lordship of Christ over Church and State." He lived and worked among the French Mennonites, one of the oldest Mennonite conferences in Europe. At this time they were divided between traditionalists committed to preserving the past and younger people eager for a more vital and spiritually satisfying Christian faith. Yoder was asked to assist French Mennonites in reconnecting with their historical and theological heritage, hoping this might help overcome division and foster renewal of congregational life. It was characteristic of Yoder that he maintained close and fruitful relations with the French Mennonites, on the one hand, and quickly forged an extensive network of interchurch and ecumenical contacts on the other.

---

[2]For a fuller biography of Yoder's life see Mark Thiessen Nation, *John Howard Yoder* (Grand Rapids: Eerdmans, 2006), pp. 1-29.

[3]Harold S. Bender to John H. Yoder, August 10, 1948, f.6, b.42, Bender papers, Mennonite Church USA Archives, Goshen, IN.

[4]North American Mennonite mission executives visited Europe, July 29–August 14, 1950, to plan for the next phase of ministry. See Wilbert R. Shenk, *An Experiment in Interagency Cooperation* (Elkhart, IN: Council of International Ministries, 1986), pp. 2-4.

During this time Yoder and French Mennonite leaders were discussing possible collaboration between French and North American Mennonites in new mission initiatives in France. He reported to Mennonite Board of Missions (MBM) that "the social service program of MCC is incomplete if it does not lead" to evangelization. But he cautioned against any North American attempt to do evangelization alone.[5] His French interlocutors emphasized the importance of this being done collaboratively with French leadership.

Already in this early period Yoder was concerned with mission strategy and theology. The spring of 1954 he was part of a group hosted by the British Society of Friends. While in Britain he and others visited the Hutterian Wheathill Colony. He reflected on this visit in an article, "Discipleship as a Missionary Strategy," contrasting the lack of attraction of the typical church made up of nominal members with the evangelistic appeal of a congregation characterized by dynamic *koinōnia*.[6]

The summer of 1954 Yoder ended his service with MCC in order to study church history and theology full-time at the University of Basel. In early September, however, a major earthquake struck Orléansville, Algeria, killing a thousand people and causing widespread destruction.[7] For several years French Mennonites and American Mennonites working in France had been discussing possible new ministry in Francophone North Africa. André Trocmé, a French Reformed pastor and the secretary of the International Fellowship of Reconciliation, had an interest in Islam and wanted to find practical ways of engaging with Muslims. He encouraged Mennonites to act.

In response to this crisis Mennonite agencies agreed that MBM would send a team of builders to Algeria. French Mennonites also recruited volunteers and helped provide oversight. Yoder directed this

---

[5]John Howard Yoder to Mennonite Board of Missions, "Report on Mission Possibilities in France," 5 October, 1951, Mennonite Board of Missions, IV-18-10, Box 2, Mennonite Church USA Archives Goshen, IN. Special thanks to Colleen McFarland, archivist, who has been unfailingly helpful in locating materials.

[6]John Howard Yoder, "Discipleship as a Missionary Strategy," *Christian Ministry* 8 (January–March 1954): 26-31. Republished in John Howard Yoder, *Radical Christian Discipleship*, ed. John Nugent, Andy Alexis-Baker and Branson Parler (Harrisonburg, VA: Herald Press, 2012), pp. 163-70.

[7]Marian E. Hostetler, *Algeria: Where Mennonites and Muslims Met, 1955–1978* (Elkhart, IN: n.p., 2003), pp. 1-7.

emergency relief and reconstruction program, which lasted from 1955 to
1958. He reported later, "From the very beginning it was planned that a
permanent missionary or missionary couple be assigned to Algeria,
both to supervise the present work and to prepare for other kinds of
missionary activity."[8]

During these years Yoder continued to develop his thinking about
the mission of the church. He had become acquainted with Bishop
Lesslie Newbigin's work. Newbigin had served as a missionary to India
since 1936. In 1952 he delivered a lecture series in Glasgow, subsequently
published as *The Household of God,* a book widely acclaimed for its fresh
thinking about the nature and mission of the church. After both Newbigin and Yoder contributed essays to a symposium on "The Nature of
the Unity We Seek" in the Spring 1957 issue of *Religion in Life,* Yoder
wrote to Newbigin, "Ever since reading your *Household of God,* I've
been wanting to ask you some questions, but didn't feel I should bother
you. Now that I've been privileged to share with you the pages of *Religion in Life* I feel better acquainted and encouraged to take the liberty
of writing you."[9] Yoder raised probing questions about the nature of the
local church and the role of the episcopacy in principle and in practice
in the Church of South India. In January 1959 he received an apologetic
and long-delayed reply from Newbigin, now in transition from India to
the International Missionary Council in London, giving a hurried and
incomplete response to the issues Yoder raised. Newbigin remarked
twenty years later: "John Yoder wrote the most searching critique of my
book that I received from anyone. And I have not yet answered him."[10]

Between December 1957 and April 1958 *Gospel Herald* published Yoder's five-part series on "Islam's Special Challenge to Christian Missions."[11]

---

[8]John Howard Yoder, "Our First Three Years in Algeria," *Gospel Herald,* February 18, 1957, 159.
[9]John Howard Yoder to Lesslie Newbigin, 15 April, 1957, John Howard Yoder Collection, Hist.
    Mss. 1–48, Box 111/7, Mennonite Church USA Archives, Goshen, IN. See *Religion in Life* 26
    (Spring 1957) for Newbigin and Yoder essays on "The Nature of the Unity We Seek."
[10]Newbigin to Yoder, 2 January, 1959, John Howard Yoder Collection, Hist. Mss. 1–48, Box
    111/5, Mennonite Church USA Archives, Goshen, IN. Newbigin's later remark was to Wilbert
    Shenk in 1979.
[11]Title of the first installment published December 31, 1957, 1142-43. Subsequent installments
    were as follows: "Islam's Challenge to Mennonites," February 4, 1958, 110-11; "Our First Three
    Years in Algeria," April 18, 1958, 158-60, "The War in Algeria," March 18, 1958, 254-56; "Mis-
    sion and Material Aid in Algeria," April 1, 1958, 306-7.

He reviewed the work Mennonites had done in Algeria following the earthquake in 1954, using this program review as a teaching moment. Noting the violence that had marked Christian-Muslim relations over the centuries, he argued that churches that dissented from the Christendom tradition ought to approach Muslims in a noncoercive and compassionate spirit. In the 1950s a new generation of Christian scholarship on relations with Islam was being published. Missionary scholars of Islam, such as Kenneth Cragg, were producing profound, balanced and sensitive studies.[12] Yoder wrote with full awareness of this new stance and urged an appropriate approach to Christian ministry in Islamic environments.

1958–1969: ADMINISTRATOR AND CONSULTANT, MENNONITE BOARD OF MISSIONS

In 1958 Yoder joined the staff of Mennonite Board of Missions in Elkhart, Indiana, as assistant administrator in Overseas Ministries. Having served as director of the Algeria program, he already had a working relationship with the Board. J. D. Graber, who became the general secretary of the Board in 1944 following seventeen of years of missionary service in India, was a farsighted leader who stayed abreast of current missiological debate and strategic thinking. He encouraged Yoder to engage especially with issues of mission theology, ecumenical relations, and mission strategy and policy. Yoder also began teaching part-time at Goshen Biblical Seminary.

During the 1950s the "crisis of missions," symbolized by the "closing of China," cast a long shadow. Graber was impatient to put the colonial period behind and embrace the future with appropriate new strategies. Yoder fully sympathized and contributed to imagining a new mission future theologically, strategically and ecumenically.

Yoder's mission theology. Yoder's contribution to mission theology can be seen in relation to historical developments in the field. Mission studies had emerged in fits and starts in response to the growing mission movement in the nineteenth century. A century passed before anyone attempted a systematic and comprehensive treatment of Christian mis-

---

[12]See Kenneth Cragg, *The Call of the Minaret* (London: Oxford University Press, 1956).

sions. Gustav Warneck's pioneering five-volume *Evangelische Mission-slehre,* published in 1892–1903, laid the foundation for the academic study of missiology. Warneck aimed to provide a theory—not a theology—of mission faithful to the Christendom vision. For him it was axiomatic that Western theology was authoritative and, accordingly, would be the basis for teaching and training on all continents. At that time, seminaries and mission training schools offered no courses in mission theology. Indeed, the development of mission theology as a dedicated field in mission studies had to wait until the 1950s.[13] The further step beyond mission theology—that is, contextual theologies— emerged late in the twentieth century.

The International Missionary Council (IMC) played an indispensable role in the development of mission theology through a series of international assemblies between 1928 and 1958. In 1952 the IMC met at Willingen, Germany. Although the assembly failed to agree on a concluding statement, the assembly is regarded as a landmark event, a catalyst to future developments in mission theology.[14] In lieu of a conference consensus statement, Wilhelm Andersen prepared an essay, "Towards a Theology of Mission," which surveyed and summarized developments from 1910 to 1952.[15] Following Willingen, the IMC Commission on Theology of Mission sponsored research and writing projects that kept these developments on track. The 1958 IMC Assembly in Accra, Ghana, approved two new studies: Johannes Blauw, *The Missionary Nature of the Church*—which Yoder used as a textbook for his Theology of Mission course—and D. T. Niles, *Upon the Earth.*[16]

Yoder entered the conversation during this creative time in the devel-

---

[13]We lack a comprehensive history of these developments throughout the twentieth century, but see Gerald H. Anderson, *The Theology of Missions: 1928-1958* (Boston University, Ph.D. diss., 1960); Gerald H. Anderson, ed., *The Theology of the Christian Mission* (New York: McGraw Hill, 1961); and Rodger C. Bassham, *Mission Theology: 1948-1975* (Pasadena, CA: William Carey Library, 1979).

[14]See N. Goodall, ed., *Missions Under the Cross* (London: Edinburgh House Press, 1953). At the time Willingen was declared a failure. Lesslie Newbigin later observed: "Thirty years later one can look back and say that it was one of the most creative in the long series of missionary conferences." *Unfinished Agenda,* rev. ed. (Edinburgh: St. Andrew Press, 1993), p. 130.

[15]Wilhelm Andersen, *Towards a Theology of Mission,* International Missionary Council Research Pamphlet No. 2 (London: SCM Press, 1955).

[16]Both published in New York by McGraw-Hill, 1962. Niles' book was criticized, especially by evangelicals, for universalistic tendencies.

opment of mission theology. During the 1959–1960 winter term, Yoder gave a lecture at Drew University on "The Otherness of the Church."[17] This brief but fundamental statement of Yoder's theological vision holds together missiological, ecclesiological and ecumenical dimensions, as does his approach in this book. Each dimension is essential to the integrity of the whole. The church's mission is to witness to the lordship of Christ over all the powers, calling men and women to give their allegiance to Jesus Christ.

Yoder's Anabaptist perspective and his doctoral study with Karl Barth and Oscar Cullmann led him to trace deviations from the biblical norm over the centuries that resulted in a truncated ecclesiology. He saw the "Constantinian" shift that linked baptism and citizenship as paradigmatic for the accommodations and compromises the church made repeatedly with the powers—economic, political, social and moral. While the New Testament maintains a clear distinction between "church" and "world," between belief and unbelief, too often the church heeded other voices and succumbed to the temptation to blur the lines between them. The Constantinian variety of mission, notorious in its crusading and colonizing forms, contradicts the self-giving love graciously offered by Jesus the Messiah and his call to voluntarily follow him. Yoder argued that a compromised and confused church will not engage the world with the liberating good news that Jesus Christ is Lord. While the sixteenth-century Reformation made some gains, it reaffirmed the alliance between church and state, thus attempting to defend and maintain the territorial character of the church, an ecclesiology at odds with the New Testament.

In his 1967 keynote address to the Believers Church Conference at Louisville, Kentucky, Yoder extended and elaborated his critique of Christendom and proposed an alternative vision of the church as a missionary people in and to the world.[18] Two years later, without changing the substance, he rephrased his argument: "The Anabaptist vision calls for a Believers' Church. With reference to the *outside*, this means that

---

[17]John Howard Yoder, "The Otherness of the Church," *Drew Gateway* 30 (Spring 1960): 151-60. Republished in *The Royal Priesthood* (Grand Rapids: Eerdmans, 1994), pp. 220-30.

[18]John Howard Yoder, "A People in the World," in *The Concept of the Believers' Church*, ed. James Leo Garrett Jr. (Scottdale, PA: Herald Press, 1969), pp. 250-83. Republished in *Royal Priesthood*, pp. 65-101. See especially "Mission Compromised," pp. 89-101.

the church is by definition missionary . . . a church which invites [people] into fellowship. Men and women [are] not born into fellowship . . . [but] are invited to enter it by free adult decision in response to the proclamation of the love and suffering of God. On the *inside* the Believers' Church means that the adhesion of a member is [by] personal, responsible, conscious, mature, adult choice."[19] This church's inner life will be marked by uncoerced mutual care.

In the 1920s and 1930s IMC assemblies had grappled with the theme of ecclesiology and mission. Hendrik Kraemer's *The Christian Message in a Non-Christian World* (1938) marked the high point in this development. After World War II a critique of "ecclesiocentrism" emerged, led by missiologists such as J. C. Hoekendijk. By 1960 Hoekendijk was arguing that the church was only an instrument for bringing God's *shalom* to the world.

Based on a careful reading of Ephesians 3 and 2 Corinthians 5, Yoder offered a different understanding that required a "basic reorientation of our thinking about mission." He rejected the classical definition of the church, that is, the church is "present where the sacraments are administered and the word of God is preached to the faithful," because it sunders the essential relationship between church and mission. Further, to assert that church and mission are inseparable "is not simply an affirmative statement about the church; it is also a radical questioning of her missionary methods."[20]

Yoder was equally critical of evangelical and ecumenical Protestant views of ecclesiology and missions. Functionally, both operated from the same Christendom model: missions were initiatives taken independent of ecclesial responsibility. Lacking a robust ecclesiology, evangelicals were characterized by their preoccupation with personal piety, and they viewed mission as the work of a special society outside the church's purview. Mainstream Protestantism was associated with state churches, which had large nominal memberships; since mission was not integral to its ecclesiology, the mission-minded among its membership formed independent mission societies.

---

[19]John Howard Yoder, "Anabaptist Vision and Mennonite Reality," in *Consultation on Anabaptist Mennonite Theology,* ed. A. J. Klassen (Fresno, CA: Council of Mennonite Seminaries, 1970), p. 4.
[20]Ibid., p. 32.

In addition to his focus on ecclesiology, Yoder brought another dimension to mission theology from his study of Scripture—a foundation for contextuality in mission. Observing that "in a very coarse-grained way we can say that the New Testament is the document of a transition made by a message-bearing community from one world to another," he cited five texts—John 1:1-14, Philippians 2:5-11, Colossians 1:15-23, Hebrews 1–2 and Revelation 4:1–5:5—that show apostolic writers, entirely independent of one another, resorting to a common pattern of response to an alien worldview.[21] For example, the writers were completely familiar with the language and thought of the host culture. However, they did not fit Jesus and his message into the ready-made categories of the host culture but presented Jesus as transcendent Lord. Ostensibly, Yoder's purpose was to address the perplexing question of religious plurality; but in the process he provided a theological foundation for contextualization that has generally been lacking in missiological discussion.

Mission and unity. In 1961 the International Missionary Council (IMC) was formally integrated into the World Council of Churches (WCC), and its work continued as the Division (later Commission) on World Mission and Evangelism. That year Yoder was named a member of the new division's subcommission on theology of mission, and he participated in its July 1–10 meeting at the Ecumenical Institute, Bossey, Switzerland.[22] The integration of the IMC into the WCC, however, had not been easy. The proposal for integration had stirred intense debate that was carried on in study papers, committee meetings, correspondence and periodicals for ten years. While the IMC Assembly in Accra, Ghana, approved the proposed integration in 1958, dissatisfaction with this decision continued to fester.

Historically, the IMC had attracted a wide spectrum of Protestants and Anglicans. Conservative evangelicals who otherwise remained aloof to church union movements had been longtime members of IMC. Indeed, the modern mission movement was essentially an evangelical

---

[21]John Howard Yoder, *The Priestly Kingdom* (Notre Dame, IN: University of Notre Dame Press, 1984), pp. 49-53.

[22]This was one of several WCC commissions of which he was either a member or theological adviser over the next thirty years.

initiative for it was the evangelical wings of the major churches that joined with believers church people in sponsoring Protestant missions. The membership of the IMC reflected this fact. Both ecumenical and evangelical Protestants had argued against IMC-WCC integration precisely on the grounds that it would inevitably alienate a significant part of the Protestant missionary movement that hitherto had worked harmoniously with IMC and Christian Councils across the world.

This experience stimulated not only Yoder's theological writing but also his behind-the-scenes relationship building among evangelical and mainline Protestant mission leaders.[23] Further, it influenced his approach to Mennonite mission strategy.

Yoder and mission strategy. World War II was a watershed event for missions. It hastened the collapse of the old system of Western domination and with it the mission model of the previous 150 years. Christian missions were at an epochal crossroads. Donald McGavran—born to missionary parents in India and himself a missionary to India from 1924 to 1954—published his seminal work *The Bridges of God* in 1955. McGavran emerged as a leading strategic thinker with his axiom that the key to church growth was to pay attention to the sociocultural bridges by which people groups could be reached. He argued that church growth is the *sine qua non* of mission effectiveness.

Yoder took a keen interest in the challenge of exploring mission strategies appropriate in the emerging environment. He acknowledged the achievement of the modern mission movement and noted that: "Church historians are already recognizing the 'Foreign Missions Movement' as probably the most significant development in church history since the Reformation."[24] Yet Christian missions were defined by what Sri Lankan Christian leader D. T. Niles called the "Westerity of the missionary base."[25] Although missionaries were not direct agents of colonialism, modern missions could not be separated from "a still broader cultural and economic tide."[26] The modern mission model was borrowed directly

---

[23]On this, see Gayle Gerber Koontz, "Unity with Integrity," in *Radical Ecumenicity*, ed. John Nugent (Abilene, TX: Abilene Christian Unity Press, 2010), pp. 57-84.
[24]John Howard Yoder, "Christian Missions at the End," *Christian Living* 8 (August 1961): 12.
[25]D. T. Niles, *Upon the Earth*, p. 195.
[26]Yoder, "Christian Missions at the End," p. 12.

from the secular realm: like colonial officials who administered Western colonies across the world, the missionary was sent from the West, supported financially from the West, and following service would return to the West. This era was now ending. Newly independent countries were taking steps to restrict or even curtail the work of foreign missionaries.

Yoder put the modern mission movement in historical perspective by viewing it within the whole of Christian experience. For most of the past nineteen centuries the expansion of the church happened through the migration of committed lay Christians: families or groups went to new regions where they settled, earned their livelihood and cast their lot with their adopted community.[27] No mission society provided financial and moral support, and there were no fixed length of terms or provision for returning home to retire. In this respect, the modern mission movement is a historical anomaly. In searching for new strategies in the late twentieth century, earlier historical patterns can be instructive.

In 1961 Yoder published a pamphlet titled *As You Go: The Old Mission in a New Day*. His textual premise was the familiar Matthew 28:19, which he retranslated: "As you are going. . . . " The thrust of the Great Commission is not finding new geography but being alert to needs and opportunities for witness wherever the Christian is. Yoder grounded his presentation in historical experience. From this standpoint the modern professional missionary does not represent the whole of Christian history. On the contrary,

> [What] we call the "foreign missionary movement" is a relatively recent phenomenon in the history of the church, beginning about 1800. . . . It would be wrong to limit our thinking about the future of missions to one particular concept. . . . Throughout the history of God's people, the Gospel has been brought to new parts of the world primarily by migration of financially independent Christians . . . [who] were dispersed, sometimes because of commercial or family interests, more often because of persecution. Where they went, they took their faith with them, and new Christian cells were planted.[28]

---

[27]Yoder makes the same arguments more succinctly in, "After Foreign Missions—What?" *Christianity Today* 6 (March 30, 1961): 12-13.

[28]John Howard Yoder, *As You Go*, Focal Pamphlet No. 5 (Scottdale, PA: Herald Press, 1961), pp. 11-12. See afterword below, p. 404. Subsequent references to afterword in parentheses.

Yoder called for cadres of people ready to experiment and take risks in order to discover fresh patterns of missionary obedience. Rather than understanding Christian mission as a program, this was a challenge to venture forth as witnesses of the gospel in neglected places, both at home and across the world. This bold, fresh strategic thinking struck a responsive chord with younger people.

J. D. Graber sent a copy of the pamphlet to McGavran for evaluation and comment. McGavran responded with a five-page review. He commented that "'migration evangelism' is a terrifically appealing idea," observing that this was the way Islam was spreading.[29] McGavran's concern, however, was that a mission board be mindful of the tendencies of migrant communities to become insular and, accordingly, take steps to insure that the main goal be church planting.

Yoder's proposal attracted considerable interest and resulted in sustained experiments in Japan, Brazil and Bolivia. But in the postcolonial world, except for countries of North and South America and Europe, migration with a view to obtaining citizenship has been virtually impossible.[30]

In addition to his fresh proposals about mission by migration, Yoder was deeply involved in strategic thinking about the role of Western missions and the churches they planted, in relation to African Indigenous Churches (AICs).[31] Shortly before Yoder joined MBM administrative staff in 1958, a group of churches in Nigeria contacted the Board, asking to be recognized as Mennonites. After some confusion it gradually became clear that longstanding Western mission policies had produced extensive unintended consequences, that is, hundreds of indigenous churches had sprung up across Africa. One such group in Southeastern Nigeria learned about Mennonites through an international radio broadcast. They re-

---

[29]J. D. Graber to D. McGavran, 9 November, 1961; D. McGavran to J. D. Graber, 12 December, 1961, Mennonite Board of Missions, IV-18-13-02/1956-1965, Box 8/35, Mennonite Church USA Archives: Goshen, IN.

[30]The nearest anyone came to writing up an evaluation of these "experiments" was Marvin J. Miller, *The Case for a Tentmaking Ministry* (Elkhart, IN: Mennonite Board of Missions, 1978). One Mennonite missionary couple tried for 30 years to get citizenship in India, to no avail.

[31]Descriptors for this phenomenon have evolved: "breakaway churches," "separatist churches," African Independent Churches, African Initiated Churches, and, recently, African Indigenous Churches. Changing terminology reflects growing understanding and respect on the part of scholars and mission-related churches. The earlier terms are now regarded as pejorative. Preferred usage now is the acronym AIC.

quested recognition and resources from MBM. The crucial question was: what kind of relationship was appropriate? Yoder was assigned administrative responsibility for this new venture. He helped shape the strategy and theological rationale for a new kind of missional partnership.[32]

In late 1959 MBM sent Edwin and Irene Weaver, who had already served in India for two decades, to Nigeria to get acquainted with these churches and determine what kind of cooperation might be appropriate.[33] The Weavers soon discovered that southeastern Nigeria could not be considered an "unworked" mission field. Indeed, major Western denominations—Roman Catholic, Anglican, Methodist, Presbyterian and the independent Qua Iboe Mission—had sponsored missions to this region since the late 1800s and had well-established churches, schools, hospitals and clinics throughout the region. A second group of Protestant missions, comprised of those who had arrived more recently, rejected the comity system followed by the older Protestant missions. In addition, there were numerous African indigenous churches interspersed among the "mission" churches. Relations between the mission churches and the indigenous churches were hostile. Most of the senior missionaries bluntly advised the Weavers to leave. A few felt the situation ought to be addressed and urged the Weavers to stay.

Shortly after arriving, Edwin Weaver reported to Yoder some of his and his wife's first impressions. In short, they felt overwhelmed. Responding to Weaver's "stimulating and disquieting letter," Yoder offered what proved to be prescient counsel: "this is more an ecumenical than a missionary task, if those two concepts can be separated." He counseled that the main task is to "decrease the confusion."[34] Before Weaver had received Yoder's December 18, 1959, reply he sent a sequel.[35] Soon after

---

[32]Wilbert R. Shenk, "Go Slow Through Uyo," in *Fullness of Life for All*, ed. Inus Daneel et al. (Amsterdam: Rodopi, 2003), pp. 329-40; David A. Shank, "John Howard Yoder, Strategist," *Mission Focus: Annual* Review 15 (2010): 195-217.

[33]See the firsthand account by Edwin and Irene Weaver, *The Uyo Story* (Elkhart, IN: Mennonite Board of Missions, 1970).

[34]Edwin I. Weaver to Yoder, 9 December, 1959; Yoder to Weaver, 18 December, 1959, both in E. Weaver 1959, Mennonite Board of Missions, IV-18-13, Mennonite Church USA Archives, Goshen, IN.

[35]Weaver to Yoder, 14 December, 1959, E. Weaver 1959, Mennonite Board of Missions, IV-18-13, Mennonite Church USA Archives, Goshen, IN.

sending the first letter, the Weavers had received books they had shipped to Nigeria. Weaver reported: "The first I got out to read again was your *The Ecumenical Movement and the Faithful Church*. I was very impressed. I didn't lay it aside until I had completed it. Your booklet has applications and implications for us here." Yoder's strategic response to Nigeria was solidly based in his theory of ecumenical relations. But the search for a viable strategy went on for many months.

Providentially, the Weavers met Harold W. Turner at a guesthouse in Lagos early in 1961. Turner, a lecturer in theology at Fourah Bay College, Sierra Leone, was in Nigeria researching the origins and development of the Church of the Lord (Aladura), an AIC he first encountered in Sierra Leone in 1957. He was one of the few scholars doing scientific research of a phenomenon widespread in Africa but held at arm's length by mission churches.[36]

Turner was convinced that Christian missions had blundered in relation to these churches. He hypothesized that AICs emerged in reaction to mission churches: they were attracted to the Christian gospel, but they rejected the noncontextual forms mission churches imposed, their inability to engage the African worldview, and the lack of scope for African leadership.[37] He urged the Weavers to continue working in a dialogical mode with these churches in southeastern Nigeria. The Weavers kept Yoder informed of the contacts they were making, especially with people like Turner, who had significant expertise to offer specific to their situation. Yoder read Turner's insightful articles. And Turner briefed Yoder on research under way by various scholars working in West Africa.[38]

In the spring of 1962 Yoder visited Nigeria. He affirmed the Weavers in developing a multifaceted strategy, with dialogue as the essential

---

[36]Weaver sent Yoder Turner's manuscript, later published as "African Prophet Movements," *Hibbert Journal* 41:3 (1963): 112-16. Turner was working on his 2-volume study: *African Independent Church* (Oxford: Clarendon Press, 1967). A few other publications had appeared, for example, Bengt Sundkler, *Bantu Prophets in South Africa*, 2nd ed. (London: Oxford University Press, 1960).

[37]See Harold W. Turner, "Religious Movements in Primal (or Tribal) Societies," *Mission Focus* 9 (September 1981): 45-55, summarizing 25 years of research, reflection and writing.

[38]Yoder to Turner, 2 March, 1962; Turner to Yoder, 11 March, 1962; Yoder to Turner, 23 November, 1962; Turner to Yoder, 30 November, 1962; all in E. and I. Weaver, 1960-65, Mennonite Board of Missions, IV-18-13, Mennonite Church USA Archives: Goshen, IN.

method for working toward reconciliation and mutual respect among various Christian groups. With the backing of Church of Scotland senior missionary R. M. Macdonald for the proposed initiative, all the mission churches in the region embraced this proposal. One outcome was a program of theological education geared to the needs of the AICs with the mission churches providing teaching staff. Tragically, the Biafran War (1967–1970) forced all missionary staff to withdraw, and the program collapsed.

One of Edwin Weaver's initiatives had been to foster and facilitate dialogue between the various ecclesial streams in southeastern Nigeria by holding a series of meetings in which the mainline and indigenous churches met for dialogue. As a part of this process, Weaver collected various documents—official statements, draft articles, brief descriptive histories of some of the groups, and statements of faith, doctrine and practice by various AICs—that by 1965 numbered more than fifty items.

In a memorandum Yoder recorded some of his ruminations on what this interchurch study process represented in *ecumenical* and *ecclesiological* terms.[39] From the beginning of the Nigerian venture, he was uneasy about the inherent tendency of the mainline churches to assume that they represented the normative vision of the church.[40] From a believers church perspective, he was alert to any hint on their part that the AICs would have proved their respectability when they accepted the "organized unity and the pattern of ministry . . . according to traditional standards of the older missions." The Yoder-Turner position argued that the indigenous churches be granted full respect and accepted on their own terms, rather than be subjected to vetting by the structures and processes of the established mission churches.

In 1969, Mennonite Board of Missions agreed to assist the Church of the Lord (Aladura) in establishing a theological college. The Theological Education Fund provided annual subsidies for capital costs while MBM

---

[39]Yoder to Shenk, memo, 21 September, 1965, Edwin Weaver Papers: Independent Churches, Yoder Historical Manuscripts 1–48, Box 85/37, Mennonite Church USA Archives: Goshen, IN.
[40]Note Yoder's sharp comment upon reading the response of the secretary of the Nigeria Council of Churches to Weaver's representation on behalf of the AICs: "Mr. Wood seems to have forgotten the ecumenical dimension of his office." Yoder to Weaver, 15 January, 1960, Mennonite Board of Missions, IV-18-13, Mennonite Church USA Archives: Goshen, IN.

supplied and paid two teachers.[41] In the process of setting forth MBM's understanding of cooperation with the Church of the Lord (Aladura), Yoder drafted a seven-page statement that included a rationale for Mennonite cooperation with AICs.[42] The essential elements of Yoder's theological and theoretical framework for his strategic thinking in relation to the church's mission in West Africa, first expressed in the 1958 publication *The Ecumenical Movement and the Faithful Church*, were further developed in the essay "The Nature of the Unity We Seek."[43] The missionary shape of the church and the call for Christian unity were interwoven in Yoder's theology and practice of mission.

1970S–1980S: THEOLOGY PROFESSOR AND MENTOR

By the 1970s renewal movements were calling insistently for recovery of the "whole" gospel: Christian base communities in Latin America, liberation theologies, Christian communes and liberation movements such as the antiapartheid campaign in South Africa—all were seeking to address profound ethical challenges with the resources of the gospel. During those years Yoder mentored through his writings and relationships a number of young evangelicals in their "radical" attempts to connect mission theology and ethics. The Yoder family spent the 1970–1971 academic year in Buenos Aires, Argentina. He lectured in seminaries and developed a network of relationships, especially among emerging young evangelical theologians. He encouraged them to challenge current mission theology and strategy.[44] In the United States, he served as a resource to Evangelicals for Social Action and to the Sojourners community and magazine.

---

[41]The Theological Education Fund was established in 1957 by the IMC. Under the WCC's Commission on World Mission and Evangelism, it continued providing grants to seminaries in Asia, Africa and Latin America for upgrading theological education: updating libraries, providing scholarships for advanced training of faculty and offering students stipends to study in seminaries and Bible schools in their own countries.

[42]Yoder, to W. R. Shenk, memo: Policy of Mennonite Missions and Service Agencies Toward African Independent Churches, 14 February, 1970, Mennonite Board of Missions, IV-18-13, Mennonite Church USA Archives: Goshen, IN.

[43]John Howard Yoder, *The Ecumenical Movement and the Faithful Church* (Scottdale, PA: Mennonite Publishing House, 1958) and "The Nature of the Unity We Seek: A Historic Free Church View," in *The Royal Priesthood*, pp. 221-30.

[44]See John Howard Yoder, *Revolutionary Christianity: The 1966 South American Lectures*, ed. Paul Martens, Mark Thiessen Nation, Matthew Porter and Myles Werntz (Eugene, OR: Cascade, 2011).

At the first International Congress on World Evangelization, Yoder played a behind-the-scenes role advising and encouraging young theologians. Sponsored by the Billy Graham Evangelistic Association and held at Lausanne, Switzerland July 16–25, 1974, this event brought together more than three thousand delegates and observers. Two of the plenary speakers, C. René Padilla and Samuel Escobar, whom Yoder had met in Latin America, represented a new generation of evangelicals in Latin America. They called for a vision of "radical discipleship" and commitment to a gospel that embraced all of human reality. Contesting the old dichotomy between evangelization and social action, they challenged the evangelical status quo.

During the Congress these "radical evangelicals" caucused in opposition to the official statement, the Lausanne Covenant. Yoder was one of several of their counselors. They argued that the Congress ought to take a more radical position on the issues of poverty and injustice that blighted the lives of millions of people in the less developed countries. They declined to sign the Lausanne Covenant, insisting that it was too passive in the face of the desperate conditions in Latin America, Africa and Asia.[45] Following the Lausanne gathering this group published *The New Face of Evangelicalism: An International Symposium on the Lausanne Covenant*, in which they developed their position in fifteen chapters of commentary.[46]

Yoder and the church-growth debate. In 1965, Donald McGavran became founding dean of the School of World Mission and Institute of Church Growth at Fuller Theological Seminary. His ideas were widely embraced among evangelical mission agencies that began sending their mid-career missionaries for retooling under McGavran's tutelage. McGavran argued that church growth was the key indicator of mission effectiveness. He amassed case studies from around the world of how

---

[45]Congress leaders tried to accommodate the group. The "radical evangelicals" drafted a statement, "Theology and Implications of Radical Discipleship," which was included in the official congress proceedings. See J. D. Douglas, ed., *Let the Earth Hear His Voice* (Minneapolis: World Wide Publications, 1975), pp. 1294-95.

[46]C. René Padilla, ed. *The New Face of Evangelicalism: An International Symposium on the Lausanne Covenant* (Downers Grove, IL: InterVarsity Press, 1976). Senior Western evangelical leaders insisted this diverted attention from evangelism, "the highest priority." This debate would continue well into the 1980s.

churches grew or stagnated and coined special vocabulary to describe his ideas. The key to McGavran's theory was the homogeneous unit principle: "[People] like to become Christians without crossing racial, linguistic or class barriers."[47] But could this claim, based solely on empirical evidence, be validated on biblical and theological grounds?

While McGavran's ideas were attracting an enthusiastic following, others were not persuaded.[48] The Civil Rights movement in the United States was gaining in strength. Asians, Africans and Latin Americans were alarmed by a mission strategy that could readily be used to give legitimacy to continuing unjust divisions in societies based on caste, class and ethnic differences. These issues were especially problematic for missiologists in situations such as apartheid South Africa. While McGavran vigorously decried these criticisms, people remained uneasy. He was a pragmatic strategist, not a theologian.

In February 1973, the Mennonite Missionary Study Fellowship met to study "The Challenge of Church Growth." The purpose was to evaluate the strengths and weaknesses of McGavran's theory and offer constructive critique. Yoder gave the major paper, "Church Growth Issues in Theological Perspective." He approached his topic carefully and respectfully. Much of his critique centered on McGavran's idiosyncratic definitions of key terms in Matthew 28:19-20: *discipling* and *perfecting*. Yoder argued that McGavran's use of the Great Commission could not be supported exegetically.[49] The papers presented at the consultation were subsequently published as a small book.[50]

Yoder was invited to a consultation four years later on the homoge-

---

[47]Donald McGavran, *Understanding Church Growth*, 2nd ed. (Grand Rapids: Eerdmans, 1980), p. 223. McGavran first formulated and introduced his insights in *The Bridges of God* (London: World Dominion Press, 1955).

[48]Already in 1962 Victor Hayward, CWME Study Department (WCC), confided to Yoder that he was interested in McGavran's ideas but was meeting considerable criticism. Victor Hayward to John Howard Yoder, 14 November, 1962, John Howard Yoder Historical Mss. 1–48, Box 85/37, Mennonite Church USA Archives: Goshen, IN. Subsequently, Hayward did convene the Iberville (Quebec) Consultation on Church Growth, which issued the "Iberville Statement on Church Growth." But it did not quell the disquiet.

[49]See David Bosch, "The Structure of Mission: An Exposition of Matthew 16–20," in *Exploring Church Growth*, ed. Wilbert R. Shenk (Grand Rapids: Eerdmans, 1983), pp. 218-48, a magisterial study showing that McGavran's interpretation was indefensible on exegetical grounds.

[50]Wilbert R. Shenk, ed., *The Challenge of Church Growth* (Scottdale, PA: Herald Press, 1973).

neous unit principle, a consultation sponsored by the Lausanne Theology and Education group chaired by John Stott. Thirty-five people gathered in Pasadena, California, May 31–June 2, 1977. Five faculty members of Fuller's School of World Mission prepared papers on methodological, anthropological, historical, ethical and theological dimensions of the homogenous principle. Five scholars prepared written responses to the position papers and another twenty-five persons participated in the discussion. Yoder responded to Peter Wagner's paper, "How Ethical Is the Homogeneous Unit Principle?" but Yoder's response was never published.[51]

Yoder's last contribution to the church growth debate was an essay, "The Social Shape of the Gospel," in *Exploring Church Growth*. This makes clear the substantial difference in ecclesiological vision that stood between McGavran and Wagner, on one side, and Yoder and C. René Padilla, among numerous other thinkers, on the other.[52] But the ground was shifting. In a 1986 reflection from an insider's vantage point, Arthur F. Glasser acknowledged that interaction with critics had changed the church growth movement in important ways. He noted that "[McGavran] no longer uses Homogenous Unit Principle in his writings but refers instead to the 'mosaic of peoples.'"[53]

Ethics and missionary practice. In his speaking and writing over the years Yoder called American missionaries to deeper cultural and ethical awareness. Because most American missionaries were reared in a religious culture that prescribed appropriate behavior, they were inexperienced in ethical discernment. The way one behaved was not a conse-

---

[51]See consultation statement, "The Pasadena Statement on the Homogeneous Unit Principle," Lausanne Occasional Papers No. 1, London: Lausanne Committee for World Evangelization and World Evangelical Fellowship, 1977, and *Making Christ Known*, ed. John Stott (Grand Rapids: Eerdmans, 1996), pp. 57-72. Wagner's paper was published in *Occasional Bulletin* 2:1 (1978): 12-19. Yoder's response, "The Homogenous Unit Concept in Ethical Perspective," is available in the conference compendium held in the Fuller Theological Seminary Library and in the John Howard Yoder Digital Library hosted in Elkhart County, Indiana, http://replica .palni.edu/cdm/landingpage/collection/p15705coll18.

[52]John Howard Yoder, "The Social Shape of the Gospel," in *Exploring Church Growth*, ed. Wilbert R. Shenk (Grand Rapids: Eerdmans, 1983), pp. 277-84. Padilla's response to one of the Fuller faculty papers was also published in this collection: C. René Padilla, "The Unity of the Church," in ibid., pp. 285-303.

[53]Arthur F. Glasser, "Church Growth at Fuller," *Missiology* 14, no. 4 (October 1986): 415.

quence of conversion but of following the practices of one's "Christian" culture. Missionaries who had never questioned the common dualism between evangelism and social action were unprepared to come to terms with the "whole gospel" vision that emerged globally in the 1970s.

In June 1983 Yoder addressed the annual meeting of the Association of Professors of Mission on "Ethical Issues for Training for Cross-Cultural Missions." He argued that American evangelical missionaries operate with binary patterns: "Certain components of the Anglo-Saxon evangelical experience have predisposed many of us, and many of those who come to our schools, to trust binary patterns of analysis which specifically tend to relegate matters of ethical concern to secondary or derivative status."[54] Examples include: nominal versus real Christianity, outer versus inner, formal versus existential, and spiritual versus material. These pairs are separated into *prior* and *secondary*. Obviously, a secondary item is less important than what is prior. Yoder observed that the ethical is "routinely in the second category."[55]

Yoder believed it was inexcusable in crosscultural situations to treat ethical thinking as a "secondary" matter to be set aside either by habit of mind or by arbitrary decision. Training missionaries for crosscultural ministry must include attending to ethics, for the ethical vision of Jesus can only be understood as constitutive of the gospel. In the life, ministry, death and resurrection of Jesus the Messiah, we have seen and received the whole gospel.

Yoder also pressed the indissoluble link between ethics and evangelization in his ecumenical interactions. The theme of the Sixth Assembly of the WCC, in Vancouver, B.C., July 24–August 10, 1983, was "Jesus Christ—the Life of the World," the evangelistic task of the church. In a compelling statement he asserted that evangelization is the test of our ethical vocation. Citing John 17 and the Sermon on the Mount, he stressed the integral relationship between visible unity and the distinctive lifestyle of discipleship—salt, light, city on a hill. Jesus connects this to the practice of enemy love as displayed supremely in God's action.

---

[54]John Howard Yoder, "The Experiential Etiology of Evangelical Dualism," *Missiology* 11, no. 4 (October 1983): 449.
[55]Ibid., p. 451.

Jesus Christ made peace between hostile peoples by the blood of his cross (Eph 2) and gave us the ministry of reconciliation.[56] Ethics and mission cannot be separated.

CONTINUING CHALLENGES OF YODER'S MISSION THOUGHT

Yoder consistently worked against the grain of conventional, taken-for-granted renderings of biblical interpretation, church history and contemporary practice. From his radically Christocentric focus, he called fellow pilgrims to deeper and more complete obedience to our crucified and reigning Messiah. As demonstrated in the early chapters of this book, he insisted on a rigorous reading and openness to the scriptural text. He was ever alert to the ways Christians in every age have over-adapted to their culture, thereby compromising their witness. Protestants have clustered into ecumenical and evangelical blocs with each group clinging to a lopsided gospel. The underlying issue, generally unacknowledged and unaddressed, is the Christendom ecclesiology that forces a choice between a church without mission and a mission without church. These insights and commitments are representative of the challenges Yoder's mission thought continues to pose today.

---

[56]John Howard Yoder, "A Comment: Evangelization Is the Test of Our Ethical Vocation," *International Review of Mission* 72 (1983): 630.

Yoder's Introduction
to the Topic

W hat is the target and function of this work? The title could be written more than one way, so we need to meditate on what *Theology of Mission* does and does not mean.[1]

THEOLOGY AND THE MISSIONARY TASK

We could focus on the place of *theology* as a discipline related to the missionary task. That is to say that the missionary witness in a new cultural context, as a church comes into being, will face questions not answered elsewhere. To face those new questions there will have to be a theologizing process: distinguishing between right and wrong adaptations to the new host culture; checking translation of the Scriptures to insure clarity and accuracy. In a new church context there will need to be culturally appropriate articulations for catechism, church order and leadership training.

In that new situation interchurch relations will pose new challenges. The missionary representatives of earlier Christianity will have brought with them their denominational or other identities, but there will be a new theological passing on and relating of traditions in the host country.

---

[1][Compare David J. Bosch, *Transforming Mission* (Maryknoll, NY: Orbis, 1991), pp. 1-11; J. A. B. Jongeneel, "Mission Theology in the Twentieth Century," in *Dictionary of Mission Theology*, ed. John Corrie (Nottingham: Inter-Varsity Press, 2007), pp. 237-44; C. E. Van Engen, "Mission, Theology of," in *Global Dictionary of Theology*, ed. W. A. Dyrness and V.-M. Kärkkäinen (Downers Grove, IL: InterVarsity Press, 2008), pp. 550-62. —Ed.]

The question will arise as to what kind of theologian or what kind of theologizing process is needed to help the church in its missionary calling. That would be important, and we cannot avoid touching on the theological process itself, but that is not the focus of this book.

The topic is narrower, with several sides. One is to ask, what issues in theology are especially important for the light they throw on the missionary nature of the church? It might be that there are things Western theologians have debated at great length that throw no light on the church as missionary. We do not have to deal with those subjects. Other issues subject to theological debate may become more meaningful or important when we think of the church in the missionary mood rather than the church as established.

Second, what aspects of the missionary enterprise call for theological analysis and illumination? What does it mean for somebody to send missionaries or to go as missionaries? What does it mean to be a sending church or a receiving church?

Finally, if there is such a thing as the church's missionary enterprise, a notion that developed in Christendom, does that reality or mandate throw any corrective light on or does it complement the nonmissionary theology of the nonmissionary churches of the West? Does the missionary concern offer a new perspective on Western theology?

THEOLOGIANS AND THE MISSIONARY TASK

One of the major figures in the field of mission theology, Johannes Hoekendijk, wrote that theologians "have been in the past among the most unconquerable saboteurs of evangelism."[2] By this he meant that the faculties of theology in European universities and the state-church structures have generally not been supportive of, or have even attacked, critiqued or undercut concern for what Hoekendijk called "evangelism" but could also be called "mission." What are the reasons for that? Doing theology as an educational enterprise in Western Europe was in a nonmissionary context. Europe thought of itself as a Christian culture, and whatever could be called "missions" belonged in some other part of the

---

[2][Johannes Hoekendijk, "The Call to Evangelism," *International Review of Mission* 39 (1950): 162. —Ed.]

world. Since the context itself did not raise the missionary question, it was natural that theology did not deal with it. If you look through European systematic or practical theology texts, the theme of mission is absent in most of the texts and even in the presuppositions with which most of the texts were written.

Part of the reason university theologians were hard on the missionary enterprise was that the wrong kinds of people were interested in it. Mission work was usually done by Pietists and separatists, people who were not representative of the established churches and their theological practice. Moreover, that work was often done by simple people who not only had minority positions but often did not think about those positions very carefully.

In European Christianity, the agencies that carried out the sending process were not the church. The church was a sociological agency responsible for governing pastors and placing them in pulpits and handling the denomination's internal affairs in any given country. The organizations that sent missionaries were missionary societies that were created spontaneously by voluntary membership who then created their own structures. A theologian in a European Protestant university (or an American Ivy League university) did not feel that the missionary enterprise was something for which his or her church was responsible. Theology had to do with domestic church management.

Early in the twentieth century, this classic polarity between the missionary and theologian shifted partly because of the modern ecumenical movement that arose out of the missionary movement's success. The missionary movement was an agent of developing churches around the world. When it became visible that there was a worldwide Christian community that took expression in different forms in interchurch relations, Western academic theology could no longer avoid the fact that the worldwide church must be accepted, related to and given meaning. The fact that it is a subject being dealt with, however, does not mean that the kind of critique of missions that Hoekendijk referred to is no longer present. In fact, critique can become sharper. It used to be that the established theologians did not talk about evangelism and missions; now they talk about missions and evangelism critically.

Pietist emphases in missions is one of the standard theological critiques. The rootage of the missionary enterprise in Pietism has had two effects that contemporary theology criticizes. One is the concentration on conversion as an individual phenomenon, for both the missionary and the convert. This is subject to some criticism from both biblical and realistic perspectives. The other effect that is criticized is the focus on a particular—sometimes called moralistic—cultural style that calls for conformity to the cultural patterns of the sending churches, for instance, forbidding use of alcohol and dancing. While the previous generation of missionaries was concerned to export the patterns of faithfulness that had been found necessary at home, theologians would say alcohol and dancing are not necessarily the most important points.

Still another critique has to do with perceived narrowness in theological understanding. One of the currents of thought in Western theology, sometimes called "neo-universalism," argues that God's love must be effective beyond the borders of the visible church. Theologians who hold this view suggest there must be ways to be objects of God's love and to be reconciled with God or to trust in God's goodness without joining a Western organization. They question missionaries who go to the rest of the world with the Christian message thinking that if they don't reach people with the message those people will be lost. But what does "lost" mean? The missionaries defined salvation in terms of European semantics, European experience and European concepts of what it means to be human, to be saved and therefore to be lost. Theologians asked, can we think this way anymore? Isn't God's purpose broader than the perdition of everybody who has not heard and joined our movement? This cuts across the traditional missionary motivation: the lostness of all people outside the Christian message.

Another critical perspective on mission comes from cultural anthropology. In our time there has arisen a much greater capacity to analyze the uniqueness of every culture, and there is greater awareness that meaning—including religious meaning—is dependent on the shape of a given culture. We cannot simply translate words and know that in another culture we are saying the same thing, because the meaning of a statement is always conditioned by that culture. It is often argued that the simple, anthropologically untrained missionary has been saying things in other countries that were meaningless, or that did not mean what they thought they said. This is another form of the "simple people" reproach with which the theologians previously critiqued or ignored missions.

Such criticisms of Christian mission, criticisms that are still present, encourage professional theology's low view of missions.

WHAT IS *THEOLOGY* OF MISSION?

But what do we mean by *theology* of mission as distinguishable from other things we might say about missions? How is theology distinguishable from missionary method and principles?

For some people theology means collecting and collating propositions or truths. They think that we have a certain number of Christian truths. We can state them at greater length with more propositions or more simply in a creed. Those affirmations, stated in the best possible language, are what we believe. Theology is simply a matter of interpreting the propositions, clarifying them, checking the definitions, keeping them straight and defending them.

Theology starts on the level of catechism. What ideas must a believer believe in order to be accepted for baptism? How much does someone have to know? One of the meanings of catechism is "what you have to know in order to be recognized by the rest of the Christian community as a fellow believer and to be ready for incorporation into the community through baptism or confirmation." Beyond that minimal instruction one soon discovers that we do not all teach the same theology. Catholics and Lutherans differ, so we have to give reasons for choosing this or that answer to one of the big questions. Controversy comes after catechism.

After controversy comes systematic thought. In systematic thought we ask how it all hangs together. What assumptions are more fundamental than others? Which reasoning processes are valid, and which do not make sense or are not convincing? Systematic theology is self-conscious. It turns in on itself and asks, "How are we thinking?" not simply "What do we think?" It asks, "Why do they think differently?" and "How do we think properly?" Systematic theology comes at the end of an evolution in theological thought within Christian history. It comes after catechetical instruction and after controversy. In church history we see this development taking place over the centuries. Systematic theology has also tended to become hardened as definitive in the thought of the church and to be taught for its own sake.

While for some people theology is organizing traditional truths systematically, for other people theology is simply a realm of talking about God. In that realm individuals can have their own new ideas, which are legitimate theology too. In this view one can even be an atheist and do theology as long as the person thinks carefully about the fact that God does not exist. *Theology* is just another word for thinking carefully about what matters the most. Given this spirit, which puts a premium on tolerance, variety and individual authenticity, there arises a new criticism of the whole missionary package: it is arrogant. The missionary undertaking does not let other people have their own theology. It tries to impose a better one, even across cultural borders.

In the last century and a half, these two schools of thought—one that held that theology means everybody doing their own critical thinking from scratch, and the other that theology is an authoritative body of truths everybody should believe—debated one another. The debates were mostly about whether to believe the Bible and what authority the Bible has. Many assumed that those in favor of propositional theology were the ones who "believed the Bible" because they got their propositions from it, and the other people were the ones who did not. This turned out, on later analysis, to be simplistic because most propositions in systematic theology draw from sources beyond the Bible. Systematic theology uses contemporary terms. It translates and paraphrases. It selects. It borrows later agendas. It debates issues that only arose in the Middle Ages or in the Reformation. Much of what it takes to make theology systematic is borrowed from other places and debates.

I suggest we back away from those classical ways of understanding what theology thinks it is doing. We should not assume that we are dealing with a total body of knowledge that is to be firmly organized once and for all, which we then unfold. Theological material always comes from history, and it is always an arbitrary selection. On the other hand, theology is not a simple transposition of biblical statements into an outline, as if one can take the whole Bible, put every line on a card and then reorganize the cards in a more logical way than they were in the written Bible. That is what some people think systematic theology is. But every transposition, every translation, every selection changes something.

To avoid both arbitrariness in our own theological selection and the idea of theology as a settled, rigid set of answers, let's look at theology as a *reasoning process* in the life of the church. This process needs to be done carefully, responsibly, in the fellowship of the church, subject to the authority of Scripture, but not in the wooden way of the past, thinking that all we are doing is rearranging biblical thinking.

If we examine this process from a sociological perspective, we can ask what the Christian church as a group of people has to talk about together. One is our common convictions or catechism: a minimum common knowledge that a new member of the community ought to be aware of to be acceptable as a member. Naming this may not take much theological conversation (although in some churches it takes more than in others). A second thing that we do with language is liturgy. We have ways of praying and we break bread together, and we have ways of explaining what is going on when we do these things. That is also theology. It may focus on the same subject matter as the catechism and it may not. A third thing that we do with words in the church is to argue. There is wrong doctrine. There is also good diversity in expression of convictions. But to distinguish between diversity that is good because it is complementary and values a variety of gifts and situations, and diversity that is wrong, the church has to think and argue. The technical term for that is *polemics*, an argumentative kind of theology.

Yet another function of theology we call *apologetics*, which simply means that we are trying to express ourselves in the language of the people we are trying to talk to. We don't tell them in our language how our position hangs together, but we try to adopt their language and speak to them in a way that will win them or at least make sense to them in their terms.

Each of these approaches has a different set of ground rules. If you are doing catechetics, then you will ask if this conviction is indispensable. Can you get along without it? If you are doing polemics, you will have a different set of questions. You will ask, "Where does error begin?" "What is consistent and what is contradictory?" We can find both kinds of thinking already in the New Testament. They produce different statements.

I suggest that for our purposes we look at the function, not the content of theology. *Theology* really ought to be a verb—*theologizing*, that is, "doing theology." Theologizing is not so much a subject—you can theologize about anything—as it is a ministry or a way of working. It is one of the functions that ought to be going on in the church— thinking about our thinking, thinking about our language.

While the New Testament assumes a variety of ministries in the church, the role of teacher/theologian is the only one that the New Testament says only a few people in the church should hold. "Not many of you should become teachers, my brothers and sisters, for you know that we who teach will be judged with greater strictness" (Jas 3:1). Why shouldn't there be many teachers? James goes on to say that language is unruly; it tends to run away with itself. We speak a word and assume it means something. We make sentences and assume they are somehow valid. We also recognize the power of abstraction and the tendency of terms to be reified. So we want only a few people working on language— and they should be careful people—because the task calls for restraint. It calls for approaching any subject with critical concern to relate it to the whole faith: with the concern for centrality (the catechetical concern) and faithfulness and coherence (the polemic concern).

In the process of theological reasoning in the life of the church, we will not put the accent on the fact that the Bible is a closed canon, but on the fact that the Spirit still speaks to make biblical criteria relevant. We will not assume that our set of answers are right forever, or even for now, but only that the congregation, the missionary enterprise, keeps asking questions to which we will keep having to find answers. In this process the theologian stands in judgment on the church, but only within the church, and only as the Spirit speaks.

GLOBAL PERSPECTIVE

The next theme to identify in delineating what we mean by *Theology of Mission* is the place of a global perspective. In the past there has been a clean distinction between foreign missions and home missions. "Home missions" is what the church does in her own culture. "Evangelism" is what the church does in her own neighborhood. "Foreign missions" is what the church does when sending people overseas.

Our increasing awareness of the commonality of situations in one part of the world and another makes that distinction too simple. Those of us who live in North America or Europe would find that there are parts of our own countries so different from our own that we would feel as if we were in a foreign country if we lived there. There are also parts of the "overseas" world that are highly Westernized. In fact we are not far from having state churches in some African countries and South Pacific islands. The problem of religious establishment is not limited to Europe or North America.

While it used to be taken for granted that Europe and North America were Christian and other continents were "the non-Christian world," that is no longer possible to assume. This is partly because of the growth of the church around the world and partly because there is increasing awareness that Europe and North America are not simply "Christian." We cannot assume the home country is a Christian country, and all we have to do is evangelize (that is, get individuals to join the church in the Christian country) or to work in certain fringe areas (that is, with immigrants or Native Americans or slum dwellers) and call that home missions. That picture is not helpful in understanding the breadth of the missionary concern.

A further issue arises over the East/West divide in Christianity. To think that there is an East that never was Christian and a West that used to be Christian oversimplifies in numerous important ways. Eastern Christianity used to be the name for the Russian Orthodox, the Greek Orthodox, the Syrian Orthodox and the Coptic people. Is that West or East? It is not quite either. Then there is the fact that neither Africa nor Latin America falls under the East-West polarization. So some people have begun talking about North and South. The North is the developed world and the South is the poor world, which means Latin America, Africa and southern Asia. No one of these efforts to get handles on the problem will work, but we cannot work without handles either.

In spite of the difficulties, we will consider the "overseas model" as typical for raising the issues we will examine. We want to put our questions in the context of the widest cultural, legal and physical differences we can—but without assuming that crossing distant cultural boundaries is categorically different from crossing cultural boundaries in some given homeland. However, looking at mission in relation to more distant places and cultures may give us samples more representative and revealing.

MISSIONARY METHODS AND PRINCIPLES

Our focus on theologizing in the context of mission needs to be distinguished from the kinds of concerns that would be raised if our title were "missionary methods" or "missionary principles." In that case we would give more attention to the actual procedures of the missionary agency or the professional missionary person. We cannot ignore those questions, because they have theological implications. But neither can we focus on them, because not all of them are strictly theological. We will touch only incidentally on items that would be dealt with in a book on principles or methods.

Missionary agency management. Some questions regarding principles or methods have to do with the missionary agency as an institution: a board, a mission society, a sending office. This kind of agency needs management and support policies. It needs to define its relationship to a constituency. It must also address the question of the status of the missionary person as an employee of the mission institution. What constitutes candidacy, call, ordination and tenure?

Mission agencies also need to determine their priorities. What is and should be the place of schools, hospitals, community development or other service agencies, which do things other than create congregations? How are service and mission related as concepts, as functions and as agencies?

Another question is the status of field management structures and their relation to the church in that country. What does it mean to have concern for "indigenous methods"? Does this mean that missionaries in a given overseas context will consider themselves regular members of the local church? Should they transfer their membership from North

America, serve the church in leadership roles only if they are elected and give their tithes to a local congregational budget? Or is that precisely backwards because that warps the genuinely indigenous nature of the local church? Should they keep out of the way of the local church as part of their presence and offering, to avoid the danger of domination? That is a theological issue, but it is also an issue of agency management. It is another issue we cannot focus on.

Focus of the missionary effort. Another set of questions that we cannot avoid but that we will not deal with directly has to do with priorities in the focus of the missionary effort. Should the mission effort concentrate on trying to reach everybody? Should it rather try to reach elite policy makers and cultural leaders because they will influence many others? Should it focus on trying to reach the poor because Jesus was in favor of the poor? Or should it focus on reaching whoever will be most likely to respond? Those are significantly different approaches. Those are elements we will not deal with in this book.

Cultural adaptation. Further decisions have to do with what is appropriate or inappropriate cultural adaptation in a mission setting. If people in the non-Christian religious culture meet under tents, should Christians meet under tents too? Should the mission effort adapt as much as possible in superficial, visible ways to the surrounding religious culture so as to be identified as also religious? Or should the Christians make the point that they are Christian by *not* using the same kinds of buildings, shrines and meeting times as the religious establishment?

Should missionaries work to have large congregations so they can have a preacher and a budget as their sending churches do, or should they work with house churches so that new Christians have an intimate point where they can be brought into community and catechized? Is the primary goal a maximum number of converts or a maximum spread of Christian values, which might be done best by not insisting on converting people? Is it more important to go to the cities because that is where more people are? Or to go to tribal areas where the Christian message has not reached because the gospel is supposed to reach "all tongues" and every city already has some type of church present? All these questions are theologically relevant. We cannot avoid touching on them and using related illustrations, but they would be dealt with more fully and carefully in a book on missionary methods and principles.

Believers church concerns. Under the heading of principles or methods we could focus on some specific concerns that those in the believers church and historic peace church traditions hold and how they ought to be expressed in mission work, if they ought to be expressed at all. For example, because of the shape of established Christianity in Europe in the sixteenth century, Anabaptist Mennonites have focused on the importance of believers baptism in contrast to infant baptism. Should missionaries insist, in a country where other people baptize their babies, that infants are not to be baptized and that the decision to become a member of the church must be a mature, personal decision? What does the concentration on individual decision mean in a culture where individuals follow family or clan decisions rather than make their own? What does believers baptism mean where there is no established church that collapses citizenship and baptism? Does the same obligation remain to make an issue of infant baptism? Is there more of an obligation to focus on this practice because the church is in a missionary situation, or perhaps less because it is a more serious matter to press an issue that could divide Christians in some other part of the world than it seems to be in our part of the world? In North America we have a pluralistic way of getting along on many of these issues. Disagreement and division are more difficult when Christians are a disadvantaged minority in an unfriendly culture.

Another question is how mission work should deal with the church-state relationship, given that it has a different form in every part of the world. To what extent should Europeans or Americans carry to other parts of the world the patterns or convictions developed in the relatively tolerant, relatively democratic West? Or should pacifist Christians promote an ethic of nonresistance and raise the whole set of questions around violence, the state and the military?[3] Minimally, missionaries

---

[3][Yoder used the term *nonresistance*, which had a particular resonance for Mennonite seminary students at the time. We have retained his usage for historical integrity and for the peaceable spirit the term connotes, even though the term is easily misunderstood. In our current context a term such as "nonviolent resistance to evil" better communicates Yoder's intention, for he consistently argued against those who assumed that *nonresistance* meant passivity, withdrawal or refusal to respond to the suffering of neighbors. See Leo Driedger and Donald B. Kraybill,

should feel as free about preaching the moral conviction that war and killing are wrong as they do about preaching other aspects of the gospel. Perhaps a message that includes nonresistance in fact clarifies the nature of God's love or the nature of Christian life.

Further, what would it mean for those who see peace as integral to the gospel to let the church's pacifist stance be a part of missionary identity and procedures? What would that mean in countries where a military government carefully supervises especially the activities of foreigners, but also the activities of its own citizens? Perhaps nonresistance is not only a message, but a way of doing mission. Are there violent and nonviolent, nationalistic and nonnationalistic, ways of carrying out the mission of the church? If so, nonresistance would not only be part of the content of the message but would also shape missionary procedures.

We will be obligated to dip into these areas for samples or guidelines, but I will make no effort to cover them systematically.

GROWTH OF MISSIOLOGICAL STUDY

In recent years there has been sizeable growth in the field of missiology. I earlier referred to this in terms of ecumenical theology. Until the late 1950s you would not have found in the average seminary library a subject heading or books on "theology of mission." That observation, however, should not be overdone, as if I were suggesting that nobody ever thought about mission theologically before. But it seems that the nature of the church's mission was not a central issue and was not dealt with in the same way as the doctrine of humanity, the doctrine of sin or the theology of sacraments had been: trying to illuminate it from the Bible and from other theological resources; trying to build it into the theological discipline and get academic theologians to recognize it.

A landmark in the development of mission theology was a meeting in 1952 in Willingen, Germany, of the International Missionary Council (IMC) who asked for a study of the theology of mission.[4] That request

---

Mennonite Peacemaking: From Quietism to Activism (Scottdale, PA: Herald Press, 1994) who trace changes in ways Mennonites have articulated their peace commitment since the 1930s and 1940s. —Ed.]

[4]On this see Willhelm Andersen, "Further Toward a Theology of Mission," in *The Theology of the Christian Mission*, ed. Gerald Anderson (New York: McGraw-Hill, 1961), pp. 300-313.

gave visibility to the missionary concern in interchurch thought. From then on one can follow meetings, reports from study conferences, and other kinds of documents on the topic. After 1961, when the IMC was formally incorporated into the World Council of Churches, development of mission theology continued to be encouraged by the WCC Commission on World Mission and Evangelism.

This rapid survey of developments in the field of missiology helps identify the agenda we will try to address in a rather obvious sequence of topics in the rest of this book.

1

THE PROPHETS

Israel and the Nations

Generally, when interpreters of the Bible look for its "missionary message," especially in the Old Testament, they identify such a message wherever there is reference to "the nations." There is implicit reference to the nations whenever Yahweh's sovereignty is affirmed as reaching beyond God's care for the Israelites. Genesis 1–11 places all of world history in a context of creation/fall/providence under a sovereign who at the same time is specifically the caring and covenantal Lord who calls Israel.

More directly, the call of Abraham is related to God's saving purposes for all the nations. Some interpreters have taken this to mean that Abraham was a missionary because he leaves and goes out to receive some promise that is not defined but which has to do with being a blessing to the world. Max Warren, for example, maintains that, "The Apostolic church came into being when God called Abraham out of Ur of the Chaldees and bade him go out into a land he did not know and Abraham obeyed. When the grace of God in choosing Abraham was met by the faith of Abraham in accepting the choice, the Church was born."[1] Thus, the meaning of election—being selected out—does not mean a selfish privilege but an assignment to be a mediator or a representative between the electing God and the nations.

---

[1][See Max Warren, *The Calling of God: Four Essays in Missionary History* (London: Lutterworth Press, 1945), p. 45. —Ed.]

A third implicitly missionary dimension of Old Testament faith is the nonexistence or the impotence of the other gods or of idols. Whenever this polemic against idols is proclaimed, there is intrinsically a message to the people serving those gods, even though the context in which we find anti-idolatry literature is the internal discipline of the Israelites.

On quite another level, the prophetic vision of the nations coming to Jerusalem to learn the law has a missionary impact. The most familiar passage is Micah 4:1-4, parallel to Isaiah 2:1-4; but it is found as well in Psalm 46, Ezekiel 28:25-26 and Zechariah 8:20-23. In this vision, Jerusalem is the center of the world, which represents a statement about the world as well as about Jerusalem (Jer 3:17, 16:19). The nations will come to Jerusalem, bringing tribute (Is 18:7). They will recognize Yahweh. They will recognize Israel's election. They will learn the law (Ps 67), and civilization will be restored. The word for such civilization is *peace*, which is spelled out in terms of economics: "They shall beat their swords into plowshares, and their spears into pruning hooks; nation shall not lift up sword against nation, neither shall they learn war any more; but they shall all sit under their own vines and under their own fig trees, and no one shall make them afraid; for the mouth of the LORD of hosts has spoken" (Mic 4:3-4).[2]

This restoration may be seen with or without Yahweh's direct intervention to "judge the nations" in the sense of exercising political sovereignty. It may be envisaged with or without an explicit relationship to the cult or the temple at Jerusalem. There is not such a relationship in most of the above texts. It is not said that there will be Bible reading or circumcision in all of the nations or that there will be no more eating of pigs. Yet the Jews would have to think that the nations would be still better

---

[2]The common picture of people coming to the city could be spoken of as salvation. They come to the true God. They recognize where God has spoken and who God's chosen people have been. They accept God's law. They go home and make peace, and everybody has his or her own garden. What more would they want by way of salvation? In one sense we can say that the future salvation that is expected for the nations is that they do not become Jews. But then what is the meaning of peoplehood? What is the place of sacrifice, of having the correct Scriptures, of the law's details and of the way of life that God wants people to live? There is a remaining ambiguity at that point. If we bring in the New Testament meaning of salvation, there are parts that are not in this Old Testament picture. If we ask on the basis of the text, it is hard to say what additional benefits the nations would want once that prediction of Micah and Isaiah is fulfilled.

if they not only heard the law and went back and had peace, but if they started doing without pork, observing the Sabbath, bringing sacrifices and observing the law.

A few texts speak directly about the possibility that Yahweh might be known and praised by the nations. Most direct is Psalm 67: "Let the peoples praise you, O God; let all the peoples praise you. Let the nations be glad and sing for joy, for you judge the peoples with equity and guide the nations upon earth" (Ps 67:3-4).

The songs of the Suffering Servant also have missionary implications.[3] In Isaiah 42:1-4 we read that the spirit of Yahweh has been placed upon the Servant and that he shall "bring forth justice to the nations" (Is 42:1). Harold Rowley, a Baptist Old Testament scholar, says this missionary implication follows logically from the dogma of monotheism: If there is only one God, then that God must be God for all people and that the election of a particular human group to know this one true God automatically calls them to become God's proclaimers.[4] He also refers to Isaiah 42:2-3—"He will not cry or lift up his voice, or make it heard in the street; a bruised reed he will not break, and a dimly burning wick he will not quench; he will faithfully bring forth justice"—which is significant for the judgment it expresses on later missionary understandings that the means of this proclamation to bring justice to the Gentiles shall not be ordinary kinds of power.

In Isaiah 49 we read that the Servant's assignment is not simply "to raise up the tribes of Jacob and to restore the survivors of Israel" (Is 49:6) but to be made a light for the Gentiles. Isaiah 50:4-9 adds the element of suffering to this ministry to the Gentiles and then the crowning passage Isaiah 52:13–53:12 adds the element of the Suffering Servant's vindication when it is seen that his suffering was as a ransom for "many." Rather than deciding that this passage had to do exclusively with the prophet or with some other person in his time or with some future figure or with a community, all of these elements probably belong. The Servant is perhaps at the same time Israel in its various shades of

---

[3]See Harold Henry Rowley, "The Servant Mission: The Servant Songs and Evangelism," *Interpretation* 8, no. 3 (July 1954): 259-72.

[4][Ibid., p. 266. —Ed.]

meaning: a faithful remnant within Israel, a man within that faithful remnant, a man yet to come in the future. In any case, if that is the kind of purpose God has avowed, then Israel's witness to Yahweh must be one of corporate servanthood for the sake of the Gentiles.

Thus there is justification for the claim that the foreign missionary enterprise is rooted in all of Scripture and not simply in the New Testament. Yet it is more important for our guidance to be clear about the ways in which this Old Testament vision is different from what we mean in modern times by *missions*.

Israel takes no action toward bringing in the nations. We do have a modest openness on the part of the Israelites to integrate into their number persons of other tribes. The Mosaic legislation provides for the rights of strangers, and the stories of Joshua and Judges support the further elaboration of archeologists and historians who believe that as the Hebrews infiltrated Canaan, many who dwelt already in the land must have joined their family federation.[5] More than we realize from the ordinary introductory reading of the story, Israel was made up of a composite population with a nucleus of people who could reach back to the Abraham story. Israel's identity was built around the Abraham story, but all along they were incorporating other people into that story. Even on the way out of Egypt—when you would think that the group would be made up of only the true descendants of the Hebrews (because who else would want to belong to those people)—there are still a few references to some who do not seem to be fully, ethnically part of the Hebrew group but who simply have tagged along.

Two different terms describe these people. At the beginning of the exodus from Egypt, Exodus 12:38 says, "A mixed crowd also went up with them." What is a "mixed crowd"? The Hebrew term for this—ʿēreb—only appears twice in the Old Testament. But the other place it occurs is Nehemiah 13:3 where it very obviously means nonethnic people; it means the Samaritans. To the extent that we can compare texts from one book to another or from one period of Hebrew literature to the next, it would seem that this term (with some indication

---

[5]For example, see George Mendenhall, "Hebrew Conquest of Palestine," *Biblical Archaeologist* 25, no. 3 (1962): 66-87.

of reaching beyond ethnic identity) was already there.[6]

There is also another term which makes this same point but less clearly. It would not carry much weight if it were not for the "mixed multitude" reference. "The *rabble* among them had a strong craving; and the Israelites also wept again, and said, 'If only we had meat to eat! We remember the fish we used to eat in Egypt for nothing, the cucumbers, the melons, the leeks, the onions, and the garlic; but now our strength is dried up, and there is nothing at all but this manna to look at'" (Num 11:4-6, italics added). The idea of being unsatisfied with the food came to the Israelites from "the rabble." Who was the rabble? Maybe it was some of the Israelites. Perhaps not. The text is not clear.

What is clear is that once the Israelite people were established in Palestine, the ultimate makeup of that nation included great numbers of people who were not Abraham's biological descendants, who were taken into the covenant along the way. This means that although it was not a very strong part of Israel's self-understanding, it was part of Israel's lived experience. God's people add others. God's people are open to membership.[7]

But that is not a missionary witness to the nations. Nor is it a witness to the nations when in Isaiah a few prophecies are directed to Cyrus or when in Amos words of condemnation are directed to all the neighbor nations. The literary form of an address to that other nation or ruler

---

[6]Of course when a term was not used very often, we cannot be absolutely sure about its exact meaning.

[7]The question arises as to how the Old Testament's war stories relate to the theme of incorporating outsiders. If we read Joshua and Judges superficially, we have the impression that the Israelites came into the land and took over the whole place right away by killing everybody. But if we look more carefully at some of the texts, it clearly does not say that. Both books repeatedly talk about people they had not exterminated and that the Israelites then incorporated. Despite the impression in Joshua of a finished battle, half of Jerusalem still belongs to the other people. So there was a long period of infiltration.

Moreover, the holy war was more of a guiding symbolic vision than it was a technique for becoming a people. Americans are taught in high school to think that their nation became a nation because of a revolutionary war. In reality the war was an episode in a long history of becoming more loosely related to Britain; the real elements of nationhood came before and after. Similarly, the peoplehood of Israel was less dependent on those holy wars than a superficial reading of Joshua and Judges makes one think.

Yet these stories also mark a point at which Israel's self-understanding did not include an affirmation of other people. In terms of mission, however, as long as we are ready to destroy any other people we cannot be missionary. That is self-evident.

does not actually mean that the prophet ever took the message there, and the impact of the message is clearly directed at a Hebrew audience. Jonah took a message to Nineveh, but that was not the proclamation of God's law. When the Ninevites repented, there is no indication that they began bringing sacrifices to Jerusalem or stopped eating pork. Johannes Blauw makes this point when he says that the attitude toward the Gentiles in the Old Testament is "centripetal"; that although the Israelite's vision is universal in that it affirmed that there is only one God of the whole world, their universality is not missionary.[8]

Even if we look at the vision of the nations coming to Jerusalem, which as we saw above is the most dramatic and widely used image, what convinces the nations is Israel's restoration by an act of Yahweh. The nations are not brought in because missionaries are sent to them either with a Jewish message or with a wider than Jewish message about God's sovereignty. The part that Israel has to play in fulfilling the promise that the nations will come is simply to wait and keep the law even at the cost of suffering. Harold Rowley represents the typical view that converting Gentiles to Israel's religious practice is not a strong concern in the Old Testament: "They are not missionaries, seeking to win the nations to the faith of Jehovah, but rather men who are so moved with gratitude to God for all His goodness to them that they can think of no worthier way of acknowledging His goodness than to tell all men about him. . . . But this was born of their sense of what they owe to God, rather than any compassion for the Gentiles."[9] Even when the vision is the most affirmative as in Isaiah 2 and Micah 4, what people come to learn is God's law for the nations, not the faith of Israel. They do not adopt the cult, temple sacrifice, circumcision or even Sabbath observance: what they do is go home to live in peace.

This Old Testament imagery shows no thought about the lostness of

---

[8]See Johannes Blauw, *The Missionary Nature of the Church: A Survey of the Biblical Theology of Mission* (New York: McGraw-Hill, 1962), pp. 38-41. [For Blauw the Old Testament has a *centripetal* view of mission in that the nations and faithful Jews come to Jerusalem to experience God. With Jesus, a directional change occurs in that his disciples go from Jerusalem to the nations, what Blauw calls *centrifugal* mission. —Ed.]
[9][Harold Henry Rowley, *The Missionary Message of the Old Testament* (London: The Carey Press, 1945), p. 36. —Ed.]

the nations beyond their lack of knowledge of Yahweh. There is in fact considerable room for the affirmation that others than Israelites can know the true God. We find pagan saints in the Old Testament story, non-Israelites who are recognized as somehow having a valid relationship with the true God.[10] These are not only righteous people before Abraham, but even after Abraham: Melchizedek, Job and the Queen of Sheba. Melchizedek is striking because through him Abraham brings his tithes (Gen 14:17-24). Jethro is interesting because through him Moses gets some ideas about how to organize the people at Sinai (Ex 18). These righteous outsiders apparently have valid morality. In Malachi 1:11 it appears that they are somehow worshipping the true God: "For from the rising of the sun to its setting my name is great among the nations, and in every place incense is offered to my name, and a pure offering; for my name is great among the nations, says the LORD of hosts. But *you* profane it" (Mal 1:11-12, italics added). Even Israel's possession of a divinely mandated order of sacrificial worship is not an exclusive privilege.

This idea that other people than the Israelites can know the true God points to something peculiar to the nature of historical faith as distinguished from metaphysical religions. If God's existence is a matter of metaphysical theory, then the credibility or knowability of that existence should be the same for all, and any limitation of that information to a privileged group of knowers is fortuitous and intrinsically unfair. If to be saved is dependent on metaphysical information or if to be saved is itself a metaphysical state unrelated to particular history, then one has to think about the lostness of everyone ignorant of that special saving information. For a faith community whose nature is historical, the sense in which outsiders are outside is very different. This is a matter needing only to be noticed at this point; we will have to return to it much later in the book.

In summary, the Old Testament neither meditates about the eternal lostness of people who have not heard about Yahweh nor about the destiny of people before Abraham.

---

[10]For more on the holy pagans, see Jean Daniélou, *Holy Pagans of the Old Testament* (Baltimore: Helicon Press, 1957).

BROADER OLD TESTAMENT THEMES

So far we have been looking for a missionary thrust in the Old Testament text itself and have noted a narrowing and modesty about what the Old Testament says and does not say about mission compared to some contemporary missionary interpretations. There are some general theological affirmations in the Old Testament that are probably more important for missions than what we have been looking at, ones that reaffirm ideas we have touched along the way. What does the Old Testament message as a whole mean for the missionary imperative?

No other gods. One of the omnipresent themes, noticeable especially in the last half of the Old Testament period, is the struggle of the true God versus false gods. It is said that those gods do not exist. They are not true gods; they are vanities and emptiness. But we still have to fight with them. The prophetic message is not the same thing as a modern cultural enlightenment message, in which we tell people, "The gods are not really there, so you do not have to think about them." Rather there is a struggle with the power of idolatry, and the struggle is something other than educating people about the fact that these gods do not exist. It is more than that because they have a hold on people. How can something that does not exist have a hold on people?

In the modern context, we think of religion versus nonreligion, theism versus atheism, and people who practice religion versus people who do not practice religion. We think that the missionary task is an apologetic task or the task of convincing people that they need the religious or transcendent dimension, or religious practice. Persuading people that there was a transcendent God was not a problem in the Old Testament. The question was whether they could recognize the difference between the true God and false gods. The issue was the identity of the God of Abraham, Isaac, and Jacob, or the Lord of Hosts. For Israel God's identity was reflected in ethics, community process, politics, family and work. This involved religious practices, but in a narrow sense, that is, in specific ceremonies like temple sacrifices. The real difference was that Israel had a God who had a different name and a different personality than the false gods; people were to live differently in covenant with that God.

Creation and covenant. Another observation from the Old Testament witness has to do with the relation of three concepts: creation, providence and election. The texts affirm God as Creator of the universe. Then there is the course of history, and we speak of God as providence, as Lord of history, as sovereign. Finally there is election. The way the story is told, it happened in this order.

But the way it happened in Israel's experience was the other way around. First of all there was the event of covenant, and then it was possible to say that the God with whom we are in covenant had been running history. Then it was meaningful to say that God is the sole Creator. This universe did not create itself. As we observe the formation of the Old Testament literature, we can see a moving out from the concrete historical experience of covenant into the less concrete affirmation of providence over all history and creation. Now when we tell the story, the story starts with creation. But the affirmation of creation is not something that stands by itself. It is the confession of the people who first experience covenant and then wrote world history in light of the covenant.

God's sovereignty. Another general observation about Old Testament theology is the vision of divine sovereignty as continuing not only back to Genesis 1–11, but as encompassing the entire world. Divine sovereignty is expressed through other nations as well as through Israel. God's governing of history is in some sense in favor of Israel, on Israel's behalf. Sometimes it is in order to use Israel to bless the nations. But God uses Assyria (Is 10), Cyrus (Is 45), Nebuchadnezzar (Jer 42:11-12) or other emperors for God's own purposes.

The first task of Israel is to be Israel. Finally, the first task of Israel is to be Israel, to live up to the identity of the covenant.[11] That emphasis still may throw light on what we should be doing today. Maybe the first task of the church in mission is to be the church. Abraham's faith, his readiness to be mobile and the willingness of his followers to be a peculiar people were prior to anything else that God could do with them. Whatever they did later by spinoff, by accident or by further vision, the

---

[11]I accentuate this argument in "A Light to the Nations," *Concern* 9 (1961): 14-18.

first thing they were supposed to do was to be faithful. Anything else that they could be used for was dependent on that vision. Distinctness was the first call, not out of pride but out of the awareness of the nature of the God who called.

Numbers 22–24 tells the story of King Balak's effort to hire a prophet to curse the Israelites. This is part of the prophet Balaam's message: "How can I curse whom God has not cursed? How can I denounce those whom the LORD has not denounced? For from the top of the crags I see him, from the hills I behold him; Here is a people living alone, and not reckoning itself among the nations!" (Num 23:8-9). That kind of prophetic aloneness, that willingness to be different, is the first requirement for Israel.

Israel is to live up to the covenant. There shall be no idolatry. The Old Testament reflects a continuing critique of settling into nationhood, kingship and statehood and of forgetting God's ways. In the exile the texts evidence a continuing hope in covenantal promises despite the loss of nationhood and statehood. There is trust of the Servant—that his servanthood is nonviolent and that his submissiveness will be the tool of election. An understanding of peoplehood has emerged that can lay the groundwork for something new to happen in the New Testament.

INTERTESTAMENTAL MISSIONARY ACTIVITY

During what we call the intertestamental period, the Israelites in the dispersion became more and more effective, convinced and self-aware about being a missionary people or about what we call making proselytes. In the later Jewish Diaspora after Ezra/Nehemiah and after the Maccabees, there was no opposition to incorporating into the believing community as full members people who were not born into Israel. This followed from Jewish conviction that other gods were not true gods, that their own law was the true law, and that there would be a time when all the nations would be brought in. If one is looking forward to that time and if somebody wants in already, then what grounds does one have not to let that person in? So the community developed a clear missionary method in the intertestamental period for letting people in who already saw the superiority of Jewish faith. The rabbinic tradition explained the rules for incorporating non-Israelites into the synagogue fellowship. The New Testament testifies clearly that Jews were accepting proselytes all over the place.

THE OLD TESTAMENT IN NON-WESTERN CULTURE

One other theme we must address before moving to the New Testament is the place of the Old Testament today in the church in non-Western cultures. Should a missionary to India, Africa or Japan take along the Hebrew story and those old patriarchs and battles? Cannot the missionary simply preach Jesus and forget about the Old Testament?

Some people argue that just as Jesus fulfilled Jewish expectations, so he fulfills the expectations of people in any other culture. If missionaries go to a new culture, they should find out what the people expect—what fulfillment they are looking for—and say how Jesus fulfills that hope. A missionary in India should find out what is the expectation or longing in Hindu Scriptures and find a way of saying that Christ meets that longing; Indian Christians can then put Jesus on whatever pedestal they have. The apostle Paul put Jesus on the pedestal of the Old Testament, for Jesus first appeared in Paul's Jewish world. Then Paul went to Athens and he started relating Jesus to the expectations and the worship of "an unknown god" (Acts 17:15-34). When this is the method, it is confusing to bring along all those Hebrew ancestors. Why not let others keep whatever patriarchs or expectations they have and let them be fulfilled in Jesus?

What is there to be said on the other side? A fuller treatment will have to wait for chapters 4 and 5, but here I will make a brief one-sided case for taking the whole Bible with us to other parts of the world and to other periods of time. To understand the New Testament as a culmination of the Old makes it clear—as it needs to be made clear in a missionary context—that the Christian message is a story of God acting in history to achieve something for humanity. The proper way to talk about an action of God is to report it. The proper way to talk about an idea is to argue it and explain why it makes sense, but the proper thing to do about an event is to tell about it.

God's actions are not simply proofs of God's truths; God's actions are the salvation that we now talk about. The Old Testament story safe-guards this biblical quality of faith and corrects the modern under-standing that the religious task is to prove the validity of theism over against atheism, monotheism over against polytheism or the reality of the supernatural over against a flat view of nature. The Old Testament story is not just another set of religious insights. If Jesus does not fulfill the Jewish expectation for the whole world, then he is just another guru or prophet in religious literature. If what a Christian brings to a Hindu is, "Look at my guru beside your guru," the Hindu will believe his prophet has more wisdom. If what a Christian brings to a Muslim is "Look at my prophet beside your prophet," her prophet will have come later than Jesus and therefore will be better. Unless there is the claim to be standing on the shoulders of Hebrew history, the character of the message itself is distorted by the expectations of the culture to which we try to take it.

As a subpoint of this, the Old Testament story clarifies the difference between a faith based on God's actions in history and a nature faith or a fertility faith. A constant characteristic of human cultures is that we explain in terms of gods the natural cycles of summer and winter or rainy and dry seasons. In family life we celebrate with the gods mar-riage, childbirth, adolescence and death. Cultures give religious meaning to the life cycle and the nature cycle. The biblical message in its struggle with Baalism and with national religion already lays the groundwork for clarifying that biblical faith is not a nature faith. That does not mean that there is no relation between the God in the Bible and nature. But there are different ways to know God, and it makes a difference which way we take. If we seek to know God through knowing nature, then we are "groping" after God (Acts 17:27). That is the word that Paul uses at the Areopagus. The result of looking for a god in nature is slavery to the stars. If we look for God in nature, in fertility, in the regularities of the stars, the result is slavery to the cyclical and the nonhistorical, to meaninglessness.

The true God is the God of nature too. But the way to know God is through God's deeds, God's self-imparting in the covenant. It is the pe-culiarity of the covenant or of God's historical working that it cannot be a message without being concrete. That is, we cannot say God is purposeful unless we know God's name. We cannot say God is a God who acts unless we can say when and where God acts. One of the peculiarities of modern existentialism is to try to say one without the other. We keep on talking about a God who is personal but we no longer know God's name, so we talk about being personal as a shape of the human experience. Or we talk about God acting in history, but we do not want to name any times and places as if this is true because it might be disproven.

We cannot affirm history without talking about times and places. The Old Testament's claim that God acts in history is only pegged down if missionaries can say what that history is before they describe God. Jesus was embedded in that history. Therefore the message of Jesus is not the real message unless missionaries take the Old Testament with them. What happens when we overlook or reject the Old Testament has been demonstrated very clearly in the second century by Marcion, who thought it would help to make Christianity more acceptable if we would amputate the first nine-tenths of the Bible.[12] The interim experience has clarified again the structural importance of seeing the New Testament as patterned with the Old Testament.

This has been a brief foray into material that we will come back to in later chapters. The peculiarity or particularity of Christian faith is really the particularity of Jewish faith.

---

[12]It has also been demonstrated in modern times by Hitler, who performed a similar surgery on Scripture.

2

JESUS' PUBLIC MINISTRY
AND THE NATIONS

We enter the New Testament materials with the question we already identified in the Old Testament: in what sense is there or is there not a specific mandate to go beyond the Jewish people to the nations? We ask this question recognizing that there has been historical development. Instead of taking the New Testament as a block, we will look for levels of development, development of two kinds. First, the texts tell the story chronologically, so we ask in what sequence things are recorded. Second, there are different kinds of literature and some grounds for knowing what was written first or what was written later. We can attempt to discern within the New Testament as a whole which are the earliest forms of thought and which are the more developed.

EARLY JEWISH EXPECTATION AND THE BIRTH OF JESUS
An element of God's promise that Israel will be a blessing for the nations appears in all of the songs in Luke 1 and 2: the Song of Mary, the Song of the angel, the Song of Zechariah. This element is clear in Simeon's prophecy: "Master, now you are dismissing your servant in peace, according to your word; for my eyes have seen your salvation, which you have prepared in the presence of all peoples, a light for revelation to the Gentiles and for glory to your people Israel" (Lk 2:29-32). Simeon's word to Mary (Lk 2:34) that alludes to Isaiah 42 and 49, the Servant of the Lord Songs, may reflect this promise as well. Here is an early statement, before John the Baptist, of the idea that "now the

end is beginning." This reinforces what we will see in other places: when the end comes, the Gentiles will get in.

The wise men who figure in the birth narratives could be interpreted as symbolic of the Gentile world coming to praise God. This could be a dramatic statement that already at the birth of Jesus the nations are beginning to come and bring their tribute. It is striking that Matthew, who so often makes a point of saying that some aspect of Jesus' life fulfills a verse from the prophets, does not give us that meaning here. Nevertheless, we might understand it this way. Since Matthew's audience already had a framework of understanding that when the Messiah comes the nations will bring tribute, they may well have seen the beginning of the fulfillment of this Jewish expectation in the story of Jesus and the magi.

JOHN THE BAPTIST AND THE GENTILES

John the Baptist obviously addresses himself to the Jewish people. As in the Old Testament, he expects a coming event, an intervention by God. This coming event will purify, empower and destroy. It will include baptism in Spirit and in fire, and violent judgment for evil. John expects all of this to happen simultaneously.

The coming event will include the centripetal dimension of mission demonstrated in John's own practice. Soldiers come to listen to John. He neither turns them away nor makes Jews out of them. He tells them that they will have to behave differently and what that change in behavior will mean. When his listeners make much of the fact that they are Abraham's children, he downplays the significance of that privilege by saying that God can make children of Abraham out of stones. In other words, the coming kingdom is not limited to people whose membership is assured ethnically. But John the Baptist clearly focuses on Israel's restoration and is not interested in Gentiles except as they respond to his message for Israel.

JESUS' INAUGURAL SERMON

Although the Gospels may differ in the extent to which they make room for their message reaching beyond Israel, they agree that the focus of Jesus' ministry was completely within the Palestinian context. As Jesus' mission begins, it seems no different from John the Baptist's. He comes to his own people: "He came to what was his own, and his own people did not accept him" (Jn 1:11). The whole organization of Luke's Gospel is pointed toward Jerusalem. For Matthew the gospel is understood as ful-fillment of Scripture. Yet there is always enough in the Gospels to in-dicate that the expectation of a wider relevance is in the shadows or just around the corner as it had been in the Old Testament.

Jesus' inaugural sermon (Lk 4:14-30) offended his listeners because of the idea of God preferring the Gentiles. Jesus did not offer this as a thesis or a teaching. Nevertheless, Joachim Jeremias has suggested that Jesus proclaimed an openness to the Gentiles when he read from Isaiah 61: "We observe that the passage which Jesus took as the text of his ad-dress breaks off strangely in the middle of the sentence. The words, 'to proclaim the acceptable year of the Lord' (Lk 4.19 = Is 61.2), are imme-diately followed in the Old Testament text by the concluding words, 'and a day of vengeance of our God' (Is 61.2). Jesus leaves out the day of vengeance!"[1] According to Jeremias, Jesus' listeners would have been waiting for that next verse concerning vengeance. Since Jesus left it out, Jeremias concluded that Jesus was opening up the covenant to the Gen-tiles. However, Jeremias's reading makes certain untenable assump-tions about the technique of quotation. The normal rabbinic way to identify a text was to quote the beginning, but this did not mean that the speaker stopped at that point. The speaker probably finished the text. One could just as well argue that the omission in Luke meant that enough had been quoted that his listeners could recognize the text. Therefore, we probably cannot argue from Jesus omitting the reference to vengeance to a positive openness to the Gentiles as Jeremias and others following him have done.

Jesus' use of Elijah and Elisha in his post-sermon debate with those who had heard him is more striking than his quotation from Isaiah 61 because Elijah and Elisha were sent beyond Israel. Jesus says that there were many widows in Israel during the famine, but "Elijah was sent to none of them except to a widow at Zarephath in Sidon. There were also

---

[1][See Joachim Jeremias, *Jesus' Promise to the Nations* (Philadelphia: Fortress Press, 1958), p. 45. —Ed.]

many lepers in Israel in the time of the prophet Elisha, and none of them was cleansed except Naaman the Syrian" (Lk 4:25-27). After this, the passage moves to the astonishing signs and wonders and to the authority with which Jesus began to minister, which were also the beginning of the new age Jesus had just announced. The new age, we know from the Old Testament, was to be an age in which the nations would be gathered. The feeling that *now* is the time when God will reach beyond Israel is clear. But this is never said pointedly or explicitly. This would be the case as well in the early chapters of the other Gospels.

THE SENDING OF THE TWELVE DISCIPLES

Apostle, in Greek, means somebody who is sent. So we might think that Jesus was already getting ready to reach beyond Israel when he chose his twelve "missionaries." Linguistically that could follow. But *apostle* meaning "missionary" was used only later and has that clear meaning only after the resurrection. It seems that the point of choosing these twelve was to dramatize Israel's reconstitution. The apostles are sent only to Israel (Mt 10:5-6; 15:24).[2]

The sending of the twelve disciples in Matthew 10, Mark 6:6-13 and Luke 9:1-6 is not the beginning of mission in the strict sense either. Drawing on Hermann Strack and Paul Billerbeck's *Kommentar zum Neuen Testament aus Talmud und Midrasch*, George Caird shows that Jesus telling the disciples to shake off the dust from their feet (Mt 10:14; Mk 6:11; Lk 9:5; 10:10-11) was based on an act meant to disassociate Jews from Gentile pollution. But Jesus directs the disciples to use this gesture against whole Jewish towns whose assemblies elect not to join with Jesus. "In other words, the sending out of the Twelve was not so much an evangelistic mission as a political manifesto." In any case, the sending is a sign not a mission.[3]

---

[2]Matthew is clearer than Mark about this limitation. That is understandable because Matthew's readers would have been more aware of the reconstitution issue than Mark's readers.

[3]See George Caird, "Uncomfortable Words: Shake off the Dust from Your Feet (Mk 6:11)," *The Expository Times* 81, no. 2 (1969): 41. With regard to mission and Jesus, Bultmann says, "The fact that in the thought of Jesus the national connotation of the Kingdom of God remains in the background does not mean that he taught its universality. He took for granted as did his contemporaries that *the Kingdom of God was to come for the benefit of the Jewish people. . . .* He never thought of a mission to the Gentiles." See Rudolf Bultmann, *Jesus and the Word* (New York: Scribner, 1958), p. 43 (italics original).

The sending is a sign that the end is coming. In fact, the sending itself is part of the coming end. The Gospels do not report membership results or that people were baptized into the new movement as a result. Elsewhere Luke 10:1-12 indicates that sometimes Jesus and his disciples baptized, but that point is not made in connection to the sending of the Twelve or in the sending of the seventy (Jn 4:1-3). The sending was a dramatic proclamation and symbol of the kingdom's nearness. But as the texts themselves describe it, it does not create a new movement.[4]

How do we interpret the fact that this sending is more a sign than a mission? Alan Richardson says that the sending was intentionally a sign. That was all it was meant to be.[5] Vincent Taylor, on the contrary, says it was really meant to trigger the end. He takes over in a modified, more modest way something Albert Schweitzer would have said: Jesus thought that the proclamation that the kingdom is at hand itself would make it come, if only that proclamation reached all of Israel. "So I send out twelve people or I send out seventy people and when they have said that in every village then it will become true." But Jesus was disappointed in that. That would be Schweitzer's thesis.[6] But Richardson, who says it was meant only as a sign, and Taylor, who said it was meant for more, would agree that there was at this point no gathering of adherents, even Jewish adherents. The scholars tell us that after this set of preaching circuits, there was no more than before a discernable membership of the Jesus movement.

THE END-TIMES GATHERING OF THE NATIONS

Jesus does predict, on the other hand, that in the future there will be a gathering of the nations.[7] Still in the future, and still an ingathering, the

---

[4]In connection to this, we should note that Jesus criticized Jewish proselytizing: "You cross sea and land to make a single convert, and you make the new convert twice as much a child of hell as yourselves" (Mt 23:15). Jesus recognizes the fact of Jewish mission, but he puts it completely in a critical light because of the nature of the convert's position. He does not say the outreach itself is wrong. But it is wrong because it brings people to a position in which they reject Jesus.

[5][See Alan Richardson, *An Introduction to the Theology of the New Testament* (New York: Harper, 1959), p. 314n2. —Ed.]

[6][See Vincent Taylor, *The Life and Ministry of Jesus* (Nashville: Abingdon, 1955), pp. 113-19. —Ed.]

[7]See Johannes Blauw, *The Missionary Nature of the Church: A Survey of the Biblical Theology of Mission* (New York: McGraw-Hill, 1962), pp. 70-71.

nations come to Palestine, and they come to Judaism. Matthew 8:11-12 is a sample of that centripetal mission: "Many will come from east and west and will eat with Abraham and Isaac and Jacob in the kingdom of heaven, while the heirs of the kingdom will be thrown into the outer darkness" (cf. Lk 13:29).

Another example is from the cleansing of the temple in Mark 11:17, where Jesus quotes Isaiah 56:7, "My house shall be called a house of prayer for all the nations."[8] Jesus did not drive out the merchants from the inner-temple courtyard but from the outer courtyard, which was as close as the Gentiles could come to the temple. Some have interpreted Jesus' action as a symbolic expression of his intent to make it possible for the Gentiles to approach the temple. The point of the cleansing was not simply to get in the way of the trade in money and animals, but to dramatize that Gentiles were supposed to be able to come there to worship. The text leaves room for that interpretation, even though the wider text does not mention it.

In Luke 11:29-32, Jesus again recalls outsiders. He says that the Ninevites believed Jonah's message and that the Queen of Sheba ("the queen of the South") came to hear Solomon. The Jews probably took this as a condemnation of themselves. Jesus says in effect, "These are outsiders who were open to a message. But you are not open to a message." Jesus does not say, "I am going to go to the outsiders who listen." But by using the examples of Nineveh listening to Jonah and the Queen of Sheba coming to Solomon, Jesus at least shows freedom to think of outsiders as related to the message, which in that sense pushes the door open for a later missionary perspective.

There are also specific passages that predict a future openness or even sending that go beyond what we have been saying so far. Note the Syro-Phoenician woman (Mt 15:21-28; Mk 7:25-30); the "other sheep" (Jn 10:16); and the Greeks who come to Jesus and whose coming he takes as the occasion for an outcry of praise: "Now among those who went up to worship at the festival were some Greeks. They came to Philip, who was from Bethsaida in Galilee, and said to him, 'Sir, we

---

[8]The parallels in Matthew 21:13 and Luke 19:46 are less clearly about the Gentiles. Both leave out "for all the nations."

wish to see Jesus.' Philip went and told Andrew; then Andrew went with Philip and they told Jesus. Jesus answered them, 'The hour has come for the Son of Man to be glorified'" (Jn 12:20-23). The Greeks coming to and recognizing Jesus was taken as a sign of the times; God's kingdom was coming.

In the story of the high priest Caiaphas's unwitting prophecy, the Gospel of John might also be predicting the ingathering of the Gentiles. Caiaphas says, "It is better for you to have one man die for the people than to have the whole nation destroyed" (Jn 11:50). John then glosses Caiaphas's statement by adding that Caiphas prophesied "not for the nation only, but to gather into one the children of God who are scattered abroad" (Jn 11:52 ESV). Those who are "scattered abroad" could be the scattered Jews. It is more likely that by the time John wrote this Gospel he did mean the Gentiles.

Oscar Cullmann has interpreted John 4 as specifically referencing the mission to the Samaritans. The text itself does not say that. Yet, after Jesus conversed with the Samaritan woman, he told his disciples: "Do you not say, 'Four months more, then comes the harvest'? But I tell you, look around you, and see how the fields are ripe for harvesting. . . . For here the saying holds true, 'One sows and another reaps.' I sent you to reap that for which you did not labor. Others have labored, and you have entered into their labor" (Jn 4:35-38). It is hard to know what Jesus meant. But by the time John wrote his Gospel, this passage could have been describing the process in Acts 8 where Philip began to convert the Samaritans through his preaching, and then the disciples came and confirmed the Samaritans' entrance into the church. Thus Oscar Cullmann interprets John 4:35-38 as predicting the first stage of missionary expansion, read back into Jesus' time.[9]

Although the idea of outsiders coming into Israel is present in the Gospels, the idea is still marginal.

Perhaps a more central passage with more explicit relevance to our topic is Matthew 24:3-14:

---

[9]See Oscar Cullmann, *The Early Church* (Philadelphia: Westminster Press, 1956), pp. 185-92. [Cullmann makes the additional point that the fields the disciples were looking at were not ready for harvest yet, so the mission put in the mouth of Jesus is still future. —Ed.]

"Tell us, when will this be, and what will be the sign of your coming and of the end of the age?" Jesus answered them, "Beware that no one leads you astray. For many will come in my name, saying, 'I am the Messiah!' and they will lead many astray. And you will hear of wars and rumors of wars; see that you are not alarmed; for this must take place, but the end is not yet. For nation will rise against nation, and kingdom against kingdom, and there will be famines and earthquakes in various places: all this is but the beginning of the birth pangs.

"Then they will hand you over to be tortured and put you to death, and you will be hated by all nations because of my name. Then many will fall away, and they will betray one another and hate one another. And many false prophets will arise and lead many astray. And because of the increase of lawlessness, the love of many will grow cold. But the one who endures to the end will be saved. And this good news of the kingdom will be proclaimed throughout the world, as a testimony to all the nations; and then the end will come."

The beginning of much suffering is a time when the gospel will be sent to the nations. It is significant to notice this link. Also, the predictions of the cross are occasionally correlated with predictions of openness to the nations. But none of these hints or predictions of possible future outreach changes the point of Matthew 10:5-6, which basically says, "My disciples do not really go beyond the Jews." At most a more generous attitude toward Gentiles is part of the expected fulfillment of the Jewish Scripture.

The connection of suffering with the ingathering of Gentiles also relates to the universal quality of the titles that are given to Jesus. Jesus is called, for example, "the Servant." The Servant of Yahweh in Isaiah 42 and 49 was going to bring justice to the nations. Some references to Jesus seem to indicate that this dimension of the title "Servant" was part of what Jesus saw himself preparing to do. For instance, Matthew 12:18-21 quotes Isaiah 42:1-4: "Here is my servant, whom I have chosen, my beloved, with whom my soul is well pleased. I will put my Spirit upon him, and he will proclaim justice to the Gentiles. He will not wrangle or cry aloud, nor will anyone hear his voice in the streets. He will not break a bruised reed or quench a smoldering wick until he brings justice to victory. And in his name the Gentiles will hope" (Mt 12:18-21). Most of the time when Matthew quotes an Old Testament prophecy and says, "This came to pass so that it might be fulfilled with what is said," he uses only a brief text, sometimes just a phrase or a pair of words (for instance, saying that Jesus was going to come on a donkey referring to Isaiah 62:11 and Zechariah 9:9 in Matthew 21:5). But in Matthew 12:18-21 we have an extended quotation, four verses from Isaiah 42, precisely the ones that talk about proclaiming justice to the Gentiles, who hope in the Servant's name. So the Servant's worldwide or Gentile-focused mission is affirmed. The passage still does not talk about missionary organization, but it has a wider relevance.

Matthew introduces the verses from Isaiah 42 as a comment on the fact that "many followed him" (Mt 12:15 ESV). Matthew does not say, however, that those "many" were Gentiles, nor does he explain why that statement fits the Isaiah 42 quote that talks about proclaiming justice to the Gentiles. There must have been something about Jesus' work at that point that Matthew thought had a wider meaning for the Gentiles than what others perceived in that immediate context.

In relation to suffering and the ingathering of Gentiles more particularly, we can look at Mark 10:45, the end of the passage where Jesus calls his disciples to servanthood: "You know that among the Gentiles those whom they recognize as their rulers lord it over them, and their great ones are tyrants over them. But it is not so among you; but whoever wishes to become great among you must be your servant, and whoever wishes to be first among you must be slave of all. For the Son of Man came not to be served but to serve, and to give his life a ransom for many" (Mk 10:42-45).[10] The "ransom for many" again echoes the Servant Songs. "The many" could just as well be translated "all." It is a universal pointer. Wherever we find reference to the Servant, direct or indirect,

---

[10]Another title we find applied to Jesus is "Son of Man." We cannot pursue here the complexity of what that meant, but we do have to look at its implication for our theme. The only clear Old Testament reference is Daniel 7 where the Son of Man is one who is going to reign over the nations. "With the clouds of heaven there came one like a son of man, and he came to the Ancient of Days and was presented before him. And to him was given dominion and glory and a kingdom, that all peoples, nations, and languages should serve him" (Dan 7:13-14 ESV). The Son of Man is not linked to the people of Israel but to the wider world.

there is by implication some idea of the wider ministry. But again these texts are not focused on missionaries going to the non-Jews.

Even when Jesus helped a Gentile—for instance, when he healed the centurion's child—he did not go into their homes. Going into Jewish homes is part of the mission in Matthew 10. If it was a place of peace, the disciples were to stay there; if not, Jesus told them to shake off the dust from their feet and go on. But they did not go into the Gentiles' homes. Jesus never did, even though he helped some Gentiles.

WHY WAS MISSION TO THE GENTILES A LATER DEVELOPMENT?

Why was this wider opening to the Gentiles still in the future even after Jesus began to minister and said, "The kingdom is at hand in my presence. Now you should repent. Now you should believe. Now you should act differently. Now you should go proclaim"? Why was the expectation that the Gentiles will come to Israel not yet fulfilled? What would turn the direction of things or precipitate a missionary outgoing? Scholars have suggested a number of different answers.

Regenerate Israel will attract the Gentiles. Some scholars suggest that Jesus' message must first renew Israel, and the regenerated Israel will attract the Gentiles. There would be no missionary going out, but there would be a new incoming because of the renewed quality of Israelite life that has received Jesus.

Israel's rejection must be settled first. Other scholars suggest the opposite. They maintain that reaching out to Gentiles is linked with the refusal by Jews to accept Jesus as the Messiah. The Jews must turn Jesus down before he is free to go elsewhere. This idea is the most fully developed in Paul, but some people have used it to interpret the Gospels. For example, in relation to Luke 4:24-27 they say the reason Elisha and Elijah went to non-Jews was that they did not get any hearing from the Jews. They say Jesus said this was happening again in Nazareth. "A prophet is not accepted in his own country. You are not listening to me, so I am going to go to non-Jews too." Although that is one passage where some have discerned this meaning, it does not seem to fit what was happening right then in Nazareth. The people had not rejected him yet. They had expressed a favorable astonishment at his ministry up to that point.

In Paul, however, this interpretation has a clearer basis. Romans 9–11, and especially Romans 11:15 and following, are along this line: "If their rejection is the reconciliation of the world, what will their acceptance be but life from the dead?" The Jews had to reject Jesus in order that the world would be saved. Because of this rejection the crucifixion took place, and that is what sends us to the rest of the world.

The priority of the Jews—that it is through the Jews the message must go to others—is also found in Acts 13:46. Paul and Barnabas were just beginning the first missionary trip. They were in a synagogue first in Antioch of Pisidia, and the people urged them to speak again the following Sabbath. That next meeting reached beyond the synagogue: "almost the whole city" gathered to hear Paul (Acts 13:44). When the Jews in that meeting contradicted Paul, "Paul and Barnabas spoke out boldly, saying, 'It was necessary that the word of God should be spoken first to you. Since you reject it and judge yourselves to be unworthy of eternal life, we are now turning to the Gentiles. For so the Lord has commanded us, saying, "I have set you to be a light for the Gentiles, that you may bring salvation to the uttermost parts of the earth"'" (Acts 13:46-47).

This is like having to touch first base before going to second. First the Jews had to have their chance, but they rejected Jesus, so now his followers can go to the Gentiles. Acts 13:47 is the only place where Paul is recorded as quoting "the Lord," meaning it in the Old Testament sense. Usually when he quoted "the Lord" it meant Jesus. Here he was quoting another of the Servant texts (Is 49:6), so "the Lord," meaning God, is a chronological necessity. The reason that Jesus went to the Jews first was that there was a sequence that needed to be followed. You do not have to ask why; it is just that God wanted it that way. Maybe it was that the Jews' rejection was the prerequisite for the cross. But of course, the rejection in the city of Antioch was long after Jesus' crucifixion, and Paul still went to the Jews first.

First, slay the Lamb. This leads us to another explanation, one that Blauw notes: the crucifixion of Jesus had to happen first.[11] Until there

---

[11]Johannes Blauw, "The Biblical View of Man in His Religion," in *The Theology of the Christian Mission*, ed. Gerald Anderson (New York: McGraw-Hill, 1961), pp. 31-41, and also Harry Boer, *Pentecost and Missions* (Grand Rapids: Eerdmans, 1961), pp. 139-48.

was the slaying of the lamb, or the atoning sacrifice, or the slaying of the Servant (Is 53:11), there would not be a ransom for many, and therefore there would not be salvation for the Gentiles. It is difficult to consider that as an adequate explanation because according to this interpretation of atonement, there would not have been salvation for the Jews either.

The concept of the atonement—the sacrificial lamb or slain Servant—developed later in the New Testament and in church history. After the fact, interpreters could say, "Well, of course they did not have a saving message before the cross." But according to the Gospels, Jesus went to the Jews with a saving message before the cross: "The kingdom is now here; believe." How could he do that before the cross? My critique is simply on the level of logic. I do not mean to say that the crucifixion did not have to happen or that it is any less central than what Blauw assumes. But the explanation that "the crucifixion had to happen first" does not answer the question why the opening to the Gentiles does not occur in Jesus' public ministry.

Moreover, this view overlooks the fact that the disciples did not go out to the nations immediately after the crucifixion, immediately after Easter or immediately after Pentecost. Neither the pre-Pentecost nor the post-Pentecost church through Acts 6–7 did any wider preaching. The event of the cross by itself was not yet enough.[12] There are other turning points besides the crucifixion—specifically Pentecost but other turning points after Pentecost as well.

Nevertheless, we must agree that there was a temporal waiting for something to happen before taking the message beyond the Jewish community. Maybe what had to happen is not something that occurred in Jesus' public ministry. Maybe it was the resurrection, or maybe it was Pentecost.

The Gospel of John may appear to contradict this waiting to reach out to Gentiles, for John 17 clearly looks beyond the present disciples to

---

[12]Our question, "What about the nations?" is not quite the right question in relation to Jesus and the early post-Jesus church. Why there was no mission to the Gentiles did not need an explanation because it had not happened yet. It would have been ahistorical if it had happened any other way. Jesus went to the Jews, and so the first church was a Jewish church. Jesus stayed at home in Palestine most of the time, so his followers did too. The absence of mission to Gentiles did not need much explanation because it could not have been otherwise.

many other sheep. Jesus says: "I ask not only on behalf of these, but also on behalf of those who will believe in me through their word," that is, later generations, the wider church (Jn 17:20). Yet this is pointedly not a prayer for the world. "I am not asking on behalf of the world, but on behalf of those whom you gave me, because they are yours" (Jn 17:9). The wider world hates the disciples: "The world has hated them because they do not belong to the world, just as I do not belong to the world" (Jn 17:14). Here *the world* does not mean the Gentile world. It means the world of unbelief and rejection. But even here, there is no reference to a formal witness, only a prayer that the church may be faithful. The oneness of the church—the disciples and those who believe through the disciples—is to be a witness. "The glory that you have given me I have given to them, so that they may be one, as we are one . . . that they may become completely one, so that the world may know that you have sent me" (Jn 17:22-23). The glory is given so even the world that persecutes and hates will know. But its knowing does not mean the world will be converted. It means the world will be shamed; it will be condemned in its rejection. The world is not thought of as being won, although the disciples will win some people.

In summary, there is and yet there is not a worldwide perspective in the Gospels. Specifically, actively Jesus tells his disciples to stay with the Jews. On the fringes, in the future, in some exceptional cases, the texts point beyond Israel. But reaching out to Gentiles is not yet said pointedly or affirmatively. This leaves aside Matthew 28:20, which we will deal with in the next chapter. On the whole, during the earthly public ministry of Jesus, the Gentiles are on the margins or waiting the future ingathering. The concept of an aggressive, organized missionary effort is not there.

3

THE GREAT COMMISSION
AND ACTS

In the last chapter, we dealt with Jesus' public and less public teaching ministry and asked how he related his mission to the Jews to anything wider. We found that he concentrated on the Jews, but there were several ways in which a wider mission appeared on the fringes. We did not deal with the Great Commission either in the form we have it in Matthew 28:18-20 or in the relatively parallel forms we have elsewhere, especially Luke and John. So in the first half of this chapter we will look at these and other texts that relate to them.

THE GREAT COMMISSION

We did not touch on these Gospel texts in the chapter on Jesus' public ministry—why not? In part we did not do so because they represent a new chronological stage. There we were dealing with "Jesus' public ministry." The post-resurrection Jesus is already moving into the story of Acts. Therefore, we might see more clearly the appropriateness of skipping over the Great Commission in the previous chapter if we go on to the story of Acts and then look back. In a subsidiary way, I left the Great Commission texts aside to avoid concentrating where traditional missionary interpretation has always concentrated. The traditional interpretation is linguistically questionable. The Commission is also one of the sections about which redaction critics are the most dubious.

The traditional popular understandings of the missionary mandate and of missionary history are based centrally on the Great Commission text or concept.[1] The last thing Jesus did was tell his disciples to go to all nations. So they did. In terms of history, it is assumed that they consciously fulfilled this command. In terms of the church's mandate, it is because Jesus said to go that the church has this authority.

In the sixteenth century, for instance, that mandate was the basis for a debate about baptism. Their translation said, "Go therefore, and teach all nations, baptizing them in the Name of the Father, and the Son, and the Holy Ghost" (Mt 28:19, Geneva Bible). It said *teach* before it said *baptize*, and that proved they could only baptize those who had been taught. So they should not baptize babies. This was a key text in the Anabaptist debate about infant baptism. Applying the concept of "institution" in the strict sense, the Anabaptists asked, when was baptism instituted? It was instituted when Jesus said, "Go baptize."

The same concept of authority was still present in the age of William Carey (1761–1834). The way Carey and his generation debated the issue of foreign missions was to ask, "Does that mandate still apply?" Jesus told his disciples to go everywhere. Is that an imperative for us? Most people said the disciples already finished that. Carey said that the mandate continues to apply until the whole world is evangelized. This concentration on the Great Commission is still present in sermons and has played a part in many people's personal vocational development. This focus, however, is what needs to be tested, partly textually, but especially from the Acts story.

Parallel texts usually interpreted as missionary mandates. There are four texts that can be interpreted as roughly parallel.

Matthew 28:18-20. Matthew's text comes closest to being what is usually interpreted as an imperative for mission. But it is not an imperative to go in the strict literal sense. The imperative in the Greek is to "make disciples." Three adverbially used Greek participles describe how to make disciples: going, teaching, baptizing. "As you go, make disciples," is not strictly an imperative to go. It does not say, "Go ye." It says, "Make disciples." It is assumed that they will be going. But when, where or why

---

[1][Here Yoder was referring to understandings that developed after 1800. The term "Great Commission" was essentially a twentieth-century usage. —Ed.]

they go is not the text's focus. So the classic sixteenth-century Lutheran tradition with no foreign missions can be perfectly honest and not at all bothered about the text when they say that by parish preaching and baptizing babies they are doing what the Great Commission says.

Acts 1:8 and Luke 24:46-49. In Luke-Acts, the sending is not a command but a prediction. In Acts, Jesus says that the disciples "will be my witnesses in Jerusalem, in all Judea and Samaria, and to the end of the earth," but that is not a command. It is a prediction. In Luke, the risen Jesus says, "Thus it is written" that "repentance and forgiveness of sins is to be proclaimed in his name to all nations," though it is not clear where it is written.

John 20:21-23. John 20 focuses on the authorization to forgive. "'Peace be with you. As the Father has sent me, so I send you.' When he had said this, he breathed on them and said to them, 'Receive the Holy Spirit. If you forgive the sins of any, they are forgiven them; if you retain the sins of any, they are retained'" (Jn 20:21-23). This is John's parallel to Matthew 18:15-20, where Jesus says that those sins we forgive are forgiven; those we do not forgive are not forgiven. So John 20:21-23 is a sending. The word "sending" is even used here. But it is a sending in the sense of authorization to function in the church.

So none of these four passages says quite what they have been taken to say, that is, that they are mandates for foreign missions.

Acts and the Great Commission. More important is the experience of the New Testament church as reported in Acts and reflected in the Epistles. There is no indication in Acts that churches ever quoted to themselves the Great Commission.[2] It would have helped if they had quoted it when they were struggling with two questions: Was it all right for Peter to baptize Cornelius? How do we apply Jewish ritual prescriptions to Gentile believers (the question of Acts 15)? But they did not quote it. The determining event that led to the decisions in those cases was not saying, "I remember Jesus said we were supposed to receive the

---

[2]This is especially argued in Harry Boer, *Pentecost and Missions* (Grand Rapids: Eerdmans, 1961), pp. 28-47. I am convinced by Boer's reading—the sources give no indication that the church before Paul ever thought about connections between what they were doing and the fact that there are texts that say Jesus told them they should do this.

Spirit, then we would go to all of Judea, then we would go to Samaria, and then we would go to the whole world." They never show any indication in Acts of either reminding themselves that this was predicted or saying that it was commanded. The mission of the church in Acts happened, but not by expositing or applying a mandate. We could say they were following out their charter but did not think to say so, but that is a funny way to read a text.

Nor did they deduce a mission beyond Israel from the Old Testament. We have observed that the Old Testament was expecting that at some future point, when the Messiah would come or when the kingdom was established, there would be an ingathering of the nations. We do not see them explaining, from the Old Testament, the church's growth into new populations, even though it would have been fitting at certain points.

Strikingly, Peter's defense in Jerusalem of why he had been so accepting toward Cornelius provides the only explanation in Acts that quotes Jesus' teaching.

> "And as I began to speak, the Holy Spirit fell upon them just as it had upon us at the beginning. And I remembered the word of the Lord, how he had said, 'John baptized with water, but you will be baptized with the Holy Spirit.' If then God gave them the same gift that he gave us when we believed in the Lord Jesus Christ, who was I that I could hinder God?" When they heard this, they were silenced. And they praised God, saying, "Then God has given even to the Gentiles the repentance that leads to life." (Acts 11:15-18)

John the Baptist is the one who said, "I have baptized you with water; but he will baptize you with the Holy Spirit" (Mk 1:8), but Peter claimed that Jesus said it. Nevertheless, it is not the Great Commission. It does not say, "You shall baptize." It says, "You shall be baptized by the Holy Spirit." Peter found in the events of Cornelius's conversion a confirmation of how the Spirit was working, but he did not find an outworking of the mandate to baptize.

In Acts 10:42-43, Peter does not quote but alludes to Jesus' mandate to preach. In his sermon to Cornelius, after he has come to Cornelius's house, Peter says that Jesus "commanded us to preach to the people and to testify that he is the one ordained by God as judge of the living and the dead. All the prophets testify about him." That is one point at which there is reference to the mandate to preach.

A further striking observation is that even when Old Testament texts that could have a missionary implication are quoted, that meaning is not drawn from them. For instance, in Acts 2:16-21 Peter quotes the prophecy of Joel that had referred to "all flesh" and to "everyone who calls on the name of the Lord," and Peter claimed that the prophecy was fulfilled. He could have exposited it in the direction of reaching beyond the Jews, but he did not. Moreover, in Acts 2:39 Peter says, "The promise is for you, for your children, and for all who are far away, everyone whom the Lord our God calls." That also would have left room to bring in other people, but that was not done. To judge by Peter's own reactions in the beginning of chapter 10, when he said "those who are far away," he could still have meant Diaspora Jews. Throughout Acts there are repeated references to texts that could have been interpreted to point beyond the Jewish culture and yet are not. In Acts 3:25, for example, which says that in Abraham "all the families of the earth" are to be blessed, the gathering is still expected, but it is only implied, not expressed. It is neither practiced nor planned. They were not thinking strategically or looking forward to next steps, as the story is told. This is even true about Paul's ministry as Acts recounts it. In Acts 13:46-47, when Paul is explaining his preaching, he quotes not the Great Commission but Isaiah 49:6, the "light to the nations," one of the Servant Songs. Even when the missionary reality is beginning to take place, the interpretation of it is not focused on "Jesus told us to go."

By the time the Gospels were written, the Great Commission was part of the record. John actually says that he is putting things into his Gospel that the early believers had forgotten, or there were things that Jesus said that they did not remember until later. I do not think it disrespectful to the canonical texts to observe that there are some things recorded in the Gospels about which the apostles and the early church were not very conscious at first. Luke is not interested in telling us that they knew what they were doing. If he has any interest, it is the opposite: the early believers struggled against going beyond Israel, dragging their

feet all the way. It was always a new, unplanned event—against somebody's resistance—that pushed them beyond old boundaries.

What then did happen if the traditional popular interpretation that
the disciples immediately set out to fulfill the Great Commission is not
correct? The alternate thesis is that a whole series of events, pushed by
the Holy Spirit, led in a certain direction. In this process the Holy Spirit
gradually used the Great Commission as a memory, but more often
used other kinds of considerations and other kinds of happenings.

This second interpretation suggests we return to the story as a whole.
So, what is the story?

THE MISSIONARY STORY IN ACTS

Pentecost: Acts 2. The story starts with Pentecost. Something like Pentecost was predicted in Acts 1:8. The disciples were told to wait, and they
were waiting. But what happened next was not at all the product of expectation or planning. A new thing happened to them, which they could
then interpret for the onlookers. But there is no indication that this Pen-
tecostal experience is what we are expected to have today.

Pentecost's impact is universality. According to most interpreters,
Luke clearly implied a relationship between Pentecost and the Babel
story, in which, as a result of sin, tongues were scattered and people
could not understand each other. In Genesis, this story of confusion and
separation laid the groundwork for world history. In Pentecost, by contrast, we have a new event that lays the groundwork for a story of universality and unification. Later historians see this as Luke's editorial perspective. But Peter did not see with the benefit of hindsight.

The church after Pentecost was still a faithful sect completely within
Judaism. They met daily in the temple and included in their membership
many priests (Acts 6:7). But they believed that Jesus was the Messiah—
something a Jew could faithfully believe. A person did not stop being a
Jew when he or she believed somebody to be the Messiah. In fact, around
133 C.E., Rabbi Akiba, a rabbi who is highly respected in the Talmudic
tradition even today, believed that Bar Kochba was the Messiah. That
did not make him any less a Jew.

In summary, if we read the story for its own sake rather than reading it from a later perspective with the concept of Matthew's missionary mandate, clearly Pentecost did not make the church missionary. Pentecost, as Luke later recorded it, pointed in that direction, but we have been pointing in that direction ever since Abraham, ever since Isaiah.

Hellenist widows: Acts 6. The next major event for our purposes is Acts 6, the tension about the Hellenist widows. In order to understand this tension and further missionary development, it is important to know that sociologically or institutionally speaking, there were two parties in the early church, both made up of Jews. One was a Palestinian messianic sect that believed they knew who the Messiah was, that he had come, that after being killed he was raised and that he was the center of their gathering. But they were still faithful Jews. They went to the temple. As far as we have testimony to their Christology from the discourses of the first chapters in Acts, it is what later theology came to call "adoptionist," that is, Jesus was a great man who was given divine status as a result of his obedience—if we take only those texts. They included in their members priests (Acts 6:7) and Pharisees (Acts 15:5). They were committed to fulfilling the entire law as interpreted by their rabbinic tradition. They sent people, two by two, to other churches that they had not founded to observe how the law was being kept. That is, they did not send missionaries but observers to see whether the younger churches were applying the rules from back home.[3]

The second party was called "the Hellenists." They were just as Jewish as the Palestinians, but with wider cultural horizons. They had been living in other parts of the world, sometimes for generations. They lived their life of faith normally in the synagogues located where they were, not in the temple. They would come back to Jerusalem for religious feasts when they could, even during their productive years as merchants or craftsmen, so they were not against the temple. But they could live without the temple because they had been living in Corinth, Ephesus, Tarsus and elsewhere.

What was the difference between the temple and the synagogues as a

---

[3]The leader of the group was James, the brother of the Lord. It has been suggested that even the calling of this James had some relation to an earlier vision of the dynasty of family leadership, which made sense in that kind of Jewish culture.

focus of peoplehood? The synagogue focused on Scripture not on ritual, on reading the scroll together and not on sacrifice. Synagogue life was carried on by elders in the community, by what sociologists would call voluntary association and not by priests and a self-perpetuating hierarchy. The synagogue's cultural form was congregational and local, not central and hierarchical.

The Hellenist Jews had their own synagogues (Acts 7). That is where Stephen did his preaching. He did not preach in the synagogues of the Palestinians, but in the "synagogue of the Freedmen (as it was called), Cyrenians [North Africans], Alexandrians, those from Cilicia and Asia" (Acts 6:9).[4]

The Hellenist Jews were at home in the wider world, which does not mean they were less Jewish. It means they were more Jewish because their Jewishness had been tested and confirmed in the wider world. They had to stay Jewish in a pagan culture. That meant they thought about what it meant to be Jewish. They compared their monotheism with the polytheism of their neighbors. They compared their morality with the licentiousness of their urban neighbors and still stuck to being Jews. They knew what it meant to be intentionally faithful and to maintain that faithfulness in the synagogue reading the Scriptures and in pilgrimages back to Jerusalem. The fact that they were at home in the wider world meant that they were capable of stating their faithfulness to Christ in an encounter with that wider world, and while it is not our business to pursue the development of Christology in the earliest church, it would show that they were capable of making stronger statements about Jesus than the Jerusalem Jews did.

This is the sociological context for the tensions regarding the Hellenist widows in Acts 6. The widows were Greek-speaking Jews who had lived somewhere outside of Palestine. When they could, Hellenist Jews would come back to Jerusalem to retire. The synagogues maintained charitable resources for people from the Diaspora: the elderly, of course, some of whom were widows. The non-Christian Jewish structure al-

---

[4]Probably for reasons of dialect, or maybe of knowing each other back home there were synagogues according to ethnic origin, and the Hellenistic Jews who came from Asia Minor did not meet together with the Hellenistic Jews that came from North Africa.

ready provided special care—housing and the sharing of goods—for widows. The gathering of followers of Jesus in Acts also included widows—both Palestinian Jewish widows, who were well taken care of because they were at home, and non-Palestinian Jewish widows, who were less well taken care of because they did not have a home synagogue. These Greek-speaking widows needed help the most but were getting the least attention from the community in its economic sharing.

The seven men who were called to correct this imbalance were all Hellenists, that is, they had Greek names. Their accreditation for this task was that they were filled by the Holy Spirit. We do not hear anything more about them helping the widows, but we hear about two of them as preachers.

The first missionary push beyond Israel: Acts 7–11. Hellenist Jewish Christians were the first people to spread because they were the first to be persecuted. They were the first to preach beyond Jerusalem, the first to preach beyond their own circle and the first to be called Christians. Their center came to be Antioch. Their leader and spokesman came to be Paul.

The story of this movement begins with Stephen's discourse in Acts 7, a major block of text in the book. His speech represents the new perspective that the Hellenist Jewish Christians brought into the church. This discourse begins by critiquing temple-oriented worship, even though traditional Jewish Christians were still going to the temple. Stephen is the first disciple to be martyred, like Jesus. Strikingly, Stephen is like Jesus in his death, saying, "Lord, do not hold this sin against them" (Acts 7:60). Also like Jesus, the accusation that gets him in trouble is that he criticized the temple.

In his long discourse, he surveys Hebrew history and makes two basic points. First, everything important in the history of God's people happened outside of Palestine. In effect, he claims "All the significant events that constitute our people were events whose meaning was elsewhere, especially the Exodus story." Second, this people's story is a history of rebellion. The rebellion is one of localizing God: making God a house when God does not want a house. As the prophet says, "Heaven is my throne, and the earth is my footstool. What kind of house will you build for me?" (Acts 7:49). As a result of Stephen, or the movement he represents, the first wave of persecution arose against the church (Acts 8:1-3).

The first persecution hit only the Hellenistic church. We observe this because later, when the scattered Hellenists had made some converts, especially Philip in Samaria, they could send to Jerusalem for support. Peter could go and ratify the conversion by laying hands on the Samaritans. That is, *the church* was not chased out of Jerusalem, only the Hellenists. This was not because they believed Jesus was the Messiah. That was not a crime. The Twelve and the other Palestinian Jews, who still lived in Jerusalem, also believed he was the Messiah, and they kept going to the temple.

Rather, the Hellenists were persecuted for criticizing the temple and the law. They were persecuted not just because this was a theological, doctrinal or even a ritual issue, but because the law and the temple were the foci of the traditional understanding of God's calling of Israel. If the calling focused on the law and the temple, it was important to stay with what we have been calling the "centripetal" definition of God's purposes for the world. The Hellenists' criticism of the temple and the law began to crack things open to see another vision of how God will relate to the world. That is why the Hellenists were being persecuted. By contrast, the Sanhedrin never persecuted the non-Hellenistic Christians.[5]

The second person who carried this outward movement was Philip. He was one of those scattered in the Hellenist persecution, and he turned up in Samaria. This is the first step of the prediction in Acts 1:8, "You will be my witnesses in . . . Samaria." Nobody sat down and said, "Let's go to Samaria; it says so in the charter. We have to go there first." Instead, the Hellenist Jews who were followers of Jesus were chased, and Samaria is the first place they landed, unintended. But once he got there, Philip shared his faith. And lo and behold there were signs and wonders. The Holy Spirit worked again to confirm the gospel. Then Peter and John had to come from Jerusalem to see whether Samaritans

---

[5]James was later killed by Herod and not by the Sanhedrin.

coming to faith in Christ was all right, and they concluded affirma-tively because again there were signs and wonders.

After this Philip met and taught a man from Ethiopia, who was from farther out yet, but still a God-fearer who was deeply interested in the Jewish tradition. He had gone to great trouble to come to Jeru-salem to worship.[6]

The story's next step is again a story of broadening. This time it is Peter and the Gentile Cornelius in Acts 10–11. Peter went to meet Cor-nelius in spite of himself; the whole story is about Peter's resistance and change. The Cornelius event is a major turning point in the book. Peter came to stand between the traditional Palestinian and the Hellenist fol-lowers of Jesus as a mediator.[7] He was open to a wider mission than the Pharisees in the church (Acts 15:5).[8] Galatians 2:7 even says that Peter was assigned a mission to Jews.

At the same time, while Peter agreed with Paul in being open in principle to non-Jews, he was subject to the Jerusalem church's over-sight. When Peter and Paul were in Antioch together and the ob-servers came from Jerusalem to see whether the rules were being kept, Peter respected them and broke fellowship with the non-Jewish Chris-tians (Gal 2:11-14).

After the Cornelius story we return to the Hellenists who were scat-tered, and we find them in Antioch. Acts 11:19-21 says that they were the first to preach to pagan Gentiles. Prior to this work in Antioch followers of Jesus interacted with some people like Cornelius who were not of ethnic Jewish background but had a relationship with the synagogue. In Antioch, however, they preached for the first time to people who had no such connection. In Antioch, they were first called Christians (Acts 11:25-27). And Antioch was to be the base for Paul's work.

From there the story traces Paul's missionary voyages and then moves

---

[6]While this is an illustration of the gospel shared with someone who was not ethnically Jewish, it represents the Hebrew Old Testament "light to the nations" theology (the Ethiopian comes to Jerusalem) rather than a "going out to the nations" theology.

[7]There were other mediating figures such as Barnabas, who hailed from Cyprus, so he was a Hel-lenist. But the Jerusalem church trusted Barnabas enough to send him to Antioch, and he was linked to John Mark, who was also from Jerusalem. See Oscar Cullmann, *The Early Church* (Philadelphia: Westminster Press, 1956), p. 191, and his book on Peter.

[8]Farther in the Hellenist direction we have Apollos (Acts 18:24-28).

to Acts 15, another crisis of broadening. Paul's pivotal role in this story will be the focus of chapter four.

OBSERVATIONS BASED ON ACTS

The missionary church of the New Testament was the Hellenist church. It was smaller than the more conservative Jewish group. It had fewer leaders and less tradition. But it was basically the Hellenist church that gave us the New Testament story, except for what we call the General Epistles, Peter and James, for it was the Hellenist church that survived.[9] The whole New Testament was written around the missionary agenda of the Hellenist church. Though careful historians can find traces of it for generations, the more traditional Jewish church collapsed after 70 C.E. Once it lost the base of Jerusalem, it could not by definition become a missionary church, so it became a tiny exile movement for a couple generations. What we normally call the New Testament church is really only the Hellenistic branch. That is the first observation: the Hellenist churches are the people who carried out mission.

Every step was unplanned as far as the story is told. There is never any indication that the followers of Jesus sat to think that they should go to Samaria and then to the uttermost parts of the world, or that they in any other way referred back to a mandate. Each step was always a new event.

Although not usually present in Protestant thinking about mission, that the disciples misunderstood Jesus is just as true after Pentecost as it was before. The usual idea is that what they could not understand was the cross and how the cross relates to the kingdom. They were Jews and Jews could not understand the cross because they were always hard-hearted. But then there was the resurrection and later Pentecost. The usual view is that after Pentecost, the disciples had it all clear; they went out and followed the Great Commission.

The real point is that humanness of learning stretches on and on, and the learner is finite. Even after letting in Cornelius, the early

---

[9]The General Epistles are the least read in the New Testament. They are the least original compared to the Jewish background, and even they are addressed to the Diaspora followers of Jesus, not to their own Palestinian church.

church was not ready for Acts 15. They had to address the question of "Christian" identity and practice again. But we can attribute this to human finitude, rather than human depravity. We cannot learn everything at once. The early followers' lack of understanding of the wider dimensions of faith was partly because there had not yet been the context in which the implications of what Jesus had said would be meaningful. They could not read the meaning of Jesus' teaching with reference to Corinth, if they had no notion of Corinth. There had to be a process. And for the Jews who followed Jesus, getting to deeper understanding was part of the revelation.

The expansion was always at the Holy Spirit's initiative. Often today, the name Holy Spirit is used to designate our own best ideas. That is, we have a committee meeting, and when we come to a conclusion we say that is the Holy Spirit. Perhaps the Holy Spirit is identified as visible to us in certain especially striking internal events in the life of the church or an individual. In the story of Acts, however, the Holy Spirit pushes people beyond the present borders of their community. Every time that happens, step by step, threshold by threshold, through Acts, there is reference to the Holy Spirit at work. The Holy Spirit pushes the church beyond itself.

The Spirit's work is identifiable, whether in signs and wonders or in ecstasies such as tongues. It is beyond human resources. And, as Acts demonstrates, the Spirit makes mission happen and makes mission acceptable. The reason the church in Jerusalem had to accept Peter's report about Cornelius was that they too had had ecstatic experience. That is the function of ecstatic experience: to accredit a new breakthrough. The Spirit does not just empower the preacher or prepare the listener and bring the listener to assurance. The Spirit does both of those and in addition gives orders to the community.

There were no missionary agencies or special training for cross-cultural mission. There were no special organizations needed. The congregation's normal functions—sending, ordaining, sharing, giving—were the organs of the missionary process. Congregations authorized people to go somewhere, and they sent funds or messages. Every step was sociologically, culturally prepared for by the Hellenistic Jews—people who served as bicultural and bilingual bridges, people who were at home already in the world to which they were going. This was more than simply knowing the language or studying another culture the way anthropology and linguistics help us to do today. It was that the other world was truly their world. That is where they grew up. They maintained their Jewish identity, but they maintained it in that wider world. And they could express their witness to Jesus in that larger cultural frame because it was their home.[10]

This whole phenomenon of the broadening Hellenistic Christian community culminates in the man Saul/Paul; we will see more of his self-understanding in the next chapter. Already in the Acts story he is a symbol and the culmination of this process. Paul was from Tarsus, though he was not simply one of the Hellenist Jews, given his Jerusalem education and connections. We see traces of his Hellenistic education when he talks to the Athenians.

The Jerusalem congregation, the home church, the Twelve ratify the missionary effort. That is as strong as we can say it. Sometimes their attitude was more negative than that. The best they did was to say it was all right that Paul's missionary work should happen, that they would not stop it or declare that Paul was not a true follower of Jesus. They agreed to state with a little more indulgence than before the extent to which they would impose Jewish law on non-Jewish Christians.

LESSONS FOR CHRISTIAN MISSION

The story recounted in Acts has some lessons both for interchurch relations and for missions, especially in how Paul dealt with various situations. In earlier work I tried to address the relevance of this story for ecumenical dialogue.[11] But what are the lessons for Christian mission?

Our culture has tended to say that the church is the instrument of mission. Proclaiming the message is one thing and making a vehicle to proclaim the message is something else. This vehicle could be the whole church if the whole church is willing, but if not, the church can create a

---

[10]Paul was from Tarsus, even though sent at a younger age to be educated in Jerusalem.
[11]John Howard Yoder, *The Ecumenical Movement and the Faithful Church*, Focal Pamphlet No. 3 (Scottdale, PA: Herald Press, 1958).

separate committee. In either case the message is not the church. Moreover, the particular events whereby the work gets done are not of high importance. In this view what really matters is the message as words, as abstractable from the church, so that we can pick those words up and take them from one place to another and preach them in the other place.

In the Acts story we see rather that the church is not simply a vehicle; the events in the church's life are themselves the fact of mission. There are events to be interpreted. There is a way to be followed, and people are invited to join that way. In fact, "way" is the first name for the Christian faith in the early part of Acts. So it is not that first they had a message, then they needed a vehicle for the message, then they got a church, and then the church figured out how to communicate the message. It is really the other way around. First the scattered believers talk about Jesus, and then they have to deal with the fact that some of the people who listen to them accept him; and that makes them move. They gradually come to see that this movement was what God was doing with them. Then they have to interpret the Jesus they have been talking about in the new language of the people around them.

What pushed them in this direction were experiences they recognized as the movement of the Spirit. This is a different perspective on the Holy Spirit than we usually have in modern Protestant thought. Acts does not focus on the work of the Holy Spirit as making us sure, converting us, regenerating us or deepening the subjective reality of our faith. This subjective dimension is where the Holy Spirit appears in Karl Barth's churchly Trinity, in Pentecostalism's inner conviction of the reality of Jesus or in Wesleyan assurance. But if we come to Acts with these modern assumptions about the Spirit working in the heart, we do not see that what the Spirit did in the New Testament was something different. In Acts the work of the Holy Spirit is outside the person. The Spirit calls on people, and the Spirit's working is discerned not in their feeling but in their talking. The decisions that are identified with the Holy Spirit are outward decisions, social decisions, travel plans. That does not mean that we do not have to talk about subjectivity in our culture. But we have to identify a certain degree of modesty in reading it back into the biblical record.

Here in Acts and in other New Testament texts we can observe the "widening of the world" frame of reference both in terms of sociology and in terms of discourse. This cultural widening and the significance of how it happened were a prejudice and profound concern of this group of crosscultural people, the early church.

4

THE MINISTRY OF PAUL
IN SALVATION HISTORY

We have a chapter on Paul, but not on James and Peter, not only because Paul wrote more, but more fundamentally because he was a pivotal person in the story. We know there was a whole broadening movement, and there may have been other key persons in that movement. But, as the story is told in Acts, Paul represents a turning point in a set of further thresholds in reaching beyond Palestinian Jewish Christianity into the Gentile world. Not only is he personally a pivot in the story, he is also pivotal in interpreting it. He represents a distinct step in interpretation. We will look first historically at Paul's ministry and its place in salvation history and then at his interpretation of it.

THE MINISTRY OF PAUL IN SALVATION HISTORY

Paul's own person gathered up two histories. He was completely and faithfully Jewish. He talked about this in many passages (Acts 26:4-5; Rom 11:1; Gal 1:13-14; Phil 3:4-5). On the other hand, he was fully at home in the Gentile world. He was born in, lived in and even after his conversion went back to live in the Diaspora. Apparently, by birth he was a Roman citizen. His church base was Antioch. He had at least some literary education—he could quote the poets, and he preached to the philosophers in Athens. His own coming into the movement is the hinge of Acts.

So what did his conversion mean? What came to him? What did he know afterwards that he did not know before? Who was he that he was not before? Uniformly, in the three reports we have, his conversion was permission to go to the Gentiles. There are many things about a modern conversion that we do not find recorded in Paul's conversion, but what we do have reported is significant. In Acts 9:15, God says in a vision to Ananias that Paul is going to "bring my name before Gentiles and kings and before the people of Israel." In Acts 22:15, Paul says Ananias told him that "you will be his witness to all the world of what you have seen and heard," but in Acts 22:21 it sounds as if Jesus gave Paul this charge in a new vision after he left Antioch. In Acts 26:15-17, when Paul tells the story again, it almost sounds as if he was given this charge later when he got to Jerusalem. He is reporting it this time before King Agrippa and claims the Lord spoke directly to him on the Damascus road: "I am Jesus whom you are persecuting. But get up and stand on your feet; for I have appeared to you for this purpose, to appoint you to serve and testify to the things in which you have seen me and to those in which I will appear to you. I will rescue you from your people and from the Gentiles—to whom I am sending you."

These texts in Acts say different things about when and from whom Paul received his commission to preach to the Gentiles.[1] This is a problem if we are concerned about Paul's biography. But if we are concerned about the meaning of his commission, it is strikingly uniform. He did not emphasize that he was going to go to heaven now that his sins were forgiven or that he was a whole man. He emphasized that he was given a commission to testify to the Gentiles.

But he touched base first with the Jews. At first Paul was occupied with testifying to the Jews that the Messiah was Jesus. "When they opposed and reviled him, in protest he shook the dust from his clothes and said to them, 'Your blood be on your own heads! I am innocent. From now on I will go to the Gentiles'" (Acts 18:5-6). Similarly, when Paul got to Rome, he checked in with the Jews and then called a meeting.

> Some were convinced by what he had said, while others refused to believe.
> So they disagreed with each other; and as they were leaving, Paul made one
> further statement: "The Holy Spirit was right in saying to your ancestors

---

[1]There are other cross-references to consider as well, such as Galatians 1:16.

through the prophet Isaiah, 'Go to this people and say, You will indeed listen, but never understand, and you will indeed look, but never perceive. For this people's heart has grown dull, and their ears are hard of hearing, and they have shut their eyes; so that they might not look with their eyes, and listen with their ears, and understand with their heart and turn—and I would heal them.' Let it be known to you then that this salvation of God has been sent to the Gentiles; they will listen." (Acts 28:24-28)

Paul's ministry was to take the message to the world. We find it in greetings (Rom 1:5; Gal 1:15-16) and other longer passages (Rom 11:13; 2 Cor 10:14-16; Col 1:23; Eph 3:1). Perhaps the strongest statement is from Acts 13:47, where Paul quoted a Servant Song (Is 42:6), the same verse from Isaiah that Luke 2:32 applied to Jesus, but here Paul used it about himself and Barnabas: "For so the Lord has commanded us, saying, 'I have set you to be a light for the Gentiles, so that you may bring salvation to the ends of the earth'" (Acts 13:47).

PAUL'S INTERPRETATION OF THIS MINISTRY

Paul most clearly stated the meaning of his ministry to the Gentiles in Ephesians.[2] A key term in Ephesians 3:1-12 regarding this ministry is *mystery*.[3] In contemporary English, *mystery* is something we cannot figure out. If we consider the "mystery religions" of Paul's time, the meaning would also have something to do with keeping secrets. However, Paul was not talking about arcane information that only the religiously initiated have, because he said the mystery is now manifest (Col 1:26) so everybody can see. Another use of "mystery" in Greek had to do with a political or military plan. Before a battle only military planners know their strategy. But once the plans are carried out, everybody knows the secret. The acting out of the plan is its revelation. It is in that sense that the mystery Paul referred to—that the Gentiles are fellow heirs with Jews—was hidden down through the ages. It was a mystery only in the sense that God's plans were not clear to the early church until they were carried out.

---

[2]It does not matter for our purposes whether Paul, his amanuensis, or one of Paul's disciples wrote Ephesians, though the topic is hardest to explain if it is not Paul.
[3]See also Colossians 1:26-29 and Romans 16:25-26.

Abolishing the law that separates. How is this mystery exposited? In
Ephesians 3:3 Paul said, "As I wrote above in a few words." Here he may
have been referring back to Ephesians 2:11-16: "Remember that you were
at that time without Christ, being aliens from the commonwealth of
Israel. . . . But now in Christ Jesus you who once were far off have been
brought near by the blood of Christ." When Paul said in Ephesians 2:12
that to be lost is to be "without God in the world," to have no hope, he
was describing the Gentile world's status: to be lost was the same thing
as being outside the promises of Israel. How was that distance or
strangeness between Jew and Gentile overcome? It was Christ's work
that made us "one new humanity" from these two kinds of people by
abolishing "in his flesh . . . the law with its commandments and ordi-
nances" (Eph 2:14-15). Jesus did it by giving everyone access in one Spirit
to the Father. So when in Ephesians 2:10 Paul said, "We are what he has
made us, created in Christ Jesus for good works," that was not a reference first of all to individual regeneration, but to a new people. This
was the work of Christ in the cross—making a new people, or "breaking
down the dividing walls" (Eph 2:14). The result is a new humanity (Eph
2:15; see also Eph 3:15). The wider social reality comes into view because
the effect of the law in separating people has been broken away.

In Lutheranism, to say that Jesus abolished the law means he abolished the law as ethical demand. The law's proper function is to bring us
to repentance. Once we have repented we are free from the law. We are
not only free in the sense that we no longer stand condemned before
God as a criminal is condemned in a court—but the law has no more
hold on us. We are free also in the sense of behavior. We do not have to
do everything the law says regarding circumcision, dietary restrictions
or the Sabbath. But once Lutheranism has done away with the law as
ethical demand, it has the problem of how to uphold ethics in the church.

Paul, however, meant something different by "abolishing the law." In
Ephesians 2:15 he was talking not about the law in its ethical content—
things to do and not to do—but about the law as that which separates.
The law represents the monopoly the Jews had on the knowledge of God,
which made the Gentiles "strangers to the covenants of promise" (Eph
2:12). Law created hostility between those who were in this law and

those who were beyond it. Law meant the exclusion of the Gentiles.[4] It meant the law's historical effect on community, not its content in terms of ethical demands or prohibitions.[5] "What is done away with in the cross," he basically said, "is the effect of the law in creating hostility in separating the Jews as a people from the Gentiles as people."

Reality of mission before theology of mission. We can ask which came first: was the broken wall of the law the basis of the mission or the consequence of the mission? Was the fact of reconciliation or the message of reconciliation prior? The question of which came first arose in the previous chapter. Did the Gentiles come into the community that followed Jesus because somebody sat down and thought, "Let's bring them in," or did they come into it some other way, and then it made sense? My suggestion is that the event of bringing in the Gentiles came first and then had to be interpreted.

When Paul joined the movement, he interpreted what was already happening. His joining gave the movement greater clarity, effectiveness and self-consciousness, but it was happening before he was drawn in. In fact, it was because Gentiles wanted to follow Jesus that Paul went to Damascus. He was trying to stop it. He was not trying to keep Jews from being messianic; if he had wanted to do that he would have stayed in Jerusalem and persecuted James and Peter. Instead, he was trying to stop Jews from letting down the fence of the law in Damascus and Antioch. He was against people like Stephen saying that since Jesus is the Messiah we do not need the temple and the law. As the Stephen story illustrates, Gentiles were joining the Jesus movement before Paul started preaching the gospel. Paul joined a movement that was already going on, became its major bearer and then, in Ephesians, its major interpreter.

---

[4]There are also wider meanings that law has in Paul's other writings: bondage, not grace (Gal 4); bondage typifying the powers and principalities to which we are in bondage. But those dimensions are not crucial for this present argument.

[5]There was an actual wall in the temple precincts, excluding Gentiles from the inner temple. An inscription on the wall, which is now available in Jerusalem museums, says, "Let no one of the Gentiles enter inside the barrier around the sanctuary and the porch; and if he transgresses he shall himself bear the blame for his ensuing death." When Paul talks about breaking down the wall, it is quite possible that he is thinking more than metaphorically. For the inscription see Michael Avi-Yonah, ed., *Views of the New Testament World* (Jerusalem: The International Publishing Company, 1961), 5:188.

Hence the fact of mission was prior to the theology of mission. The way it actually happened in the church's life was that the experience of mission was prior to the missionary mandate. Moreover, this is how Peter finally described the process, as he thought about his experience with Cornelius:

> You know that in the early days God made a choice among you, that I should be the one through whom the Gentiles would hear the message of the good news and become believers. And God, who knows the human heart, testified to them by giving them the Holy Spirit, just as he did to us; and in cleansing their hearts by faith he has made no distinction between them and us. Now therefore why are you putting God to the test by placing on the neck of the disciples a yoke that neither our ancestors nor we have been able to bear? On the contrary, we believe that we will be saved through the grace of the Lord Jesus, just as they will. (Acts 15:7-11)

Even at that late date, Peter does not refer to Matthew 28, the Great Commission or anything Jesus had ever said. Peter refers to his experience with Cornelius.

If the fact of mission is prior to the theology of mission, then we still have to ask, "Where did the facts come from?" The Christian Jews, according to many scholars, thought in terms of what could be called a "syllogism of fulfillment."

- In the messianic age the nations will come to Jerusalem. (That is the general premise.)
- This is the messianic age. (That is the subordinate premise.)
- Therefore, the nations will come.

Perhaps somebody in the Jesus movement sat down and thought that through in relation to Gentiles, or perhaps everybody simply said, "That is the way it must be."

It is doubtful, however, that the first twelve disciples thought this way. Remember that the promise—in the messianic age the nations will come to the light—did not call for going anywhere, did not tell them to go preach to Gentiles. Even though they had Jesus' predictions in their memories, and even though once Pentecost happened they cited the prophet Joel, the disciples were still surprised by the event of Pentecost.

In fact, the only thing the disciples contributed to Pentecost was to be there waiting. Thus, the only explanation for its happening was that God was behind it. That is how they made sense of it. The place of theology in the church's life was to explain the coherence of what had happened and how to talk about it. God did something, and then people had to think about it.

While the argument I have just made applies other places as well, it applies even more specifically to Paul—an intelligent, abstract thinker with a vision of history and a depth of interpretation—explaining what was happening. "It happened first. I got drawn into it. So now I see. This is God's nature. This was God's plan from before. Praise God for it!"

PAUL'S CONVERTED WORLDVIEW

Another set of readings from Paul that help us see how he interpreted his ministry might be called his "converted worldview."[6] This may be understood by asking, "What did Paul mean when he talked about knowing 'no man after the flesh' (2 Cor 5:16 KJV)?" Before examining what he meant by this, we need to consider 2 Corinthians 5:11-15.

Paul defends himself. In 2 Corinthians more than anywhere else, Paul had to defend himself against two kinds of people who critiqued his ministry. On one side were the Apollos people who could not understand why he made so much of Jewish history and why he did not simply preach religion in the philosophical way that Gentiles could understand—without people having to learn Aramaic prayers and other such things. On the other hand, the Peter and James kind of people wondered why he was troubling the community by integrating people who did not have a Jewish background and had to be taught the prayers and the Old Testament. So in 2 Corinthians, Paul defended his missionary strategy on both sides. There seem to have been three reproaches.

First, Paul may have been criticized for being a people pleaser. Although almost all English translations put the first part of each verse in 2 Corinthians 5:11-13 into the indicative mood, there are grounds to put

---

[6]Some of what I will say under this heading is condensed from my *The Politics of Jesus: Vicit Agnus Noster* (Grand Rapids: Eerdmans, 1972), pp. 212-27. [See also John Howard Yoder, *To Hear the Word,* 2nd ed. (Eugene, OR: Wipf and Stock Publishers, 2010), pp. 1-24. —Ed.]

it into the interrogative, as James Moffat's translation does. Since there was no punctuation in the received Greek text, we cannot tell whether the original was a declarative or an interrogative sentence. I suggest that the beginning of these verses should be put as questions. For example, in 2 Corinthians 5:11 instead of Paul stating, "knowing the fear of the Lord, we try to persuade others," Paul would be asking: "Do you think that I who fear the Lord am 'trying to please' others?"[7] Most English versions translate the Greek word *peithō* in 2 Corinthians 5:11 as "persuade." But the Greek word has a negative connotation. It does not mean "I win people over" or "I convince people." It means "I sell out to people." To be a people pleaser is a reproach. If the first part of this verse is posed as a question, Paul was quoting his accusers and defending himself against reproach: "Do you think that I, who fear God, 'am trying to please people?' What I am is known to God, and I hope it is known to you."

Second, in the following verse Paul would have been quoting his accusers to the effect that he was inappropriately recommending himself: "Do you think I am 'commending myself again' to you? No. I am just giving you something to explain. Giving you cause to be proud of us so that you may be able to answer those who pride themselves on a person's position."

Third, in 2 Corinthians 5:13 Paul answered the accusation that he was insane and basically said, "They say I am 'crazy.' Well, that is all right if it is for God. God is worth my being eccentric. But, on the other hand, if I am in my right mind, logical, that is for you. There is a certain rationality to my being a minister to you, to my having the missionary style and stance that I have. It is logical for me to be the missionary that I am. For the love of Christ constrains us." The love of Christ urges us on.

The love of Christ. What did Paul mean by "the love of Christ" that urges us on? There are two primary meanings of this Greek phrase that grammarians would identify.

The objective genitive. "The love of Christ" can be the love I have toward Christ. It comes from gratitude. I want to please him. I want to

---

[7]The old translation, "Knowing therefore the terror of the Lord, we persuade men," is the only basis for hellfire preaching in the King James Bible, and it has become a motivation for some missionary preaching.

do his will. This is how most Protestants have interpreted the basis of Christian ethics. I am grateful to God. I want to praise God. Therefore, I do things that glorify God. The "love of Christ that urges us on" is the love in me toward God. It is my subjective stance that makes me want to do these good things. There is some doubt about whether this interpretation is adequate since the word that is translated "constrain" in the King James Version and "urge" in the rsv seems to be a stronger word than the objective genitive interpretation supports. The tone of the Greek word is closer to "coerce." The New English Bible says, "The love of Christ leaves us no choice" (2 Cor 5:14).

The subjective genitive. So it must be that the love that is at work here is to be interpreted in what is grammatically called "the subjective genitive," the love that Christ has, the love that Christ shows. This love lives out through me, but it is his love not mine that we are talking about. Paul said that Christ's active power and not his own was working, and that is why Paul had no choice. He could not help himself. 1 Corinthians 9 talks at greater length about how Paul had no choice. He had no merit. He had no praise coming for being an apostle. Since he wanted to do a little something of his own, he worked for nothing so he could have something to boast about. But he had no choice about being an apostle; Christ's power at work brought it about. It did not depend on him.

This whole discussion is not about Paul's motivation in a modern Western individualistic sense: What is it that makes me do this? Why do I feel like doing this? Paul was talking about a *history*, about the love of Christ that gave him no choice in the set of events that dragged him along despite himself. There is no indication that Paul sat down and asked if he was going to do what he was told. His comment in Acts 26:19 is as close as he comes to the possibility that he might have done otherwise: "I was not disobedient to the heavenly vision." He did not think about his motivations. He thought about a story he had been pushed into and about a new worldview imposed on him by events. It was not that he had something new in his heart that made him happy or made him want to share.

What is this new view that Paul has? It is described in a complicated sentence, but the point is simple. "For the love of Christ urges us on, because we are convinced that one has died for all; therefore all have died. And he died for all, so that those who live might live no longer for themselves, but for him who died and was raised for them" (2 Cor 5:14-15). If we diagram that sentence it would go round and round. But there are really only two parties involved: (1) Christ (his death and resurrection for all) and (2) other people (whose lot is death but who live for Christ by identifying with his death and resurrection). That is said in a grammatically complex but intellectually simple way. Christ took our place, and now we are in his place. Christ died for all, and "all" is the word that matters. There is no distinction between Jew and Greek.

Regarding no one from a human point of view. We can return now to Paul's "converted view" represented by 2 Corinthians 5:16: "From now on, therefore, we regard no one from a human point of view; even though we once knew Christ from a human point of view." The King James Version reads, "Know we no man after the flesh." The superficial, traditional interpretation of that translation is that to know someone after the flesh means to care about his or her historical humanity. That is an understandable argument—that Paul was defending his apostolicity against those who said that since he had not been with Jesus physically, he was not as good an apostle as those who had been. So Paul needed to make the point that it was not essential to have known Jesus. This is a reasonable argument; apostolic authority might have been of concern to Paul. However Paul's statement "though we once knew Christ from a human point of view, we know him no longer in that way" is made only as background for the fact that he does not look at *anybody* from a human point of view. The people he was writing to and being scolded by were all still in their bodies. So knowing Christ "in the flesh" cannot be what this text means.

What then does it mean? The Greek words that Paul used in 2 Corinthians 5:16—*kata sarka*—that are translated "after the flesh" or "human," are most fittingly translated "ethnically." That is, "I do not see people ethnically anymore. I do not perceive people in the category into which their biology and genealogy put them. I do not evaluate people on the basis of whether they are Jews or Gentiles. I do not do that anymore because Christ took the place of all and all live in his stead. So then I also have to see them that way."

We have often missed this because one of the worst mistranslations in several of our English Bibles is 2 Corinthians 5:17. "Therefore, if any man be in Christ, he is a new creature" (KJV; see also RSV, NASB).[8] In the original Greek text, the word "he" is not there. It is not a sentence. It is an exclamation: "If anyone is in Christ, new creation!"—exclamation point, no sentence. The other mistake in translation is that the word translated "creation" here cannot possibly mean a creature, in the sense of a single person seen as an object of creation. In New Testament Greek the word means the act of creating, the event when God created the earth, or it means all that God created. What the Greek says in this verse is that if somebody is in Christ, that is, if someone sees the world in view of the fact that Christ died for all and all live for him, then there is a whole new world. It is the world that is different, not the individual. All of the modern digging around to know where conversion happens inside the heart—is it in the nerve cell, is it between the id and the superego or is it in the process of education—had nothing to do with what Paul was talking about when he spoke of the new creation. It is a different subject. He was not against modern conversion and its preoccupation with what happens inside the person; he just did not know about it.

Paul said that he did not see a person anymore as what he or she was culturally, genealogically or ethnically, or in terms of class, status and education. What he recognized in his relationship to other members of the people of Christ was their place in the new humanity. To see the world in faith is to see it in light of Christ having broken down the wall. Christ's death makes it impossible any longer to discriminate between "in people" and "out people," according to the flesh.[9] There is a new worldview, a new way of putting reality together. That includes something new about personality, reflexes, complexes and all the rest. But it

---

[8][The New Revised Standard Version corrects this mistranslation. —Ed.]

[9][Yoder noted Markus Barth, *The Broken Wall: A Study of the Epistle to the Ephesians* (Chicago: Judson Press, 1959). By the time Yoder taught Theology of Mission in 1976, Barth had published *Ephesians: Introduction, Translation, and Commentary on Chapters 1–3* (Garden City, NY: Doubleday, 1974). See pp. 253-325. —Ed.]

starts with what God did by opening Israel to the Gentiles in Jesus.

We have not come yet to what usually is seen as the climax of the passage:

> All this is from God, who reconciled us to himself through Christ, and has given us the ministry of reconciliation; that is, in Christ God was reconciling the world to himself, not counting their trespasses against them, and entrusting the message of reconciliation to us. So we are ambassadors for Christ, since God is making his appeal through us; we entreat you on behalf of Christ, be reconciled to God. For our sake he made him to be sin who knew no sin, so that in him we might become the righteousness of God. (2 Cor 5:18-21)

Sin is the estrangement that Christ has overcome. That is what he took on himself. Atonement is reconciliation. There is no discussion here of other theories of the atonement that appear elsewhere in the Bible. Elsewhere sin and atonement have to do with blame and innocence, and we use the imagery of the court, or it has to do with pollution and purity, and we use the image of the altar. Here atonement involves reconciling groups of people.[10] Christ's work has to do with the barrier between Jews and Gentiles and their new relationship made possible by the breaking down of the barrier in his death.

PAUL AT ODDS WITH MODERN MISSIOLOGY

Our task in developing a theology of mission is not to take the understanding we have inherited from recent practices that are called missions and simply reaffirm them. Rather, we should test for coherence in understanding and identify differences between the New Testament situation and our place in culture and history. There are some notable silences in Paul's expression of his ministry when compared and contrasted with the way we have recently expressed a sense of mission. That does not mean we are necessarily wrong. It means we need to be aware of this difference and to evaluate it in view of our place in culture and history.

---

[10]This is not the only place where Paul talks about categories of people more than individuals when he is interpreting his ministry (cf. 1 Cor 1:21-24; 9; Rom 9–11).

Paul's silence. First, Paul did not say it is our major duty to go and talk to our neighbors or to go to the other side of the globe and talk to our neighbors there. Edwin Roels, writing on Ephesians, clearly makes this point:

> Paul generally does not urge his readers to proclaim the gospel to their neighbors, nor to go to the ends of the earth with the saving message of Christ. Rather, he urges them and commands them to live a life of holiness, to walk worthily of their calling, to demonstrate in loving and harmonious unity the new powers which have entered into the world in Christ, to demonstrate through victorious living the present victory of Christ over the powers of evil. It has been suggested that the reason why Paul does not urge his readers to a life of verbal witness is primarily because the early churches were not deficient in this respect. Though this is possible, it should be emphasized that what Paul is really doing in his letters is stressing the significance and importance of the believer's life as mission.[11]

Second, Paul did not express concern for the subjective reality of the listener's religious experience: offering personal counseling, pressing for decision, describing the Damascus Road experience that he had in hope that others might have a similar one. Maybe this silence is accidental. Maybe we do not happen to have the tracts he wrote on the four spiritual laws or how to do personal work. There are some things we cannot argue from silence. But at least we can say that a preoccupation with how to help an individual person respond to the message in a saving way is not central or it would be there in the canon.

Paul's focus in mission. When Paul did speak about mission, the character of his thinking was somewhat different from the mission thought that has come to dominate our culture in the past two centuries.

Paul had an ongoing attachment to and "yearning for" Israel. Even though he spent most of his time going out on missionary journeys, Paul did not see any meaning to this unless his going was of one piece with God's promises to Israel. He could not leave Jews behind. By contrast, Western missionary thinking inherited the medieval view that

---

[11]Edwin Roels, *God's Mission: The Epistle to the Ephesians in Mission Perspective* (Franeker: T. Wever, 1962), p. 57.

either Jews are the one category of people Christians do not deal with or that Christians ought to convert Jews by coercion if necessary. What is new in modernity is the idea that the Jewish people have special strategic importance because of their place in salvation history. But the wider meaning for Paul—that the church of Jews and Gentiles is an extension of the identity of Judaism—has not had much of a place in most Western missionary thinking.

Paul said that part of the point of the mission is the message that all people belong. This will raise questions for us later when we come to the missionary method that says we should go to one kind of people at a time because they will respond better that way.

Paul repeatedly showed concern for the community's growth and faithfulness. He called the church to mutual admonition, to be a disciplined community, not only to faith in Jesus. This is different from missionary approaches that lack a strong ecclesiology.

Paul was self-conscious or self-critical about wanting to be found a faithful servant. He pushed himself. He did not take for granted that he had no problems. He pushed hard at his ministry, sometimes to the point of jeopardizing the respect people had for him. In contrast, some of our missionary efforts have not been adequately self-critical.

Paul used his fate, even if it was being in prison, as a chance to proclaim Christ. He did not mind if other people with bad motives were preaching the same message, as long as the message was preached (Phil 1:12-18). Our mission history has too often been marked by groups who have been suspicious of each other and competitive in communicating the gospel.

Paul did not tell his own conversion story as a model for other people's conversions. Conversion testimony is a standard way that modern Western visions of conversion are projected and enabled, by seeing how somebody else thought about his or her sin and calling. Twice in Acts Paul told the story of his calling. But both times it was before a hostile audience to explain the divine sanction for what he was doing. Also, he described his Damascus Road experience as the basis for his becoming a missionary, not as a basis for becoming a Christian. Otherwise he was hesitant to speak about his own experience. He referred to the fact that he talked in tongues more than the Corinthians (1 Cor 14:18). But he referred to that fact only to tell them it did not matter. He referred to the fact that he had visions, but he said it in a veiled way (2 Cor 12:2).

Where he did explain himself at some length is with regard to his suffering. Then he said, "Imitate me" (1 Cor 11). Then he said that he is proud of his weakness (2 Cor 12). As far as I have been able to find, in the New Testament there is no report of a conversion experience seen from the convert's subjective perspective. We have reports about people coming to faith, but nobody says how it felt, talking about his or her assurance of sins forgiven, or a prior struggle with guilt, or what the voice that came to the person said—all elements that have characterized modern preaching. Paul uses his suffering and his work as a leader, a witness, a moderator and a bridge builder as a model, rather than his conversion experience.

PAUL'S STRATEGY AND TACTICS

We can also observe elements of Paul's method that illustrate his understanding of mission.

Community precedes converts. Wherever Paul went he began with the synagogue. That is, he did not plant a movement from scratch by dropping the seeds of a message or by winning individuals through close personal work and hoping that later out of those individuals would grow a community. He started the other way. He started with the community that was there, which meant the synagogue, and he proclaimed to them that Jesus was the Christ for whom they were waiting. Some people accepted the message, others rejected it. So the synagogue split, which became public agenda, and thereby drew the Gentiles' attention. But the sociological base of Paul's work continued to be the believing half of the synagogue to which the believing Gentiles then came. Paul never gathered individuals and then tried to make a group out of them, worrying about the next generation and at what point the mission board should recognize them as an independent church. There was a community before there were converts.

Mission means renunciation. The second major dimension of Paul's method might be titled "renunciation." Not with a lot of accent, and yet visibly, Paul saw his participation in Christ's ministry and in the cross not only in his being nonviolent or being persecuted, but also in his working at being a servant of all people. He spelled it out at the greatest length in 1 Corinthians 9 where he says, "To the Jews I became as a Jew, in order to win Jews. To those under the law I became as one under the law (though I myself am not under the law) so that I might win those under the law" (1 Cor 9:20). This is to be taken literally. He made vows and went to the temple because of those vows, just as a faithful Jew would do. "To those outside the law I became as one outside the law (though I am not free from God's law but am under Christ's law) so that I might win those outside the law. To the weak I became weak, so that I might win the weak. I have become all things to all people, that I might by all means save some" (1 Cor 9:21-22). This was not accommodation, which would have meant making things easy for himself. It was clarification. It was to avoid giving the Gentiles the impression that his message was irrelevant because it was a Jewish message, and vice versa.

Paul was not trying to develop several different churches to serve different clienteles. Some people seriously propose that: there should be a black church and a white church, a middle class church and an upper class church. They propose that Christians adjust to society's divisions by creating a church for every group of people. By contrast Paul's entire ministry made a point of getting different people together. Because Jews and Gentiles were together in the Jesus movement, when he went to the Gentiles he did not alienate them by making much of his Jerusalem vows, and when he talked with Jews he did not emphasize his freedom from the law.

In what sense was that renunciation? It was renunciation of time to be himself. Someone who is "all things to all people" is accused of being without character, of being unreliable, of trying to please people, of not having a mind of their own. Paul, however, accepted this costly flexibility because the self he was called to be was a minister to both peoples. This meant he always had to be determining how he was going to behave on the basis of his concern to win the people he was with. He never said this was easy or came naturally. In fact he said, "I punish my body and enslave it" (1 Cor 9:27). It required serious psychic discipline to make himself into that kind of cosmopolitan person. He did not say everybody could do it.

Another element of Paul's renunciation was his abandoning the right to financial support (1 Cor 9:3-12). He could not help being a preacher, but he could choose whether to renounce financial support, which he did so that he could put something of his own in the cause.

Because his was a dramatically different world from ours, Paul also made no use of the cultural gradient that is so typical of modern missions. We cannot separate mission efforts of the last two centuries from Western Christian nations' economic and political superiority and our self-perceived cultural superiority. Western missionaries went from independent countries to dependent countries or colonies. They went from industrialized countries to countries that were not industrialized. They went from countries with efficient education systems to countries without schools. They went from countries with modern medical understandings, staffing and hospitals to countries without those. In the last two centuries missionaries moved down the cultural gradient from places of strength to places of weakness. So at the beginning of the twentieth century someone with a high school education or two years of college and no further specialization could go from the American Midwest to the middle of the Congo and have significant status just by knowing more about farming, medicine, electricity and how to make an automobile run than most Africans. That cultural gradient did not exist in New Testament mission.

Gentiles share in Jewish history. The next observation about Paul's methods is that he made a point that Gentile believers should share in the Jewish history. He did not say, "We Jews have a message that is fortunately now translated into Greek, so go worship God yourselves." He said they had to care about Moses, Jeremiah and Jerusalem. He took collections in the new churches for the old churches. He gathered money in Corinth and all around Asia Minor and took the money to Jerusalem (Rom 15:25-26; 1 Cor 16:1-4; 2 Cor 8–9; Gal 2:10). Partly this was mutual aid because there had been a famine in Jerusalem. That is when one of these collections started, and there were more poor older brothers and sisters in Jerusalem than elsewhere. But his concern may well have been more than mutual aid. It may have been he sensed a fulfilling of what the prophets predicted: that the nations will bring tribute to Zion. There are some interpreters who suspect that Paul saw in these collections for Jerusalem the beginning of the nations' riches flowing to Jerusalem. It is at least clear that Paul's teaching ministry included introducing the Gentiles to the content of the Old Testament and introducing the Jews into a Jesus-oriented reading of it.

Another striking element of making the Gentiles share the history is that Paul taught Greeks to pray in Aramaic. Some rote learning of Aramaic prayers seems to have been part of Paul's missionary method. He did not teach them much, probably not all of the Jewish prayers. But he could write to the non-Jewish believers and throw in an Aramaic word—*abba*, *maranatha*—and assume they knew what it meant. Paul reminds us that we cannot come to the faith without caring about the people from whom we got it.

Conversion is not manipulated inwardness. On the level of method, how did Paul perceive conversion as far as we can tell from the record? We have already noted that the passages concerning "the new creation" (2 Cor 5:17) or "the new person" (Eph 2 and 3) should not be understood, as they have been taken to mean in the West, as preoccupation with the converted individual's regenerate subjective psychic structure. Indeed, this element, of concern in contemporary missionary method, seems to be missing in Paul. We do not see him recording his observations about where a certain person stands along the way of becoming open to the gospel, admitting guilt or need, trying to make an initial commitment or coming through with a full commitment. In the modern missionary movement these are things we hear reported and about which we hear requests for prayer. Through articles and prayer letters, the missionary's non-Christian neighbor becomes a person in the minds of the people back home. We look for a series of ethical and emotional steps that we expect as a person moves toward faith, and we want to help them in this process as much as we can without doing violence to the person.

Modern psychological and cultural anthropological points of view object to any "manipulative" or "pressured" approach. That is not my point. It would not have been Paul's point. He believed that the truth of the message he preached was the missionary focus, not the manipulation and evolution of a person's inwardness. This difference is worth more time in order to understand it better. How can we understand what we observed in Paul? I will make several suggestions.

Proclamation and persuasion are not the same things. Persuasion or *peithō* in Greek is a negative word for Paul. Persuasion, in contrast to proclamation, seeks to bring someone to an affirmation, and the focus is more on whether he or she has really accepted what God has done than on the fact that God did something. The New Testament witnesses said, "Christ is risen. Whether you believe it or not, that is true. We are telling you." That is proclamation. But if we say, "Can't you believe it? Don't you see? Doesn't it speak to your need? Don't you think you would be happier if . . . ?"—that type of questioning moves the focus of concern from the event to its acceptance, from its public quality to its private meaning. That, I am suggesting, is the difference between proclamation and persuasion.

The figure of speech that I use to illustrate this is the difference between the train and the taxi. The taxi will not go somewhere unless a person wants to go and pays for it. The taxi is on the client's schedule. If the taxi driver contributes at all to the decision about whether to go, it is by inviting the passenger to make the trip and saying that the rider would be happy when they get there or that the driver will get them there more cheaply, safely or quickly than somebody else. The individual's decision, however, is what determines whether the trip will be made and what the destination is, even whether the taxi will run. By contrast, when a train leaves depends on the schedule, not on any passenger's choice. Where the train will go depends on a combination of the schedule and the tracks. There is objectivity and reliability, a fitting into a plan that does not depend on any given passenger. Whether somebody gets on the train is completely his or her decision. But if somebody does not get on, they do not go anywhere. Moreover, what constitutes the destination does not depend on them at all.

Think of that difference as it relates to evangelism. Modern Western evangelism says, "Won't you please get on so I can have a fare? Because I have to make my living running this taxi." Kingdom of God proclamation says, "This train is bound for glory. Get on or get left." The objectivity, the fact that the train is going to leave without us if we do not get on, the fact that the kingdom is coming whether we want it or not, is the way of the kingdom whether we like it or not. As it happens, we will find that it is a good trip. But whether the conductor gets paid does not depend on whether we get on. Whether the engineer burns the fuel does not depend on whether we get on. The train is simply going. The kingdom is not a taxi. The kingdom is more like a train.[12]

We do not get conversions by describing conversion; we do not get faith by expositing the doctrine of justification by faith. That is an overstatement, because we do get conversions by describing conversion. But such converts might be people who have gone through the model conversion but have not understood the objectivity and sovereignty of the kingdom. We can gain converts also by expositing justification by faith. But then we may have people who have been convinced about an idea and do not know what it means to subject their minds to the lordship of Christ.

The cross cannot be communicated by domination, by lordship, even the domination of personal magnetism. This is a way to speak about an approach to conversion in deeper, more biblical language. There are some things that we can communicate by personal psychological power—rhetorical, therapeutic or Socratic. There are ways to guide people into the conversion experience we would like them to have. My thesis is that we cannot communicate the meaning of the cross of Christ using a manipulative power technique—whether it is that of Socratic power, pulpit pounding power or counseling couch power. The ends and means have to fit. The content and form have to relate. The meaning of the cross is a renunciation of such power as God's way to be reconciled.

---

[12]When I contrast persuasion and proclamation I do not mean the difference between Paul as a preacher and Paul as a teacher. The difference between preaching and teaching for some people is a matter of communication style. For others the difference is a matter of the audience; that is, preaching is to people who have not accepted the message and teaching is within the community of faith. But this distinction does not add anything to what we have said. Paul stood on the pedestal of the synagogue and said, "Jesus is the one to whom the covenant pointed." Even the Gentiles came to that message. Once they were in, he taught them. But we do not know much about what he taught them, except that he taught them the Old Testament and how Christians stand on its shoulders. When I was differentiating persuasion or proclamation, I meant that both are messages to those outside the community. The question is how we communicate to the listener.

Summarizing these various observations based on Paul, we do not find in the texts we examined the standard contemporary sequence of conversion either in time or in logic. That sequence runs as follows: There is a message. It reaches a listener. The listener accepts and is saved. Then he or she joins a group. Since we do not want to be divisive, we open that group to everybody. Therefore, the New Testament church had to be open to everybody. For Paul it was the other way around. The diverse group came first; the message developed in response.

We could say also on the practical level that this standard sequence tends not to work. If the sequence is that we have the messenger, then the message, then the listener, then the response, then we gather together people who have responded, then say "let's not be divisive," it is too late to take that final step. The way the process worked has already produced a clannish group. So we end up with closed churches and lone ranger Christians. But that is a practical observation. Theologically, this approach is heresy.

In Paul's message the more important objection to this standard approach was theological: Christ's work reconciles people into one new social reality—a community of Jews and Greeks, people from the law and people without the law, people with a heritage of worship and people without a heritage of worship, people with a structured personality and people with disintegrated personalities. That is not the only way to describe what Christ did. But it is the way 2 Corinthians 5 and Ephesians 2 and 3, among other places, described it. The very work of the church requires awareness of those outside the church, for their involvement in the church is part of its purpose. We cannot do our internal work first and, once the momentum picks up or when we have solved certain problems or when we have reached a certain size, then reach beyond the church. The New Testament church, as we see it in Paul, was always relating to those on the edge of its membership.

WHAT IF PAUL HAD GONE WHERE THERE WERE NO JEWS?

This brings us to a problem we have not touched at all, one that will concern us further later. What if Paul had gone where there were no Jews or no synagogues where he could begin to preach? There is only one case of this in the New Testament, and we can never be sure it is safe to reason from one case. In Acts 14 Paul and Barnabas fled to Lystra. Maybe there were Jews there, but the text says only that "there they continued proclaiming the good news" (Acts 14:7). It does not say to whom Paul was preaching. It does not say he was preaching to the synagogue, as previous texts do. Then there was a miracle; a man lame from birth was healed (Acts 14:8-10). People began to shout that he and Barnabas were gods. They called Barnabas "Zeus" and Paul "Hermes," the Greek god of orators. After that the priest of Zeus came out to welcome them, which makes sense. If American diplomats arrive in Hong Kong, it is the American embassy that comes out to meet them. Since "Zeus" was at the city gate, the priest of Zeus came out to welcome them with oxen to sacrifice. Paul was extremely troubled by this and said,

> Friends, why are you doing this? We are mortals just like you, and we bring you good news, that you should turn from these worthless things to the living God, who made the heaven and the earth and the sea and all that is in them. In past generations he allowed all the nations to follow their own ways; yet he has not left himself without a witness in doing good—giving you rains from heaven and fruitful seasons, and filling you with food and your hearts with joy. (Acts 14:15-17)

Note that Paul said nothing about Jesus here. He offered the Jewish argument against idolatry and polytheism and for a God-Creator who loves all people in every time and place, a God whose main focus is to keep people from the practice of polytheistic sacrifice. This is what Luke chose to report. Maybe there is more to the story, but to the extent to which we can do anything with it—the only story of its kind that we have in Acts—these two men acted just like Jews. That is, they had to bring the Jewish message first before it was meaningful to talk about Jesus. Some people may have believed the gospel; it is not reported. A congregation may have emerged, but it is not reported. The apostles stayed there a while until Jews came from elsewhere to denounce them. Later Paul and Barnabas visited that place again, so there may well have been a church founded. Argument from silence does not prove a lot. But argument from affirmation does prove something. What the people in

Lystra clearly affirmed was Jewish monotheism, the doctrine of one Creator-God who does not want sacrifice to false gods and who does not want a multiplicity of temples in the town. Luke, who is so interested in telling us about the church's progress, has no interest in telling us how this church progressed, how a church without a Jewish base started. The only chance he had to tell us about a purely Gentile church, he did not take. At least this passage identifies the problem that we have. Paul's message was so rooted in the Jewish story that it is not easy to conceive how he would have given it without that Jewish story.

To leap ahead, what does this Jewish foundation of Christian faith mean for mission today? There would be three obvious answers. One would be that it makes no difference. We could pay no attention to this observation, not caring whether we speak to that Jewish base or not. It seems that it mattered a great deal to Paul, however.

Second, it might mean that, when they move to new areas, Christians move as a community of Jews and Gentiles. If there were Jews in towns such as Tarsus and Ephesus, it was because Jews had migrated there. They had migrated not to be missionaries, although some of them may have had a little of that vision. They migrated to make a living and because they were pushed out of where they had lived. But they took their faith with them. One way to think of what to do in a place where there are not any Jews, or to say it more broadly where there is not a religious people, is that there should be a migration of religious people there. Go as a congregation. Let that be the base, so there is never a time of proclamation or witness before the community is present. The old Greek word for scattering or dispersion is *diaspora*, and most often in church history we get a diaspora when we do not want it: through persecution or the loss of territory. But how about being in diaspora on purpose? How about being a missionary people?[13]

If we return to the Great Commission with this question in mind, we see that it does not talk about sending at all, it talks about going. It expects those to whom Jesus is reported to be speaking, to be going some-

---

[13]For a more extended argument along this line see John Howard Yoder, *As You Go*, Focal Pamphlet No. 5 (Scottdale, PA: Mennonite Publishing House, 1961), reprinted in the afterword to this volume, pp. 399-421.

where. It is also collective. The text does not say, "When you send a couple of people and the rest of you stay home, then make disciples of all nations." Rather, the *you* is plural. Whatever you do, wherever you go, *together* make disciples of all nations. So that is the second alternative: let's take some Jews along.

The third alternative is to encourage conversion to Hebrew faith. That means to propagate a moral monotheistic culture for its own sake. Teach people that idolatry is wrong, that morality is necessary to be human. Give them the notions of respect for parents, marriage, property and truth found in the Ten Commandments. Propagate that as valid culture and a reasonable worldview whether people become disciples or not. Never mind that the people who accept that culture do not all convert, because there is at least a base on which it is meaningful to stand to say, "Jesus points to a new creation." This might have relevance for contemporary discussions of the place of cultural transmission in missionary method: the place of schools and the place of nonchurch agencies like the YMCA, which was such a great part of the missionary concern in China.

In examining the New Testament so far, we have stumbled onto the fact that it does not speak clearly to the question of the foreign missionary movement in the modern sense of going to places where there is no Jewish faith community. New Testament writers knew about Persia, but they did not say or do anything about it. They even knew something about Africa—beyond the northern parts that were part of the Roman Empire—but they did not do anything there that was recorded. Foreign mission is a topic to which we have to build a bridge theologically and historically. We must recognize that we cannot simply leap into it from the New Testament example because of the pervasive importance of the Jews in the world to which Paul went.

5

OTHER TEXTS AND THE
NEW TESTAMENT'S THEOLOGY
OF MISSION

This chapter will address certain strands of New Testament literature that we have not yet considered and will review New Testament theology of mission as a whole.

Prior to dealing with Paul we might have asked whether we have any New Testament witness to church life that was never impacted by Paul or by the events we have been pondering. Vincent Taylor uses the word "primitive" to refer to certain sections of the New Testament.[1] By this he means sections that witness to the simplest and first way in which the apostolic church lived its faith prior to Paul's thought and missionary activity or to the development of theology represented by the letter to the Hebrews.

JAMES AND PETER

The picture of the missionary church we have in James and Peter is of a people in a hostile world being tested by suffering. That the world was hostile was taken for granted. That they were a people rather than just an accidental pile of individuals was taken for granted and sometimes strongly argued (1 Pet 2:9-10). The idea of being tested by suffering runs all the way through 1 Peter 1, 4 and 5 and James 1 and 5.

---

[1][See Vincent Taylor, *The Formation of the Gospel Tradition* (New York: Macmillan, 1968). —Ed.]

Suffering itself becomes the occasion for witness:

> Now who will harm you if you are eager to do what is good? But even if
> you do suffer for doing what is right, you are blessed. Do not fear what
> they fear, and do not be intimidated, but in your hearts sanctify Christ as
> Lord. Always be ready to make your defense to anyone who demands
> from you an accounting for the hope that is in you; yet do it with gen-
> tleness and reverence. Keep your conscience clear, so that, when you are
> maligned, those who abuse you for your good conduct in Christ may be
> put to shame. For it is better to suffer for doing good, if suffering should
> be God's will, than to suffer for doing evil. For Christ also suffered for
> sins once for all, the righteous for the unrighteous, in order to bring you
> to God. (1 Pet 3:13-18)

Strikingly, this passage connects witness and the community's visible
nonconformity. "Be ready to give a reason to people who ask you what
your hope is." This assumes that people were going to ask Christians
where their hope lay. In what context would others be asking what their
hope was? In the context of the community's innocent suffering. That is
clear before and after the passage. They suffered innocently as Christ
did. That was their solidarity with him.

This peoplehood is both a privilege and a witness. First Peter 2 offers
literary expressions of this. First, we find frequent quotes from the Old
Testament.[2] For example, the quotation in 1 Peter 2:9-10 is from Hosea,
who loved an unfaithful wife but first had to make it clear that he rejected that unfaithfulness. Hosea did that by naming her children "Not
My People" and "No Mercy." "Not My People" is obviously a significant
name to give your wife's child. "No Mercy" is a judgment on the whole
relationship. The rest of Hosea says that a time will come when "Not My
People" will be called "My People" and "No Mercy" will be called "Mercy."
Hosea's message is a symbol of God's relation to God's unfaithful people.
Peter picked up that whole package, not just a verse, and set it in his
letter saying that this promise was being fulfilled right then. "Once you
were not a people, but now you are God's people; once you had not received mercy, but now you have received mercy" (1 Pet 2:10). This text

---

[2]When Peter thought something was important, he found an Old Testament quote to support it.

did not refer to a Jew/Greek polarity. That polarity had not yet come into view. It referred to the polarity between faithful and unfaithful, mercy and no mercy, my people and not my people, acceptance and rejection. But God had now given the genuine peoplehood they did not have, the peoplehood and belonging to God that was unfulfilled under the other covenant.

Furthermore, in Hebrew parallelism, when two symmetrical phrases rhyme or when their rhythm and grammar are the same, the phrases generally mean the same thing or have some close relationship. Being God's people and having received mercy are not two different subjects; they are one subject. To have received mercy is to be a people; to be a people is to have received mercy. The two clauses are parallel.

In the preceding verse we have a striking line up of four nouns, all of which are collectivity words—race, priesthood, nation and people. These define the new people. Each of the four nouns has an adjective that points to distinctiveness, novelty and difference. "You are a *chosen* race, a *royal* priesthood, a *holy* nation, *God's own* people" (1 Pet 2:9, italics added). Moreover, being a peculiar people shows forth "the mighty acts of him who called you." It is the peoplehood itself that proclaims. Thus, to be different from the world is the prerequisite of witness, of visibility, for James and Peter.

But the people were dispersed. James and Peter talked about being scattered. First Peter was even addressed "to the exiles of the Dispersion in Pontus, Galatia, Cappadocia, Asia, and Bithynia" (1 Pet 1:1). They were visible in the world because of their different lifestyle. Their economics were different. James radically critiqued the way in which any closed community caters to the prestige of its wealthy members. There was a different communication style. For example, James 3 warns about transparent communication and the dangers of the tongue.

What did Peter and James say about the church's witness when it was scattered, visible, different and persecuted? The witness was simply to explain how it made sense to be this kind of people. It meant giving account of Christian hope (1 Pet 3:15). It was to put to silence those who were reproaching believers unfairly (1 Pet 2:15). And it focused on the possibility that the persons closest to them may be won by their style.

"Wives, in the same way, accept the authority of your husbands, so that, even if some of them do not obey the word, they may be won over without a word by their wives' conduct" (1 Pet 3:1). The lifestyle itself, and specifically servanthood, was the witness.

This outlook remained forward looking, centripetal. Peter still expected that the period of God's triumph, when the nations will glorify God, was yet to come. Following the peoplehood passage Peter wrote, "I urge you as aliens and exiles to abstain from the desires of the flesh that wage war against the soul. Conduct yourselves honorably among the Gentiles, so that, though they malign you as evildoers, they may see your honorable deeds and glorify God when he comes to judge" (1 Pet 2:11-12). "The day of visitation" is coming. Some new thing is still to be expected in the future. When that time comes the nations, the Gentiles who are persecuting you, will see and will glorify God. The church in James and Peter, the pre-Pauline church, still saw itself as looking forward to the age when the Gentiles will respond. But when they respond, they will respond by affirming the righteousness of the peoplehood that meanwhile is waiting for that event. This is a different set of literature from what we have previously examined, but it has a very similar kind of content. It is the community's lifestyle that is the occasion for verbal witness, and its servanthood and its morality are the content of the witness.

THE JOHANNINE WRITINGS

John's Gospel is somewhat different in style from the Synoptic Gospels. The author has a slightly different purpose.

The word *witness* is found in John and so is the concept "witnessing." In the basic legal or cultural sense, a witness is somebody who comes to a courtroom or to a place where something is being contested, and says, "I saw that."

- John the Baptist witnesses in John 1:19.

- John 20:31: "But these are written so that you may come to believe that Jesus is the Messiah, the Son of God."

- John 21:24: "This is the disciple who is testifying to these things and has written them, and we know that his testimony is true."

- 1 John 1:1-2: "We declare to you what was from the beginning, what we have heard, what we have seen with our eyes, what we have looked at and touched with our hands, concerning the word of life—this life was revealed, and we have seen it and testify to it."

In Johannine literature, witnessing does not have the distinct modern meaning of a particular message to a particular audience. It means certifying facts, attesting to the identity of what we are talking about, taking sides with the story.

The concept of *world*, to which the witness is directed, is significant in Johannine literature. The writings say both affirmative and negative things about the world. First of all, the world is hostile and that hostility is recognized and accepted.

- Jesus says in John 17:9, "I am not asking on behalf of the world."
- 1 John 2:15: "Do not love the world."
- 1 John 5:19: "The whole world lies under the power of the evil one."

And yet there is affirmation.

- John 3:16: "God so loved the world."
- In John 17:21, the reason for the oneness of the future believers is "that the world may believe."
- In John 16:7-8, Jesus promises the coming of the Spirit, who will convict or convince the world.

While the fact is accepted that the world is hostile, there persists a love for the world, a perspective that envisions its salvation.

The parallel to Matthew's Great Commission, John 20:21-23, is not outreach oriented. It puts together what in Matthew is separate: the mandate to bind and loose or to forgive and not forgive (Mt 18:15-20) and the concept of being sent (Mt 28:18-20). In John 20, the two are identified in the same passage. "As the Father has sent me, so I send you. . . . If you forgive the sins of any, they are forgiven them; if you retain the sins of any, they are retained" (Jn 20:21-23). The Johannine concept of sending is more focused on the authority to speak in God's name than it is on the disciples going anywhere.

Yet despite the lack of any outspoken missionary vocabulary or subject matter, we might note something relevant for mission if we step back and look at the Gospel of John and the Johannine letters as documents or cultural products. In language and style these are the least Jewish books of the New Testament. While John's Gospel contains Old Testament allusions and themes and relates to Hebrew history through the person of John the Baptist, debates about Abraham and conflicts with the Pharisees, there are no Old Testament quotations from known Hebrew versions and no Hebrew words. These documents have gone into the wider world. They talk Greek. The Gospel of John uses a simple Greek style as one would if he had not studied the classical language. The Greek has Aramaic tinges to it according to careful scholars. But there is a Greek style of reasoning, using, for instance, abstractions like *Logos*, which does not translate anything Jesus said.[3] When John says "The eternal *Logos* was with God and became flesh," he has moved into the Greek world, talking abstractions. The Hebrew mind did not work this way.

That does not mean John sold out to the Greek world, because the next thing he said about the *Logos* was that it became flesh, which any intelligent Greek knew the *Logos* could not do. So John made a strong statement, but he made it in the Greek world. Many scholars have commented that the darkness and light imagery, the two realms, is Hellenistic. In fact, that is why many people say the book must have been written much later. I think it was written rather by a different kind of person than the Synoptic authors, a person plunging into the Hellenistic world with his message.

As I pointed out in chapter 2, there may even be a few elements of specific mission awareness in the Gospel. There are the other sheep in John 10:16, the others who will come to belief in John 17:20-26, and the conversation with the Samaritan woman at the well in John 4 that references the fact that Samaria was the first place to which the church spread.

---

[3]It is more or less equivalent to *ḥokmâ* in the Proverbs, but John does not use the word *logos* as a translation, because *sophia* translates *ḥokmâ*.

THE EPISTLE TO THE HEBREWS

The other major writer in the New Testament is the author of the Epistle to the Hebrews. Almost every one of the points I made about John could be stood on its head when talking about Hebrews. The book is all about the Old Testament and has long quotations from it. A Gentile would have found it meaningless to talk about priesthood, the furniture in the ark, the shape of the temple and how the priest is chosen and functions.

The author of Hebrews did not develop missionary dimensions where he could have done so easily. For instance, he told the story of Melchizedek, which could have been used in a missionary sermon. He argued that the old covenant was inadequate. That would have been a good basis for saying why the new is different. But, for the author of Hebrews, the inadequacy of the old covenant was not that it was limited to Israel. The newness the text talks about would not need to extend beyond the Hebrews. Further, the suffering of faith in chapters 11 and 12 are not related to the conversion of the world, not even the way they are in Peter and James. The statement that repentance may be impossible to some (Heb 6:4 and 12:17) is not exploited with urgency for preaching the message.

Yet, as was the case with John, as a literary event Hebrews says much more than what is first apparent. If John was the least Jewish writer, in some ways the author of Hebrews was the most Hellenistic writer. This is evident in his literary style, writing and reasoning, and careful use of Old Testament quotes. Hebrews does not quote the Old Testament like a rabbi. The author used quotations as an essayist would, as a person who knows literature. He took a whole passage in its context and carefully said what it meant, which was not the way a rabbi or even Paul used an Old Testament text.

The author simply assumed he could take the Old Testament story and that temple and sacrifice business into the Hellenistic world. He assumed the Old Testament history could be read within the Greek literary framework. He was confident that his Greek-reading audience would find it worth the trouble to figure out what priesthood, sacrifice, altar and meeting God on the mountain meant.

Hebrews also includes a striking image of the new replacing the old in chapter 12. The Hebrews came to a mountain that thundered and frightened them. They did not want to go to it and said, "Moses, you go." "But you have come to Mount Zion and to the city of the living God, the heavenly Jerusalem, and to innumerable angels in festal gathering, and to the assembly of the firstborn" (Heb 12:22-23). Again the church is the new thing that replaces the old.

In different and almost opposite ways, John and Hebrews were doing what Paul did: reaching beyond Palestinian Jewish Christianity into the Gentile world. They did not talk about it or argue it as Paul did. They did not say, "It is a revelation to me." But they were theologizing, communicating and producing a literary monument that simply assumed they were both Jewish and Greek. They put those two pieces together very differently. Hebrews referred often to the Old Testament but clearly used a Greek thought style. John used a Greek vocabulary but a distinctly Jewish thought style. Yet they were both doing the same thing. They were expositing the new peoplehood in the new culture.

THE BOOK OF REVELATION

The remaining New Testament section is the Book of Revelation. It is not only a special type of visionary literature but it weaves in elements of hymns that were already being used in the churches. That is especially the case in the first vision of Revelation 4 and 5.

This segment begins as a vision of the heavenly throne room. Around the throne are twenty-four elders and four living creatures. The four living creatures "day and night without ceasing . . . sing, 'Holy, holy, holy, is the Lord God Almighty, who was and is and is to come'" (Rev 4:8). Already in that quotation we have the structure of the hymn that is being worked into this vision. It has three tenses, "who *was* and *is* and *is to come*" and later there will be three verses relating to those three tenses. The four creatures sing three times, "holy," and then there are three responding verses each of which begins with the word *worthy.*

The first verse looks backward. "Whenever the living creatures give glory and honor and thanks to the one who is seated on the throne . . . the twenty-four elders fall; . . . they cast their crowns before the throne, singing, 'You are worthy, our Lord and God, to receive glory and honor and power, for you created all things, and by your will they existed and were created'" (Rev 4:9-11). This corresponds to the "was," the past, the praise for creation.

Then comes a long narrative interlude: the vision of the scroll sealed with seven seals that no one was able to open. The word *worthy* is used again in the sense of having authority or proven capacity. "No one in heaven or on earth or under the earth was able to open the scroll. . . . And I began to weep. . . . Then one of the elders said to me, 'Do not weep. See, the Lion of the tribe of Judah, the Root of David, has conquered, so that he can open the scroll and its seven seals'" (Rev 5:3-5). Then John sees the Lamb. The Lamb takes the scroll. "When he had taken the scroll, the four living creatures and the twenty-four elders . . . sing a new song: 'You are worthy to take the scroll and to open its seals, for you were slaughtered and by your blood you ransomed for God saints from every tribe and language and people and nation; you have made them to be a kingdom and priests serving our God, and they will reign on earth'" (Rev 5:8-9). That describes the present, and what is going on in the present is that people "from every tribe and tongue and people and nation" are being made a kingdom and priests, or a kingdom of priests, reigning on earth.[4]

The scroll is a routine symbol in this kind of literature. Through the rest of Revelation, every time one of the seven seals is opened we learn a little more about what is to come. The sealed scroll is destiny or the meaning of history, what God is doing or about to do. The image of the opening scroll recalls Paul's reference to the unveiling of the mystery hidden until his time—that Gentiles are fellow heirs with Jews. In Revelation the slain Lamb is seen as the one worthy to unseal the meaning of destiny. He is praised specifically for the fact that through his sacrifice he brought together a priestly community "from every tribe and language and people and nation" (Rev 5:9). The process that mattered for them in the present, in the unfolding meaning of history, was the calling of the church. This was a new song. It was not the song they sang before. Previously they praised God for creation. Now they were praising the

---

[4]This is another quote that goes all the way back to Moses.

Lamb for being worthy through his sacrifice not only to unseal the meaning of history but to carry it out in the creation of a new people in the present.

The third verse refers to the future. The Lamb that was slain is worthy "to receive power and wealth and wisdom and might and honor and glory and blessing" (Rev 5:12). Here is the third tense, the "is to be," and the third "worthy."

The vision of history exposited out of this early church hymn is that the Lamb is sovereign. He moves history as he breaks the seal. The scroll does not unroll automatically and God, sitting on the throne, does not unroll it. The unrolling must happen in history, and it is the Lamb who unrolls it. Beneath the other things that are happening on earth is something of deeper meaning—the creation of a priestly kingdom. This is very different language from Ephesians 2 and 3, but it is the same point. The purpose that God had before is now being carried out, the creation of a people made up of all peoples.

NEW TESTAMENT THEOLOGY OF MISSION

Generalizing from the New Testament experience as a whole, we do not see reflected in most of the New Testament writings, nor in church practice, a formal recognition and carrying out of a textual mandate to send missionaries or to go to new places with a message. In his book, *The Missionary Nature of the Church*, Johannes Blauw was looking for a textual mandate, and he found it more in the New Testament than in the Old. But, even there, the "going" was neither studied nor automatic. It was taken for granted. It was unavoidable and even sometimes accidental. The Diaspora base was in place before the gospel. In this sense the "new people" *was* the message before it became the vehicle for the message. In the simple literal sense—which mattered so much in the debates in the age of William Carey—the New Testament is not as missionary as has been assumed.[5]

But because the reality of this new people was the message, it also became the vehicle for proclaiming it. The New Testament as a fact and

---

[5]Did Jesus say that his apostles should go? And has that mandate been carried out?

as a worldview is missionary all the way through, and most visibly so when it does not talk about it. We observed this in looking at the literary mood and cultural assumptions of the authors of John and Hebrews, who did not talk about the church's mission at all, but just took for granted that it was that kind of a church.

This church inherited the particularity of the Old Testament and, more than we usually recognize, stayed with Abraham and the law. A later story, especially the nineteenth- and twentieth-century European Protestant way of interpreting the New Testament, spoke of breaking out of the bonds of Judaism, positing Paul against Jesus or the next generation versus the first generation, so that finally Christianity became a non-Jewish Hellenistic religion. Something of that happened with time, but it did not happen in the New Testament period. Much of what has been seen as Christianity moving into the Hellenistic world was not movement out of the Judaistic world. Paul, who for some was the symbol of leaving Jewish loyalty behind, clearly said he was reaching out to Gentiles in the name of a better understanding of Jewish loyalty, not in opposition to it. Jewish particularity remained; the New Testament church never outgrew Abraham.

The universality in the New Testament vision comes from the Old Testament too: the expectation that in the messianic age all the nations will learn God's law. Peter and Paul saw this expectation as beginning to be fulfilled, but the expectation was nothing new or anti-Jewish. Hebrew particularity and messianic universality are not in tension. They are not alternatives as they have so often been made out to be in efforts to understand the New Testament church. They are mutually supportive; neither would exist without the other.

This new people found itself scattered and suffering, but the dispersion and suffering were meaningful because of the promise of victory. Did the promise mean that if they would just stick it out for a couple more years the tides would turn and their suffering would be replaced with lordship? No. It meant the coming victory of this new unity in Christ; what will stand in the end will be that God has made a new kind of humanity.

This new humanity is not simply the *instrument* of the mission that carries the message. It is not simply the *object lesson* of the mission: "Look how they love each other." It is not just the *deposit* of the mission: all these people were saved and here they are in a pile. The new humanity *is* the salvation. It is already real. The being of the church is the salvation story as well as being the instrument, the object lesson and the deposit. It is the new community's faithfulness to its universality that leads to its dispersion. That is what we saw in Acts.

Proclamation was part of the event. The process of proclamation was itself part of the meaning of the event; that is, the proclamation did not just say that something happened, that it was important and that God did it, but the telling was also part of the event. God was at work in the process of the telling. Thus part of the claim was that God had brought about the messianic age; there was now a messianic people as a sign of that age. The in-gathering had already begun to happen in the reality of the church, and the fundamental proclamation was to be that in-gathering.

This proclamation was not primarily directed toward the outside world. Many ministries that were talked about in the New Testament church were not directed in this way. This is striking, considering the great number of ministries listed in 1 Corinthians 12 and Romans 12. Some of them might be focused toward the outside world, but none of them are by their very nature.

Ephesians 4 is the third passage that has a listing of ministries and, given the context of chapters 2 and 3, is clearly talking about building up the community's internal life. Chapter 4 begins: "Lead a life worthy of the calling to which you have been called" (Eph 4:1). The calling is the unity of the preceding two chapters. The virtues of Ephesians 4:2-3— "humility and gentleness . . . patience, bearing with one another in love, making every effort to maintain the unity of the Spirit in the bond of peace"—describe what it takes to make church unity real. The purpose of the multiple ministry is that "all of us come to the unity of the faith and of the knowledge of the Son of God, to maturity, to the measure of the full stature of Christ" (Eph 4:13). The "fullness of Christ" refers to the variety of ministries within the community. It does not refer to individual, spiritual maturity or to ministry to the outside world. The contrast in Ephesians was not between church and world but between what the community was and what it had become.[6]

The church's proclamation was also connected to the end of the age. Two texts—Matthew 24:13-14 and 2 Peter 3:11-12—are sometimes taken as affirmation of a specific almost causal linkage between the church's proclamation and the end. In the midst of a discourse on the Mount of Olives concerning the coming of Christ and the ending of the age, Jesus says that things will get worse and worse and many will fall away, "but the one who endures to the end will be saved. And this good news of the kingdom will be proclaimed throughout the world, as a testimony to all the nations; and then the end will come" (Mt 24:13-14). This text is used in certain conservative circles to give a special priority to the missionary concern for unreached tribes, taking the word "nations" as meaning some kind of ethnic or cultural unit. They assume that as long as not all have been reached, then preaching to all the nations has not been concluded. When the gospel is preached to all the nations, then the end can come.

The other text interpreted in that direction is 2 Peter 3:11-12: "Since all these things are to be dissolved in this way, what sort of persons ought you to be in leading lives of holiness and godliness, waiting for and hastening the coming of the day of God, because of which the heavens will be set ablaze and dissolved, and the elements will melt with fire?" How would one go about "hastening the coming of the day of God"? If we have understood already from the other text that the actual carrying out of the proclamation ministry has some relationship to reaching the end time, then this second text would say the same thing. The Revised Standard Version has a footnote that says "hastening" is not the only good translation.[7] It could be simply "earnestly desiring," and then, of course, it would not make that point.

---

[6]This is not to downplay what we observed before about the church's presence in the wider world. It might be that in some other places (for instance, in the Pastoral Epistles) certain identifiable functions of the church might point outward. But even that is not sure. The one that modern English speakers would think most likely to point outward is the word *evangelist,* which is found in the Pastorals. But there is no reason to assume that the word *evangelist* meant in the Pastorals what it means today. That would have to be studied first.

[7][The NRSV includes the same note. —Ed.]

Principalities and powers as objects of mission. When we looked at Ephesians, we did not note that the objects or audience of the proclamation included more than people, that "through the church the wisdom of God in its rich variety might now be made known to the rulers and authorities in the heavenly places" (Eph 3:10). What "principalities and powers" meant is a debated area of New Testament thought. New Testament scholars over the last century have mostly debated whether to pay any attention to that kind of language in the apostle Paul. Most of them have thought that it reflects a prescientific worldview. More recently it has been studied more respectfully. There seems to be some agreement that these powers have something to do with the structures behind history, the way in which the whole is greater than the sum of its parts. There is a persistence to the patterning of social behavior. Things happen as if there were a structure behind the course of events, including such things as the power of law, the power of habit and the power of cultural assumptions. There is the claim that on this level of invisible but real structures the presence of the church has some impact. Hendrik Berkhof suggests that the best kind of translation of principalities and powers would be any words that we use in English that end in "-ology" and "-ism." An "-ology" is not something we can see. We cannot pin one down and take its license number, and yet an "-ology" is real. An "-ism" is not something we can photograph, and yet it is real. It has a power. It has a structure. Maybe that is the simplest lay translation. For instance, one of the principalities and powers to which we proclaim, one of the addressees of the proclamation of the new peoplehood, is the structure of racism. The church's proclamation is not simply to individuals, some of whom will listen and some of whom will not. The proclamation "Christ is Lord" is to the structure of reality. It is to the whole course of history.

6

Mission and
Systematic Theology

Without covering every topic, this chapter deals with those usually under the heading of systematic theology and their relation to mission.

Mission in the Nature of God

Traditionally, theology proper talks about God and God's nature, a subchapter of theology talks about the work of salvation, and theology of mission focuses on how we report and propagate this theology. We have reason to ask whether this separation is, in fact, helpful. What if sending were itself part of God's nature? That is, what if God did not simply make a creation that happened to fall and that God happened to save, so that we now need missions? What if the very nature of God were to reach out and to send?

In fact, the Hebrew vision does not give much attention to what God would be like if God were alone, not acting or reaching out, not sending and speaking. Abraham, as the prototypical believer, leaves home trusting that he is being led somewhere, even though he does not know where. The God of the prophets is the God who speaks. The concern to see the missionary movement and missionary mood rooted in God's character grows out of the biblical narrative and has effects that we have been turning to in systematic theology.

P. T. Forsyth, a relatively conservative British Congregationalist in the early twentieth century, wrote:

The first missionary was God the Father, who sent forth his Son in the likeness of sinful flesh. That is the seal and final ground of missions—the grace, the ultimate unbought, overwhelming grace of God, the eternal heart and purpose of the Father, who gave us not only a prophet but a propitiation. The second missionary was that Son, the apostle of our profession as the New Testament calls Him, the true primate of the apostles, of those that he sent forth who himself came forth from the bosom of the Father to declare Him; who exiled and emptied Himself in this foreign land of earth, and humbled Himself to death, even the death of the cross. The third missionary is the Holy Ghost whom the Saviour sends forth into all the earth, who comes mightily and sweetly ordering all things, and subduing all lands to the obedience of the Kingdom of Christ. The fourth missionary is the church.[8]

The Son is sent. We hardly need reminders of how often that is said in the New Testament. The Spirit is sent not only in John 14 and 16, but also at the end of Luke and in the Pentecost account itself.

A later Hellenistic theology will talk about the Father, the Son and the Spirit and ask whether they are substantially the same, whether they have the same nature (*homoousia*). This theology perceived nature as something relatively stable. That which is more real is that which changes less. If we were to say this in a more Hebraic mood, we would talk about Father, Son and Spirit as the same in function, movement, mission and mandate, which is the point that Forsyth was making.

If the nature of God is to send, the God of the Bible is different from gods who must be approached. People must approach a god who has a location, such as the *ba'alîm*, the nature gods on hilltops in Canaan. People also had to go to Delphi to hear oracles from the gods who told secrets. Some gods a person must approach by self-emptying, by meditating, by casting off consciousness, will or knowledge. Some gods must be appeased when they are angry. But the God of the Bible is one who comes, who takes the initiative, who reaches across whatever it is that separates us.

That the biblical God comes to humans means a few obvious things.

---

[8][Peter Taylor Forsyth, *Missions in State and Church: Sermons and Addresses* (London: Hodder and Stoughton, 1908), pp. 270-71. —Ed.]

It means we reaffirm our incapacity to save ourselves. With a god that we must approach, we contribute to our own salvation by making a pilgrimage or by going to the mountaintop with our sacrifice. When we approach a god by emptying ourselves, we contribute enormously to our salvation through the disciplines of contemplation. When a god must be appeased, we contribute to our salvation by offering gifts. But if God is the one who does the moving, the going and the removing of barriers, then we do not in the same way "cause" the salvation we receive.

Second, the belief that God sends or comes to us affirms the ordinary place where we are as the place where God meets us. There is not a special divine realm, a place where we must go to find holy ground. We do not need to back out of ordinary reality into another reality where God is more at home. God breaks in where we are.

That God sends or comes means one more thing. If God chooses to work in history, it means God is taking the risk of incarnation, of *being* in history. God is choosing to identify with the uncertainty and weakness of existence within history. God is not afraid of history and risks losing God's own self within it, as the other gods do not.

This nature of God, it can be claimed, is the real meaning of the doctrine of the Trinity. What God sends (the Son sent in one way; the Spirit sent in another way) is no different from God's own self. This is simply another way of stating what is traditionally called the economic understanding of the Trinity. Economy (*oikonomia*) is how one manages a house. So *economic* is how something is carried out. The primary distinction in texts dealing with the Trinity is between the economic and the ontological Trinity. The ontological understanding of the Trinity says that in God's very being there is threeness *in* oneness. The economic understanding of the Trinity sees three-in-one in God at work, carrying out divine purposes. There is the Son who is sent, the Spirit who is sent in another way and the Father who sends—and they are all the same. When God comes as Spirit, that is really God's own self. When God comes as Son, that is really God's own self. When the Father sends the Son and the Spirit, that is really God's own self, and those three are all one self.

If we are concerned about a particular philosophical view of ultimate

reality, we will make the difference between the ontological and economic understandings of the Trinity important. But if we believe that
history is where God reveals God's own self, then we do not have to care
so much about the difference. Perhaps the self-revealing God is the real
one, and the economic Trinity is the real Trinity. But God is always also
ontologically what God would be like if there were no world. God is still
the same God—the sending God, the loving God.

During the patristic period theologians tried to find figures of speech
for how the three persons of the Trinity would relate to each other if
there were not a world in which to do it. That was not easy because they
had to imagine things based on the words they coined. So they discussed
whether the three persons of the Trinity were in session in and around
each other, sitting in a circle, or whether they were in a procession—
circuminsessio or *circumincessio*. *Circuminsessio* means sitting around
and *circumincessio* means going around. Both are feeble images for the
idea that the threeness in oneness is in God's own self; God is by nature
a God who sends. Even if we try to think of God with no world, we have
to think of God as relating. If God cannot relate to anything else, God
has to relate to God's own self, and there are three aspects of God's own
self, which are always there in the eternal being.

I can sympathize if you do not have the philosophical imagination to
find this conversation very meaningful. I do not either. But in church
history, the Trinity had a significant function as a way of saying that
sending, reaching out, loving and being gracious is God's very nature and
not simply an adjustment God made to the presence of a fallen world.

ANOTHER APPEAL TO THE TRINITY: A DISTRIBUTIVE VIEW

We have reason to look especially at another understanding of the
Trinity, one we might call a *distributive view of the Trinity*. That is, each
of the three persons of the Trinity has their distinct role. The Father is
responsible for what came before and exists outside the church: creation,
culture, nature and reason. The Spirit is responsible for people's inwardness. The Son is identified with the historic, visible community of
faith. This view of the Trinity contributed to thinking about mission in
both evangelical and ecumenical communities in the 1950s and 1960s as

Christian theology of mission was being formulated.

At the meeting of the International Missionary Council at Willingen, Germany (1952), there was special emphasis on the triune God as the basis of mission.[9] They had two ways of saying that "mission is the work of the triune God." One was that they did not want an overly church-centered view of mission, one centered on church planting or church fellowship. They wanted mission to be more forward-looking, more aggressive in taking on the world, more eschatological. So *eschatology versus church* (or church-centeredness) was one of the ways they put it.[10]

The other way they talked about the triune God in relation to mission was to say that there should be a better balance of three elements of the Christian message: incarnation, resurrection and eschatology. Incarnation looks to the past and affirms the Creation; resurrection created the church and the movement; eschatology looks forward to what is still unfulfilled and takes on the world. Those at the Willingen conference made that distinction in terms of these different dimensions of Christology, but it soon came to be made in terms of a distributive understanding of the Trinity.

At the same time as the Willingen meeting, the National Council of Churches produced a report on the missionary obligation of the church. Theodore Gill, former editor of *Christian Century*, wrote a summary beginning with three dimensions of the work of Christ—priestliness, meaning church-oriented missions; the prophetic dimension, meaning social action-oriented missions; and kingship:

> His kingship, so long undervalued, is now reaffirmed, and this makes important changes in the reason for missions as well as the ways of missionaries. If Christ is mostly priest, then, of course missions are meant for building altars, sprinkling baptismal water, and sharing the sacraments. If Christ is mostly prophet, our missions are naturally an extension of His teaching, training, exhorting career. But if He is king as well—and

---

[9]Willhelm Andersen, "Further Toward a Theology of Mission," in *The Theology of the Christian Mission*, ed. Gerald Anderson (New York: McGraw-Hill, 1961), pp. 300-313.

[10][Since 1938 the Missionary conference had used the term "church-centric" to describe mission. The 1952 conference challenged the idea that missions should be church-centered. —Ed.]

perhaps above all, if Christ is Lord, then we are involved in a new kind of obedience and bidden to a wider activity. The progress of Christian theology requires the reorientation of Christian missions.[11]

Gill then moved to a trinitarian understanding of mission.

The overwhelming missionary emphasis upon the Person and work of Jesus Christ . . . left out or at least underrated Him Who was revealed and with Whom we are reconciled [meaning the Father], as well as ignoring the revealing, reconciling Spirit. . . . Our eyes must never become so fixed upon Christ as to be blind to the whole God revealed in him. . . . The Great Commission makes a direct and unmistakable coupling of the mandate of the Lord Jesus and the triune name of God. In Christ we see and are related to God the Creator and God the Preserver, as well as to God the Saviour. In Him we are put next to our whole God, One who is concerned for our salvation because He is at work in His world, sustaining and redeeming His whole creation.[12]

Gill represents the concern to reach beyond the Jesus story and the church to wider dimensions of God's work. He references H. Richard Niebuhr, who is an important key to understanding how some people use the Trinity in theology of mission. Niebuhr warned against what he called the "unitarianism of the second person," that is, centering everything on Jesus.[13] What do we miss if we center everything on Jesus? If we read critically these passages from Niebuhr, we find it said in different ways, and they are not all consistent. But we can try to line up what they seem to say.

What do we miss that the Father does? First, the Father is responsible for creation. *Creation* means all aspects of the world to which we usually pay no attention: nature, the natural sciences, culture, institutions, the nature of things and reason as the structure of understanding things as they are. All of that is the realm of the Father, and we do not deal with that if we are too narrowly focused on Jesus.

---

[11][Theodore Gill, "Christian Missions: Whence and Whither?" in *The Missionary Obligation of the Church, Group I* (New York: National Council of the Churches, 1952), p. 2. —Ed.]

[12][Ibid., pp. 2, 11. —Ed.]

[13][See H. Richard Niebuhr, "The Doctrine of the Trinity and the Unity of the Church," *Theology Today* 3, no. 3 (October 1946): 377, 379. —Ed.]

Second, we miss providence. *Providence* means that God works in the arena of history apart from Jesus. Because we affirm that, as Father, God is in charge, we can read events in history as having meaning for us. The lessons of history are lessons from God. If over the centuries we have learned some things about, for instance, needing to be responsible for running the political order or needing to be responsible for ecology— things the early church did not know—we can give the Father credit for these lessons. We must affirm them apart from Jesus (or beside Jesus).

Third, reference to the Father sometimes means we should reach beyond Christianity and Judaism to a broader theism. That is, if there is one true God of the whole universe, when anybody outside of Hebrew history affirms that there is one god, it must be the same God. This view does not want to be narrow, clinging to Hebrew-centeredness, Bible-centeredness, Abraham-centeredness and Jesus-centeredness. If we affirm the fatherhood of God, then we must be willing to recognize and welcome joyfully the testimonies to theism that arise in other places than the stream of history dominated by the Hebrew story.

By concentrating on Jesus, what do we miss of the Spirit? The Spirit is the name given to the church's experience of God's guidance. If over the years the church evolves or comes to some new impression, that is understood to be the Spirit's leading. If through the centuries the church evolves into a hierarchy of bishops with a pope at the top, then that is seen to be the Spirit's leading. This view does not want to reject something simply because it did not begin in the New Testament. If the church under the leading of the Spirit took on the task of political responsibility, including baptizing Constantine and developing just war theory so that Christians could run the government, then that is a development we cannot deny.

Second, we miss flexibility in ethics or dependence on the Spirit to lead us to find the right thing to do in a situation. This concern is emphasized in "situation ethics." We do not always find a word from Jesus or from Scripture to speak to situations that we face, and we must trust the Spirit to lead us. Third, if we affirm the Spirit, we will be open to God's speaking to people who do not know Jesus' name or to God's speaking through the moral insights of nonreligious people. Fourth, we could certainly expect to find people appealing to the Spirit's work in ecstatic experience, visions, revelations, wonders and prophecies. This would be closest to the New Testament understanding of the Spirit's work, but it certainly is not what H. Richard Niebuhr meant.[14]

This trinitarian challenge is fundamentally about the church's place in the world, about Christian understanding of culture and ethics. It is not just a new or different light on the missionary obligation of the church. It uses discussion of the nature of God to push some other concerns in modern Western Protestantism.

How should we evaluate this particular thrust? First of all, this is not what the doctrine of the Trinity meant when the early church developed it. In the Niebuhrian thrust, the Father, Son and Spirit have separate tasks and say different things, and we have to balance them. We are the umpires who decide which person of the Trinity gets to speak and at which points, and we make sure that none of them dominates the others. This concept was not part of the original doctrine of the Trinity. When it developed in the third and fourth centuries, the issue was not whether there were three dimensions of God; the three names, concepts and stories were already there. The issue was the oneness of God and the status of the Son; they did not talk much about the Spirit as a separate problem. They asked if the Son was of the same authority and nature as the Father. What the doctrine of the Trinity meant to affirm was the priority of the Son in the order of knowing God and to deny that the Father has a different nature from that revealed in the Son. The whole Nicean debate was about the dignity and sovereignty of the Son. This emphasis is opposite to what those who learned from Niebuhr's 1946 essay are now arguing.

Second, the idea of a distinction of domains—the Father is the Creator and the Son is the Redeemer responsible for the church—is also missing or even contradicted biblically and historically. To the extent to which the New Testament talks about the Son and the Father, the Son participates in creation. John 1, Colossians 1 and Hebrews 1 are three different strands of the New Testament literature, and they all

---

[14]One could wonder why not, once one begins to reason that way about the separate works of the three members of the Trinity.

say this. In addition, the Spirit makes the Son present. The Spirit is not one who reveals things that the Son did not want to say or different things from what the Son said. That the Spirit makes the Son present is especially clear in John 14–16, which is the fullest description of the Spirit's identity.

We have to conclude from the perspective of systematic theology that this argument, although it claims to be orthodox because it talks about Trinity, is unrelated to what the doctrine of the Trinity has ever meant in the past. It might still be a good argument for some other reason, but one would have to make a case on that basis and not simply appeal to the terminology of Christian dogmatics for authority. If the point about theological balance or competition is valid, it can be stated in terms of Christ alone, that is, in terms of incarnation in relation to resurrection and return or in terms of Jesus as *Logos*, rabbi, sacrifice and Lord. That would be a way to talk about having all the pieces in the picture, and it is a proper concern to have.

To look a little closer at one case in point, consider the Holy Spirit working among all people. We saw that one of the things said about the Spirit is that the Spirit is moving somehow beyond Jesus, beyond the church. This came to the surface in the 1960s especially with the phrase "God is at work in the world." People said, "Let's join God at this work." That did not mean, "The church is growing; let's help it grow some more." It did not mean, "People are getting more and more profound in their Christian understanding or more and more de-voted in their Christian obedience; let's help that." It meant, "We can discern certain currents in world history that are the work of God. We can discern the current of liberation, anticolonialism and anti-imperialism. We can discern that people are coming to see the world as a unity. We can discern the growing awareness of how wrong social injustice is. Those movements that make the world more human we can celebrate and join." We will come back to this theme in later chapters, but our immediate question is whether talking about the Trinity, and specifically about the Holy Spirit, helps or confuses when dealing with this.

My thesis, which we will have to test in later chapters, is that there are real and good values about which it is *not* helpful to say they are the Holy Spirit's work. We do not need to identify Christianity with everything that has value. Within the church and the covenant, the Holy Spirit is clearly tied to the church. If we want to affirm some basis for value outside the church or the covenant, it would be more like the New Testament to talk about the cosmic lordship of Christ than to talk about the Spirit at work outside the walls of the church. The question that the doctrine of the Trinity meant to answer was not, "How can God work outside the church?" The question this doctrine meant to answer came later: We know God is working in the church as Spirit. We know God as having worked in the incarnation. We know God as the reality behind those two realities. How can we relate these three ways of knowing God? That does not mean we have closed off the question of how God cares about the rest of the world. But we need something other than Trinity language to get hold of the point.

CHRISTOCENTRIC OR THEOCENTRIC MISSION

Rather than speaking of the need for theological balance among the persons of the Trinity, another way some have put the trinitarian challenge in relation to mission has been to more directly question Jesus' centrality or normativeness in favor of a broader theism. Missionary theologian C. Stanley Smith represents the view "that the basic category in terms of which all creative theological thinking must be done upon the missionary obligation of the church is, God the Father Almighty—the basic category of the Apostle's Creed and of every great creed of the Church. . . . Christianity may take its name from Jesus Christ but it is founded upon a revelation of God, without whom there would be no Christ."[15] Smith's appeal is twofold: he says that Paul's first message to Gentiles was a message about God, not Jesus, and he points out that within the historic creeds, the confession of Jesus Christ as Lord comes second after a statement of belief in God the Father.

---

[15][See C. Stanley Smith, "An Exploratory Attempt to Define the Theological Basis of the Church's Missionary Obligation," in *The Missionary Obligation of the Church: Report of Commission 1 on the Biblical and Theological Basis of Mission* (New York: National Council of the Churches of Christ, 1952), p. 7. —Ed.]

There are two samples in Acts of Paul's preaching to people who did not have a Jewish worldview. We have already referred to Paul and Barnabas's preaching in Lystra (Acts 14). The other case is the Athens story (Acts 17:16-34). Paul had gone ahead of his traveling companions and, while in Athens, not only met with Jews in synagogues but met with Epicurean and Stoic philosophers and preached in the middle of the Areopagus where people aired their ideas. What did he say? He said the Athenians were already very religious people, for there were all kinds of temples in the town. Did Paul mean that was a good thing or a bad thing? Did he assume that their being religious was a solid pedestal on which to build or was he critical of it? We have the linguistic problem that the superlative in the Greek (*deisidaimonesterous*, translated as *very religious* in the RSV, Acts 17:22) can be either descriptive or evaluative, that is, it can mean they were extremely religious people or it could mean they were too religious.[16] Paul either started the conversation with an ingratiating complement or the opposite; as far as the language of the text is concerned, we cannot tell which.

Paul also mentioned a temple to an unknown god. Who would have built a temple to an unknown god? One possibility is that this god was part of a mystery religion, a particular god or understanding of god whose peculiarity was unknowability. Even the name of the divinity was unknown. "The unknowable god" could have been a meaningful religious statement, comparable to some strands of Buddhism, for instance. The most affirmative thing that can be said about such a god is that humans should not say anything about the god because anything said, including a name, would be false.

Another possibility is that in this polytheistic situation where every religious movement had its own building and rituals, and the mood of the culture was not to overlook anybody, somebody wanted to make sure that no god or religious group was missed. They had gotten a messenger from Persia who gave them one god's name, and they had gotten a messenger from Ethiopia who gave them another god's name; maybe there was a god from whom they did not get a mes-

---

[16][The NRSV translates this phrase "extremely religious." —Ed.]

senger. In case there was a god that did not yet have a temple or in case there were people who had not found a god of their choosing, they may have thought, "Let's build a place for that god too." Concern for equality of opportunity could have led someone to make room for one more god.

It is hard to believe that Paul accepted as a point of departure for his witness either a god who, by definition, is unknowable or the polytheistic, free enterprise, cafeteria approach of the Athenians. A god whose essence is unknowability cannot withstand talk about revelation, and not only revelation in general about that God's nature, but revelation about a man whom that God has appointed. Affirming an unknowable god could hardly be Paul's point. Nor could he accept the polytheistic approach because that is counter to what he goes on to say about the one Creator of heaven and earth. It seems more believable, if we try to reconstruct the situation Luke is describing, that Paul was making a pun and not really standing on the shoulders of the cult of an unknown god and affirming it. He was merely saying, "There is something you do not know, and I am going to tell you about it." What he said about the temple of the unknown God was no more affirmative than that.

But he was talking to an audience for whom some kind of a theistic worldview or at least some kind of an affirmation of divine being was thinkable. That is, he was not talking to modern atheists for whom the word *God* does not mean anything. Nor was he talking to a precultural animistic world where the idea of a god being personal or having a story or a will was unthinkable. It was not even that Paul was talking to seriously convinced polytheists. Greco-Roman polytheism was moving toward the philosophical idea that all of these divine figures and cults were inadequate symbols for one reality. It was rather a situation where there was a lingering theistic mood.

Paul's real thrust was anti-idolatry. That is where the passage began: he saw "that the city was full of idols" (Acts 17:16). He was in Athens waiting for his traveling companions. He did not go there with a clearly defined mission, so he did not start out as he had in other cities by attracting the synagogue as an audience. But he got so worked up about the concentrated idolatry that he started arguing both with Jews in the synagogue and other people in the marketplace about how wrong this was. The two words he used that the people who did not understand him caught in listening to him were *Jesus* and *anastasis* (resurrection). They thought that *anastasis* was another deity's name. Paul argued against idolatry in favor of the oneness, the uniqueness, the providential sovereignty and the not-wanting-a-temple character of the true God. This God had historical purposes and wanted to give every nation its place, determining the course within which their history could move with the hope that they might seek the one true God. But the nations did not do so. Paul warned that God had been patient with them so far, but there will be a judgment, and the center of that judgment will be the man whom God has appointed and raised from the dead.

Is this or is this not preaching theism—a message about God the Father—before preaching Jesus? Or is Paul rather identifying first as a Jew talking about Jesus and resurrection, and then explaining how that position meshes or clashes with the idolatrous polytheism of his audience?[17]

Smith's argument from this text that general theism should be prior to preaching about Jesus is clearly a possible one. If theism is absent, we proclaim it. If it is present, we respect it and build on it. This is not just a question of communication techniques or whether one takes the audience seriously. It is a question of who the true God is. Is the God in whom others already believe a creator, or invisible or unknowable? The thesis is serious, but it is not the only way to take the Athenian story, and in a wider sense it is not the only possible position. A worldview in which divinities were real was taken for granted in Greek culture. So Paul and Barnabas did not import theism. They did not bring a theistic metaphysics into a culture where it was absent. So this text would not in itself be a basis for saying that in speaking to the so-called secular modern man or to a nontheistic Buddhist culture, we must first talk about a personal Creator-God-Father and leave Jesus for later.

Second, in this particular situation Paul's strong thrust against

---

[17]The worldview that is taught here is much the same as in Lystra (Acts 14): because of creation or nature there was a situation in which humans should have been able to perceive God. In Athens Paul again rejects idolatry and refers to God's patience with humans.

idolatry, against a plurality of gods, against giving offerings to these various gods, and against conceiving of gods in human form (such as the Lystrans thinking that Paul was Hermes) was antireligious in the culture of the time. Speaking against idolatry was disrespectful of their religious business. It would have been a radical rejection of their theism in favor of the particularity of the Jewish way of talking about God, which insists that humans not make statues or link worship of God closely with fertility or political power. All of these elements of the Jewish message were counter to the theism that was there in Athens. Paul and Barnabas were culturally particularist. They made specifically Jewish points.

Several things Paul said about God were significantly different from the theism the Athenians affirmed. Paul said that God is benevolent. God is undiscriminating. God made the whole world, not just one province. God is not the deity of such and such a territory from which a prophet comes. God cares equally about all nations and gives each of them their place under the sun. These things were quite different from the character of the Athenians' gods.

Finally, Paul moves firmly into a historical perspective by saying that the period of God's patience ends with Christ as judge. I agree with Smith that Paul's message included statements about the specific Jewish, and therefore also Christian, understanding of God as loving, powerful, Creator, Father, invisible, Spirit and having a holy will. But Paul's preaching was not therefore any less Christocentric. When he found theism, he pointed away from it to the resurrection. When he encountered polytheism, he challenged it and rejected it.

When we enter a polytheistic situation, there is reason for saying that the true God is the one who sent Jesus and raised him from the dead, rather than some other divine entity in whom people have been taught to believe. In situations where there is no theism, the Athenian example is not an adequate basis for saying we have to argue first the metaphysics of God's existence. In Paul's message, there is an affirmation of God the Father, but this is precisely the God whom Jesus taught us to call Father, the one whom Jesus in a peculiar way claimed as the Father from whom he had his mission.

Trinitarian Formula as a Potential Hindrance to Mission

One other hypothesis to test is the possibility that trinitarian dogma—in the sense of classic creedal statements that Christians hold to because they are taught that they rise out of the history of the faith—may be a hindrance in mission.

The clearest demonstration of this comes from Islam. Because Islam is younger than Christianity, it came into being with an awareness of Christian faith. However, Muhammed did not know a refined Christianity. In fact there is some basis for thinking that the Trinity that Muhammad believed Christians affirmed was a threeness of Father, Son and Mother and that the third person of the Trinity was not the invisible Holy Spirit, but Mary. The Egyptian mystery cult of Isis and Osiris had that same idea of a husband, wife and son, all three of them gods. In the Nile Valley, syncretistic forms of Christianity had transmuted this tritheistic pattern into a Trinity where Mary was one of the three persons.[18] But, even apart from that crude distortion, to say that God is three, for a radical monotheist like Muhammad, was a form of polytheism. For Muhammad, God's oneness was jeopardized by the things said about Jesus. The Muslim reproach that Christianity is tritheistic has been part of the intellectual problem that has marked respectful cross-cultural conversation and Christian mission to this day.

This should push us to redefine what the doctrine of the Trinity means. Often in Western understanding when we do not face critiques like those from Muslims, there *is* movement in the direction of tritheism; that is, thinking of Father, Son and Spirit as three persons in the modern sense, as if there were three centers of consciousness that could talk to each other or have committee meetings. Billy Graham once used the figure of a pre-Creation committee meeting in which Father, Son and Spirit said, "If we make a world and they do not obey us, then what will we do?" Jesus

---

[18]There seems to be some archeological basis for this in Egypt. [Yoder seems to be referring to the ancient Christian group, the Collyridians, who worshipped Mary as divine. Epiphanius (315–403 C.E.) described the group and condemned them in his book *The Panarion*, 79. The Collyridians were active during the fourth century C.E., far earlier than Muhammad, who lived in the late sixth to the early seventh centuries. Their ideas, however, may have lived on in other minor heretical groups. —Ed.]

said, "I will go."[19] That is not completely useless to make some points. But Muhammad would certainly misunderstand, and rightly.

This understanding of *person* is different from what the Latin word *persona* meant when it came into the ancient creeds, where it referred to something more like a mask an actor wore. The real meaning of the doctrine of the Trinity is that there is only one God, and the revelation of God's self in Jewish history, in Jesus and through the Spirit all truly reveal God's nature. The threeness is evident; the affirmation of the doctrine of the Trinity is that God's nature is one, not that it is three.

A similar kind of problem, but on the other side, arises if one tries to make much of trinitarian dogma in Hindu culture. Hinduism is not one faith in the same sense that Christianity, Islam or even Buddhism is one faith. It is rather an enormous plurality of practices and understandings whose very pluralism is affirmed and thought to be great, glorious, inclusive and rich. If Christians say, "Even among us there are three deities, or three forms in which the deity is made known," Hindus can take this as one step in the direction of their own pluralism of divine forms. They may ask, "As long as you have three forms, why not three thousand?" If we Christians need to talk about God in three ways in order to speak meaningfully, this appears to be a concession to the polytheistic thrust of the Hinduism which says that to put God in only one form is to do violence to the plurality of divine being.

A pluralistic understanding of divine being also would be a misunderstanding of the Trinity because the point of the doctrine as it arose was to explain the authoritativeness of the incarnation as the only fully valid point at which we can know who God is. The original meaning of the doctrine of the Trinity was to affirm particularity—the authority of the Son, known in Jesus. But—both for a Muslim, who would be offended by it, and a Hindu, who would greet it—trinitarian language, *when inadequately understood*, can be a hindrance to the meaning of the witness to Jesus.

---

[19][See Lewis Drummond, *The Evangelist* (Nashville: Word Publishers, 2001), p. 72. —Ed.]

7

CHURCH TYPES AND MISSION

A Radical Reformation Perspective

In the preceding chapters we moved from the New Testament story to New Testament thought to a more systematic effort to grasp theologically what it means that God's purposes involve the Christian world mission. Before turning to specific debated theological topics that arise out of the church's missionary experience, we need to bring to our awareness the variety of available social types or concepts of the church because of the difference this makes for our reflection in the rest of this book. Different understandings of the nature of the church illuminate and shape mission questions and issues.

There are many ways to conceive of the church and her relationship to the world, but we will look especially at three of them: Christendom, Radical Reformation and Pietism. These are types of thought or ways of putting things together that have arisen in church history. Although we will refer to historical names in describing these types, our concern is not to be completely fair to past personages and events, but rather to identify various ways of thinking as thought types or models that help interpret the issues at stake. Mission literature is well aware of the problem of church/world relations and the light that it throws on the missionary task. By now everyone is critical in some sense of how missions were done in the colonialist framework. Thus to critically call into question some of the historic models in this respect is a similar approach to what we find in mission literature today. We will be asking what difference ecclesiology, and especially the church/world relationship, makes for understanding the meaning of mission.

My thesis is that there is a fundamental difference in understanding the way the church ought to be in the world, which throws a great amount of light on discussion about mission. It can be claimed that the difference between the Radical Reformation or free church model and the Christendom model is the deepest one in Christian history. This difference was present before the Reformation, although it took the most visible form in the Reformation. The free church versus Christendom division was the first division within the Protestant Reformation. That is, it was not until the 1530s that the social form of the Lutheran and Reformed movements was settled. Church/state relations and which territories were going to be Protestant were not decided, neither in Luther's nor in Zwingli's home territory, until the late 1520s and early 1530s. But the division between the free churches and Christendom began cracking in Zurich in 1523; it was definite by 1525 and irreparable by 1527.

This division is deeper than those the ecumenical movement has addressed. The ecumenical movement in its modern forms of Faith and Order and of Life and Work has compared doctrines, theories of ministry and concepts of episcopacy and asked whether we can find some common understanding through which church organizations could be less separate from one another. That is not useless. The ecumenical movement has made a significant contribution in working on many of the divisions between churches. But this free church–Christendom division runs deeper. It is of fundamental theological importance, and it has not been the subject of serious discussion in ecumenical work.

TERMINOLOGY

There are a variety of names that properly could be given to the two poles in this tension. For one pole I use *Christendom*, which in its historic origins accentuates the geographic character of the merger of church and world in European experience. That part of the globe has been thought of as "Christian," and to think of a part of the globe as Christian we have to have an understanding of the merger of church commitment with a total culture and its geography. The term *Christendom* only started to be used when Christendom was on the defensive, that is, when Islam was gaining ground from Eastern Europe and North Africa. That defensiveness meant there was a much firmer sense that this was the "Christian" part of the world. Other possible names should be identified as well because they have slightly different shadings. They are:

- *People's church* (*Volkskirche*) accentuates the concern to involve a unit (that is, people as a singular noun, the *Volk*) and the identification of a church structure with the German people, the French people, the Dutch people or wherever.

- In some other languages, especially French, the concept that is used is the *church of the multitude*, which makes the point of inclusiveness, not simply of a national or cultural unit (a *Volk*), but everybody, all the individuals and possible kinds of people are the church's business.

- Sometimes we talk about the *state church*, focusing on a narrower question of how the church as a structure for the administration of preaching and sacraments relates to the government. Of course, a Christendom church is a state church, but the tension is focused at different points. Sometimes the name of Constantine is used as a symbol for this mood because it was with his epoch that it began.

This demonstrates some of the variety of terms. Sometimes they are used interchangeably. My preference is still *Christendom*.

On the other side of the polarity, there are also several alternative terms. I use the term *free church* as the mostly widely used and the least precise. It is the least precise because in older British usage, the concept included any churches that were not established by the state. That included the Congregationalists and the Methodists who baptized babies, and thereby were not a pure type in terms of the alternatives we will discuss. Even the Presbyterians, who in Scotland were an established church, in England were a free church. In Scotland the Queen was the head of the Presbyterian Church and in England she was the head of the Anglican Church; therefore the English Presbyterians were a free church. That is the widest use of the term. More often *free church* is used for

those groups where membership is voluntary and infants are not baptized. That would exclude Presbyterians, Methodists and Congregationalists, but it would include Baptists and other groups that baptize adults.
There is a still smaller circle called the *peace churches* that could include
Methodists. But the historic peace churches are more "believers
churches" than the Methodists are. There are also various other ways of
speaking about the "free church" model:

- *Believers church* is a phrase that Max Weber coined. This was taken up
  various places including *The Concept of the Believers Church* and in a
  series of subsequent conferences and publications.[1] This term puts
  the accent at the point of voluntary membership. *Believers church*
  means that the community is made of those who have themselves
  made the choice to be its members.

- Others prefer the term *disciples' church* because those who have
  chosen to be members are not simply people who say they believe
  something but who have taken on themselves a discipline, a commitment to a distinct lifestyle.

- Others use the term *pure church*, which is problematic because of its
  ambiguity. But it points to the fact that this community is concerned
  for her identity, includes fraternal discipline and asks whether everyone who claims to belong is a member. In that sense it is an understandable term. When it amounts to the claim that the community is
  free of sin, it is confusing and inaccurate.

- Some people talk about the *Anabaptist* or *Radical Reformation* type,
  taking one particular historical stream as representative of the movement's whole approach and applying it in other centuries as well.[2]

---

[1][James Leo Garrett, *The Concept of the Believers' Church: Addresses from the 1967 Louisville Conference* (Scottdale, PA: Herald Press, 1969). This first Believers Church Conference was followed
by fifteen others, the most recent in 2008. —Ed.]

[2]The use of these terms as well as "Radical Reformation" for this type is problematic also because
many people assume that modern Mennonites represent the Radical Reformation. Current
Mennonites are heirs of a movement that is the result of many kinds of experiences and input,
of which the Radical Reformation of the sixteenth century has been only a small portion. In fact,
the assumption in recent years that Mennonites are "Anabaptists" probably has made for more
confusion than clarification.

DIFFERENCES BETWEEN CHRISTENDOM
AND FREE CHURCH MODELS

We have talked about labels. What are the substantive differences between them? Here we could set up two columns, rather simply and firmly, of extreme alternatives. There is no special order in which I will list them.

Belonging. An individual belongs to the body of Christendom by automatic baptism at birth. Historically, Christendom baptized adults at the fringes of its conquest, people who somehow got missed or who had broken out of the system and returned, or Jews when they were forced to become Christians in the Middle Ages. But normally in this model of church, somebody becomes a Christian by infant baptism. In fact, the verb *to christen* says just that: to become a Christian is the same thing as to be given a name in baptism, and that is when somebody becomes a person in Christendom.[3]

The alternative is obvious. A person becomes a member of the free church by their own choice in response to the message. The person should not only be adult, but should also be aware of the decision's meaning, content and cost.

Membership. It follows from this that membership in the church is the same as membership in the society in Christendom. There is one merged power structure and people are not really free to belong to one and not the other.

Membership in the free church is not identical with membership in society. A person is free not to be a church member and still to be a member of society with full rights. This may reflect an individualistic view of humanity but it does not have to. The free church model can combine a strongly communal view of the person and yet insist on decision at the point of membership.

Ethnicity. The Christendom approach has assumed (until modern pluralism) that community life is ethnic in the simple sense that a total Christian culture passes itself on from parents to children as a unit.

---

[3]Jews were not really "persons" in the Middle Ages. In South American Spanish, the word *cristiano* simply means a civilized human being. The alternative is a donkey or an Indian, who was also not a person in the cultural background of South American Latin until recently.

The free church can, if its geographic limitations are firm, become an ethnically identifiable unit. But its theology and practice do not call for that. If its understanding of voluntary membership continues to be applied, it will constantly break out of that ethnic temptation.

Persecution. The church of Christendom may persecute unbelievers, dissenters or unfaithful members with any kind of power necessary to keep them in line. The free church, by definition, must not persecute. There are groups with this background that pressure dissenters, but at that point they no longer fit the model.

Organization and leadership. The word *church* in Christendom tends to be used to describe the administrative agency that provides ritual worship. It is an organization. If we talk about membership in the widest sense, everyone is a member. But if we mean the church that we can complain about or address a request to, then it means the priest and above him the bishop or the consistory in a state church.

For the free church, the church is the community, the total membership, and only in a derivative way its organization and leaders.

Education and discipleship. In Christendom a person becomes a more faithful Christian through education, through nurture and through accepting the content of the faith that the church structure and its schools teach. Those responsible desire that people become more faithful Christians. Sometimes in debating enthusiasts the spokesman of the Christendom stance would say, "Do not be so demanding, God is very patient and tolerant. You do not have to be so good." But this did not mean that they wanted to be diluted or unfaithful Christians. Christendom churches want to foster faithfulness through as many tools as possible. But they are gradualistic tools that exclude no one.

The believers church sees people coming to faithfulness because they respond to a call. The Holy Spirit drives that response, so it is not simply a natural, gradualistic acceptance of nurture. That does not mean that there is no such thing as gradual growth in a person's life, especially a young person born into a family related to the church. But certain elements of that decision are discernible at a point of decision, at the point of defining and consciously accepting membership. People become more faithful by making a decision of which they are aware and for which they take responsibility.

Church/state relationship. The powers of society, especially the state, maintain the structure of Christendom. In this model it is proper that it should be that way and not just an emergency rule, although sometimes the Reformers spoke of the prince's place in introducing the Reformation as an emergency measure. Martin Luther talked about the prince as an emergency bishop. But, in the long run, it is proper that a Christian government should support church structures emotionally, financially and even with police power to discourage dissent.

The believers church's own voluntary process, the way believers interact with each other, maintains its visible structure. There are organizational structures, of course, but the structures are not propped up by outside power. The process itself does not focus so much on maintaining a constitution and offices, but on what the Anabaptists called "the rule of Christ." This refers to a conversational process that is undertaken when church groups need to deal with an issue. They talk about it with the conviction that the conversation itself and its conclusions as ratified by the wider group are how the Spirit leads.

Empire and mission. For Christendom, the link between empire and mission, or between cultural colonialism and mission, is normal. It is nothing to be ashamed of if Christian rulers and Christian business people propagate the church in the rest of the world as they propagate their rule and their business. In this sense Roman Catholicism was less consistently "Christendom" in the late Middle Ages than Protestantism came to be. When missionary orders such as the early Jesuits went around the world, they went as the pope's emissaries. They took with them Latin forms of worship and theology. But they went to places over which they had no political control. They did not feel that it was somehow a defective situation that when they got to China, Japan or South India that they were not under the Holy Roman Empire's protection. So the monastic form of mission does not represent the Christendom concept in its pure form. The monastic order is a kind of believers church. But for Christendom's high age, the age of empire, the linkage of empire and mission was normal not only for Protestants, but also later for Catholics, such as the Belgian mission in the Congo in the last half of the last century.

For the free church, the linkage of mission and empire is fundamentally problematic. It is not only a problem if it fails, if later somebody objects to it or if the natives get "uppity." It is fundamentally problematic that the Christian message should be linked with power—business power, political power or the structure of colonialism.

War. In a parallel way, in Christendom war is a theological necessity. If you have linked the identity of the Christian movement with certain peoples and governments—their structures, survival and effectiveness— then it fits that these governments should incline toward justifiable violence not only to maintain their inner peace and order, but also to defend themselves against wider threats. Since their normal social and political outreach includes the creation of colonies, it is not improper that they should use war to defend their colonial possessions and interests. So the doctrine of the justifiable war is part of the Protestant confessions and the Catholic tradition, not as a highly holy cause, but as a regrettable necessity in some cases.

For the free church, war is fundamentally to be questioned. The concept of the believers church or the free church as defined by historians is wider than the peace churches, but there is a sense in which the circles are concentric.

Place of mission. For Christendom the world mission is marginal or optional. It is not a bad thing to do, but it is certainly possible to be a true church without it. The traditional doctrine of the church in these Christendom traditions does not include the idea that the church must reach beyond herself with a message. By definition the center of Europe did not have any pagan neighbors during the time we are discussing, and there was not any strong awareness of how they might take a message to the rest of the world, especially if the message was the unity of church and society. So the place of mission in the Christendom church's self-understanding was marginal. It arose later; it was not built into the concept of the church.

For the believers church some kind of ongoing missionary activity defines the church even at home. There is no place where the believers church does not have both the possibility and necessity of an ongoing missionary thrust. Since this group is not identical with the whole society, and usually at its beginning is a small minority, gaining members for this group is conceivable emotionally and sociologically, as it was not for a state church in Europe between 1000 and 1900 C.E. But more than this, because only individuals who have responded freely to Christ's invitation can be members, the church will die out if it does not win people. Of course, there is a shortcut at this point: if the church can hang on to its children without their making costly decisions for Christ, then sustainability is a little easier. But the point remains that the believers church will not exist fifty years from now unless new people choose to join it. The free church not only can be but has to be missionary in its structure.

Role of doctrine. Not only does the church of Christendom have to make much of the state as a safeguard of identity, it also tends to make much of doctrine and of the agencies that handle doctrine. For Christendom, creeds and confessions are important because criteria for faithfulness must come from somewhere outside of individual loyalty and personal experience so that it can be handled objectively. If propositions, creeds and confessions define faithfulness, then it is also important to have in the church intellectuals and teachers who are qualified to handle those words. The Reformation's formal basis was the University of Wittenburg, the preacher's school formed by Ulrich Zwingli in Zurich, and other schools such as those formed by Calvin in Geneva and Bucer and Sturm in Strasbourg. Church reformation was a reformation of doctrine carried on by reforming teachers. This is why Harvard historian, George Williams, uses the term *magisterium* to refer to the official Reformation. This is a kind of pun, since *magisterium* in this context meant two things: the magistracy reformed and the teaching body reformed. The state and the university carried out the Reformation. Without the university we would not have had the Protestant Reformation, because the state had to authorize somebody to discern true doctrine. The bishops were Catholic, so the Reformers replaced the bishop with university professors like Martin Luther. Thus, for Christendom, theology is a profession, institutionalized in the theologians with their own power structure, criteria of faithfulness and financial base, relatively independent of the grassroots communities with their own life of piety or belief.

The free church does not reject concern for doctrinal statements, but it is located in one of the gifts, offices or ministries within the fellowship. Doctrinal statements do not define things once for all so that the church must defend the proper statement of the truth with great care. In the sixteenth century the free church was concerned for the flexible but faithful restatement of the truth in the situations they faced. The difference this made can be seen in the way in which Lutheranism from 1550 to 1570 became a history of university politics, of this phrasing against that phrasing, of who understood rightly what Martin Luther meant in 1527 or Philipp Melanchthon in 1530, and which was the right draft of the Confession of Augsburg. The way to make the Reformation faithful, for official Lutheranism of the time, was to work at those kinds of questions.

My point is neither that everybody who ever baptized a baby believes all the things I just said about Christendom, nor that everybody who was ever baptized as an adult believes all the things I said about the free church. Nonetheless, there is consistency to those two positions, the various assumptions they make and the various observations we have made about them.

MEDIATING CHURCH TYPES: THE NORTH AMERICAN MELTING POT

The use of church types is a delicate matter because we easily can be unfair to the facts or to people's intentions, and because there are often real cases that do not fit into those extreme types. One way we can correct for the possible injustice of these types is to look for more types that are different in some significant way. Another is to observe that there are mixtures, as in North America.

In the North American melting pot, the Constantinian or Christendom churches became freer in form, and the free churches became less purely free. Immigrants brought with them the assumptions and forms of different understandings of the church when they began to live together in the new country and move toward speaking the same language and sharing the same institutions. The migration set up a pluralistic society.

People from Christendom churches came from a situation where there was only one kind of people, and they were in control. They came to a situation in which they had to live side by side with people from other cultural and religious groups. Even closely related groups such as Lutherans and Catholics, or Irish Catholics and Polish Catholics, found that while they brought the same Christendom assumptions to the new world, they carried different content, so none of them could establish the old forms of Christendom in New York or Chicago.

In addition, the U.S. Constitution did not permit the legal establishment of a given denomination. While Christendom was retained on the state level in the original colonies, it gradually faded away there as well. In place of legal establishment there were religious competition and pluralism. Churches that still had Christendom assumptions in their creeds and practices had to depend increasingly on their good members' voluntary commitment rather than on state-supported structures of authority. The Catholic parochial school was an effort to reproduce the social reality of a total community by making all its children Christians through nurture, but support of the Catholic parochial school had to be voluntary because there was a public school system that was free. Parents had to be won to support the school because they believed in it, which was not the case in the old country. In the U.S. the Christendom churches had to become freer in their form.

At the same time, the free churches—Baptists who came from England or the Anabaptist descendants who came from the Continent— became less purely free, especially as they accepted the new nationalism. They thought, "The nationalism of the old country oppressed us. The nationalism here frees us and gives us more religious liberty. This is a better country." Some of the dynamics that led them to critique authorities in Europe—an antinationalist, cosmopolitan feeling and readiness to migrate if pressured—flipped over in this culture and the immigrants fostered an identification with the national government and its attitude toward the church. A "magisterial" concern for true doctrine and for having reliable schools that are the organs of maintaining faithfulness of doctrine also grew to have an importance among North American free churches that it did not have in Europe.

Ironically, the Congregationalists, who were a free church in England, became the quasi-established church in Massachusetts. It took a while for them to back away from this status even after the Revolution. Others became the *Volkskirche* of a minority group.[4] For example, the Mennonites in Switzerland were clearly a minority. Most people around them were not Mennonites, but everyone spoke German. When these Mennonites moved to Pennsylvania or Ohio, they were suddenly the only people around talking German. So the Mennonite church became the "established" church of their American cultural enclave. The church that in Europe had talked the same language and shopped at the same stores as their neighbors, through the process of migration, created a mini-commonwealth or Christendom in the new world.

If Christendom and the free church are polar alternatives, then we see in North America the fuzzing of the distinctions, movement toward each other, and development of some of the characteristics of the other group. That is mediation between or dilution of the two church types.

PIETISM: A THIRD FORM

Another corrective to the two-pole typology is noticing a completely different form, Pietism being the best example. Pietism both accepts and criticizes Christendom but does not break with it, does not get thrown out, does not form an alternative church, does not critique the state/church relationship, and does not challenge infant baptism and its expression of societal unity. It does not challenge fundamentally the existing orthodox doctrinal formulations, but says they are not enough. In addition to them, there must be personal authenticity, some kind of personal conversion, not at the point of baptism or accepting Christian truth (because those steps have been taken already) but at the point of faith becoming real for the individual. This not only calls for individual decision but it almost always demands the creation of voluntary groups— small groups, cells, house churches—that do not call themselves church but that do challenge the existing church by saying or implying it is not enough. In the sociology of the village, this form of renewal sometimes

---

[4][In nineteenth-century Europe there was a conscious shift to speaking of a people's church (*Volkskirche*) as a state church equivalent. See explanation by James Urry, *Mennonites, Politics, and Peoplehood: Europe – Russia – Canada 1525–1980* (Winnipeg: University of Manitoba Press, 2006), p. 127. —Ed.]

threatens considerably the existing church. Personal conversion (ceasing to be a formal Christian and becoming a genuine Christian in the heart), piety, good works and mission will be structured in these voluntary groups, but the groups do not reject the overarching Christendom structure. They do challenge Christendom in the sense of inviting Christians to a higher authenticity and inviting individuals to join this voluntary movement.

The nature of the Pietist movement in the seventeenth and eighteenth centuries in Europe is not our focus here. Rather than watching the history of that movement, we will use the type "Pietism" as a description of a structural approach to mission. We should note, however, that this historical movement is the place from which the missionary movement of the modern world came. The Anabaptists were in some typical sense, in some potential sense and in the practice of a few decades, the first Protestant missionaries. But they did not survive, and they did not create a worldwide missionary movement. Neither did the Christendom church at large create a missionary movement. But given the pedestal of Christendom, Pietism became the source of the great missionary movement of the last centuries. We will come back to what that means in the next chapter.

TWENTIETH-CENTURY CRITICISM OF THE FREE CHURCH TYPE AND ITS IMPLICATIONS FOR MISSION

The main contemporary representatives of those who accepted the typology of the church types described above as helpful were H. Richard and Reinhold Niebuhr, and before them Ernst Troeltsch. Troeltsch delineates the same three types we have noted: the Pietists, which he calls "spiritualist"; the Anabaptists, which he calls "sect"; and the Christendom type, which he calls "church."

Given this framework, what are the shortcomings of the free church position? Its critics noted that it rejects participation in culture. It obviously rejects war, or even the use of the sword within the law and order structure of a peaceful state. By implication it rejects any political involvement and even rejects the goods of culture, that is, education and economic productivity. Sectarians grudgingly accept a certain involvement because they have to stay alive (so they have to be part of the economy), but they do not take it seriously. They do not affirm culture. The clearest statement of this view is in H. Richard Neibuhr's book *Christ and Culture*.[5]

According to this interpretation, the radicals reject culture for a number of reasons. First, because the gospel is a spiritual message, they do not want to mix it up with cultural content or to accept cultural values for the wrong reason. Moreover, the radicals do not want to muddle politics with the gospel, which calls people to repent and turn toward God who is in another world.

Second, free church people avoid these issues simply because they do not see them as important or central. The radical free church witness is always concerned with what is central and with setting aside secondary things. Cultural power is one of the things they want to avoid; it is not central for Christians. All of this paraphrases H. Richard Niebuhr's way of stating the critique.

The critique has implications for mission, for it suggests that the radical free church position only makes sense in the West when one is trying to critique Christendom; that is, Anabaptists can only be Anabaptist when they have a Christian society to be Anabaptist against. In a worldwide missionary context, the argument goes, Christians cannot avoid culture; it is the missionaries who build hospitals, start literacy training, teach people to farm and in some places help people organize their village life. According to H. Richard Niebuhr's outlook, which is widely present in modern missionary thinking, the Radical Reformation position is parasitical. If it is managed well, it can have a function within the Christian West. But in the non-Western world, missionaries cannot avoid affirming culture, power and structure. Free church missionaries will either do culturally productive things such as building schools and hospitals with a guilty conscience saying, "Well, the natives will not listen to us unless we do a little of this," or they will do them for the wrong reasons, as bait. In some cases they may try to maintain integrity by refusing to affirm existing social and economic power, and then the

---

[5]H. Richard Niebuhr, "Christ Against Culture," *Christ and Culture* (New York: Harper & Row, 1951), pp. 45-82.

mission will founder because they do not have a Christendom system on which to rely.

RADICAL REFORMATION PERSPECTIVE ON MISSION

What claim would the Radical Reformation model make for itself regarding mission? The validity of the free church claim depends on the theological validity of its critique of Christendom. Although the Anabaptists—and others like them before and after—took positions deviant from the majority on many questions (of which infant baptism, the church/state question and the war question were only a few), this flowed from their rejection of the identification of church and world, which was Christendom's fundamental axiom. The Protestant Magisterial Reformation criticized (on the grounds of its understanding of the Bible) specific doctrinal and practical aberrations of which it accused medieval Catholicism, but it did not challenge the church/world identification as such.

That is the difference we have to evaluate. The originality of the Radical Reformation over against the Magisterial Reformation was at the point of the relationship of church and world, and making a clear distinction between them is the presupposition of mission. If there is a rejection of the visible distinctiveness of church and world, then there is less reason or capacity to conceive of a mission beyond the church because everybody baptized as an infant is in it already. There is also a built-in trend toward ethnocentricity, that is, toward assuming that the way to be Christian is the way it is done in one's own nation. With clear affirmation of one's own religious culture over against other cultures, conflicts can turn not only into wars against Turks or Arabs, who have other faiths, but also against other Christians. Pacifist Christians are used to thinking of such wars as an ethical abuse because it is wrong to kill people, which is true. We can also talk about these wars as an abuse from the missionary perspective: when we kill people we cannot evangelize them. We do not see them as potential members of our community. We do not apply to them the relationship to the nations that the New Testament says God's people should apply.

The Anabaptist separation of church and world is logically in key with a New Testament understanding of the missionary church that

overcame local and ethnic identification. We can also observe historically that the Radical Reformation already to a considerable extent in
the Waldensian experience, again in the Anabaptist experience and later
in the Quaker experience, restored a church that goes and sends. They
did not go around the world the way the Franciscans and the Jesuits did
in that epoch, but they did go beyond their own nation—and not only
because they were exiled.

The claim for the free church type as it affects mission is centrally a
theological claim made on the basis of the New Testament understanding of the church's mission. It is not a claim being made on the
basis of the performance of the early generations of the Radical Reformers. It is not a claim made on the basis of the preservation of
this heritage across the centuries or for the particular denominational
incarnations of Radical Reformation ethics or the conscious self-
understanding of these groups.

Because the free church position sees the church as somehow radically
unfaithful in entering into a cozy relationship with "the world" in Europe,
a relationship which came to be called Christendom, it identifies the
need for a change that goes back to the root and relates church and world
in a different way. This means that the ethics and structure of the church
and state relationship and the membership of the Christian community
as dramatized by whether you baptize babies or not will be significant
keys to the restructuring of a mission theology and church that tries to
do again what the New Testament church was doing in its time.

8

PIETIST PERSPECTIVE
ON MISSION

W hat has set up our current problems and vocabulary regarding mission was not the Radical Reformation but the foreign missionary movement of the last two centuries. This movement has been the source of the mission models that have dominated in our culture and churches. The missionary movement was the fruit of Pietism, an event in European church history in the late seventeenth and eighteenth centuries. This particular renewal movement created missionary institutions, methods, motivations and concepts. Other renewal movements and theologies did not. That gives us reason to ask about Pietist theology as a missionary theology.

DEFINITIONS

With regard to Pietism two things can be distinguished. First, the term refers to a historical movement in European Protestantism from the seventeenth and eighteenth centuries, including its results to the present; second, *Pietism* represents a theology or set of attitudes that can be found outside that movement or can be discussed for their own sake. Like *Anabaptist*, the term *Pietist* may be descriptive or evaluative. My intent is to use *Pietism* in the descriptive sense on two levels: a real phenomenon in history and a type of thought.

ORIGINS

Pietism arose in the age of orthodoxy. The Magisterial Reformation made the university one of the Reformation's pillars of security, reliability and faithfulness. The Reformation leaned on the state and on true doctrine. Therefore, it was the business of the state university and the state church to elaborate and clarify true doctrine. By the mid-seventeenth century there was already an intellectually and sociologically impressive body of orthodox literature being preserved, propagated and further developed by the teaching office of Christian society, whether Lutheran, Reformed or Anglican.

It became so clear what correct doctrine was that people could hold to it without the need for personal commitment or inward experience, without testing their relationship to a community, and without other interesting, live options for viewing faith ever arising. The defense of official Protestantism against Anabaptism had helped move Protestantism in that direction because it was the Anabaptists, not the official church, who made an issue of whether every individual was committed. As a result, orthodoxy moved toward being satisfied with a minimal level of commitment from individuals, as long as the total society continued to be committed to the truth. That was the situation Pietism sought to correct.

A second basic cultural observation is that Pietism arose as an elite movement. Later it became a popular grassroots movement, especially in southern Germany, but it began as a movement of the urban elite and the nobles. For a long time it was small in actual numbers of participants, but it was nevertheless significant because the participants were important people in the society.

WHAT ARE THE CONCERNS OF PIETISM?

The three central Piestist concerns were personal experience of the received faith, organization in small voluntary groups for study and prayer, and participation in mission and social service ministries.

Personal piety. As a type of thought, Pietism's first concern was to develop and express personal piety or faith as experienced. It did not involve new theological content or ideas. It involved truly making one's own the doctrine one already knew. That doctrine was Lutheran theology focusing on justification by faith. Pietism encouraged people to appropriate the deeper meaning of justification by faith as something more than a saying in a creed or ritual. It meant feeling and experiencing this truth; struggling with whether one really believed it; rejoicing that one really did believe it. Pietism was an innovation in practice not doctrine, helping people make their Lutheran identity more whole or complete.

The movement appealed back to Luther who had said in 1526 that there should be three church orders. One of them would maintain a traditional Latin liturgy, minimally corrected to keep it from teaching Catholic heresy but otherwise retained as the high cultural celebration of Christian worship. Although he did not keep the Latin liturgy as history developed, Luther had wanted to keep it because he thought it would please young students, who in that culture were taught to think in Latin. The Latin liturgy would give students the impression that for the intellectual elite Christian faith was culturally respectable.

Second, Luther thought there should be a German Mass, which would be the parish's ordinary liturgy. He prepared his own draft of the German Mass.

Third, he believed there should be an assembly of people who seriously wanted to be Christian. That would have to be a different kind of group with different structures from the established parish. Based on what Luther said about it, this assembly would have been similar to an Anabaptist group: it was to have church discipline, economic sharing and separate offices, among other things.[1] Philipp Jakob Spener, who founded one of the offices of Pietism, appealed to that text to say that Luther wanted people like the Pietists to have additional meetings in which people would help one another become more serious Christians.

Voluntary groups. Pietism was also concerned that personal piety be expressed in small voluntary groups. These groups would cultivate piety by meeting to read a book or other literature, to study the Bible, or to share personal experience and prayer. In that epoch, freely organized small groups that met at some other time than the parish worship were already to some extent an elite phenomenon. In the seventeenth century,

---

[1] [See Luther's Works (Philadelphia: Fortress Press, 1966), 53:62-64. —Ed.]

the common person did not have time for such meetings. A village
peasant did not have the literate or other communication skills needed
to participate freely in that kind of small group. The group form itself
was an elite phenomenon.

Luther had said these small voluntary groups would be a third form
of church. The Radical Reformation said these groups are *the* church.
But the Pietists maintained their groups were not the church because
they did not have sacraments, ordain ministers, define doctrine or
handle the support of the established church. The Pietists were doing
something that the official church structure was not doing. The Pietist
circle was a supplementary ministry, not an alternative church.

Pietism provided a critique of the established system, but not a fundamental critique. It said the established system was not doing everything that needed to be done: it was not bringing faith into an individual's heart or giving a person a chance to express faith voluntarily in a
small group situation. But Pietism did not critique what the established
church was doing.[2]

Sacrificial services. The Pietist perspective emphasized that personal
piety and the small group experience would express themselves in sacrificial services relating to newly perceived social needs: orphanages,
schools for poor people, Bible printing and distribution, overseas missions, and home mission efforts dealing with needy segments of the
population. For these ministries the Pietist movement created new voluntary institutions called societies. They were supported spontaneously
by people with money to give and time to do good works that expressed
Christian love for needy neighbors. The movement did not work
through the church because the church was an old institution designed
for something else. The church remained the first institutional track; the
second institutional track was the missionary society.

---

[2]The Pietists had their own social meeting, but they still went to the parish church. However, the
church service was very dry. So they wrote and printed little pocket books that Pietists could
take along to church and read during the sermon and even during the Lord's Supper so that
something meaningful could be going on while they were affirming their allegiance to the
church as structure. Both of these things could be going on at once: they could be listening to
the sermon because they did not believe in attacking the established church, and they could also
be communing with the Lord on their own.

PIETISM'S MODEST CHURCH RENEWAL AND MISSIONS

Thus Pietism, which created the modern missionary movement, was the product of Lutheran theology plus the additional elements of personal motivation, small groups and institutions with more active motivation than Lutheran theology itself had produced. Pietism centered its program on visible works carried on by societies—schools, hospitals, Bible distribution—and it said both yes and no to the established church at large. The missionary work it did was not the church's work in the strict sense, as Pietism understood it. The movement created new agencies that the church did not govern, although they respected the church.

Pietism did not expect the whole church to join the Pietist movement. They were willing to let the church as a whole remain uninvolved in mission if they could obtain the official church's tolerance of this work. A Pietist knew a person had to have had a renewing Christian experience to have the motivation, the vision or the grasp of what it means to be missionary, to be service-oriented or to be critical of the way widows and orphans are treated in one's own society.

At the same time, those things that the established church was committed to do were done well enough that the Pietists accepted them. This meant that when their missionaries went overseas they took, for example, the ordination practices and the liturgy that the state church dictated. So Pietism was a modest renewal movement, claiming only to add the missing dimensions that would fill out the faithfulness of Protestant Christendom, but not claiming to be or to restore the church.[3]

PIETISM'S NEW DOCTRINES

This attitude toward the established church meant there was an ambiguity about the place of theology in Pietism. There was first of all an af-

---

[3]John Wesley was part of the Pietist movement in England both before and after his special experience at Aldersgate where his "heart was strangely warmed" as he meditated on Luther's *Commentary on Galatians*. The primary structure in Wesley's movement was also the small group he called "the class." The established Church of England would not recognize Wesley's movement as a renewal movement the way the established churches of the Continent had done for Pietists there. Because the Church would not ordain Wesley's missionaries to North America, he ordained them himself. This and other tensions eventually led to denominational separation between Pietists in England and in North America, though Wesley wanted to work within the established church.

firmation: "We want to be orthodox. We do not want any new doctrines." But then there was a double critique of orthodoxy. On the one hand, the affirmation of orthodox doctrine was not enough either morally or experientially for the Christian believer or the theologian. On the other, orthodoxy's content was not adequate because there was not a doctrine of Christian experience.

The Pietists stated the first of these limits of orthodoxy in terms of the opposition between religion of the head and religion of the heart.[4] A person can affirm true doctrine and not internalize it at all. The orthodox were also saying this, but one of the debates was whether somebody had to be converted to be a good theologian. According to orthodoxy, conversion was a superficial thing that happened to some people and did not happen to other people, but in any case had nothing to do with true doctrine. True doctrine had to do with whether someone read the Bible or creeds rightly and whether one's statements of doctrine were in a faithful relationship to earlier statements of doctrine. Determining true doctrine was a linguistic operation, a propositional exercise. What did the state of one's heart have to do with that? Orthodox theological faculties all over Protestant Europe expressly affirmed that whether somebody was a faithful theologian was not related to their personality or attitudes, whether he beat his wife or gave a tithe. Orthodoxy had to do with doing theology correctly. Then the Pietists came along and said, "We agree about right theology. But we will not accept a theologian unless he is converted." So there developed the "theology of the born again."

This brings us to the second limitation of orthodox theology. The Pietists said true doctrine is all right, but a person had to "get it in his heart." That meant theologians needed to debate what this entailed and to add a new set of doctrinal themes related to the theology of religious experience. The new doctrine focused on questions such as these: How does one have an experience? What does such an experience mean? What is the content of experience? What is the validity of experience? What is a nonvalid experience? Before this, religious experience had not been part

---

[4]This opposition was not invented by modern clinical psychology; it is two hundred years old.

of theology in any deep sense. So the Pietists not only affirmed the orthodox doctrinal heritage but actually called for additional doctrine.

AMBIVALENCES IN PIETIST APPROACHES TO MISSION

As Pietists began to engage in crosscultural mission they found that their assumptions and emphases regarding doctrine and experience, salvation and ethics, and the relation of church and state required adjustment. They faced new tensions.

Start with orthodoxy or experience? When the Pietist missionary societies went overseas to brand new cultures where people did not have these traditional doctrines, they had to consider what to take along. If they took religious experience because it had been an important part of their identity at home, it would not have the same meaning; it could not stand as a corrective to orthodoxy in the new place, since orthodoxy was not established there. One of the first debates in Pietist missionary thought was whether to take orthodoxy along or not. Should they repeat a valid experience by taking first what is not adequate—orthodox doctrine—so that other people could have the experience that the Pietists had of adding the capstone—religious experience? Or should they just take the capstone along without the orthodox inadequacy?

If they emphasized experience, they would systematize the corrective and lift up what was most meaningful to them, for example, how each had appropriated forgiveness. Orthodoxy was not particularly meaningful, and the people back home who believed orthodox doctrine were not all serious Christians. Religious experience was the live thing. But in another culture this raised a difficult question. Instead of talking about God, Jesus and the Holy Spirit, they would be talking about each person's experience. Is that the gospel? On the other hand, if they were to take along the whole block of classical doctrine then they would be simply exporting European culture with its established religion.

The problem of orthodoxy and experience in Pietist mission theology follows from the way in which Pietism did not claim to be the church, but to be a complement and corrective. Pietism's taking more than one position on the adequacy of the established church is a clear tension and ambivalence.

Empire and mission. A second problem about which Pietism had some ambivalence was its relationship to Europe's political structure, which at the time of the great missionary movement was also spreading out over the world. The great age of the missionary movement was also the great age of European empire. The Pietist movement in Europe was critical of numerous injustices in society, especially the fate of certain categories of poor people, but it was not fundamentally critical of the structure of society. As mentioned before, Pietism was based in the elite classes. At the later end of the Pietist period it was based on the wealth of the first industrialists of the Industrial Revolution, new elite who had money to give for missionary societies. Therefore, the Pietists accepted the existing political structures of nation, Christian Europe and the economy. Probably the fact that these societies were not simply congregations but administrative institutions existing on donated money meant that they felt at home emotionally with the early factory owners or nobles.

The Pietists assumed that the favor of the colonial powers, which not always but often supported the missionary endeavor, was providential. It could have been otherwise. The colonial administrator made things easy for the missionary and protected his freedom of movement. Colonial power did not always support directly the missionary's proselyting intentions (in some early periods there were administrations that protected the traditional religion of the indigenous population), but at least it protected the missionaries' freedom of movement and service institutions and often became even more supportive than that. Yet Pietist missionaries had the moral courage to freely criticize local, inhumane abuses by colonial administration. They were not uncritical or culturally so ethnocentric that they did not see specific injustices. There was some courageous anticolonial talk at certain points when a colonial administration was nasty. But the idea of colonialism in itself was thought to be a good thing because they saw it as the Christian world coming to the help of the rest of the world.

Colonialism was also, in the wider sense, part of the mission. Just as the Pietists brought from Europe the capstone of Christian cultural experience in the form of personal appropriation of salvation, so the colonial administration brought the foundation of Christian political culture, a culture that was the deeper basis on which orthodox doctrine sat. Because of its ambivalent attitude toward the established church, Pietism had the capacity to critique empire but only at the point of abuses such as when a colonial administrator unnecessarily massacred people or let people be enslaved. But that there was a colonial structure in place was seen to be one of the ways God was helping the mission.

Pietist ethics and mission. We have noticed tensions regarding doctrine and also empire. How about ethics? In Europe the Pietist stance with regard to ethics was about the same as their stance toward true doctrine. There was no intended critique of the established ethical vision, but there was a much higher degree of earnestness in living it out. For example, nobody was in favor of drunkenness. The state church was not in favor of drunkenness, it simply did not know what to do about it. Pietism took this critique of drunkenness and made it instrumental by saying a person who is really born again will not drink or get drunk. The established church was in favor of family structures, loving parenthood, and family loyalty and solidarity. Pietism would make that work. The established society was in favor of economic productivity and honest hard work. Pietism would make it work. In fact there was genuine moral renewal all over Europe to varying degrees, as a result of the way in which Pietism translated society's already existing moral commitments into personal character and day-by-day social process. People were more honest. They were harder workers. They loved their children and their parents more than before. But again, the existing standards were strengthened, deepened, clarified and radicalized, but they were the existing standards.

Pietism helped people be good through the processes of mutual support in fellowship groups. But at the same time they taught that it is not enough to be good because "justification by faith" is not based on one's goodness. There was a built-in, self-critical tension at this point: a truly higher level of moral performance together with the insistence, straight from Luther, that higher moral performance does not do a person any good in God's sight. The Pietists encouraged ethical action anyway—because it might do Christians good in their own sight, and they will feel better if they do good or their action does their neighbor good. But this should not be motivated by desire for salvation. This tension between salvation and ethics needed to be communicated somehow in the mission setting.

PIETIST PERSONALIZATION AND MISSIONARY STRATEGY

What effects did Pietist emphasis on religious experience have on self-understanding and on missionary strategy? In a general way, the effect of this personalization was emphasis on small groups and inward appropriation of the faith. In European culture, Pietism arose in the age of Enlightenment. Personal meant subjective. For something to be personal it had to be inward and individual, that is, located in just one person. Any social form it had was that of one person relating to other persons on a basis not derived from existing structures. Small groups were part of the corrective. Personal religious experience was another.

The established communal definitions of faith were the frozen, inadequate and unreal ones. A Pietist might have said: "When I think back, what I appropriated in my individualized experience was not that Christ is Lord in the New Testament sense of cosmic providential power, but that Christ is mine, as nearness, not as object. It was not that I was overwhelmed all of a sudden by the cosmic and historical dimension of the claims of Christ, but that I took more and more seriously its subjective significance, its inward significance for my own self-understanding. That was what I needed, because as the product of established orthodoxy, I was inhibited and care-laden. Moral teaching made me feel individually guilty, and then as a Pietist, I received individual release."

But the more seriously one takes this focus, the less clear it is what the message would be to two other kinds of people. One is a person who is carefree, who does not have orthodoxy to react to, and who has not been impressed by guilt through Christian culture, parents and the parish parson. The other is someone who is so communally oriented because of personality or culture that he or she is not prepared to process subjective individualistic experience. What can a Pietist say to a person who has not been taught to think about inwardness? Emphasis on personal experience raises a question about the content of the missionary message. The cosmic, historical and peoplehood dimensions of the biblical message are less manageable from a personalistic perspective than from some other theological perspectives we might establish.

A second effect of the personal nature of experience was at the point of motivation. Why did a Pietist want to go somewhere with the message? It was to save individuals, to share with them the satisfaction the missionary had found and to save them from what the Pietist had been saved from—feeling lost, rejected, guilty, knowing that they were personally estranged from God. The motivation was to help individuals appropriate faith and see its personal value for them.

Bringing to another culture this personalistic orientation, two different things happened. Those individuals who responded—that is, those who were already marginal to their communal culture in another part of the world, or those who made of the missionary their father, mother, community or extended family—could have this experience in a way that was much like the one the missionary had had. But then where were they socially? As new Pietists, they could not be the capstone of a Christian culture as the missionaries had been in Europe. Rather, they were isolated from their culture, at least at the beginning of the missionary effort.

A further effect of personalization on missionary strategy was related to the orthodox doctrine/religious experience tension noted earlier. In order for people to personally experience renewal, missionaries first had to plant churches and get masses of people into the cultural orbit of the established churches back home; after that there could be renewal. But along with the total institutional church framework came the propagation of European culture. Because the Pietists also believed in good works, they contributed to cultural colonialism through hospitals and schools. Literacy, teaching of trades, teaching health and saving people from epidemics were major cultural contributions, but they did not make Pietists of people. However, the total framework did lay a foundation for a possible revival. From our historical perspective, we recognize that the mission church was nevertheless completely foreign. Missionaries had real trouble getting a mission church to be Indian, African or indigenous, because it started by being totally foreign.

Effects of Pietism's Ambivalent Relationship to
the Church on Mission Strategy

At home in Europe there were basically three church structures. There was the established church with its parishes, consistories, bishops (in England), doctrine and rituals. Second were the local fellowships, which were within that church and subject to it. Third, there were the free societies, which at home were meant to be merely instruments for doing certain jobs: people who wanted to distribute Bibles created a Bible society; people who wanted to help orphans created a society to start an orphanage. These were simply administrative societies. They were not Christian communities, not churchly. The foreign mission association or missionary society was likewise just an administrative tool. It is probably important also that the main missionary societies were not territorially identified with a given provincial or state church. They gathered support through the mail from many places. One of them was based in Hamburg, another in Basel and another in Stuttgart, but these societies did not serve only those areas. Their funds and missionary personnel came from all over.

However, once the missionary societies moved overseas, the significance of these three forms of church was reversed. The mission society, instead of being the least important of the three, became the most powerful. It had the money. It placed the personnel. It defined the structures not only for the missionaries themselves, but even for people who came into leadership in the younger mission church. Back home the society was set up only as an administrative agency. But when it became the only form of the church in the mission setting, it was the boss. If a spontaneous fellowship of individuals developed, it was under the mission, not under the established church at home. When a legitimate ministry began, one that included practice of the sacraments, it was under the mission as well.

At first the missionary societies did not notice this problem. But once they noticed it, they wondered what they should do. They could say the church was already in the new place. While it did not look like the church back home, believers were there. In Europe, most of the churchgoers were not as committed as the people who were also in prayer groups. Within those smaller committed groups were the elite people who actually tried to do something, those who had created this missionary society. The missionaries could say, "Perhaps this new group of believers *is* the church—without all the dead wood."

The other approach to creating a church, rather than focusing first on personal conversion and nurturing groups of believers, was to start by building many institutions. Schools and orphanages especially tended to bring into relationship with mission personnel individuals who were somewhat open to Christian faith. They might not be profoundly open, but among them might be an elite group who would want to study and become more devoted. There would come a time when they would have enough education that they could be pastors and bishops, and the mission group would meet the European criteria that would make it a church. But that would take a long time. Until then, the new believers would not be in a recognized church.

Whichever way was chosen, there were serious drawbacks. In either case mission and church were two separate agencies, different in membership and resources, and there was a built-in conflict between these two agencies. The second serious drawback was that a normal and adequate experience of Christian life could be had for years, that is, decisions could be made and structures developed, without asking, "Is it a faithful church?" because, of course, it could not yet be. Missionaries could not ask that of it initially. So they set up patterns and created precedents and attitudes before asking, "Is it church?" They also could not ask, "Is it a faithful church?" before a mission church was truly indigenous because that would be a premature question. The new group had not been in existence long enough to meet those requirements. So the mission could go on being Christian and doing good works, without testing whether the developments fit their own ecclesiology or a biblical theology of the church.

This is not to suggest that non-Pietist missionaries were any better at this point. But the Pietist theoretical distinction covered up the problem by enabling the work to go on without them being embarrassed about the fact that their societies and new groups of converts were not really "church." The church back in Europe trusted the mission to say when there was a recognizable mission church, and until they did so the established European leaders were not responsible for it. The mission trusted the church back home to say what the standards were whereby they would know when a church existed. Meanwhile missionaries worked for sixty or a hundred years and never needed a local church.

What does that say to new believers overseas and others around them about the meaning of *church*, and especially of worldwide Christian fellowship, in relation to the importance of mission schools and hospitals or of the importance of the (usually) warm fellowship of the missionaries among themselves?

THE EFFECT OF THE PIETIST HERITAGE ON SOCIAL ETHICS

There has been a widespread polemic in European ecumenical and academic theological circles against Pietism at the point of social ethics. The accusation is that in social ethics there were four mistakes. One was that the Pietist social ethic, especially in the missionary situation, was individualistic. Another was that it was centered on avoiding certain vices discouraged back home: do not drink, dance or smoke. Third, critics said Pietism was uncritical about certain abuses: slavery and colonialism. Fourth, behind the shelter of these three things, Pietism was fundamentally unconcerned, dualistic and withdrawn. What little it had to offer was overshadowed by these shortcomings. In the more sweeping sense it was not affirmatively, actively involved in the course of history.[5]

This simply is not true.[6] Pietist noblemen and industrialists were another case of the general social phenomenon in the West that minorities are culturally and socially the most creative groups. Pietists were the makers of world history. They were disproportionately strongly represented in politics, trade and social leadership. These same men were the backbone of the missionary societies and of many other kinds of charities. They may have taken wrong positions on some issues. They may have been too paternalistic in their sense of how to organize a factory or

---

[5]Philippe Maury popularized these unfair concerns in his book *Politics and Evangelism* (Garden City, NY: Doubleday, 1960).

[6]I have a chapter that defends Pietism on these points in John Howard Yoder, *The Christian Witness to the State* (Newton, KS: Faith and Life Press, 1964), pp. 84-88 [reprinted by Herald Press, 2002. —Ed.].

a charity. They may have been too conservative in their attitude toward colonialism. But they were not withdrawn, uninvolved or irrelevant. They were not without caring. They did not avoid taking a position. If someone disagrees with their position, he or she should disagree because the Pietists took a position perceived to be wrong but not accuse them of being unconcerned, as this wide stream of anti-Pietist polemic did.

I would further disagree with this stream of polemic regarding where it locates the trouble. If the Pietists were wrong or did not always do the right thing, what were their basic mistakes? I would say that one was that they had no problems with involvement in the state, war or political violence as a proper or even a Christian duty. Many missionaries would come home from the field in order to fight if their country went to war. Second, they critiqued social and economic patterns when they conflicted with the Puritan ethics of the establishment more than when they conflicted with the New Testament. Another critique would be that their vision of sharing wealth was not a critique of the economic order itself but rather focused on surplus wealth: "Give to charity all you can. But first you have to accept the system and make as much money as possible." Those two chapters are quite separate in the factory owner's economic life. The Pietists also did not foresee the revolutionary impact of what they were doing overseas in education and medicine, initiatives that would help to explode the whole colonial system later. I am not saying they should have thought that through. I am saying if they had a limit, then it was at this point.

SUMMARY OF ANABAPTIST AND PIETIST RENEWAL PERSPECTIVES

The previous chapter and this one have been oriented around two concepts of renewal. There are more concepts of renewal than these two, for instance, the monastic and conciliar movements within Catholicism or the Magisterial Reformation. But we have looked especially at two post-Reformation concepts that go further than the Magisterial Reformation claimed to do: the Pietistic and the Free Church (or Anabaptist or Radical Reformation) models. We have observed the claims to be made for each, especially the fact that the Pietist movement as a historical phenomenon has been at the origin of what we call the modern missionary movement, even when Lutheran or Baptist churches carried out that missionary activity. Pietism throws light on mission far beyond the work of the particular societies that brought it into being. We will deal in the coming chapters with the alternative types of church that come out of that movement.

But first, I will posit some summary theses about the forms of renewal and what they say to the rest of our theme.

The free church model is biblical and normative. The New Testament church was a free church. That is simply a factual statement. It had no link with the powers of society. It did not propagate itself by any supportive relationship to economic or political powers of the age. Membership was voluntary. Its ethic was countercultural. It was missionary in the sense of continually reaching into new populations. This was the case by conviction, not only by accident.

The official historical position of the Magisterial Reformation, most bluntly put in the Reformed tradition, was that God wanted a theocratic relationship of church and society but had to start at a disadvantage in the New Testament. Finally, by the time of Constantine, God returned the situation to the theocratic vision of the Old Testament. The "free church" status of the followers of Jesus in the New Testament or apostolic age was a fact, many Reformed would agree, but it was not a norm.

I am suggesting that the New Testament is normative. It is the nature of the gospel itself that calls for a clear distinction between church and state and between church and world. The points at which the gospel most clearly calls for that stance are in slogans identifiable as missionary, especially with reference to ethnicity. The church by conviction understands Jesus to have "broken down the dividing wall" (Eph 2:14) between peoples and that the church must have a distinct ethic especially with regard to power or "the powers." If "Jesus is Lord," then other lords are not. Those two convictions of the New Testament church are not simply making the best of a disadvantaged situation but are convictions identified with the gospel itself.

The early church's missionary stance involved commitment to change. By definition, if the church is going to go into new cultures, absorb new kinds of peoples and talk new languages, there will have to be reformulations of theology; new lifestyle issues will have to be dealt with and new decisions will have to be made about how to respond to new questions. A missionary church cannot be culturally rigid. We do not have many samples of how the New Testament church entered into new worlds. But we do have their basic encounter with the Hellenistic world, which was very different at certain points from the Palestinian Jewish world. We can see some of the shifts that they made in formulating the faith as a result.

If the church is to be missionary, change and faithfulness must not be alternatives. We must find ways of defining both of them so that they belong together. Faithfulness must not be conceived of as timeless rigidity. Change must not include a blank check for all kinds of adaptation, but rather modification within the nature of the original mandate. The two New Testament slogans—mission and ethic as over against ethnicity and lordship—are perhaps the keys for our purposes.

The Constantinian relationship is a fundamental apostasy. If mission and ethic are the keys, then the Constantinian relationship of church and state is a denial of mission or a simple failure to maintain these two key criteria. The Constantinian relationship represents a fundamental shift away from the nature of the church as mission-oriented. Historically, after the church became the officially supported state religion, it could be assumed that the church's mission was complete because there was finally a Christian civilization, one that extended throughout the whole Roman Empire.

Likewise, there was a shift at the point of the political and economic power structure: Christians began to bless, accept, baptize and use it for the sake of the church's security. Again the meaning of mission was at least hindered and perhaps firmly denied. Once the gospel or the bearers of the gospel in the visible church were identified with the existing power structure, then the gospel could not be fundamentally critical and the church could not call for a basic change. Constantinian Christianity was fundamentally conservative. Even though placing the church and power together meant the church could call for a certain kind of movement or change by the bearers of that culture's power (for instance, those who carried out the expansion of the Christian Roman Empire or those who later managed colonialism), it did not make for change at the heart of Christendom.

One of the arguments that keeps arising in the debate about styles of renewal has to do with the concepts of *Constantinianism* and *primitivism*. Primitivism is an often used label that is subject to several different meanings. When used as a negative term, it points to people who naively and legalistically assume we can repeat the New Testament pattern on any given subject, whether it is ministry, church organization or doctrine. They assume we can revoke the change that has taken place over the centuries and simply reaffirm the origins. So primitivism means rejection of change. When used in a more positive light, primitivism is a particular understanding of reformation or renewal that does not assume we can get back to the original pattern but rather says that we can move forward to see anew the original pattern's relevance. That is, the image of the Garden of Eden or of the New Testament church is a criterion for critique within present history that seeks to move us forward and not to deny change.

When the language of primitivism is used with reference to Constantinianism, the general picture is that the Christendom or Constantinian thesis favors change while primitivism does not. This view believes we have made progress since the New Testament and might say: "The New Testament church had two strikes against it, but now we Christians have won status. The New Testament church could not dictate morality to the world, and now we can. That is progress. That is change. The primitivist wants to revoke that change and return us to the disadvantaged position." This analysis assumes that the Anabaptist type is against change and the Christendom type is for it. But that is a misapprehension. Once church and ruler are merged in one partnership, people are *less* open to change than before. They make the fourth century normative, or the ninth century, or whatever century their king tries to reign, because they have put the established church on the side of the established state. Therefore, the motor for change that was constituted by the difference between church and world at home and by foreign mission has been neutralized.

The Magisterial Reformation hardens Christendom. The Magisterial

Reformation identified medieval abuses and precipitated movement at many points. It called into question the way in which the church's teaching authority had been defined, challenged a type of sacramentalism that confused the meaning of salvation and reaffirmed biblical authority as a source of critique and renewal. In many details the Magisterial Reformation was helpful, but it was not at the two fundamental points of mission versus clinging to ethnicity and the critique of society's power structure. At these two points the Magisterial Reformation agreed with medieval Catholicism. In fact, the Magisterial Reformation hardened the dimension of ethnicity by making the basic ethnic unit the nation or province instead of Christian Europe. Saxony, Switzerland or the Netherlands could make itself an autonomous, self-determining political and religious people of God that could fight other Christian countries. Likewise, the ethic of blessing the power structure was sharpened rather than weakened by making the prince or the city council not simply a Christian government, which it had been for a thousand years, but the organ of church reformation. Having given up on the bishops to reform the church, the reformers took the strongest Christian laymen available to reform the church, and that happened to be the government. Since the government reformed the church, Christians were even less likely than before to be critical of the government's ethics. One superficial specimen of this is the fact that in Catholicism the just war theory is standard doctrine, but it was never proclaimed as infallible or thought to be the only possible Catholic position. In all the Reformation creeds, by contrast, just war is confirmed in the creed.

Pietism is a valid critique and corrective. The merger of church and society is called into question by the renewed focus on personal appropriation of faith in an adult, conscious, authentic way. With the discovery of the Christian's call to be a servant, to identify and address flaws in the social structure that creates victims, and to care for the needy comes a rediscovery of vision for the rest of the world and a corresponding ethical critique. But Pietism presupposes and confirms the Constantinian framework, and wants to work in symbiosis with it, leaning on it at the same time it critiques it. Pietism does not claim to be an alternative strategy, but rather a permanently needed corrective strategy.

The Radical Reformation is a more basic corrective. The Radical Reformation focuses more clearly on the two issues to which we referred—ethnicity and ethics. It is, therefore, closer to the New Testament in tension, practice and theological conviction. Compared to Pietism it is a radical corrective. But compared to the New Testament it is still a corrective and not a new start. The Radical Reformation is still talking back to Constantine or to Zwingli. So it is also marked by what it critiques.

The Radical Reformation is also marked by its Christendom heritage in that it does not critique everything. It assumes certain things from the common heritage that it has not thought of criticizing. For instance, most of the Anabaptists, the Czech Brethren and the radical Puritans never thought of denying anything in the Apostle's Creed. Where there was a critique at specific points like ethics or believers baptism, those elements were emphasized in the polarization between them and Christendom authorities and, therefore, were overemphasized in comparison to the place those issues would have had in the New Testament.

The two particular dangers for Anabaptists are primitivism in the bad sense and isolation from surrounding society. The primitivist temptation is the naive claim to be starting again with the New Testament without the awareness of how much even the Radical Reformation picture was determined by the centuries that had passed. The second temptation is to accept the status of an enclave, to find a niche in society to be different but not to be missionary about it.

Where this leaves us is that the missionary experience of Western Christianity in the modern centuries has actually been carrying four different Christianities in mixtures: Christendom, Protestantism, Pietism and the free church. Mission efforts have not been very conscious of these separate heritages and their implications. To some extent, especially in the high age of colonialism, part of the Christian message to the rest of the world has been that of Christendom: Christianity linked with its civilization, military domination, commercial power and cultural expansion. A second heritage has been the critical stance of official Protestantism, which makes more of the Bible and less of church hierarchy or the sacraments. Third, there is the stronger corrective of Pietism. Finally, there is the still more critical free church vision. These four Christianities are always there in the missionary experience. We will try to sort them out insofar as that process can throw light on the issues we will address in the rest of the book. One thing is clear: none of them replicates New Testament Christianity. The one that in some ways is the nearest to it— that is, the free church stance—remains colored by the fact that it arose in the post-Christendom West and therefore is marked by its dialogue with what it was critiquing.

9

THE CHURCH AS MISSIONARY

In this chapter we will deal with a subject that would be given much more attention in systematic theology or ecumenics: the concept of the marks of the church (*notae ecclesiae*). The list of marks has varied and has had different functions in theology and different implications for mission.

One function of a list of marks of the church is to help people recognize a true church when in doubt or conflict. That is, if there are two quite different entities claiming to be the church, which is the faithful one? To answer, we need a criterion. For instance, in the fourth century controversy the Donatists argued that the church was to be *holy*, as in the creed: "We believe in one, holy, catholic, and apostolic church." To them this confession meant that if they saw two bodies trying to be the true church and one of them was holy and the other was not, the holy one was the faithful one. Augustine answered the Donatists by saying Christians also believe in the *catholic* church, which means that it is everywhere. If Christians see two competing bodies, each claiming to be the true church, they should ask which one exists in the whole world; that is the catholic one. In each case, one of these marks became a criterion for judgment as to where the faithful Christian ought to stand.

The Reformation was the first major division in the church that resulted in two separate doctrinal traditions. In the division between Eastern and Western Catholicism, doctrine was not very significant. The Reformation created a new doctrinal criterion for the faithful church. They could not say the Protestant church was catholic in the sense that it was in communion with all other Christians. Instead they said the true church would be found where the Word of God is properly preached and the sacraments are properly administered. *Properly* meant "our way." For purposes of debating with other Christians, this was not a particularly helpful criterion, but at least they knew what they were going to measure. They would measure how the preaching was done, what the message was and how the sacraments were administered.

The marks of the church as criteria for judgment would become especially important in mission and ecumenical relations when a young church emerged from a Western agency's missionary work. Could this young church be recognized as a church in its own right? What were the criteria for that? Or to say it the other way around, what was the mission responsible to provide to the young church? Christian unity and division had new meanings in the missionary context, so there was greater need than before to understand what constituted faithfulness or unfaithfulness in the church. What were the relevant marks of the church in that place?

Our initial work with the concept of the marks of the church assumed that we have two options: Is a group the true church or not? Ongoing divisions among Protestants are the practical demonstration that we need more categories than yes or no. Logic also suggests there may be degrees between them. For instance, there may be a community that can be recognized as a community of fellow Christians, but that has visible flaws. Another example would be when there is clear evidence that a group is *not* a true Christian community, and yet there is other evidence that indicates that these same people are indeed following Christ as Lord. We might find a church that is apostate; it is clearly a church, but it took a wrong turn so as to deny the faith. Further, there may be something that is not a Christian church at all and never was, although it may be using the label.

Another way of describing different degrees of the church's faithfulness is language that has come to be used in Anglican and Catholic circles. They distinguish between the *esse,* the *bene esse* and the *plene esse* of the church. The first term specifies what it takes for the church *to be* (*esse*). If a church does not have this, it is not a church. The term *bene esse,* the church's *well-being,* indicates characteristics that would be good, though not necessary, for the church to have. Language about the church's *full being* (*plene esse*) permits Anglicans to say that they are the only ones that have all three dimensions, but some of the rest of us have enough that they can say we are also church, but a limping or defective church. In order to be a full church, there must be bishops standing in apostolic succession.

In addition to the role of the marks as criteria for judging the presence of the true church, there is another function of the marks. They state ideals or a vision of the faithfulness toward which we strive. They are meaningful as foci of direction. This is what Protestantism has usually meant when it says that the church we believe in, based on the creed, is made up of true believers, even if it is not a visible community. In his book *On Our Common Calling*, Visser 't Hooft outlined three marks of the church that can be used as firm criteria to identify a faithful church but that more often function as ideals or pointers to qualities that the church ought to have. He noted the functions of witness (*martyria*), fellowship (*koinōnia*) and ministry or servanthood (*diakonia*).[1] Lesslie Newbigin identified another triad of ideals: faith, order and experience.[2] But neither Newbigin's nor Visser 't Hooft's marks usually serve as tools of historical discrimination. When he was Secretary of the World Council of Churches, Visser 't Hooft would not go to a given member church and say, "Sorry, there is no *martyria* here so you cannot be a member church." That would have been unthinkable. Still the marks offer a significant focus of ideals.

WEAKNESSES OF THE MARKS

If we want to use these criteria more firmly, we have to come back to the question of how we would use them to discriminate among churches. To whom would we apply a yardstick? To the clergy? To the constitution? Or something else? The official Protestant criteria apply to the clergy: "Where the Word of God is properly preached and the sacraments

---

[1][Willem Visser 't Hooft, *The Pressure of Our Common Calling* (Garden City, NY: Doubleday, 1959). —Ed.]

[2][Lesslie Newbigin, *The Household of God: Lectures on the Nature of the Church* (London: SCM Press, 1953). —Ed.]

properly administered." We do not look at the members but at the preacher, and we ask whether the preaching contains the gospel message that, for us, is at the heart of Christian faith. In considering "where the sacraments are properly administered," we ask if the clergy name the Trinity in performing baptisms and whether in celebrating the Lord's Supper they affirm the presence of Christ and deny transubstantiation.

Assuming that the criterion is applied negatively, that is, a church does not measure up, so what? Does that justify schism? Does the absence of any one criterion justify schism? Do none of them justify schism but they justify something else? Is it, for example, the basis for increased concern for renewal?

Still another question is what to do with the criteria in the next generation. Assuming there was once a division, by the use of the right criteria (whatever they are), we might say that the division was justified because one group of people was right—whether they stayed, were kicked out or left voluntarily. But where are we three generations later when each of those groups has propagated itself, its orthodoxy and its membership? Is there such a thing as permanent guilt by heredity, so that, for example, every Presbyterian to this day is guilty of what Huldrych Zwingli did to the Anabaptists? Is a historian's statement that a division was justified only the clearing of his or her conscience, doing nothing for the present? What should be the relationship of Roman Catholicism today—especially in view of the changes that have taken place not only in its behavior but in its structure and its doctrine since Vatican II—to Luther, Zwingli or the Anabaptists?

THE MARKS OF THE CHURCH AND MISSION

This discussion relates to mission in a number of identifiable ways. One is whether being missionary is itself a mark of the church. Is a nonmissionary church a church? Can we say that missionary identity and commitment is a good thing, but dispensable?

The suggestion that to be missionary is a mark of the church would add something significant to debates within Western churches and the ecumenical movement, especially to Faith and Order debates about the nature of the church and its renewal or about the faithful structure of the church. To say that to be missionary is a significant mark of the church also relates to Western Christianity's church and society discussions. The ethnicity and the ethics dimensions of a missionary church would make a big difference in these various debates. In relation to the ecumenical movement, we would need to ask, "What is the meaning of separation? Is there a possibility of apostasy, or must we assume that all churches are faithful? What is it that we meet about when we can meet with Christians of other movements?"

In relation to mission, we would see the light this mark throws on the home church and the continuing temptation to fall back into an ethnically defined identity even though the church may have a missionary theology. Also, this mark may be a criterion for recognizing the point at which a younger mission church is identifiable as a sister church. For instance, if we were discussing missionary methods and principles we would pay a lot of attention to the concept of self-propagation as one of the criteria for the church's maturation out of the tutelage of the missionary organization.

The concept of the marks of the church has to say at least this much: there is such a thing as not being the church. I would argue that it is proper to say this much despite the difficulties in knowing what else we can say. The concept of "not church" is thinkable in two forms. One is that there is something we call *world* that is not the church, and that is a significant thing to say since Constantine. This distinction is not simply tautology or playing with words. We have to be able to say it meaningfully.

Unity, apostasy and mission. Second, there is such a thing as *apostasy*, something that is so fundamentally unfaithful that either its message or its status as church must be denied. Apostasy is different from error or weakness. It is commitment to some specific and basic error that makes the "church that calls itself church" an effective adversary of the true church's mission. Where the empirical church is an adversary of the church's biblically defined mission, we need the term *apostasy*. Our theology has to provide for that possibility even though it threatens contemporary ecumenical manners. An example would be the Inquisition or the Crusades in which the linkage of the church to a particular power structure, including its military, was such that the people the church dealt with could not conceivably perceive it as embodying a reconciling mission. This example, along with anti-Semitism, racism or the Judaizing of the far right wing of the earliest church in the time of Paul, is a form of apostasy with respect to its missionary character. To be apostate often means having the wrong doctrine. The New Testament itself talks about people who went out from us and are not of us because of what they did or did not say about Jesus. But in relation to the missionary mark of the church, apostasy can also be a matter of the church's form or structure.

Concern for the missionary mark of the church can also throw light on other possible errors that fall short of apostasy and are still worth debating. There are divisions, for instance, among the churches. Should we try to bridge them all right now? Are some of them deep enough that we would do well to proceed with Christian mission without waiting for one another, or without concentrating our effort on bridging those old divisions? Use of the marks of the church will illuminate how far apart we are and how worthwhile it is to try to get all of those different movements together.

I hope we can use these marks in a new mood, not use them in the self-righteous way as has often been done. If any given community is truly the church, that is the gift of grace not a possession. The marks are not a bludgeon with which to hit other people. The mood in which we search for the shape of faithfulness must always be one of response to grace and grateful sharing of gifts. It should never be "us against them." Any visible denominational organization in the modern form, denominational in the strict modern sense of a group that excludes most people and includes the rest because they have a common bureaucracy, is intrinsically apostate to the extent to which it takes itself alone seriously as the church. No denomination can honestly use the marks of the church to prove it is right. What we can properly do is to use them to find sister churches or other communities which we recognize as also right. We should use the marks of the church as signs of grace and in a mood of gratitude and acceptance, rather than in a mood of self-righteousness and self-accreditation.

I also hope we will use the marks in a new way in measuring faith-fulness; we will have many degrees of "yes, but," "no, but" or "maybe" in addition to a simple "yes" and "no." We may still need to say "no" where the church has accepted Constantinianization or the crusade form in her relationship to Western power because such an error is so funda-mental as to be nothing but a scandal. There will be other times when we will say that our own church is so far apart from another tradition that we cannot do anything together, but we recognize there is some-thing Christian about that tradition as well. There will be other places where we will say that we do not see how we could meaningfully col-laborate, but we do sense an obligation to dialogue with one another, admonish one another and invite one another to look at an issue that had not been previously discussed. In these ways there can be different degrees of mutual recognition.

What does this mutual recognition of each other as "church" have to do with missions? First, the modern missionary movement has renewed the concern for church unity. The modern ecumenical movement is a child of the modern missionary movement. That is one connection. An-other is that mission is one of the missing marks of the church that might be recovered through mutual recognition and ongoing dialogue. For instance, Stephen Neil picked up the traditional Calvinist marks of the church—the Word of God properly preached, the sacraments properly administered and discipline—and added three: fire on earth (an aggressive self-propagating quality), suffering and pilgrim mo-bility.[3] Those are all marks of the church's missionary dimension.

In the sixteenth century, Menno Simons also added some marks. He accepted the Protestant marks of proper preaching and sacraments properly administered, though he defined them differently than Luther and Calvin. But he added four more marks: holy living (a nonconformed lifestyle), brotherly love (a visible community), unreserved confession (meaning we do not let a hostile world's threats keep us from mission) and suffering.[4] Menno's originality at this point was that these four

---

[3]See Stephen Neill, *The Unfinished Task* (London: Edinburgh House Press, 1957).
[4]See John Howard Yoder, "A People in the World: Theological Interpretation," in *The Concept of the Believers' Church*, ed. James Garrett (Scottdale, PA: Herald Press, 1969), pp. 250-83. For

marks were missionary. They applied to all church members, not only to the clergy as the two Protestant marks did. Menno's four marks describe a community, and it is a community that is in but not of the world. These marks *cannot* refer to a community unless it is distinct from the world, yet in it. If it were not such a community, there would not be marks of nonconformity, suffering or unreserved confession. The missionary stance of a minority church within the wider society is a prerequisite for these marks being present.[5]

Another reason why using the marks to recognize a sister communion is important for mission, if my claim is true, is that what is most wrong about apostasy is the denial of mission. That is, other failings such as having the wrong doctrine of the Trinity or leaving out the wine in the Lord's Supper are bad, but they are not as fundamentally bad as the denial of mission. It is at the point of mission that apostasy becomes the most visible and damaging.

Marks of a faithful missionary church. That leaves us with the question of the relevance of the missionary marks for the *bene/plene/esse* discussion, as well as for ecumenical relations and mission. For example, if we go to the Church of Scotland, how do we apply a list like Menno's? On this matter, I have a few theses for critical evaluation.

Apostasy is not first doctrinal, but historical. The doctrinal explanation of why a given body has taken the wrong track will probably be a breach of fellowship before it becomes diversity in doctrine. In this sense apostasy is not something we *think* wrong; it is something we *do* wrong. That does not mean apostasy will not have doctrinal implications. There always will be a doctrinal dimension if the church denies Christ. That is, the denial will be talked about; it will be interpreted. But that denial will take new forms in different times and places.

If the breach, or the unfaithfulness, is first of all not doctrinal but historical, then only the fact of the break can explain the break.[6] That

---

Menno, proper administration of the sacraments meant believers baptism and that the Lord's Supper should be given only to believers.

[5]It might be illuminating to note that where the church suffers persecution is where the church has these additional qualities of the fellowship that we want to recognize.

[6]One classical sample where history preceded doctrine is Zwingli and the Anabaptists. They agreed on everything that mattered in systematic theology. And yet Zwingli thought it was

is, we do not say we broke fellowship because they think this and we think that. Rather, we broke fellowship because they stopped talking. The question is not "What do we differ about?" but "Who stopped talking?" Deeper than the sixteenth-century question of whether people who baptize babies or people who baptize believers are wrong is the question of commitment to the unity of the church. Who broke off the conversation? Was it the Anabaptists or their persecutors? Functionally, apostasy means somebody stops talking with fellow Christians about the meaning of faithfulness. The particular thing they stop talking about can vary and can be important or unimportant on some other scale.

Apostasy is local and temporal. This is a response to my earlier question about guilt by inheritance. Apostasy is not permanent, and is not contained in a hierarchy or a creed. A creed can develop out of the fact that the Lutherans rejected the Anabaptists. But that does not mean that three generations later the Lutherans who repeat that creed are in the same sense closed to an Anabaptist reading of the gospel. The pope, the cardinals and the bishops put Anabaptists to death in the sixteenth century, but that does not mean that the attitudes of Mennonites or other Anabaptist groups today toward cardinals, archbishops and popes have to be the same. It might be the same. But we will have to ask the question anew rather than simply inheriting an answer.

The denial of mission is apostasy. Denying mission is apostasy because it solidifies in-group identity and ceases reaching beyond its membership to incorporate others on the basis of God's love.

Apostasy is not a statement about a church's salvation status, but about the usability of their visible community in mission. The only place that the New Testament, Anabaptism or Quakerism authorize us to talk about salvation status is in the process of congregational discipline (Matthew 18 and parallels). There it is the church's business to say of someone who has totally and repeatedly refused congregational process that God has authorized the visible community to say that it acts in God's name in

---

worth turning them over to the cops to be executed, and the Anabaptists thought it was worth holding to their view and being turned over to the cops to be executed. That means that something other than the standard outline of doctrinal issues mattered more. And what was it? It was whether there should be a church whose very stance was mission. That mattered more than the regular doctrinal issues on which they agreed.

deciding what to do. But we cannot say that about a church. We can only say that about a brother or a sister who has refused to listen.

However, the concept of apostasy has a function in relation to how we deal with people or communities as we carry out the church's mission. When we encounter apostasy, we must disavow that witness. It means we cannot function together as witnesses or as servants with those people. The effect of apostasy is that rather than share in the unfaithfulness of other Christians, we must be ready to suffer at their hands. All of this is self-righteous language, but it is to be used subject to the qualifications stated before.

Central to the definition of faithfulness and therefore of apostasy is whether a church proclaims reconciliation. That is just another way to say that mission is a mark of the church. Just as proper preaching and proper use of the sacraments need to be defined, so also "proclaims reconciliation" needs definition. It begs the question in one sense, yet reconciliation is built into what the church is supposed to be. It is different also from some other kinds of faithfulness, like holding to the right creed. Proclaiming reconciliation is not something we can possess without living it.

THE IMPACT OF THESE THESES

The church used to define heresy in doctrinal terms. When it was defined doctrinally, the church could find those who held the wrong doctrine and disqualify the whole church or group. I am saying we should start rather at the point of function: mission is the measure of fidelity. The mark of apostasy that matters the most is when we structure the denial of mission.

Then we have to ask, can a theology be condemned as apostate if it does not point to mission, if it rejects the necessity of mission or does not contribute to mission? There are theologies that deny the usefulness or necessity of mission or that reject the conversion of non-Christians to Christianity as a goal. This is something we will see later in the discussion about other religions. But that question is ambiguous. When someone rejects the conversion of non-Christians to Christianity as a goal, which Christianity are they talking about? Are they talking about the Christianity of the Crusades or the Christianity of Jesus? We may not call "missionary" the way the medieval crusading church forced the Spanish Jews to become members, for instance. But if that is what we think Christianity entails, then we may reject conversion to Christianity. We always have to ask which Christianity we are talking about before we know whether the affirmation or the denial of its particular form of mission is what we want.

We have not discussed what the mark of the church as missionary means for relations to other religions or what we think about the meaning of Jesus in the context of other contemporary religions. But suppose that were all cleared up and there were a theology that would deny the duty of Christians to call people to follow Jesus and be members of his covenant people. An adaptation of my thesis would say that to exclude any category of persons from the imperative to make disciples is apostasy. It affirms wholeness before God on other grounds than the movement of God in Jesus. That is possible to affirm, but when we affirm that, we are not following Jesus. Apostasy in this sense is defined simply by a historic reading of whether the imperative to make disciples of all persons is part of the Jesus movement or not. It is not a reading about whom God loves or what categories of people God can tolerate. Faithfulness or apostasy depends on whether the church is a community that is propagating the Jesus message.

10

THE CHURCH AS RESPONSIBLE

In referring to the church as *responsible*, I do not mean the sense that is current in social ethics. I mean rather that a given church body overseas has the maturity and the responsibility to be the church in its own name, not simply as an extension of the missionary agency. This concern reaches far into details that a course in missionary principles or methods would address. But it also depends on theological understandings of the church. The shape of the problem is itself a product of our theology of the church and not only of missionary methods.

The subtext of this chapter is unity. Perhaps we should begin with why *unity* relates to the *responsibility* of churches that have issued from the missionary enterprise. If we are to affirm the younger church's relative independence, that is, its responsibility, we must at the same time deal with Christian unity. In the eyes of some, the autonomy of the new local church would seem to jeopardize this unity. The alternatives to recognizing the independence or responsibility of the local church—alternatives that some people would call sectarian and others paternalistic because they want to keep linking the young church to the mother church—are concerned for the church's unity.

The second reason for seeing the responsibility of the younger churches as closely related to that of unity is the fact that the missionary movement has had a major impact on the ecumenical movement. The younger churches of the Third World and their leaders were first given recognition and a serious hearing in those agencies that have come to be called "the ecumenical movement."

DIFFICULTIES IN RECOGNIZING YOUNGER CHURCHES

We move now to the subject proper: the relationship of different theologies of the church to the independence and responsibility of churches that have grown from mission activity. We begin by recognizing the fact that the church as planted is not easily recognized as being the church, according to the standards that many missionaries bring with them from home. For instance, the home church usually sets criteria for ordination and defines them in terms of a certain level of education and the capacity to act like a scholar, organizer or counselor. Since the younger church's leadership cannot meet those requirements quickly, the missionaries create lower levels of leadership: the catechist, the teacher, the leader. These are terms found in overseas churches that are not recognized back home. The missionary organization usually chooses the persons who fill these roles rather than members of the local church choosing them from the congregation. They are generally not dignified with ordination in the Western sense. Yet they are the ones who lead the local teaching and worship life in the missionary's absence.

This means that most people's normal church experience must take place week by week in the absence of the ministries that the home church deems necessary for the younger church to truly be the church. For instance, if the home church is Anglican, it believes that a bishop is necessary to have a genuine church experience. Yet, in the first generation, no one from the national leadership is qualified to be a bishop; the only bishop in their experience is a foreigner in a distant city. So the new church must live its Christian life led by deacons and catechists. For other denominations, the criteria are different. It may be that the pastor must have a baccalaureate degree. For some American denominations, the criterion is the capacity of the local congregation or district to keep minutes on its deliberations.

At the same time that the normal village church must function without these structures in place, the churches in the major centers theoretically have all they need. They have bishops or pastors who meet the requirements, but they are foreign. When the requirements for ministry brought from home cannot be met in the first generation, only two options are available: to have a theologically recognizable church life led by foreigners or to have an indigenous church experience that is theologically defective.

Usually in the process of development, a second stage occurs where the younger church is recognized as a branch of the home church. For instance, for a decade the Mennonite Church of Argentina and the Mennonite Church of Madhya Pradesh in India were considered to be district conferences of the former General Conference of the Mennonite Church in North America. Many thought this recognition was progress. Of course Argentinians and Indians did not participate in the Conference sessions in North America except by naming as delegates missionaries who were home on furlough. However, considering these new churches as districts of the North American church was the most affirmative thing the North Americans knew to do at the time.

The next step in development is usually what missionary agencies have come to call *devolution*, or becoming indigenous, which means that certain functions that the mission had administered are turned over to the local church. These are usually functions such as baptism and catechism that have to do with the regular internal congregational life. They are usually not functions related to missionary outreach and often are not functions that require foreign staff and funding, like schools and hospitals. In this stage of development there are two organizations side by side—a nationalized church and a mission that has the staff and money.

The next stage in development is typically a crisis called *integration* where it is seen to be offensive that church and mission are separate organizations. Operations such as schools and hospitals that had been administered by the mission are put under the local church. But that change makes the church incapable of self-support. In addition, it clutters the agenda of the national decision-making body with management of foreign funds and staff, creating artificial problems of power and prestige as well as tensions with the supporting bodies back home.

After integration, there is usually a disentangling effort to move the institutions away from church control, giving them separate local governing boards. There is emphasis on partnership: neither the church nor the mission agency is in charge, but both must consult. Then, usually at some point of crisis, the mission administration will make a firm, unilateral decision to withdraw from certain services, which the national leaders often say is spiritually healthy.

Still another set of questions arises when the local church wants to cooperate with other churches in the same territory, churches that the mission did not plant and that may have quite different denominational names. As the local church becomes increasingly self-determining, leaders may also ask if there is a way to relate to the missionary agency and its churches other than being administered by them. Concern for "world confessionalism" often emerges: might the local churches participate as equals in a Lutheran World Federation gathering or Mennonite World Conference?

PIETIST ORIGINS

This pattern of evolution and devolution fits with the Pietist missionary assumptions we previously examined. It fits with that movement's axiom that the definition of ministry standards is the function of the official state church or the home church's convention. The mission agency does not claim to be the church, and therefore does not claim authority to ordain ministers or define the criteria for ordination.

Second, we observed that what devolves, what the mission management passes to local church management, is bureaucratic and financial control. That is, the problem devolution addresses is the problem of centralized structures brought from outside. Devolution accepts the colonial structure and then tries to correct it by changing the occupant of the driver's seat. But the corrective keeps the flaws of what it rejects, namely the driver's seat, which had been necessary in the first place only because of the mission agency's foreign management structure.

A third Pietist assumption is the legitimacy of denominational identity. In the new country, missionaries and mission churches do not start from scratch being biblical Christians or New Testament disciples and relating to all Christians who have similar convictions. They are Lutheran according to the Augsburg Confession or Presbyterian according to the Westminster Confession. That identity is assumed to be legitimate even in a completely new place.

Finally, the Pietist structure creates the identity of the missionary as a person and defines this distinct ministry. The church the missionary serves in the host country does not define the missionary; the sending and supporting church does. Whether he or she is a teacher, a counselor, a bookkeeper or a medical doctor, in the first generation this person has the status of missionary all the same.

In observing that these patterns and problems come in this shape from Pietist history, we are not saying that the situation definitely could have been otherwise, but we do ask the question: Could there have been an alternative? What would it have meant to say that the church is constituted by two or three people who meet in Jesus' name? What would it have meant to say, as soon as elders could be identified in that new local congregation, that it would become the responsible entity? In that circumstance the home church would still have a powerful link with the new church in the person of the missionary who, if he is resident, is a member both of the home church and the new church. If the missionary itinerates, he would be an esteemed visitor at the new church, but he would not have any formal or unique right to define the local church on the grounds of a sacramental understanding of ministry, especially when absent.

This more local definition of the church would not stand in the way of maintaining the world confessional body, but would be less exclusively denominational in local settings. A given overseas church would not be hindered from fraternal relations with other groups with similar convictions and practice simply on the grounds that the others are not Mennonite or are not Presbyterian. A given overseas church would be able, given this understanding, to receive missionaries from several sending bodies, and thereby to be less dependent on a single body.[1]

This will sometimes pose problems that administrations have difficulty handling. What if the young church, given from the start this much recognition of local elders, would differ from the home church on some important issue? That would be significant. But we differ from one another at home too. Fraternal disagreement is not something that can be stopped by maintaining a formal subjection of the new church to the church at home.

---

[1]We had a little of this in Mennonite experience. The Mennonite Church in Java has received personnel from both North America and Europe.

Also, granting this much church status to the younger group introduces the danger of it taking advantage of having several connections
overseas. It could play, for example, European and North American
sponsoring churches against one another. If it were a union church related to the mission boards of several denominations, it could go from
one to the other to get the best kind of support. This is threatening to a
mission administration, but it is simply the other side of what the mission
board has always done. A mission board that works in Japan, India and
Africa is always deciding which relationships to invest in and emphasize.

World Confessionalism

World confessionalism is usually the last stage of the devolution mentioned earlier. This new kind of agency, such as the World Federation of
Lutherans or the Presbyterian World Alliance, might possibly be a new
form of foreign missions that the rich nations support. Through these
agencies they may still control the movement of their finances and personnel around the world. Even then, it would be a somewhat better
form of foreign control in that decisions would be internationalized and
no one donor country would control the funds.

We have to recognize, however, that the world confessional body assumes that the issues that define denominational identity are important
and those that do not do so are unimportant. It is dubious whether
many issues that define differences between Presbyterians and Lutherans or between Lutherans and Anglicans are truly important in the
life of the local church overseas.

The value of confessional identity is not so much its definition of
theological identity as the way it enhances relationships. Because of
where they went to school and the agencies they traditionally related to,
church leaders in the older and younger churches became personally
acquainted and aware of one another's orientations. They also learned to
trust in each other's processes. This makes the international relationship
human and manageable, as it would not be if we simply declared the
total unity of all churches and accepted the corresponding need for constant ecumenical visits. We need to protect world confessionalism by
the awareness that this is all that it is: a link with people who have had

common experiences and trust one another. World confessionalism does not refer to a group of people who have a common theological commitment at all points or even at the most important points of contemporary mission and witness; such a group may not be able to speak as a unit except on ancient issues. On the other hand, it may function as a warning against nationalism and cultural narrowness.

THE ROLE OF THE MISSIONARY IN THE LOCAL CHURCH

The next general question is the place of missionary personnel in relation to the definition of the church in the new place. Traditionally, initially, automatically, the missionary was the first bishop. But that was not a lasting solution. If it was healthy, the local church created congregations that the missionary did not found. The next generation of missionaries, if they came as young foreigners after the church had been in existence for some time, clearly was not acceptable as bishops.

There are two simple ways to conceive of the status of the missionary. One is to speak of the missionary organization and therefore of the missionary person as "scaffolding." We need scaffolding while the church is being built, and then we tear it down, leaving only the building. Since the church is to be indigenous, missionaries should stay out of it. The Christian and Missionary Alliance follows this pattern. The missionaries do not even attend church conference meetings because that would interfere with their indigenous character. The shortcoming of this approach is that the scaffolding often does not come down. The mission stays and continues to govern education, medicine and outreach—which contribute to the local church's character even though they are not part of the ministry of the local congregation.

The other alternative is for the missionary to be a "fraternal worker." The separate mission organization is dropped and the missionary is integrated into the local church. Wherever placed, he or she is no longer a missionary whose authority is derived from being sent from overseas. A fraternal worker exercises his ministry under local supervision. Stephen Neil would say, for instance, "A missionary ceases to be a missionary on the day on which he sets foot on the shores of the land in which he has been called to work. From that moment he is a servant of the church in that place and nothing else."[2] It is theologically proper that home churches send missionaries. But once the missionary arrives, he or she is a fraternal worker, used as that church may please.

But this has problems as well. Culturally the young church is not ready to make the best possible use of this foreign resource. It is not staffed to deal with the fraternal worker's counseling needs or placement problems and does not always have the vision to use well the worker's special capacities. Generally, the younger church is not able to commit resources, including this fraternal worker, to continued outreach. In addition, this approach is not clear whether there is a real value to being foreign, whether there is theological significance to the fraternal worker's foreignness being integrated into the local church.

If the local church fully accepts the missionary with his cultural power, the fact that he is an appreciated guest and a gift to the church means he will be disproportionately weighty in his speech and actions. If the missionary tries to minimize this weightiness, he will always be cramping himself in his effort. Not to fulfill the role he is expected to fulfill and not to become more powerful and more needed are also sources of artificiality or confusion.

THE DISTINCTNESS OF MISSION AGENCIES

We spoke of the Pietist missionary society or board that did not claim to have church status, but this understanding was true for other denominational traditions as well. In this view, conferences or conventions determine churchly identity; mission societies do the sending business. Yet mission boards do function episcopally by overseeing the church's mission work.

At the same time, because the missionary society is organized along business lines and excludes sacramental and ministerial agenda, it is cut off from direct links to its supporting church population. It has to promote itself. Since often its funding is gathered through other channels than those of the church proper, it must advertise the importance of its cause and how well it is doing. One of the marks of Western Protestantism is the visibility of missionary outreach as a distinct cause for

---

[2]Stephen Neill, *The Unfinished Task* (London: Lutterwort, 1957), p. 92.

which fundraising is done. The missionary, then, functions as a professional in an agency increasingly driven to focus on urgent needs, dramatic poverty or ignorance—dimensions which threaten to change the shape or mood of the ministry itself.

Since the mission in its day-to-day operation is not the church, the missionary is cut off from the critique that the church's traditional standards provide. Because a Protestant missionary leaves to the church at home the definition of "the gospel properly preached and the sacraments properly administered," that standard cannot exercise critical impact on the way he or she works. A Baptist or a Mennonite missionary who rejects the idea of infant baptism may be serving in a mission that has an orphanage; it is not automatic that they will teach the faith in the orphanage in a way consistent with the rejection of infant baptism. Since the mission is not the church, neither the mission nor the home church assumes that the church's standards automatically govern the mission.

However, a mission agency often functions as a churchly body despite itself. A mission board may simply take missionaries when they are ready to go and provide support for them, but later find itself responsible for a new denomination. For example, if the mission is not a denominational missionary agency, the churches that come into being overseas will become a new denomination. When the Hebrew-Christian Alliance, which in North America is simply a supportive agency to enable mission to Jews, works in Palestine, it creates a Hebrew-Christian Alliance denomination. The Christian and Missionary Alliance, which in North America claims not to be a denomination, in other places creates churches identified with it. The Latin American Mission, the Central American Mission, the Chinese Christian Mission are all nonchurch agencies in North America, but the result of their work overseas are new denominations. Even denominational mission boards, because they do not intend to be "the church" and neither ordain nor fix theological standards, do not face the problem of inconsistency when the local churches they bring into being form a new denomination.

The other problems noted earlier associated with centralization of structure and the nonchurchly character of the mission societies still also must be faced.

WHICH AGENCY DOES OUTREACH?

An additional ongoing problem is related to the organizational separation that exists between the local church and the foreign agency in the mission setting. Which of those agencies is responsible for ongoing outreach? One response is that once the missionary has planted a young church, the leadership potential of the young church is needed for internal catechism, pastoring, counseling, housekeeping and management. The person available for further outreach is the missionary. Missionary personnel also have linguistic capacities and special training for mobility or cultural adjustment. So the missionary pulls out and goes somewhere else to be a new missionary again. While it is hoped that the younger church will eventually have surplus personnel to send elsewhere, the usual assumption is that the young church is not missionary. The mission is missionary.[3]

The alternative view would be to say that after the first generation the one thing the missionary should *not* do is further outreach. The foreign missionary should stay in the oldest churches to offer his or her specialized resources and training, concentrating on providing the resources that will help the church become more responsible. Outreach is the first thing that the mission agency should turn over to the responsible local body because this is where the missionary's foreignness is the most problematic. The local body can rejoice in that foreignness and the missionary's special capacities and resources without them getting in the way of the church's own life and outreach, whereas people outside the church are the ones least likely to get the right message from the foreigner.

CHURCH UNITY: MESSAGE AND METHOD

The next subtheme deals with the question of church unity and its interrelationship with the missionary message and method. If mission were thought of only as throwing a message over the fence from one culture to another or of fishing individuals out of the world into the church, then mission could have its own mandate and technique

---

[3]The Christian and Missionary Alliance churches have been most successful in doing this compared to other missions.

without any relationship to ecumenics or concern for unity. But we saw that the experience of unity in the early church was the root of mission, that the reconciling of Jew and Gentile was the mystery God was unfolding (Eph 2–3). This is the case in practice in missionary experience as much as it is in theory.

The missionary agency in most of church history was the Christian community. That is still largely the case despite the function of specialized missionary personnel. If the church community is the missionary vehicle, and if unity is part of the message, then the separateness, the dividedness of Christians is a hindrance to witness.

This was noticed first of all as a practical matter at the origins of the so-called ecumenical movement in the early part of the twentieth century: the overlapping of geographical coverage, the waste of personnel and the confusion of the audience—given mission efforts by multiple independent groups. What did it mean for people in India to find fifty-seven varieties of Christians telling them it matters whether we baptize babies or not or whether we have bishops or not? What does that still do to the meaning of Christian witness in the world? More important than the practical waste, overlap and competition is what happens to missionary morale, confidence and even to the message itself when part of the proclaiming has to be competition between denominations.

Still more profound is whether the message itself is being compromised; whether it is itself denied by the fact that separated agencies proclaim it. Denominational walls have their origins several decades or centuries back in theological issues. But denominational identity today is primarily ethnic. For separate denominations to project their separate ethnicity as if it were theological unity denies, formally speaking, the witness of Ephesians 2 and 3. How can we expect the whole message to be meaningful to the pagan if we deny it in the form in which we communicate it?

Missionary experience has thrown considerable light on the concern for Christian unity. Practically speaking, the greatest degree of fellowship beyond organizational borders has usually been experienced in the missionary context and by missionary people. That is, people who would not fellowship back home, who would not go to the same schools or to the same worship services in their local town, do so when they get to Timbuktu because there they feel Christian unity more than they feel differences. It is also historically the fact that the concern for Christian organizational unity first grew on the mission field or from mission agencies: comity, cooperation, international missionary conferences.[4] For instance, a concern for coordination of mission agencies' choice of fields for mission work, which assumed a degree of mutual recognition, arose in the nineteenth century. Interdenominational agencies such as the YMCA, the Evangelical Alliance and the student volunteer movement also developed. Frustration from competition overseas and the fact that missionaries, who met doing normal socializing, found themselves close to one another despite their theological differences, developed further the concern for cooperation.

For example, the International Missionary Council is older than other forms of the conciliar movement. The formal World Council of Churches movement began at the point of mission. The slogan from John 17:21 where Jesus asks for church unity so that the world might believe has become the ecumenical movement's slogan. The phenomenon of intercommunion happened first overseas. The phenomenon of united churches happened first overseas. Indeed, without the missionary perspective we would not have the ecumenical movement we have today.

What kind of unity do we seek? But beyond noting the close ties between mission and the ecumenical movement, it would be fitting to ask again what kind of unity we seek and to ask this in the light of missionary concern. There are as many visions of Christian unity as there are denominations. Lutherans believe that Christian unity around the world needs to meet Lutheran criteria; Catholics and Baptists believe no less regarding their own.

Generally, we can discern in the conciliar movement two foci for understanding how to work at the unity we seek. William Carey, the National Missionary Councils, the Life and Work movement and the inter-

---

[4]William Carey actually proposed an international missionary conference long before there was a church merger movement in the West.

church aid movement—all of which contributed to the creation of the World Council of Churches—say, "Let us work together as if we recognized one another. Let us recognize one another for purposes of cooperation without committing ourselves to the approval of one another's theology, sacraments or ministries." It is in this conciliar cooperation that the most has happened: the most money and staff have been sent, the most contacts have taken place. This is church unity in practice, in operation, in ministry, in service. The second focus has been Faith and Order, the context for sustained theological conversation about doctrine and ministry, sacraments and church order. Here Lutherans and Anglicans, and more recently Catholics, have been concerned for ecumenical conversation.

These two thrusts—the conciliar cooperation thrust and the Faith and Order thrust—have in common that they can be run by hierarchies quite apart from grassroots control or congregational expression. In addition, they do not need to refer to the pagan world or to mission. They were defined within Christendom: one focusing on the church as a service agency and the other focusing on the church as ritual agency. Most of the World Council of Churches' and National Council of Churches' work has been on these levels. That is not wrong, but it is a limitation.

This limitation means that the conciliar movement does not deal with the deepest estrangements within denominations: between right and left, between old and young, between rural and urban. It means that Southern Baptists cannot relate to the World Council. It means that the Council does not deal easily with nonhierarchical denominations such as the Pentecostals. So we have a paradox in the ecumenical movement. On the one hand, the preoccupation with unity that led to the creation of these conciliar organizations came from missionary concerns. Yet this conciliar movement now centers on nonmissionary, non–free church problems and does so in a nonmissionary way.

What kind of unity enhances mission? Might the renewal of a missionary perspective throw new light on the unity concern? Instead of asking what kind of unity Christians should have with one another, what if we asked, "What kind of unity, if lacking, hinders mission?" Then we would see that this unity is not first of all the separateness of organizations; that is a matter of management efficiency, and it is not even certain that a totally centralized organization is more efficient. Unmerged agencies can work together smoothly in mission if they recognize each other's memberships and ministries. This is not just spiritual unity, but the unity of a visible body.

Evangelical emphasis on spiritual unity as over against organizational unity has a point, negatively speaking. Unity of organizations alone is not enough. But emphasis on spiritual unity is also wrong in that it interprets this unity as invisible. For the sake of mission, we need church unity that is marked by visible mutual recognition among congregations and agencies so that we do not continue to project the offense of ethnic separation.

Finally, the way the church deals with difference in unity affects its missionary witness. I would argue that to deal with unresolved tension is more important than to ignore it to ease collaboration. The New Testament church dealt with tensions, as is evident from Matthew 18. The conciliar movement and much of the church merger movement (like the church of South India) did not seek to reconcile or handle major differences. They saw where they could cooperate despite differences. They did not seek to be the church in the sense of Matthew 18 where binding and loosing takes place and brings about a unity that was not previously there.

There would be more to say if this were a discussion of ecumenics about the interlocking of concern for mission and concern for unity. My point now is simply to observe that they are mutually reinforcing, have been historically in the past, and can be now.

THE MISSIONARY CHURCH'S DISCIPLINE AS A THEOLOGICAL PROBLEM

Mission workers often bring ethical rules from home, for example, rules forbidding polygamy and dancing. Most missionaries say Christians should care for the government; Mennonites say that is not the business of Christians. All missionaries reject cannibalism. Such culturally based discipline dramatizes the young church's foreign cultural style. The younger church is tempted to take over the new rules in a legalistic way that is much more rigid than it was in the missionaries' home country. Christian obedience is translated into taboos rather than being seen as ethically functional in serving the neighbor, in personal discipline or in communication.[5]

The corrective for this, some say, is that the mission should never have anything to do with Christian discipline. But that seriously limits the message, because the message does include a new kind of life. How can the young church learn this if the missionary does not teach it? Is there some way of teaching that would not be paternalistic or foreign? If so, should teaching be done before or after recognizing the responsibility of the local church? The example I have used here is that of ethical discipline, but it could apply as well to doctrinal identity. The present concern is not to ask whether a particular ethical position is right or wrong, but to ask what the problem of foreign standards means for unity and responsibility in mission.

Criticism of importing foreign standards is quite wide in recent missionary thought, but it is not necessarily deep. People like Donald Mc-Gavern would say that if there are such elements of foreignness, the new church will not grow. Therefore, the mission should give the local church more liberty to talk the language of their neighbors and to identify the issues that make sense in the local culture. But this emphasis does not speak to the concern noted above that part of being Christian involves adopting moral and theological identity.

Roland Allen is more theologically concerned than Donald Mc-Gavern but makes analogous points. He argues that focusing on matters of structured church discipline is not found in the New Testament at the point of creating churches, that it is not effective in reaching the wider world, and that the more narrowly we define what it takes to be a faithful church, the more we tend to deny the fullness of church experience to most Christians in a pagan culture. But he would make assumptions

---

[5]There are times in the first generations when a young church's concern for morality is so rigid that they really need Luther's message of grace. But if the missionaries had started with Luther's message, it would not have fit. All of the live agenda of valid church history will eventually find its place in the new church. Until the agenda arises out of the life of the younger community and they develop their own transcultural leaders, the missionary has to be there as the pipeline for this kind of communication.

also about a minimum amount of Christian moral teaching and doctrinal identity that we cannot do without.

A FREE CHURCH PERSPECTIVE

Without working out the details, let me state what a free church perspective would be regarding this list of problems. In addition to the New
Testament data, the free church perspective is a critique of Christendom.
That means it identifies the dangers of magisterial structures that take
the church's life away from the grassroots. It focuses on the centrality of
the congregation and on the necessity of personal decision.

At these points Pietism, as well as other denominations' boards and
agencies who did mission work in the same way, retained the form of
Christendom. These missions created local congregations, but ministries and ritual were not defined locally. The local church brought
common people and poor people into its life, but the administrative
structure was magisterial and the political orientation favored the authorities in that colony and in the home nation. There was a concern for
personal piety but a tendency to create a new ethnic enclave in the pagan
country. Pietism, despite its intention, propagated Christendom. It
wanted genuineness, but it taught Puritanism, that is, an imposed
faithfulness. It wanted personal experience, but it exported dogma and
bishops as the definition of church order. Back home the Pietist
movement claimed that most people were not true Christians, and then
when it went overseas, it took along that Christian culture from home.

The counterclaim is that a free church orientation—this does not
mean a Mennonite denomination—could do something toward solving
these problems. Recognizing local churches in the mission setting
would be easier, clearer, more responsible and more manageable. Recognizing these new churches as truly the church would affirm that the
local church's experience is itself necessary to the life of the church, not
optional or dispensable. Their need to have a valid church identity is not
only one of pastoral psychology, but of theology and morality.

To immediately recognize church reality in the mission setting, the
standards for recognizing the church must be minimal. I would say that
in the first generation, even in the first months, one must be able to rec-

ognize whatever is central to one's definition of the church. The standards must be those "without which no church is present." That means that where there is a body of believers with elders we have to distinguish the criteria for recognizing minimal church identity from the ideal identity that includes such things as education for ministry, specialization of tasks and moral insight. I said this systematically; we could say this from the New Testament example as well. Paul named elders in every church soon after forming those communities.

What would those minimum requirements be? I would suggest the following: two or three people gathered together; recognition of leadership and discipline; common worship which includes baptism, the Lord's Supper and reading the Bible together; a link to the past in the form of the Bible and affirmation of the meaning of the faith; and a link to church fellowship around the world, that is, visitation and mutual recognition in relation to Christians elsewhere.[6]

Anglican Roland Allen said we need four things: creed, gospel, sacraments and ministry. But he assumed the other dimensions of what I mentioned. He also noted extensions of these concerns that are not minimum demands: higher demands that the preacher have a baccalaureate degree, that one accept the Augsburg Confession and that leaders have to know how to manage a synod and take minutes. In a missionary context, we may need to get along, but I think it may be healthy to get along for a long time without keeping conference minutes.

The danger of this free church orientation to mission is trusting inadequate churches. Certainly if we use this minimum concept of what it takes to recognize a sister community, there will be inadequacies and incompetence. But if the Holy Spirit moves the church to mission and unbelievers to faith, maybe we could trust the Spirit to keep order. How does it happen that we trust the Spirit for the former and not for the latter?

Roland Allen said, although in Anglican language: if we trust the Holy Spirit for order, if we enable the local congregation to act, if we say that structured ties to the forms of faithfulness found in the West are

---

[6]This means a creed, in some sense, but not necessarily a historic creed: "Jesus Christ is Lord" might be enough.

dispensable, we are making a free church point. This does not dodge or solve all of the problems of foreignness, of immigration, of the status of the missionary or the status of the young congregation's discipline. But the shift from Pietist assumptions to free church assumptions throws new light on some of these questions, makes some of them more solvable, perhaps removes some and helps us identify new ones especially at the point of radical discipleship and Christian nonconformity in the new society.

11

THE CHURCH AS LOCAL

The theme for this chapter is usually dealt with under the adjective *indigenous*. It is a discussion that arises as a corrective for the foreignness of the missionary enterprise: the fact that it brings with it cultural, ritual, intellectual and economic forms from Europe or North America. These forms are identified with the faith and yet not the same thing as Christian faithfulness. The more blatant the missionary operation's foreignness, the more evident the criticism becomes. The obvious alternative is to let the new church be Christian in its own culture. Rather than teaching people foreign words or practices, why not make Christianity indigenous in its form?

The fact that foreignness can create blatant offense and evident critique does not mean it is always clear what to do next; after all, by the nature of the case the new church's culture is not Christian. What it means to be Christian in "their own culture" is not self-evident but will have to be found. It certainly will not be the same thing as what they were doing before they became Christians.

One side of the question about becoming indigenous is the matter of ecclesiastical structure, dealt with in the previous chapter. In this chapter we will look at the cultural side: its language, ritual, group process and worldview. Once again I will argue some theses in relationship to this theme.

THERE IS A WRONG FOREIGNNESS

There is something wrong when the missionary process estranges people from their own cultural base. We can observe this wrong foreignness in the modern missionary enterprise where European forms have been exported and established, forms that were not necessary, did not belong and which cut off the young church from her world. We have a model for this in the Judaizing movement in the New Testament, which was already bringing a wrong foreignness into the mission. Paul and the Judaizers both wanted to bring the Jewish heritage to the pagan world, but they had different ways of doing it. The so-called Judaizers brought too much with them, or the wrong things. The gospel came with a cultural form that did not relate essentially to becoming a Christian. This wrong foreignness denied mission by being irrelevant.

In our case, if the wrong foreignness comes from Europe or North America, it may raise ethical questions by putting the mission on the side of political and economic power. This is not just a cultural question such as communicating understandably would be, but a moral question. If the missionary personnel are good friends of the colonial administrators or the foreign commercial establishment, that says something about the message. If they approve of the colonial techniques, it is even more questionable. This degree of wrong foreignness falls short of love and servanthood by not fully appreciating, caring for, loving and respecting people in their own cultural skins.

THERE IS ALSO WRONG ACCOMMODATION
TO INDIGENOUS CULTURE

On the other side of the debate about becoming indigenous, a strand of religiously neutral non-Christian anthropological analysis critiques missions not just because they are European or North American, but because they are foreign. Mission destroys the old culture by raising new questions or bringing in different ethical considerations. This anthropological critique may idealize the old system's adequacy. It may say, "These people were happy and had a good thing. Their society was healthy. Why did you interfere?" without really testing whether that society actually was healthy or whether it was going to be knocked over anyway by other elements of Westernization, such as railroads, mines, schools, alcohol or rifles. Western culture would come, even if the missionaries did not.

Both the excessively foreign missionaries and the excessively pro-indigenous, antimissionary anthropologists assume that the host culture is monolithic, a single block. With this view, either we accept the new culture and gradually try to infiltrate certain constructive ideas into it, or else we smash the new culture because it is all of the devil.

Christianity does change culture. If what the missionary message brings with regard to Jesus is not somehow new to the scene, then it is not a missionary message. There must be something added if the meaning of the gospel is not to be simply another slogan for the same old life. We should not need to decide between the two classic alternatives of total indigenous authenticity, on the one hand, or total inauthentic foreignness on the other. There must be a third option.

AFFIRMING AND CRITIQUING CULTURE IN MISSION

Jesus was genuinely, irreproachably Jewish. Yet he presented an alternative to the ways of being Jewish that most people were pursuing at the time. Paul was genuinely a Mediterranean Hellenist. Yet he presented an alternative to other people's ways of being Mediterranean Hellenists. These sample models are by no means the only ones, but they are our classical ones. What theory fits those examples? These models push us to develop a theory that denies our only alternatives to be total indigenous authenticity and total inauthentic foreignness. The question is not "Are you going to go or are you going to be foreign?" in the indigenous culture. The question is, what are the *alternative ways* to be in it?

This framing of the question is another example of the issues we have inherited from the old European alternatives. The Christendom approach, including the Pietist correction, assumes that we have a unified Christian culture. We cannot see how to fiddle with its unity, so we accept the whole block, or we make minor corrections while respecting its integrity. If we make that assumption about our home Christian culture, it is no surprise that we make it also about the host non-Christian culture. We assume either it is a unity that must be smashed or it is a unity that we will respect, and then we sow our seeds of renewal in that new soil.

The believers church or free church, on the other hand, denied the monolithic quality of the Christian culture. It pushed for a pluralistic society back home and by its very existence created it. Therefore, its concern is that there be a new option, which is neither completely native nor foreign but a new thing.

What happens in a new culture when people hear about Jesus? How can we affirm a culture at the same time that we critique it? What will be the criteria for trying to do this? We will use Africanization of the gospel as a sample in considering these questions, though we could ask the same questions about any part of the world. However, there is more thinking and writing in English concerning Africa than concerning some other places in relation to these questions.

Assuming that we are not satisfied with the two polar ways of defining the options—total indigenous authenticity and total inauthentic foreignness—and we want something more like the New Testament models, how would we get hold of that? What would be the test questions? Most often I have the impression that the people who think and write in this area are aware of the extremes as we have stated them and know that neither extreme is acceptable. So they talk about "balance," about not selling ourselves out to either extreme but remaining in the middle. That means we do not have a clear position, but only a sense of being torn in both directions.

The modern balance approach is more political or psychological than it is theological. We can understand somebody trying to live that way, especially if his or her role is a politician or a bureaucrat; where they stand depends on how loud the shouts are from either side. The apostle Paul, in contrast, did not try to balance two extremes. He had something new, which was his own integrity.

Another more widely used criterion in approaching gospel and culture is to distinguish between form and content and say that the content must be the same message always, but it will take different forms. A different way to say this is to distinguish between things that matter— the essence—and things that do not matter—*adiaphora*. They do not matter because they do not make a difference. *Adiaphora* is the same root that we have in the English word *differ*. But *adiaphora* are the "no difference things." There are some things that matter—we have to affirm the Trinity—and there are some things that do not matter—we can speak German, French or tribal languages.

The form/content split and the essential/*adiaphora* split, I suspect, are anthropologically or culturally naive because that difference is not really there in the subject matter. If I think something is unimportant, I have made a prior decision about its place in culture, but that is precisely the decision we are trying to test. If I decide something is essential and therefore I must keep saying it the way I did back home, I have made a prior decision that it is essential, which is again what we are trying to test. For instance, was the question of whether Jews and Greeks eat at the same table essential or nonessential? Peter said it was nonessential, so they could separate the two groups and get along better. Paul said it was essential and that they would deny the whole gospel if they would not have table fellowship between Jew and Greek. This appeared to some to be purely a matter of form, just housekeeping details, but that is where the gospel content was stuck at that point. The distinction between form and content is probably deceptive. It is anthropologically naive because all content dictates something of its form, and every form assumes some content and bias.

First Corinthians 8 also shows the complexity of choosing between form and content or between what is essential and nonessential. This document deals with whether it mattered for Christians that certain foods had been involved in idolatrous processes, either as they were slaughtered or as they were prepared for eating. Paul first addressed the question theologically and said there was nothing wrong with that meat. That was truth. There was nothing wrong with eating it as long as they gave thanks for it. But then he pointed out that not everyone had that knowledge. If a brother or sister thought there was something wrong with that meat, that it belonged to an idol, then there *was* something wrong with it. The other person's culture mattered. If he or she would eat it or see you eating it, Paul said, they would fall back into idolatry. He decided that he was ready to be a vegetarian for life, to let culture, not theology, determine whether there was something wrong with that meat. That is, he let what was theologically inessential—or cultural form—rather than what was theologically essential—or Christian content—determine his own missionary practice. This raises serious questions about whether the form/content split or the essential/nonessential split is truly a help in determining how we want to be both indigenous and faithful.

In recent missionary experience in many parts of the world, first generation missionaries, not knowing any better, brought their religious music from home. Music is one of the worst things to bring to a new culture because the musical idiom is enormously varied in different cultures. For instance, Western languages lack a meaning difference that depends on tone. Whether we say something in a high or low tone might matter for emotional meaning but not for word meaning. The same syllable whether spoken high or low or with a rising or falling tone has the same meaning. We can string the words of a poem along the notes of a melody, and it does not matter what the melody is. Some words fit better depending on the accent or the melody's dynamics, but it does not change the meaning proper. In numerous other languages tonality does have to do with the meaning. One example, pulled from an African language, is a syllable that when spoken in a high tone means "take," and when in a low tone means "chew." The missionaries did not know that. So they set their words to music and had the Africans singing, "Chew the name of Jesus with you." Music is one of the last things missionaries ought to have taken along unchanged. But they all did it.

When later generations of missionaries came—those who had learned some musicology—they became interested in African culture and discovered that it was sophisticated musically. They said, "Let's write words to some native melodies. We want to help you become more indigenous again." Then it was the national Christians who said, "We cannot use that music. That is pagan, idolatrous music. That music symbolizes the devil's hold on us. Maybe we can use some other kind of folk or work song, but we cannot use *that* kind of music. It is like 1 Corinthians 8: it symbolizes the pagan past from which we have broken free, and we want to remain free." The missionary and the church cannot take something of the pre-Christian national culture in a simplistic way. The practice might be an element of idolatry, of sexual celebration or something else that is not usable.

If either a touchy balance where we try not to go too far either way toward indigenous culture or toward foreign importation, or if a simple split between form/content and essential/nonessential are inadequate, we could go back to our New Testament models to see if we could find firmer criteria for navigating local culture.

Criteria from the early church's Jewishness. From the New Testament story we see Paul and the early church bringing with them into the pagan world some things that simply reflected the fact that the early church was Jewish. They brought along into the Hellenistic world at least three things with no concern about whether they were foreign or acceptable.

First, they rejected polytheism, and not just in the superficial sense of how many temples a town had or whether the people had a theory about the existence of more than one god. Polytheism had implications for cosmology, a sense of history, the view of the nation and many other things. Second, the true God is creator. That is, they affirmed a worldwide, historical, creative purpose on the part of the God who then sent Jesus. Third, though it is not spelled out in Paul's missionary speeches, wherever they went the Jews brought with them the Decalogue, that is, a fundamental moral outline. It is true that they had not been keeping all the Old Testament rules as they moved around. They had, in fact, developed the institution of the rabbinate to make adjustments and connections so they could be faithful to the old law's intent without being bound by its specific forms, which reflected another century. But the Decalogue as such, the concept that God had given certain basic moral limits as props for humanity, *that* they took with them wherever they went, and so did the church.

I suggest that we also would have every reason to take those three things with us wherever we go and expect them usually to be foreign. That kind of foreignness is something we can have a good conscience about in any part of the world.

Criteria from the early church's newness. The next set of criteria for navigating a new culture, criteria we find operative in New Testament practice, is related to the early church's newness. It is, after all, a *New* Testament.

First, the early church emphasized the name and story of Jesus. The faith that we bring with us in mission is not only "new" but also historical. It is not only about how to be happy where we are; it involves a past. If we do not know something about that past, we do not know about that faith. We cannot transpose Jesus' name into some other name or savior figure that those in the new culture already know, even one that resembles Jesus in being a son of a god, being born supernaturally or who died dramatically. The name of Jesus and the fullness of the Jesus story belong in crosscultural mission; otherwise we do not have anything to bring.

Second, the early church brought with them the meaning of Jesus' work, which was to break down walls between peoples and create a wider humanity, making their kind of people and our kind of people into one people. As Paul wrote, "There is no longer Jew or Greek . . . for all of you are one in Christ Jesus" (Gal 3:28). Likewise, we are not Europeans or Asians; we are the new humanity in which, for example, Asian elements and European elements interrelate, fuse and converse to create something new. Wherever we go, that new humanity has to be affirmed not only as an idea, but also in practice.

Third, the New Testament church took a further Torah with it wherever it went: the Sermon on the Mount as a catechism. That is a distinctive model for dealing with the fundamental human conflicts that are found in any society and dealing with them differently. The way the Sermon on the Mount tells people to deal with these problems is "foreign" to any culture, but not because it comes from another culture. The Sermon on the Mount is foreign anywhere, not because it is European, but because it is hard to live. The Europeans never did live up to it. This foreignness cannot be handled on the old-people/new-people or home-land/foreign-land scale. It is a judgment, a promise and a new possibility that goes beyond any cultural pattern and therefore calls us to be demanding or hopeful in a way that is a source of renewal in any place.

Finally, a criterion we learned from the New Testament that might be applicable in mission today is the acceptance of minority status for the church. We do not start by assuming the church must take over the place. We start by assuming the number of believers will be modest and that the decision to follow Christ will be a costly one, therefore a decision that not many will make. That does not mean an a priori decision that there should never be a mass movement or that we would not want many people to follow Christ. It means we do not hang our hopes or strategies on the effectiveness of the message in getting a wide hearing quickly or gaining support from powerful people.

Criteria from the experience of Christendom and the Reformation. There are also criteria learned from Christendom and the Reformation. What have we learned about being the church from all these centuries of history? I suggest that there are certain elements of the church's self-awareness that have been sharpened through this history that will be helpful in guiding the crosscultural move.

One is a deepened awareness of political power as a threat to and contradiction of the gospel. It did not occur to the New Testament church to use political power in favor of the gospel, because it was not available. If it had occurred, they would have said no, just as Jesus did. It did not occur to Paul or Peter as a problem because Constantine was not available as a friend. Later, Constantine was available as a friend of the church and the churchmen all accepted his help. Now we know we should know better. We have learned through the years that Jesus' rejection of the zealot option and Paul's and Peter's getting along without Caesar was not simply because they did not have political power, but because they knew that using such power to spread the church was itself a mistake.

Second, we have a deepened awareness of ethnicity, nationalism and provincialism as an offense against the gospel. Therefore, we have additional theological tools to guard against an ethnically provincial way of conceiving the gospel when we seek to commend it in another place.

Another side of the same issue is voluntarism. Voluntarism is the view of humanity or the philosophy that emphasizes the freedom of the will. Voluntarism is that view of the church which insists that membership should be a free choice of responsible adults; it is not based on birth or ethnic identity. We have learned through the Reformation that this is something to be more careful about.

We are also more conscious that the community be aware of itself as God's people making decisions and doing God's work. The new local church should not think of itself simply as a reaction to the mission, the missionary, the leader or the foreign institution, but instead be aware of itself as a people making decisions, sharing resources and so forth.

The criteria's translatability across cultures. All of the criteria in the three categories above focus not on content, but on form; not on theology or spirituality, but on process. These criteria can be expressed crossculturally precisely because they are issues of process.[1] They can find an expression in any other culture, while certain theological affirmations or particular patterns of personal religious experience might not be able to be translated. The theological term *Trinity,* for example, is one that theologians who spoke Latin invented to make a point. By definition, the word *Trinity* does not exist in non-Western languages. It is not immediately translatable. The title *Son of God* in its particular biblical meaning or in its other postbiblical theological meaning, and the concept of justification which mattered so much for the Reformation, cannot be directly translated into other cultures. But we can test the faithfulness of the transformation of the process concerns we mentioned, because they are sociological or related to form. They are not peculiar to our culture. In fact, they are not popular in our culture either. I suggest that in response to the question of how to be both foreign and authentic in any other place, we pull out the criteria that had to do with our being both critical and authentic at home.

INTENTIONAL ACCOMMODATION

There is a specific theme that underlies what we have been talking about: intentional accommodation. This means making a point of looking in the host culture for existing elements acceptable for Christian use. In

---

[1]For example, I would tend to think that the things the Sermon on the Mount identifies are portable enough that there would be a fairly direct applicability in most places, though anthropological experience could challenge that. The Sermon on the Mount does not say there cannot be polygamy, for instance. It just says marriage is permanent. So it would not justify the smashing of polygamous marriages that has been done in the name of Western understandings of monogamy. But it would forbid separation. To say that those marriages that exist shall remain is a possibility in any culture.

the sixth century Pope Gregory wrote to Augustine of Canterbury, who went to England to be the first missionary, telling Augustine not to destroy the pagan shrines, but adapt them in Christian worship.[2] The Pope said that if those people decorate their meeting places with pine branches because the pine tree was a religious figure in the Germanic culture, use pine branches in Christian worship. If they kill pigs, kill pigs. Try anything that is not condemned by a church council, in order to make the faith meaningful. Christmas was originally a pagan holiday, given some Jesus-oriented meaning. It appears that some of the saints in the earliest Roman calendar were not even Christians, but leftover local, pagan deities that were baptized together with their hillside and their chapel.

Contemporary church growth theory makes use of the concept of the *functional equivalent*—that we have to bring, find or create something in the church's life to cover everything that people needed done for them in their pre-Christian culture. One of the classic expressions of this was a sixteenth-century controversy in China, when the Jesuit missionaries accommodated Chinese culture to such an extent that the Roman authorities had to call them to account. If the accommodations go that far, then we do not need to have missionaries.

There are also Western forms of accommodation, some of which have been seriously proposed and practiced and others of which have been suggested as types only. For instance, in our culture where bread is not the most basic food and wine is not the most basic drink, some people think we should use something else for the Lord's Supper, such as hamburgers and Coke or, as one congregation I know has done, use Ritz crackers and fresh grapes. Since we no longer walk on dusty roads wearing sandals, shouldn't we shine each other's shoes instead of washing feet?

My suggestion with regard to intentional accommodation is that we should not say "never" or "always" but rather ask, what does a specific activity mean in that host culture? There may be some practices—for

---

[2][See Bede, *Ecclesiastical History of the English Nation*, Book 1, chapter 30, in which Pope Gregory, among other accommodations, instructs missionaries going to England not to destroy temples, only the idols in them, and to let people make animal sacrifices, provided they are done to the God of the Bible. —Ed.]

instance, a civil ritual that introduces people into adolescence or adulthood—that perhaps we should not tell people in that culture they cannot have. Maybe we should work for the secularization of the activity, seeing it as part of civil life rather than the life of the new Christian community. That is, we do not look for a functional equivalent of idolatry. We get rid of it by secularizing it. However, if the activity is clearly linked to the cult of other deities, then we might need to chop it down as some of the early European missionaries did with pine or oak trees that represented the presence of the deity. If, on the other hand, certain of those cultural forms can fit with the new kind of community that we bring, with the meaning of fellowship and love of neighbor, then we can borrow it and baptize it. We can be happy to have found something local to pick up and use.

These three possibilities—make it civil, get rid of it or baptize it— obviously are not pure alternatives that we will automatically find. But asking the question that way is a way to get some clarity. So we do not ask, "Is this activity right or wrong?" First we look case by case at whether a cultural form is usable and whether it says what we have to say.

Relevance. Certain New Testament passages specifically attend to the principalities and powers, to the devil, to spiritual forces that are quite distinct from human forms and experiences. That is not typical of the modern, Western, science-oriented worldview, but it is typical of the earlier African worldview. Therefore, in Africa it may be that a priority agenda should be how the African preoccupation with the existence and character of spirits relates to God and what Jesus does to the spiritual forces. It is fitting to let that indigenous priority guide us in selecting what it is about the biblical message that they hear first. Instead of hearing first justification by faith, costly discipleship or the coming kingdom, what they hear first is God's power to protect a person against evil spirits and a concern for straightening out the ontology of beings beyond the visible and the human.

One strength of this approach is what is currently called *relevance*, that is, it is obvious that people in the new church care about the issue. If missionaries would ignore cultural relevance and say, "That is not important agenda at all; we have to emphasize justification by faith because we are Protestants," "We have to focus on costly discipleship because we are Mennonites," or "We have to give priority to the gospel of the kingdom because we are dispensationalists," they would actually accept irrelevance in the short run.

But assuming that we do not take that path and we accept the priority agenda put to us by the host culture, we still have to make a choice. What are the alternative ways of being relevant? Are we going to use that host culture's language in a syncretistic way and merge the local way of dealing with the nature, reality and power of the spirits with the biblical worldview, saying that they are basically the same thing? We might take their worldview as predisposing them for belief, thinking it should be easy for these people to understand the gospel because, unlike the modern Western person, they already believe in the spirit world. But this also opens the way for the serious danger of syncretism, fusing elements of the biblical message with people's existing religious views in such a way that one is never quite clear at what points one becomes or ceases to be Christian.

Radicality. The other alternative, which is rare in mission literature but which seems to be just as possible, is to make this congeniality of form the framework for a new radicality. That is, we might say, "Okay, this culture believes in the spirit world. So does the Bible. But what does the Bible do with the spirit world? It casts out the spirits, and it proclaims that their power is broken." We would make an issue of stating the radicality of the gospel's call in relevant terms—for instance, making much of the burning of fetishes, ceremonies of exorcism and disciplines of staying away from spirit-laden places. We would take seriously the worldview from 1 Corinthians 8 and 10 as a way of underlining the radicality of the newness that we bring. We would state the newness in relation to the old cultural terms in order that the call for a break would be firmer.

Is that difference between syncretism and radicality meaningful? Both are framed in culturally relevant ways, but they are different.

Another example often found in popular church literature—the story of Abraham—can be used to illustrate these two ways of being relevant.

One approach emphasizes how much the Old Testament—especially the patriarchal period with men like Abraham, his flocks and his many wives—is much like ordinary life in certain non-Western cultures. A man who has many sheep is wealthy, and if he has many sheep he can probably afford to have many wives. His power and self-respect are related to that kind of measurement. Indeed, the African can understand Abraham better than a modern American missionary can. Some American missionaries testify that they now understand the Bible better because they have learned to understand African patriarchal culture.

While this approach highlights continuity between Abraham and certain cultures today, I would suggest that the story of Abraham is rather an occasion for sharpening the choice between short-sighted accommodation and radicality. Abraham was a man of his time and his culture, but he was also very different. He left home and did not know where he was going. In the Bible, he is the archetype of the one who goes out, who trusts a call to a future that he has no way of understanding. The Abraham image in biblical theology is not one of cultural adaptation and fitting in, but one of costly pilgrimage. It would be possible for missionaries to use this parallel between ancient and contemporary nomadic cultures to make meaningful the newness of the gospel and the cost of obedience, rather than use it to make it easier for some Africans to slide into the Christian movement because it is so much like their familiar culture.

A further example of the tension between accommodation and radicality is ancestor veneration, common in most African tribal cultures. People make much of remembering ancestors and care deeply about whether their posterity will remember them. One approach to this situation has been to say that as long as they venerated their ancestors they could not be Christian because that is what tied them to the old world, which they would have to leave if they were going to be Christians. There was a strong thrust of trying to slice off that element of the culture at the point of church membership. The other extreme was to Christianize ancestor veneration and make the ancestors saints so that we could say that they were somehow in the story. Some of the African indigenous churches still reinstate or maintain the veneration of ancestors in some form of syncretistic relationship to Christian practices.

Once again my suggestion would be that we find a way between un-critical acceptance and rejection, that we accept the need, but find a new solution. One solution that has been seriously suggested is to accept the practice of honoring ancestors—the need for the past to remain present— but with a radical change. As Christians, our ancestors are no longer simply our own great grandfathers, grandfathers and fathers, but Abraham, Isaac and Jacob. We take on biblical history as our history. We change histories and ancestors. When people have a new lord, they also have a new grandfather. Loyalty to Christ means that a person enters into another history that cares just as much about the fathers, but they are different fathers. That is the most radical way to put it.

The other alternative, which has also been seriously suggested, is the rare and obscure affirmation in the New Testament that Christ went to preach to the departed spirits, to the saints in prison or to the patriarchs in the underworld. Maybe that could be stretched to say that a believer has the right to trust that the work of Christ relates somehow to his or her history, just as most Christian theology affirms that the work of Christ relates to Abraham or to the Old Testament saints in general, even though in terms of time that could not logically be.

We could identify the same problem of accommodation and radi-cality at the level of the church's ethical discipline. The simple solution— the old solution—was to bring to the host culture the clarity of the Western answer. For instance, take the problem of polygamy. The Western solution was that marriage is to be monogamous and per-manent; it is to be given legal form. The church and state agreed in rec-ognizing and defining it. In the West, this may be with or without the possibility of divorce—dealt with as an exception. This was a point on which until recently church and state agreed.

There are difficulties on several levels of bringing this ethic to a culture where these rules have not applied in the past. One is that it is hard to prove on the basis of biblical proof texts that polygamous union is illegitimate. It is possible to argue on the basis of biblical themes and other kinds of reasoning that monogamy is healthy or good. But a radical rejection of polygamy is not something that can be firmly argued on the basis of proof-texts. A second difficulty is that the Western models have been falling apart back home. For some, the existence of divorce meant a kind of sequential polygamy, which undercut the capacity to argue firmly that Africans should accept the Western church's guidance concerning marriage. Still another built-in tension is that bringing the demand for monogamy to a polygamous culture by saying that existing polygamous relationships must be broken up contradicts the permanence of marriage, which is clearly biblical—whether on the level of systematic theology or proof-texts. If we say that the existing polygamous unions must be broken up, we take the side of monogamy against permanence.

On a practical level, there are major social disadvantages to missionary outsiders demanding the destruction of a polygamous union. The rejected woman or women are usually socially stranded. Sometimes they can go back to their home clan, but often not. The theology of Western monogamy does not provide guidance about which wife a man should keep out of his three or four. Should he keep the prettiest one or the first one, the one that is the best gardener or the one that is the better housekeeper? Theology does not help at that point.

The alternate extreme is to say that polygamy is no issue at all— remember Abraham and Jacob with their multiple marriages. If we want to accept the local culture, we will completely drop our concerns. These concerns are foreign, irrelevant and hinder the growth of the church. There are African indigenous churches and Africanized Christian groups that make no issue at all of polygamy; that is one of the reasons for their popularity and growth potential.

An alternative which has been followed more recently by some mission groups is to note that of the two biblical concerns—monogamy and permanence—permanence is the most fundamental biblically, the most clear and the deepest in its mandate. It is not the church's business to destroy present unions, but from now on the church should teach that monogamy is preferable. This approach can be implemented quite simply at two points: the church does not celebrate additional marriages for already married members, and a polygamous person cannot be an overseer in the church. There are proof-texts in the New Testament for the latter, which helps on the practical level. In any culture someone can say, "It says here, an elder must be a husband of one wife." In summary, there can be built into the church's practice a bias in favor of monogamy, without being legalistically against polygamy, especially for new members who already have more than one spouse.

The Christian basis for monogamy is not Western-centric, because by now Western society is no longer monogamous. Instead, the basis is a theologically and spiritually profound affirmation of the personhood of the other partner, which in most cases means an affirmation of the woman's personhood. That is close to what the gospel is about and to what Jesus was saying about the foundation of the permanence of marriage in the concept of one flesh (Gen 2:24), according to God's original purpose.

In each of these cases, all we can do now is identify the theme of finding in the host culture specific cultural challenges that call for response. Sometimes the response has been accommodation and syncretism; sometimes it has been radical foreignness and rejection. I have been suggesting that we must look for something in between these two: a radical call to decision for Christ but stated in the form of the available, relevant cultural options.

By now there is in most of the overseas host cultures a body of informed, intelligent, competent intellectual leaders who know both the Western world and their own. There are also well-oriented and flexible missionaries who know both worlds. Therefore, local and foreign Christians can work together as a team to sort out faithful relationships to culture, not starting from scratch, but clearing away past mistakes and clarifying past confusions.

12

THE CHURCH AS LAITY

Laity is a theologically laden word as it has come to be used in modern times. At its root it simply means "of the people." In the New Testament the *laos* or the *laikos* is everybody that belongs to God's people. To differentiate the laity from the clergy, further evolution was necessary. In its modern meaning, *laity* presupposes the specific ministries of priests and ministers; the laity is people who do not have specific, usually sacramental, ministries. How we use the word *laity* is, therefore, already theologically prejudiced because the New Testament says that *everybody* has a specific ministry, and our current use of *laity* assumes that there are people who do not.

We can explain this shift in terms of cultural accommodation or syncretism. Every society, whether highly developed or not, has the medicine man function. Sometimes this religious leader is qualified by special capacities, sometimes by special rites and initiation. Sometimes he or she is qualified by heredity: they are a shaman's son or granddaughter. In the Old Testament we can identify the priestly class, which was hereditary. There were the sons of Levi, the sons of Aaron, the sons of Zadok.

The New Testament does not, as is often said, abolish either the priesthood or the prophet as a special office, but rather abolishes the laity. Everyone is in some sense a prophet and priest. Everyone shares the rule of Christ. Everyone has a gift (1 Cor 12:7) and everyone has been called to use his or her own gift as it has been assigned (Rom 12:6-8). There is a multiplicity of recognizable ministries carried, in principle, by all members. A specific ministry is knowable because a person can be exhorted, as in Romans 12, to serve God according to the function and grace given them. If they are going to exercise a gift or live up to the assigned ministry, they have to know what it is.

None of the ministries in the New Testament is firmly tied to financial support, although some of them merit it, especially teaching. None of them is tied to heredity. None of them is tied to schooling, training or special ritual, although some may be helped by special training. None are more religious than the others in the sense of being sacramentally powerful or set apart in some peculiar status. In later church history, however, the concept of the priesthood—a few set-apart people who are special because of their training, ordination or function—resurged. Once this concept had sprung up again, as *clergy*, we had a corresponding change in the concept of laity.

I suggest that this is like the syncretistic cult of the dead or the other similar adaptations that happened in the second to fifth centuries when Christendom was formed. This is part of the fall of the church. It pervades and persists in places where we cannot explain its presence. For instance, the Zwinglian Reformation, where there is no concept of sacramental rites either for ordination or administering the Lord's Supper, maintains the concept of clergy. Even in the free churches like the Mennonites, Plymouth Brethren and Quakers, who even more radically affirm a variety of ministries or the critique sacramental ministry, the clergy still arises again and again.

The phenomenon of clergification is, I suggest, not simply an adjustment to pragmatic needs but a normal degeneration of a social group when it no longer grasps the concept of the multiplicity or the universality of ministry.

VISIONS OF THE LAITY IN FOREIGN MISSION

Most discussion of the laity as a theme in books about the ministry or the laity fall short of rediscovering the New Testament abolition of the laity. The two most popular statements of this have been that of Yves Congar from the Catholic world and Hendrik Kraemer from the Prot-

estant world.[1] We will look especially at three understandings of the
ministry of the laity as expressed in Reformed and Pietist theologies.

According to Kraemer, lay people are part of the church's mission and
ministry because they act as Christians in their professions and thereby
serve their neighbors and transform society. This is the modern restatement of the Reformed doctrine of vocation, or the Lutheran doctrine of the station. The classic Reformation took the monastic concept
of vocation, which said that a few people have the special calling of
the monk, and stood it on its head in order to fight monastic self-
righteousness and the salvation by works concept that the Protestants
thought underlay the monastic orders. The Reformers said, "Everyone is
called to be whatever he is *in* secular life. It is not only monks and nuns,
who pull *out* of secular life, who are called to be ministers." The concept
of vocation is a good way to think about one's job as being part of God's
will for society. But it is not new. It is very conservative.

Also, the Reformation concept of vocation is not missionary, because
the job in which one finds oneself is by definition something that is already there in society. Vocation is found within a structure of stability,
not of mobility. This approach does not critique society, because it assumes that the nature of one's job is given and everybody knows what it
means to be an employer or an employee, a lord or a serf. It assumes that
social structures, or at least the ideal as expressed in these structures, are
proper. We simply need to live up to them. In fact, it favors powerful
jobs over unpowerful jobs, which, of course, is not the image we get
from the Epistle of James or from the Gospels.[2]

Further, it is increasingly questionable in our society whether this
understanding of vocation—in the secular job sense and the sense of
being the place where I find meaning in my life as a Christian—is fea-
sible. First, there is a lot of work that is drudgery, work which one cannot

---

[1][See Yves Congar, *Lay People in the Church: A Study for a Theology of Laity*, 2nd ed. (Westminster,
MD: Newman Press, 1965) and Hendrik Kraemer, *A Theology of the Laity* (Philadelphia: Westminster Press, 1958). —Ed.]

[2]*Christianity Today* had a column titled, "A Layman and His Faith" that pulled together statements of people who wanted the clergy to stay out of politics and economics because they are
the business of the laymen. But all of the laymen they asked were wealthy. None of them were
employees. [The column, "A Layman and His Faith," ran from June 10, 1957, to September 26,
1975, in *Christianity Today*. —Ed.]

make important or meaningful by saying, "I am building a cathedral." Second, not everybody has work. The shape of society is such that increasingly we will need to find meaning in things that are not productive in the simple sense. These factors undercut the Reformation approach to the meaning of the lay vocation.

But those are all objections to the Reformation concept of the ministry of the laity that come from around its edge. To compare later understandings of the laity's ministry to New Testament thought is more fundamental, and it highlights a contrast. Jobs in the world, however important they are, and however desirable it is to take them seriously as Christians, have no correlation to the gifts in the New Testament. Romans 12, 1 Corinthians 12 and Ephesians 4 give us actual lists of the gifts or ministries, and scattered references elsewhere fill out the list a little more. And what are these ministries? They include apostle, prophet, teacher, presider, prophesier, speaker in tongues and healer. There is no reference to social functions or to the gamut of things that we do to make a living and make an economic contribution to society. It is said that some of these functions are worthy of financial support in the church, but even they are not identified that way as the province of the clergy. We misunderstand the New Testament concept of the multiplicity of gifts if we try to correlate it, as the Reformed doctrine does, with the multiplicity of social jobs. The New Testament gifts, which are spread among all members, are ways of participating in the Christian community, not ways of being socially useful in the world. The New Testament is in favor of both, but it does not use the same language for both.[3]

Witness through secular vocation is the central Protestant way of taking laity seriously. It does not call the clergy's distinctness into question at all, but tells lay people that they have their ministry to do also.

The other way of taking laity seriously appears in Pietism, the revivalist traditions, Christian Businessmen's Committee, International

---

[3]Although I cannot reduce the gifts to learned or innate skills, neither do I want to systematically distinguish such skills from New Testament gifts. If somebody has the gift of a prophet, that person is probably a good speaker. If someone has the gift of teacher, that person can probably make ideas become clear. There is a correlation between humanly discernible, physiologically based capacities to do things and gifts in the New Testament sense. But I do not think we can boil one down to the other.

Christian Leadership, the Gideons and the Presidential Prayer Breakfast. Here the layperson is seen as an individual who ought to talk to his or her neighbors about Jesus. The individual should be articulate, courageous and responsible in speaking to people about the faith. To encourage this, these agencies organize along socially segregated lines. That is, a Christian Businessmen's Committee is by definition socially stratified. International Christian Leadership is an organization that specifically focuses on people in high places. Like the Reformed approach, it favors the powerful people in a given society. There is an International Christian Leadership organization; there is not an International Christian Followership organization. The fact that some of these organizations give special visibility to people who have political or economic clout recreates in a new way denominational problems, because each of these organizations will have its own staff, fundraising techniques, particular theological slant and way of praying.

There is one more approach to the laity that is also constructive but does not quite reach the New Testament vision of the ministry of the laity: the Western loyal Christian layperson who goes to Japan, India or Africa not because a mission board sent him or her but because the person is working for Gulf Oil or for the government. How is that person a resource for church and mission? Mainstream American Protestant groups have tried to do something about this by creating American Protestant congregations in the major cities overseas. Sometimes this has been simply a counseling and liturgical resource for people who want to go to a familiar church. But in some places it has helped such people become aware of the national Christian church or of local social issues or economic needs to which they might address themselves at least in an amateur way.

The possibility of this becoming significant for a deeper missionary vocation rises as we have growing job mobility and growing difficulty of getting special missionaries into certain countries. A teacher, an engineer or a consultant for some complicated agricultural development problem can get into a country overseas that would not give a visa to a professional missionary. There is increasing attention being given, even by mission agencies, to self-supporting lay people who are making economically functional contributions to the life of countries where they are working, as a way to contribute to the church's missionary concerns. However, while there is increasing attention given to the laity overseas as a resource for the mission, it is not with great success in developing new forms.

But here, too, in this lay resource for mission, agencies assume the differentiation of laity and clergy. They set the sacramental and doctrinal life of the church apart from evangelism, service and fellowship. They do not usually think of the layperson overseas as a missionary but rather as an adjunct to or substitute for the clergy or as one who in advance opens up the terrain for the truly clerical or religious function that somebody else will have to do later.

All of these ways—the traditional Reformed way, the revivalistic way and the lay-people-working-overseas way—while all functional, useful, significant and positive in their place, do not get back to the New Testament message about universal ministry in the life of the church. For none of them is peoplehood the message. For none of them is a new style of being the people of God itself part of the Christian call and scandal. That observation does not immediately say what we can do differently, but it should make us more modest about the value of those particular correctives.

LIMITATIONS OF THE PROFESSIONAL MISSIONARY

Looking back at the vocation of the professional missionary from the perspective of the New Testament and subsequent history, we can observe some limitations of the missionary agency process. Again, the fact that the missionary organization is a distinct entity for supporting missionaries is a peculiarity arising out of its rootage in modern, post-Reformation Pietism.

In some specific respects the single professional missionary—the model in the modern missionary movement—cannot represent the reality of the church. First, the single professional missionary is not several people, and the church is always minimally several people. The fact that the missionary usually goes somewhere alone, especially in the initial missionary effort, means that neither at first nor afterward when a group of people have responded is there a church in the sense of a community, because the new Christians are respondents to this person's initiative rather than being simply his or her brothers and sisters.

More fundamentally, the single professional missionary by definition cannot dramatize the multiplicity of ministries in the community. It is difficult for the new local church to grasp the reality that everyone has gifts for ministry and that they need each other when the missionary is a highly gifted person who is trained, qualified and supported far beyond the resources of the local church in that society. They believe the missionary is able to do everything better than any of the new Christians will be able to do for at least the first generation.

Another limitation is that single professional missionaries in the modern form do not usually earn a living by economic involvement in the societies where they serve. In the New Testament church, a few traveling apostle-prophets lived from gifts of the church, but most of the congregation supported themselves. That was part of the church's missionary presence in that economy. While this is not the crucial way to understand the *ministry of the laity,* it is a crucial way to understand the church's *missionary presence in society*: most church members are doing something that their neighbors appreciate enough to pay them for it.

Perhaps still more deeply, what the single professional missionary cannot represent by definition is the coming together of Jews and Greeks. By definition the professional missionary cannot dramatize the reconciling of differences between antagonistic cultures and estranged communities in the new community that gathers in confessing the lordship of Christ.

In the initial period of the missionary effort, the professional is not a minister to an existing church in the same sense as would qualify a minister back home. The missionary is neither needed as a bishop nor as a theologian-teacher, for there is not yet a flock to be shepherded or a congregation of learners. The fact that the missionary usually retains church membership back home underlines this. The legitimacy of this person's ministerial status is even harder to explain in the new church than back home, where there are also questions about the propriety of the clergy image for missionaries.

There are additional efforts to redefine the laity that move in the direction of correction. The writings of Douglas Webster especially have given currency in modern interchurch missionary thinking to the phrase "tentmaking ministry." Webster tries to decrease the social and economic difference between the ministerial leadership in the young church and the surrounding society by having the person who is a priest or minister also earn his living.[4] But there is still a radical difference between a new tentmaking Anglican priest or a new tentmaking Presbyterian pastor and a tentmaking layperson. The sacramental specialization remains. The pastor or priest is still a clergyman. The distinction between clergy and laity is done away with at the point of whether one earns a living, but not at the point of congregational and theological uniqueness.

The other kind of widespread modern corrective, found especially in certain ecumenical circles, is to take someone who has been trained, assigned and working as a minister, and assign him or her to do something else—work for the city planning office, become a social worker or become a teacher. This is not for the purpose of having that person pay his or her way, but in order to say that many other things besides preaching are also worthy in God's sight. That is a good thing to affirm. That is what the old Reformed doctrine of vocation meant to affirm. But it is backwards to affirm that by sending some ordained person to work in a secular vocation, as if we could not affirm its worthiness by having anybody else do it.

In summary, we still have not found ways of reconstituting the vitality of the multiplicity of ministries by correcting here or there the way ministerial concepts have functioned in the missionary enterprise.

THE NEW TESTAMENT AND PROFESSIONAL MINISTRY

Let us back up and ask a different question. Was there such a thing as a missionary in the New Testament church? We have a handicap in figuring out an answer to this, because the particular concerns in the passages where we find the lists of ministries—Romans 12, 1 Corinthians 12 and Ephesians 4—are always interior concerns. That is, it is not the

---

[4]This does not affect the missionary, though.

writer's prior agenda in any of those cases to provide a complete list of all possible ministries or functions but only to talk about those that are present when the congregation is thinking about the community's inner life. But that should not keep us from asking the question.

The first candidate for a missionary function is the *apostle*, a word that means "one who is sent." This seems to be the obvious linguistic equivalent of *missionary*. Yet most of the people called apostles in the New Testament did not go anywhere. If we look more closely at how the concept of apostle functioned in the debates about apostolic status, the word *sending* or the root *to send* had to do more with the question of having the authority to represent the Lord than it had to do with traveling to a new location, itinerating or founding new churches. Paul debated with others about whether he had seen the Lord or witnessed the Resurrection, but not whether he was supposed to go to Rome or to Corinth. This apostolic status, according to recent scholarship, is clearly understood to be unique: it was there for one generation and was not transmitted further. If the apostle is the only New Testament equivalent of the missionary, there is no biblical basis for missionaries since the office of apostle was not continued in the church.

We find a second possible term for missionary in 2 Timothy 4:5: "Do the work of an *evangelist*." We know what a contemporary evangelist is, so we assume that this is what it meant in the New Testament too. However, it could not mean what today is meant by *evangelist*. Our society conceives of an evangelist in a quite specialized way: one who does a particular kind of public speaking to large audiences in a tent or stadium. Obviously that is not what 2 Timothy meant. If we look at the context of 2 Timothy 4, the concern was for a function within the community that could deal with false doctrine. The evangelist had a teaching function, a ministry of relating the message to the doctrinal issues of the time. Everything else that we know about Timothy confirms that he was a pastor, in the sense of responsibility for the local congregation's faithfulness. So it would seem that in New Testament usage, if we want to be careful in our exegesis, the evangelist upheld one aspect of the teaching ministry's concern for the faithfulness of the local church, rather than being a specialist in outreach. That does not mean that the New Testament church was not missionary in its character. But these texts call us to doubt that the missionary function was delegated to one person or to a particular small category of people. In Acts, the church's mobility was the whole church's mobility. The word *you* in the Great Commission is in the plural.[5] There is the assumption that the church will be going, but only in the sense that everybody will be going: "As *you* go."

MIGRATION EVANGELISM

For many centuries the church grew by migration and the subsequent incorporation of their new neighbors. It was not until the Middle Ages that monks went places as specialists to plant churches. Augustine of Canterbury was sent to England. Many others went into the Germanic territories. Later, missionary orders like the Jesuits came into being. But the Jesuits were not founded until the sixteenth century. The growth of the church for the first thousand years was the growth of the whole church going places, as slaves, merchants or economic refugees. They went to places where they could or were forced to make a living and then expressed their Christian faith there.[6]

It would make sense from the perspective of theological critique and vision to try to restore a sense of the church's mission being that of the whole church, to be discharged neither by envoys nor specialists, but by the community itself. If this is the case, let mission be done by a community that migrates to live in the new place. Such a community can meet its neighbors ordinarily in the business of making a living. Such a community can demonstrate what a loving relationship is like in this new peoplehood. Such a community can take on the task of adapting

---

[5]I say this apart from the observation we made earlier that it is not technically a commission.

[6][In his pamphlet *As You Go*, Yoder wrote, "This church growth was not a matter of organized 'missions.' Christians, often serving as artisans or merchants, . . . established themselves farther and farther from their original homes, taking their faith with them and making an economic contribution to the society into which they moved. . . . The place of 'ministers' in this expansion was definitely a secondary one. Teachers and bishops were called to the frontier areas when there were already sufficient Christians there to have need of their services in teaching, and in organizing common worship. Still later, when the Germanic tribes of Western Europe were also progressively brought within hearing of the Gospel, this work was not done by specialized preaching ministers sent from a distance. Instead, colonies of monks supported themselves in the economic and cultural life of their people." John Howard Yoder, *As You Go*, Focal Pamphlet No. 5 (Scottdale, PA: Mennonite Publishing House, 1961), pp. 13-14 (405-6). —Ed.]

the faith to a new culture, of deciding together when it is worthwhile to maintain a foreign cultural form and at what point it is wise to adopt a local form. A group of people dealing with this problem is more likely to be responsible and reasonable than a lone professional. If a missionary community actually migrated to a new place, there would be no crisis of devolution, where first the mission runs the church and then at some point it flips over to local management. The migrant community would not be a mission agency, but would already be a new local church. There would not be the problem of the church being self-supporting, self-multiplying, or of not having long-range identification with that culture.[7]

But this New Testament model—which is also to some extent the model followed in some Anabaptist, Mennonite and American frontier experience—has limits in applicability. We observed in earlier chapters that the New Testament mission did not go to all societies. Paul did not go, as far as we know, anywhere except to those parts of the Roman Empire where there was already a Jewish Diaspora. We have no New Testament examples, and therefore no guidance in concrete form, about how to plant the church in a primitive African tribal culture or in the highly developed religious culture of a place like India.

CONCLUSION

The choices then seem to be between two logical alternatives. One is the cultural colonialism or imperialistic model—to move in bringing one's own civilization. We have dealt with the wrong kind of foreignness that this establishes, the cultural anticolonial reaction, and the problem of deciding when the church will become national. The other extreme would seem to be full respect for the existing culture. In relation to this, we dealt with the difficulty of the missionary knowing at what point to adapt or to refuse to adapt to the local culture. We have noted how this approach does not avoid foreignness, because the missionary is still a foreigner in talking about Jesus and probably in financial status. We rec-

---

[7]I do not mean to be saying that there are not many ways to be a Christian witness wherever you are. I am trying to speak in the framework of the church sitting down to say, "Now we want to proclaim in the best possible way and in the most possible places the most faithful possible message."

ognized the fact that the professional missionary's effort to respect the native culture will probably be overrun by other less conscientious kinds of invasion, such as corporations. This missionary approach is only thinkable as long as the individual specialist has an outside base to keep his or her foreign status clear.

My suggestion is that in between these two alternatives with their shortcomings is the migration evangelism model. Despite the difficulties and the fact that the New Testament does not speak to this model, I believe we have sufficient reason to consider the migration of groups of Christians as an alternative form of mission. We cannot always migrate everywhere. There are countries that do not want immigrants. But there are others that accept them if they come with a desire to stay.[8] The immigrants who would come would be less shocking than a mission agency, in that they would likely keep their own culture through their first generation of children, but only in their own circles.[9] Very few host societies would hold that against them. Missionary migrants coming to stay in a place will in the long run feel much freer and more mandated to make the adaptations of cultural identification. That is not to say that the New Testament doctrine of the church demands that the only way that the church spreads must be by migration. But there seems to be a certain correlation between New Testament ecclesiology and migration evangelism, enough to make it worth looking at this model of mission more deeply than our churches have done thus far.

---

[8][Yoder did not note this, but in the current situation where mission is beginning to flow from the South to the secularized West and North, the theology and model of migration mission may well serve immigrant Christians in these areas. In class discussion, Yoder did indicate that the model might be applicable for urban or crosscultural mission by Western churches in their native lands. He referred to people from rural churches who gradually move into town, form a congregation and become a new "center of witness," even without an aggressive vision for this. —Ed.]

[9]If there would be a large migration like a half million Lutherans coming from Germany to live in South America, there is a new danger of the creation of a cultural enclave and a group that will not be missionary.

13

MINISTRY IN A
MISSIONARY CONTEXT

There is an obvious overlap between the last chapter on the laity and this chapter on ministry, in that both are traditionally defined in contrast to one another. This chapter carries on an issue that was already raised: namely, the peculiar understanding of the missionary as minister. What is the theological understanding of the missionary vocation as a distinct ministry, and how does it relate to emerging local leadership?

THE PROBLEM IN HISTORICAL CONTEXT

We observed that the two most obvious terms in the New Testament which would at first sight seem to point to a distinct missionary profession do not quite fit. *Apostle* has nonrepeatable elements—an apostle is someone who had seen the risen Lord—and *evangelist*, on closer examination, referenced a teaching responsibility within the community, especially as the community was faced with heresy. Although the mandate to be on the road or to be witnesses "as you go" was clear to the New Testament church, this function was not assigned as a specialty to particular individuals. The missionary vocation arose in the late medieval Catholic orders when outreach became a specialty and then in the great Protestant, Pietist-oriented missionary movement beginning with the late seventeenth century.

In established religion—that is, Catholicism and Protestantism before Pietism—ministry or clergy was a particular class of persons, relatively small in size, but important. Those few people's activities constitute the church's work. In Catholicism this is defined in terms of sacraments the clergy may perform. In Protestant form, it is less focused at the point of sacrament and more focused at the point of teaching and preaching true doctrine and administering proper order. But in both cases it is what the visible, specialized clergy does that constitutes the church.

The Reformation in one way and then Pietism in another renewed the clergy. The Reformation said a minister ought to be a faithful believer in the sense of true doctrine and ethical living. The minister should do a good job of proclaiming the Word. Then Pietism said that the minister should not only be orthodox and moral, but also personally pious, meaning a person with a changed heart and vibrant inward faith. The Radical Reformation orientation and some later revivals, at least in tendency but never thoroughly, created a new leadership from among the membership rather than simply renewing the concept of clergy. They seldom fully affirmed the universality of ministry as the New Testament does, but they experienced the plurality of ministry. Thus starting with the Radical Reformation, various revival movements at least began to call into question the clergy's peculiar status. The most extreme forms of an alternate pattern were Quakerism and the Plymouth Brethren, who in one way or another actually denied the concept of a special clergy.

PREVIOUS ATTEMPTS TO ADDRESS THE MISSIONARY'S STATUS

Missionary experience in the modern sense—that is, an organized movement going to other parts of the world—met this issue of clergy at two specific points.

The status of the missionary as minister. What was peculiar about the person who left the home church to be a missionary? In what sense was that a particular ministry? The normal pattern was taken for granted. The home church—in Germany the *Volkskirche* or structured people's church—validated the missionary vocation and granted missionary status. It tested whether the person was acceptable in the European pattern and decided whether or not to ordain a person and whether to assign them to the mission society or to a parish.

From this beginning—assuming that a church overseas came into being, became increasingly responsible and grew in time to maturity—there were three ways in which the status of the missionary minister could proceed in the local setting and two ways the missionary might move on from that place.

First, in the beginning of the nineteenth century, the most prevalent way for the status of the missionary to change was *withdrawal upwards*. That is, the evangelist helped bring into being a congregation and then became their pastor, taking on a new local responsibility. As more churches developed, this missionary pastor became the bishop or senior overseer of the process. The leadership of the overseas church fellowship remained in the hands of the missionary who brought his or her status along from the home church. In this pattern, foreign leadership tended to remain longer than in some other patterns.

In a second pattern, the missionary became a specialist instead of a generalist. That is, instead of moving from evangelist to pastor to bishop, the missionary moved from generalist to specialist. This was a *horizontal withdrawal*. The missionary started out having to do everything but increasingly did fewer things with greater concentration. The person may have become only a hospital administrator or only a Christian education resource person and, gradually, more and more precisely the specialist in this task. If the mission lasted into the second and third generation, the mission agency recruited people for those specialties rather than for a general missionary. Once the agency sought a hospital administrator, the home church did not see any need to ordain that person. Where did the missionary status go in that process of change?

In a third form, the missionary was no longer a missionary at all, but a fraternal worker. This change of status could be called *withdrawal and return*. Once there was a self-governing local community, the missionary was not a missionary anymore in the sense of representing the home church in planting a church. That had been done. So the missionary became a fraternal worker on loan to the local church as needed and under its government.

In a fourth pattern, rather than trying to evolve in the role, the missionary moved on to be a missionary somewhere else. Because the local church was established and responsible, the status of the missionary became *withdrawal without return*. This pattern is most firmly incorporated in institutional form and self-understanding in the Christian Missionary Alliance, in which the missionary makes a point of not being part of the local church. As soon as the local church is organized and able to do its own business, the missionary will not go to its meetings and consciously stays away from the local church's conference sessions so as not to become a powerful member of the ongoing church life, which would denaturalize or denationalize its function.

Finally, some missionaries became truly incorporated into the host culture, a status we could call *integration* or *identification*. There are some cultures where integration is impossible because the people are hostile to outsiders, because of political barriers or because the cultural leap is so great that it is not thinkable to be part of it in any deep or permanent sense. There are other places where it would be possible to go rather far in integrating oneself into the host culture. Should the missionary do that? Which missionaries should do that? If the missionaries were ready to take on economic self-support and perhaps formal citizenship, educate their children in the host country and be willing to see them marry there, and plan to retire in that place, the missionaries would cease to be technically missionaries sent from back home. They would become permanent members of the local community. They would still bring the particular gifts associated with having come from somewhere else, but they would progressively seek to release their status as missionary and to become a permanent immigrant member of that community. This is, of course, easiest in an immigrant culture, that is, a culture in which many people had grandparents born somewhere else. This would be the case for Australia, the United States and Canada, but it is also true for Argentina, Uruguay and Brazil. In these countries it would be possible to become naturalized socially, culturally and politically and to identify not only one's own future, but also one's children's future, with that place.

In summary, there seem to be five options for the status of the missionary in his or her distinct ministry: withdrawal upwards, withdrawal horizontally, withdrawal and return as a fraternal worker, moving on to a new mission setting and integration into the host culture.

Dimensions of foreignness. We have already identified some of the issues related to the foreignness of mission efforts in chapter ten, "The Church as Responsible." They result partly from the home church's established status. At this point we will look more carefully at what foreignness means for the status of the missionary person. One issue that has come into focus more clearly in the last generation is to affirm the importance and the validity of foreignness: it is not simply negative. However, there are several quite different approaches to the problem of foreignness that are worth spelling out more fully.

Assuming foreignness on only one side. In the early missionary period there was not much awareness that the missionary was foreign. The missionaries thought the other people were foreign, which clearly assumed that normative Christian identity is what they had back home.

An embarrassed foreignness. A second approach is to assume that we are the foreigners. We are embarrassed at being in the host culture. We ought to step aside as soon as possible, because our presence interferes with the authenticity of the local church and we make them unsure of their responsibility. Our foreignness also makes the church suspect in the eyes of the surrounding pagans and even in the eyes of the national believers. The anthropologist, cultural sensitivity and political awareness all push in the same direction. There is the tendency to assume that foreignness is completely bad, dangerous or a threat to the authenticity of the local church's life.

New Testament foreignness. The next possibility is that some kind of foreignness is a good thing. But what kind? What is the valid foreignness that should be maintained, a foreignness that is theologically desirable to have represented in the church's life whether at home or in the host culture? After having observed the pendulum that swings between being too foreign and being embarrassed about foreignness, we are pushed toward taking more seriously what we observed earlier—that the crossing of borders, the breaking down of walls of hostility, is part of the church's meaning and identity. Part of what it means to be Christian in India is to care about the perspective of Christians in Europe, North America and South America, and vice versa. But we have not built this caring about others adequately into the structure of our own communities. If we really care about the fact that there is a Christian community around the world, we will send some people to other places, and we will invite some people from there to our home churches. The old way to talk about this was that if we do not send somebody to the people who have not heard the gospel, they will be lost. That is simple and proper and a way to get the concern for relationship started, but that is not the only reason. New Testament foreignness—the reality that Jews and Gentiles, and by extension all peoples, are one in Christ—calls for it.

Prophetic foreignness. Another reason why every Christian community needs the presence of people from elsewhere is to protect the church against selling out to the local cultural spirit of the times: provincialism, cultural idolatry, self-centeredness and new forms of paganization.[1] Christians in India would be helped if there would be among them people from other parts of the world to ask whether they are too patriotic or not patriotic enough. Christians in North America would be helped in the same way. If we are going to take foreignness seriously as protection against provincialism, then we should highlight the importance of people who come from other places as representatives of another church's perspective. A shortcoming of how we have understood missionary ministry is that it goes only one way, usually from the West to the South. The recovery of a prophetic foreignness could mean that missionaries are sent from India or Indonesia, Taiwan or Japan, Colombia or Africa with a message to the European or American community, rather than the other way around. The need for prophetic foreignness is a reason for churches to continue to support a missionary ministry. That missionary purpose does not run out; rather, the vocation of a prophetic missionary becomes more and more visible as a needed element in the global church.

Itinerant foreignness. Another way to work at this problem is to assign to specific individuals with rare, narrowly focused skills the status of

---

[1] [Yoder associates pagan and paganization not simply with non-Christian religions (which he does in a descriptive, not intentionally derogatory sense), but also with consumerism at Christmas and Easter, the assumption that Christians should never challenge military budgets, and blatant disregard for prisoners as human beings. —Ed.]

itinerant leaders. Their missionary vocation and function is to be an agent for linking communities in a variety of settings, as the apostle Paul or Menno Simons were. This is different from what the established missionary profession has meant, but it is a special function that is extremely strategic in some cases. A person who has been so many places, has so much insight and has sufficient mandate as a visiting authority makes a contribution everywhere he or she goes.[2]

THE STATUS OF THE MISSIONARY AS MODEL

Another issue that derives from the status of the missionary as minister is the practically unavoidable fact that the missionary becomes the model minister for the new local church, at least initially. In early mission work, the first example new Christians had of how to be a minister was the missionary. Already for most missionaries coming from Europe, the ministry had been defined in a somewhat high church way. But in the host culture and young church, the understanding of the authority and style of the minister was almost unavoidably higher, more specialized, more sacramental and more authoritative than back home. This was so first of all because the educational standards for the minister were much farther from the average educational and cultural level of the first-generation people being served than was the case between ministers and people in the home country. This would be different if one went to urban centers overseas. But, in the average case, the cultural distance in terms of education, specialization and capacities between the missionary and the members of the new church was greater than back home. This led the new church to see missionary ministers as having a special theological status, as rare and uniquely qualified persons.

A second reason the younger churches had a higher view of the missionary than the European or North American churches did was that the missionary minister arrived before there were many Christians, whereas back home he or she was one of hundreds or even thousands

---

[2]The Methodist E. Stanley Jones is perhaps the best twentieth-century example of this kind of ministry. Though he had left the mission field many years before, he was a world figure always traveling and making his particular contribution, and he could not have done this had it not been for some recognition of that peculiar ministry.

of Christians. Because the missionary minister was more select in proportion to the population in the new church, the tendency to dominate that small group of people was greater. In all these ways, the missionary as a model minister projected a more high-church vision of the role than was the missionary's own self-understanding back home.

This model of the minister proceeded into the first generation of national leaders because the first leaders were usually chosen and trained on the basis of their aptness to receive the education the mission planned to give. The status that the mission gave to local church leaders on the basis of their qualifications for ordination or formal education was not a status that grew gradually out of the community that first called the local leaders. Rather it was given from outside—from the mission, from the school or even from the foreign entity that had approved of their ordination. Even the sociology of the missionary situation made the thrust toward a sacral or high-clerical vision of the ministerial status much stronger than back home.

This status was a special problem for the integrity of missionary ministers because it failed to mesh with what they thought their ministry identity was back home. It was even more of a problem if one of the conflicts between the people of God and the host culture concerned the concept of a sacral office: a clergyman, a medicine man, a priestly person, a shaman. One mark of pagan religion is the function of the sacral religionist, a role that extends back into primitive forms of tribal community. The priest figure goes all the way back into high cultural forms like ancient Babylon and Egypt. A few specialized people doing religious things is part of any non-Christian culture, whereas the originality of biblical faith, beginning in the Old Testament with the fact that Abraham is a layman but going much further in the New Testament, is the abolition of priesthood. As we noted in the last chapter, although there were many ministries in the early church, there was no priesthood. There was no sacred person on whose status the church's identity depended. But reclerification came back into Christianity, and that is one of the elements with which we have struggled since.

That reclerification of institutional religion is somewhat undercut in the West by pluralism, by the fact that the minister comes from our midst rather than being a uniquely qualified foreigner and by our socio-logical self-awareness, so that we no longer believe in the mysterious set-apartness of the ordained. But if in the first-generation missionary situation, there is something about the structure of the ministry that quickly tends to create a high-church clergy concept, then we have to ask whether that development is a syncretistic accommodation to the pagan expectation that there be a holy man figure. This question of syncretism and the clergy would have to be tested in many places, of course, and we might well get different answers. There were places where—because the missionaries wanted to undercut their foreignness, or perhaps in other cases because they were not watching—the local culture clearly made the culture's medicine man and the church leader equivalent. For in-stance, in some Indian tribal cultures when a tribe converted, the med-icine man or his succeeding nephew became the preacher. A missionary in the South Pacific reported to me that the same person would lead a proper Presbyterian worship service in the church and then go around behind the church and sacrifice a chicken. His ministry was usable on both levels of cultural awareness. I suggest that this kind of syncretism and split life is at least questionable and that something about the shape of the missionary as a unique minister makes it hard to struggle against this tendency; it might even feed it.

There are various ways to try to dismantle the handicap of the high status of the missionary minister as a model for church leaders in the new churches. One is to address the issue of economic support. The fact that the missionary is economically supported by the home church or mission board is one of the reasons that the model of ministry is unique. But this is something that could be changed, and it is one of the elements carried over from the missionary to the local pastor that creates difficulty for the local church. In the first generation of missionary operation, the initial native ministerial leaders were supported from mission funds, as was the foreign missionary. That had a number of questionable effects. For one thing it drew more people into church professions than the local church could support later. When support for church professions could not be continued or expanded, it began to discredit ministry as a vo-cation, since other elements of society made room for economic promotion and the church did not. The university, medical systems and government all opened up as avenues for professional promotion. But the church was no longer a main place for career advancement as it was in the first two generations. This is one of the big developmental problems in Africa. People do not respect church leaders as they did before because they are not the unique, culturally prepared native people in this generation that they were several generations ago.

One alternative for dealing with the issue of economic support for local leaders has been to try to restore the vision of the tentmaking ministry. This runs against the stream of Western professional promotion, which by now is pretty well implanted in the rest of the world. To tell an African minister that he or she should not think of becoming a pastor as a path to professional promotion, after such promotion is what local leaders had been led to expect two or three generations ago, is problematic.

In addition to the loss of prestige and opportunity for professional promotion, emphasis on tentmaking ministry places a heavy load on the local church leader. According to Episcopalian standards, for instance, it is not that everybody is a minister and everybody makes tents and each ministry is a fraction of the community. It is rather that this one person is the priest of the parish and will have to continue that ministry and earn a living on the side. Since the local church does not have a theology for shared ministry, the priest has a much heavier work burden than anyone else in the community.

The issue of foreign economic support for the missionary is being looked at again. There are experiments with missionary self-support in the local economy. That looks like a new idea since the 1940s, but actually it is very old. That is the way William Carey started in India. But, of course, there are only certain parts of the world where it is likely to be workable.

Another way to dismantle the problem of economic support is to look at the issue of sacramental authorization itself. What does it mean to be an ordained minister? How will we recognize the qualification of local leadership to be ministers? If we use the standards from the church at home, standards that are so high and so distant culturally, then new Christian leaders will require economic support as they study and prepare for ministry.[3]

What would it mean to begin to dismantle that set of assumptions about church and ministry? Roland Allen, an Anglican, said that it is theologically improper to say that people should prepare for recognition as a Christian community without having available resources for being recognized as a Christian community, namely, the Lord's Supper, local ministry, and capacity to bind and loose in the church. If the foreign church does not let the local church have that experience by ordaining a bishop right away, how can it ask them to grow until they meet its requirements for authorization as a church? That is Roland Allen's argument: whatever we think is necessary for the Christian life we ought to make available immediately.

A second argument, which Allen also used, was an appeal to the apostle Paul, who quickly named elders in every church. We have to be careful about that argument because in the cases that are reported, the elders that Paul named probably had been synagogue elders in the Jewish congregation for some time. So they were not new converts. But it is still the case that Paul immediately equipped a congregation to be self-governing and provided whatever authorization it needed in terms of recognized leadership.

A third argument is that the church and its ministers are already truly present. For instance, the people that a mission calls *leaders* in rural churches are genuinely ministers; we just do not recognize it. But we ought to, because the church and the ministry are real.

---

[3]What often happens is that rather than leaving local communities without any leadership, the missionary structure creates—without any theology for it—a number of different levels of leadership, with lower standards for ministry than what is required for ministers back home. In one Mennonite overseas context there were three such levels. One was called *the leader*, and this person was authorized to be in charge of local rural meetings. The next highest level was called *the teacher*. The government recognized this person as authorized to have a school, and he was supported through that function but was also the head of the congregation that met in the school building. Then there was a *catechist*, who was above the teacher and was supported partly by the common church fund, which was largely subsidized by the mission. None of these people were ordained in the sense that back home it would entitle them to celebrate the Lord's Supper or to baptize. So these particular Mennonite churches lived for years with no national leadership that the mission recognized as qualified for full ministerial status. It was the missionary alone who had the communion glasses.

14

People Movements and the Free Church

The free church critique of the way Christendom merged people and church, and the use of the believers church model in the missionary context, have become subjects of criticism. A particular challenge—the subject of this chapter—comes from people movements: concern to respect cultural patterns of group decision and the church growth mission strategy. Some insights from cultural anthropologists with regard to both the practice and theory of mission seem to militate against a theology of the believers church. Therefore, we have a decision to make. We must either reject these missionary insights—even though they have anthropology on their side—because we claim they are theologically wrong, or we must change our theology to fit the insights.

Radical Reformation Critique of the Christendom Model of Church

While one thrust of the Radical Reformation was to question sacramental ministry, another thrust questioned the relation of the church as a new people in relation to the existing cultural, national, provincial and imperial unity. The believers church critique said that Christendom was basically wrong to merge people and church, and wrong in two dimensions: wrong at home by including every citizen in the church and wrong in the wider vision by identifying the church with Christendom and no other people.

These two mistakes were linked. Church, society and state were identified in one happy synthesis. Since everybody was a church member, membership was not very demanding at the outset. But education followed membership and sought to move each person at his or her own pace toward greater understanding of and devotion to Christianity. On a wider scale, the leader, such as Clovis or Charlemagne, spoke and made decisions for the whole population. The leaders decided whether the whole society was to be Christian, and once they decided it would be, the church became responsible for everyone's needs.

The Radical Reformation rebelled against this with numerous criticisms. First, it insisted on individual conversion and baptism. A Christian was someone who had made a personal, responsible decision to confess faith and be baptized. Second, within society, people's needs were not all the same; some needs were higher priority than others. Without saying that other needs were unimportant, the Anabaptists believed that spiritual needs had priority and therefore focused on forming communities for meeting those needs. They believed the way one became a Christian was by conversion, not by education. Both of these emphases—the priority of the spiritual values and individual conversion—entailed a new community that was different from the given group that was Christendom.

THREE CRITICISMS OF THE FREE CHURCH VISION OF MISSION

Three strands of criticism raise questions about the theology of the free church and its impact in the missionary context. While the three critiques can be separated, and should be separated for some purposes, they line up together in the present discussion.

The first critique arises within the longer-range discussion of Christian social responsibility. The perception is that the free churches are concerned only for spiritual needs, not broader society's needs. The criticism is that the church, even when a minority within a society, should not be responsible only for evangelism or cultivating internal community solidarity, but should care about neighbors, justice, social structures and human needs more generally. Social responsibility *cannot* be set aside because even if one claims to do so, as some Pietists would, we live within the wider social realm. We noted earlier that those missionary agencies and people, who claimed to address only spiritual needs and individual conversion, started building schools and hospitals because they could not help it when they saw the need. The critique is that free church missionaries, in fact, do those things which have a Christendom orientation, things based not on conversion but on caring for nonspiritual needs, even when they think they are not doing so.

However, the critics' connection of free church separateness from wider society with lack of social concern lines up differently from the way their superficial argument assumes. We do not have to grant that the distinction between church and world means that free church groups are less concerned for the structure of society, for injustice or social ethics, as I have argued elsewhere in my theological work.[1]

A second set of critical responses to the free church vision is to say that it did not work in missionary situations when tried. One problematic dimension was how missionaries understood the holiness or purity of the church. Some earlier Mennonite missionaries in one Third World country, for instance, were guided in their efforts by a vision of a called-out, pure church. When a revival movement came into the area, it uncovered considerable evidence that the bride of Christ was not pure. All those who confessed to be living in sin were excommunicated and slowly reinstated. The critics are right that the effort to establish a pure church in this sense did not work. But this understanding of the purity of the church is faulty. The free church vision does not claim the church is pure. However, the *calling* of the church to purity is instrumental in her discipline process. It is the process—meaningful baptism and binding and loosing—to which the group is committed, not the claim to have arrived.

Another difficulty is that it is not always clear when people are being baptized on genuine confession of faith and when they are baptized simply because they wish it. Critics point out that the effort of Baptists or Mennonites to plant churches in another part of the world

---

[1] [The most accessible place where Yoder addresses the issue of a free church vision of social ethics is in his book *The Priestly Kingdom* (Notre Dame: University of Notre Dame Press, 1984). —Ed.]

has resulted in little Christendoms; not all their members seem to be deeply committed and not all congregations seem to function like believers churches.

The third challenge, which backs up these other challenges, comes from people movements, concern to respect cultural patterns of group decision, and the church growth mission strategy. The earliest term, *people movements*, arose in the 1930s to describe phenomena in Africa and India where certain tribes or ethnic castes would open themselves rapidly and massively to the missionaries and want to become Christians faster than the missionaries were ready to deal with them, according to their traditional one-by-one process. The missionaries usually found ways to accept a whole village or tribal territory, but it raised new questions. *Group decision* is the phrase that anthropologists use to talk about this phenomenon and its nature in certain cultures. *Church growth* is a school of missionary thought that seeks to make the most of the decision potential of any culture, especially with regard to missionary strategy and tactics. These challenges we will explore further in the remainder of this chapter.

SOCIAL-SCIENCE GROUNDS FOR THE CRITIQUES

Several disciplines and areas of thought contribute to these three strands that critique the free church vision of mission.

One is an anthropological observation. Group decision is the way decisions are actually made in certain other cultures. The Western individualistic idea of making a decision all by oneself is foreign to the way many people make their decisions in other parts of the world. The way they decide about getting married, the way they decide about what ethical standards apply, the way they decide where to live and what work to do is in a communal way. Therefore, it is foreign to the local culture to bring the invitation to follow Christ as a decision for individuals to make, because this projects a model of "real" conversion as an individual process. Therefore, critics say, the believers church approach does not work because it is based on individual decision.

Second, the sociology of church growth—most strongly represented by Donald McGavran and his colleagues—focuses on the statistical pattern that emerges after people have decided to convert. This applies in pluralistic urban societies as well as in simple tribal societies. The church grows through homogeneous cultural and social units. In a pluralistic society there are different class and cultural groups. For instance, in East Africa before they started being expelled, the Indians were one particular group of society. In much of Southeast Asia, there is an expatriate Chinese class. In India there are caste lines. Even in a culture that has only one race, there are different social and professional classes. Church growth theory claims the church grows most rapidly through the links that already exist among people in a homogeneous cultural unit. So we should accept that kind of identification and establish a church of the poor, a middle-class church or an immigrants' church. We should recognize and exploit the fact that a special group is particularly open to a shift of loyalty and try to get as many people as possible to become Christian through that collective decision process. We should identify target populations for the growth of the church and make it as easy as possible for that category of people to accept the faith by stating the faith in terms that they can accept. McGavran called *discipling* the process of sweeping people as rapidly as possible into membership. Once they are members, lead them to a fuller understanding of faith just as any new believer is to be nurtured—but in greater numbers. This capacity to take in great numbers of new disciples is hampered if we are too concerned about the quality or purity of faith. Therefore, to get maximum church growth there should be less concern for discipleship in the Anabaptist Mennonite sense.

The third critique results from evaluation of past individual-centered missionary efforts in the majority world. When missionary efforts have been effective in winning individuals, it has meant winning them out of the family or clan, resulting in that person being cut off socially. They were social castaways who depended on the mission for fellowship and sometimes even for economic survival. They could not help but create a new caste, a new group of people whose only real access was to each other. In addition, they had no further evangelism potential in their own social contexts. This critique notes that this individualized, conversion-centered missionary approach did not win many individuals, and those who did become Christians did not create missionary churches but defensive enclaves, even in situations where there was great need for Christian ministry and mission. This negative argument reinforces the other positive argument that claims we need tactics and patterns of church growth that can follow and mine the lines of openness in the social stratification without breaking natural links. This means not asking the first person who listens to forsake all for the gospel, because we still want that person to reach his or her neighbors or relatives. We do not baptize the first person who comes, but wait until the family comes. We might not even baptize the first family, but wait until they bring the rest of the clan or at least the chief.

Based on all of these lines of critique, some would say that for the sake of the believers church, we must reject the church growth movement. Others would say that for the sake of church growth, we must reject believers church theology. Both answers are too simple. We should expect to spend more time and effort on a less black and white resolution of the questions raised here. Therefore, I will put forward a few theses in the direction of that resolution, but will not claim to resolve it. My overall thesis will be that we do not have to choose between these two alternatives. The question has been put wrongly. But we do learn something by working through it rather than dodging it.

A FREE CHURCH RESPONSE TO THE SOCIAL-SCIENCE CRITIQUES

The first thing we need to test is whether the analysis that contemporary missionary anthropology has made about the free church truly reflects its theological assumptions or whether the analysis is based on prejudices that distort the free church position. According to this analysis, church growth advocates have a tolerant, flexible understanding of minimal commitment. On the other hand, the believers church demands an excessively high level of Christian maturity as a precondition for baptism. But, as a matter of both historical experience and theological commitment, what is distinctive about the believers church is not that it demands a high level of maturity at the point of membership but that it demands commitment to a process of binding and loosing, admonition and ongoing growth which makes for maturation. It does not expect a person to be on top of all his or her problems or to have a high level of understanding before baptism. There are second, third and tenth generation Mennonite and Baptist churches making that kind of demand, but there are also many that are not. To critique the believers church for having too high discipleship demands at the point of membership is a red herring.

Second, the assumption that free churches would unilaterally reject a people-movement decision to become Christian because it is the opposite of individual conversion fails to distinguish between decision making by political control backed by superior force and genuine political spokesmanship. There is a difference between Clovis deciding that all his Franks would become Christian and a Central American Indian chief speaking for his village in asking for baptism, after having heard anyone who wanted to speak give their response to the missionary's visit. The latter is genuine spokesmanship; the former is the power of the sword. Both are group decisions, but they are different kinds of group decision. Moreover, there is certainly a difference between the creativity and adequacy of a communication event that wins the listeners' assent noncoercively and any kind of pressure that brings forth a less-than-genuine decision.

The anthropologically oriented critics of the believers church concept do not usually distinguish—as believers church people have done ever since the sixteenth century—between the sword and peoplehood, that is, between recourse to formal violent political power as a sanction for the authority of the one who governs and the fact that a social group exists. It is at the point of the sword, not at the point of peoplehood, that the believers church has critiqued Christendom, and that issue has not been identified in the recent debate about how concern for church growth should call us to abandon believers church commitment. The perception that the believers church is opposed to group decision does not take its history seriously enough.

Third, cultural anthropologists wrongly assume that personal decision as a basis for membership in the believers church is the same basis as Western individualism provides. The cultural anthropologist takes for granted that the form in which a Baptist or a revivalist preacher within the last century would have put the call to individual decision is similar to that of the believers church. That is, they assume a high level of concentration on how every individual is an isolated self and makes his or her own choices. That is understandable, but it is again historically shortsighted, because the believers church vision had origins other than Western individualism. In fact, its origin in the renewal movements of the fifteenth and sixteenth centuries emphasized peoplehood. The point was not that every individual makes a heroic decision for Christ as a lone self, but simply that assent to the community's identity must be personal. There was no emphasis in the fifteenth, sixteenth or even much in the seventeenth century on how individualistic an anthropology one must have for a decision for Christ to be valid.

Finally, the believers church versus group decision debate assumes that the only alternatives for becoming part of the church are Western individualistic personal decision on the basis of full information, doctrinal understanding and independent self-awareness, on the one hand, and a collective pattern on the other that involves infant baptism and automatic membership for all the community's members. This means excluding before the discussion begins precisely what we ought to be discussing, namely, whether the believers church is properly understood as a collective reality in which the individual and group are held together in relationship within the whole, rather than being set up as alternatives.

DEPOLARIZING THE SIMPLISTIC DEBATE

It is obvious that if we look at this debate in the classic polarized terms— believers church individualism on one side and group decision collectivity on the other—the choice becomes difficult. But can we depolarize the terms? Can we call into question the simplicity with which the question has been put? Is it necessarily the case that every collective decision has to include the whole village? Must everything that is more than personal be universal in that given social setting? Is the only alternative to completely voluntary decision the taking of action without individual decision, or are there shades of degree in how much every individual goes along with a group decision?

From a free church perspective, what would be the points of dissent to the polarized picture above? First, we could claim that free church experience is more communal and respects more openly and consciously the corporate quality of being human than the Constantinian church does. The free church is not more individualistic. In fact, individualism as a cultural movement is a product of the Constantinian West. Individualism developed as a reaction to the way in which the dominant religious political unity pushed individuals out or down. As a cultural thrust, individualism is not an outworking of Anabaptism or Quakerism, but rather an outworking of the mass movements against which both they and the dissenting movements for individual rights were pointing. Thus, there are two alternate ways to oppose and correct Constantinianism. One is to focus on the individual. The other is to form the believers church.

Revisiting the anthropological phenomena. When we look at data from missionary experience and from anthropological observation of people movements, what would be the minimal axioms that we would want to affirm from a believers church perspective? The first axiom would be that *the church is defined by a decision.* That is, the church is not defined only by the past, by a power structure or by an already present institution that spreads. The church at any place is defined by a decision at that place. Second, *the decision that defines the church must be made in any place the way decisions are made in that place,* that is, in the terms of that culture. We cannot ask that they be made in forms that were dictated by a different cultural place. That is something that anthropology affirms, and I see no reason for believers church theology to deny it.

If we look at anecdotes and other descriptions, there was always a point in people movements where a decision was concluded and implemented in baptism. There was no baptism without decision. This was a conscious decision not only for most of the people participating in the baptism but for the community as a whole. That is, the act was public. It was adult. It was related to Jesus. The simple meanings this decision carried, meanings that the missionaries working with this kind of tribal or village decision describe, are understandable at that point. We might boil it down to a creed: Jesus is my Lord, our Lord; the Bible is our book;

the Christian community—the church—is our people. That was a conscious decision of all those who were baptized.

It may be that in this situation babies were actually baptized, maybe not. But that is not intrinsic to the way the decision happened. All social groups, and especially those groups we call "primitive," distinguish between full membership and immature membership in the decision-making process, as in everything else that happens in society. In fact, one of the ways we can tell the difference between what the anthropologists used to call a "primitive society" and a complex one is the clarity with which we know who is a full member. This depends on the degree of solidity of the rites of passage, that is, the points at which puberty and adulthood are celebrated. In a simple society we always know which youth are not fully responsible in group decisions. But even if levels of assent varied in group decision, there was a clear, conscious public decision regarding baptism.

There was always in this kind of tribal group decision also an element of free acceptance of foreignness. It was free because it was their decision. But what they made a decision about was Jesus, the Bible, the church and the missionary, none of which was from their culture. Their decision, therefore, was a valid acceptance of foreignness rather than the imposition of something inauthentic to their culture. The general embarrassment about missionaries who feel guilty about past "wrong foreignness" can easily be overdone. What the village wanted to receive—to receive validly but really to receive—was a foreign message. That meant they wanted to introduce into their experience a source of change. Their decision would introduce elements of instability and discipline. They would not go on as they had before they were baptized. As people committed to knowing more about Jesus, hearing the Bible's teachings and relating to the Christian fellowship from other places, they would consciously and validly begin shaking up their society. That their decision to follow Christ became a source of change and trouble is not something about which the intervening missionary needs to feel guilty; the missionary does not need to worry about distorting the local situation. The missionary's concern is that the people's decision is conscious and valid in their own cultural form, but he or she should not be ashamed of that decision. That was why the missionary was there, and that was what the people wanted.

This does not mean that change was easy. Based on anecdotes from anthropologically conscious missionaries, once a group started hearing more about Jesus—his promises and his demands, including the moral content of discipleship—divisions in the community that were not previously there would come to the surface. They were not there before because the Jesus message was not there to provoke them. Some individuals, sometimes many, broke out of the tribal group in order to fall back into the old life, into unbelief and nonconformity to the new norms. The freedom not to believe had become real, in fact, more real than before, because before there were no other options than the traditional tribal one. The initial group decision opened the door to Christian belief. Before that decision, unbelief had been a prison; afterwards it was an option. It was the novelty of the gospel that created the freedom not to believe. The free church would expect this kind of development: increasing pluralization, polarization and therefore personal responsibility driven not by a philosophical or cultural individualism but by the fact that people have to make decisions for or against Jesus as he is now interpreted in the committed group.

The newly committed groups did not hesitate to apply their commitment in practicing church discipline. They had decided when the missionary came around that they would all be baptized and follow Jesus. Later they saw what Jesus said about monogamy. By the next time the missionary came somebody would already have said, "I do not want to be in this church because I want to maintain my former lifestyle," and the group would have let him out. Then the missionary had to talk about how they should love somebody who has shut himself out of the community. The group's action, however, was not an inauthentic position imposed by the foreign teacher; the group did this itself. Both the unbeliever backing out of the newly formed Christian community and the genuineness of the decision process within that community reflect a "free church position" in this context.[2]

---

[2]In fact, the very dominance of the concern for process, for church discipline or for binding and loosing, which is a communal experience, is much more the definition of the believers church

All of this means that there is no necessary conflict between the believers church vision and the anthropologist's realism about how decisions are made in traditional tribal cultures. The process of the church coming into being and the freedom of decision becoming visible is different in the tribal culture from what it was in the so-called Christian culture and in the mass church being broken up by renewal, but the same theological concerns can be respected. It is not a matter—in the actual experience of the tribal culture—of getting everybody into the church based on a minimal decision and then hoping all will gradually grow into mature Christians. What happens in these primitive social decisions is that everybody is baptized after a valid group decision. Then some people back away from it. Thereby they recreate the church/world distinction and relationship, a natural one in biblical perspective.

We look from the Bible at individualism in the West and say that it is not adequate. The heroic and lonely disciple is a work of Western culture; that is not a biblical vision. Should we be any less critical of group-centeredness in the non-Western countries, whether this be the primitive groups that we have been talking about or the more communal lifestyles of the older Asian cultures?

If we are guided by the principle that decisions must be made in any place according to the way people decide in that culture, that would mean different things for a culture that emphasizes individual decision and for one that emphasizes group decision. The principle applied in the West would mean that, for missionary purposes, we would not object to individual conversions, because that is the way isolated people operate. For example, even those committed to a believers church vision of communality would not say that when Billy Graham gives an altar call, do not answer because that cannot be valid. We have to accept in the West the validity of decisions that are made the way we make decisions here. But that is different from accepting the theory that the human person is a lonely individual by definition and that the more valid one's faith, the more solitary it will be. It is also a different matter from sharing the

---

than anything we say about the status of an individual. Also, historically, Anabaptism began with a discussion about whether there shall be church discipline, not with the discussion of the basis for baptism.

modern person's preoccupation with psychic processes—how one made a faith decision, whether it was real.

In a group society, on the other hand, the effect of biblical standards will be to start with the group and then break up the group. In an individualistic society, the effect will be to start with the individual and then lead him or her toward group awareness. So the approach is analogous. It starts with cultural patterns of decision, and the biblical agenda will move the group society toward individualization or pluralization and the individualist toward community. In terms of strategy of approach to a culture, it is the same.

Revisiting the church growth arguments. We now have to return to the call of the church growth movement for a minimal decision at the point of membership; this is representative of a policy commitment that should be identified perhaps as a problem in its own right. "Make the decision easy" would be the slogan way to say it. We make the decision easy not only by going to a part of society which will have the least trouble making decisions to follow Christ—a particular group that is mobile or a particular class or caste that is looking for a new option— but also by shaping the nature of the decision itself. The anthropological language is *functional equivalent*, which means you find what deeply mattered to people in their earlier social, cultural or religious life, and you make sure that there are available ways for Christians to meet those same needs. For example, missionaries will create some kind of ritual marking adolescence or a harvest ritual if that was important in the previous culture.

This commitment to making the decision easy raises the question of whether a less radical decision is a better base for further growth than a more radical decision. Is an easy decision a good way to start Christian life? That is partly a strategy question, but it may be more than that.

Even more fundamentally, what does it mean theologically to commit oneself or a mission effort to serving only one part of society? McGavran's originality lies in what he calls the *homogeneous unit*, which means finding the vein that is responsive in a given culture—the ethnic vein due to certain migrations, or the class or the economic vein due to industrialization or urbanization—and only work with those people because there the church can grow. What does it mean theologically to leave out of this mission process other categories of people?

The best example for dramatizing the issue is if we were trying to build a church in southern Mississippi. We would build black churches and white churches, and we would not make an issue of racial segregation as a moral problem or as a social problem until the second generation—until we had a chance to nurture members. We would be committed to integration on theological grounds, but we would not start there because if we did, we would not get any response from local people.

Is that a theological question? Is that a strategy question? Or is it something else? If the particular ethical issue about which we are willing to be patient is in some sense an issue appropriate for people who have had a long time in the faith, then postponing it for a generation may be all right. But if the ethical issue has to do with breaking down walls between ethnic groups, it is at the heart of the gospel. Can we then justifiably postpone it? Have we not already denied the gospel message by accepting segregation as the shape of growth?

Here we would need to debate how seriously to take the New Testament example in which Paul said that if we do not have a social form showing that we have broken down the walls between peoples, then it is not the gospel; it is another gospel regardless of who preaches it. Paul wrote, "But even if we or an angel from heaven should proclaim to you a gospel contrary to what we proclaimed to you, let that one be accursed!" (Gal 1:8). That would be the radical way to critique this approach.

Those are the issues which will remain as we proceed, in addition to the ones at the heart of the debate about how the challenge of people movements are a new way to illuminate our understanding of the church and how she carries out her mission.

15

SALVATION IS HISTORICAL

When we say that salvation is historical, we may mean that God works among people in ways we can observe, experience and discuss. This contrasts with mysticism—which says that we cannot talk about God's work—and with Platonism—which says that God is really in some other world. Both are already significant points in the discussion between the biblical worldview and other worldviews. Saying salvation is historical obliges one to identify the events and experiences in which God works. Why say God works in that event? What did God do? Why are those events more important than others?

If we say that God has been at work in Israel's history or the missionary church's history, the next set of questions arises: how does this set of events relate to other events that people call world history? Is there overlap? Are they easily separated, or are they the same thing? The International Missionary Council and World Council study commission on theology of mission asked as its first question, what is the relation between the course of the gospel and what is going on in the world? What is God's redemptive purpose in and for world history?

If we affirm that there is some relationship between mission history and world history, we have still another question: how do the events happening in world history relate to God's purposes? Does that mean, for example, that there is some specific theological meaning to Western history because the church—or at least the Judeo-Christian heritage—has penetrated Western culture? The slogan "the end of empire" points in a similar direction. There was an epoch of successful Christendom in

Europe. Then European Christianity expanded successfully through politics and military might in the rest of the world. That was the age of empire, but that age has in the simple sense ended, and secularization as a cultural trend is replacing it. Does that mean anything about God's purposes for the world?

"GOD IS AT WORK IN THE WORLD"

We begin with the slogan "God is at work in the world."[1] God is at work not only in the church or only in Christendom; God is at work every-where. God works in nonreligious events as well as religious events. The church is the place where we recognize, affirm and rejoice that God is at work in the world. Also we must join to some extent God's work in the world. The rest of the world does not recognize that God is at work there.

Several different sources inform this thrust in mission thinking. One source is popularized biblical realism, where the exodus or concept of a promised land has meaning beyond the religious and theological. It reaches into people's daily lives in how they understand geography, food, power and wealth. This view emphasizes that the Old Testament story is about the instruments of God's working, which the New Testament neither denies nor changes.

During the time this slogan was popular, the American civil rights movement gained a degree of visible success in Montgomery, Selma, Birmingham and in civil-rights legislation. These were things about which Christians cared and things they promoted. Moreover, many Christians began to see colonialism as an evil collapsing on itself as new nations came on the scene. They thought they should approve of that. Medical help was getting to more and more parts of the world. Chris-tians ought to approve of that. Both from cultural experience and from biblical studies there was a new readiness to affirm the nonreligious and non-Western dimension of where God is at work.

Another source of the idea that God is at work in the world was self-criticism. The institutional missionary enterprise was neither gaining ground, nor self-confident, nor impressed by growing openness and

---

[1]This slogan was current at the New Delhi Assembly of the World Council (1961) and in the Mexico City Assembly of the Division of World Mission and Evangelism (1963).

perspectives in mission. It was rather increasingly aware of its short-comings: failures of the churches to grow; difficulties in transferring missionary institutions to local responsibility; and the institutional dimensions of moving beyond the first and second generations of a missionary enterprise. Part of the polemic turned inward: Do not be preoccupied about what God is doing in the institutional church. That will take care of itself if Christians help further God's purposes in the world. Then they will know why they come to church, namely, to mobilize themselves in order to share in God's larger work.

DOES GOD CARE ABOUT WORLD HISTORY?

The longer-range theological issue is whether God cares about world history. Arendt Van Leeuwen said that Western history is an outworking of what God wants. New nations, industry, rejecting fate, and the human capacity to administer the universe and use nature for human purposes: these developments result from a Christian understanding, and we should affirm them.

After 1965 the World Council developed a series of studies on "the finality of Christ in an age of universal history." "An age of universal history" meant that we look at history worldwide. There is no longer such a thing as local history free from the impact of world history; there is only world history. This was not the case before the last few centuries and was not radically the case until the development of modern communications. Given this development, what are the possible options or the classical ways to answer whether God cares about world history?

The dualist option. One possibility is dualism, in its various forms from Plato to Pietism, which claims there is no fundamental or intrinsic connection between God and history. There are two different levels of being, and we relate to both. In this view the Bible's monotheistic or spiritual thrust tells us we should not focus on history but rather move toward God through mystical contemplation, inner experience and relativizing the details of time and place. Whether more people have enough food next year than ten years ago is not of ultimate concern. It is not unimportant, because history is the substratum. We do not know how to produce consciousness apart from bodies, and we do not have bodies apart from history, so we cannot get along without it. But reality—the spiritual, the ideal or the eternal—is on the other level. In its different forms, dualism places emphasis on the disjunction between God and history.

The Catholic option. Another possibility, at the other extreme, would be the classical medieval affirmation that God is slowly but progressively taking over world history and the church is God's presence in the midst of it. The church has to have clergy. Clergy have to have a head. The head has to be at a certain place. So we have to say "Roman Catholic Church." That is the concreteness in which God has committed to history. This option affirms the epoch of church leadership, beginning in the Constantinian age, as one step forward. Many more steps forward are still needed, but patiently the church is conquering the world. Sometimes there will be setbacks and sometimes there will be major victories, but it is clear that history matters.

The theocratic option. The theocratic vision—Puritanism, Calvinism, the Reformed vision—would agree with the Catholic vision in seeing God's purposes in history for a whole nation or cultural unity such as the Christian West, but it would be less patient and more critical. Instead of saying God gradually tries to Christianize this total mass, theocracy says we know enough about the specific shape of God's will to aggressively shape culture in that way. We must not be satisfied with slow patient penetration. We must seek power. We must engineer. We must teach and proclaim the Word of God to help shape the world to God's purposes. This view also differs from the Roman Catholic position in that it is more secular. That is, it does not simply try to get more people coming to confession more often and fewer people committing mortal sins. It talks about charging interest, marriage legislation, care of widows and orphans, movement toward democracy, a work ethic, capital accumulation for production and giving people jobs. The theocratic vision is driven, like Catholicism, by a vision of Christian society, Christian statesmen and an established church. But it emphasizes the lifestyle of this Christian culture and how it has to change in order to achieve God's will.

The Lutheran option. The Lutheran vision also dramatizes secularization. It takes certain elements of the dualism mentioned earlier, but instead of a yes/no dualism it is a both/and dualism. It affirms both God and history but insists on keeping them separate. In the so-called doctrine of two kingdoms, or two realms, God cares about history or the realm of law, but God also cares about spirit or the realm of gospel. Theology's task is to keep the two apart, not to merge them as the Catholic and Puritan visions do. The end toward which world history is moving is sure in God's providential purposes, but it cannot be calculated, we are not responsible for it, and it is ultimately irrelevant. Salvation history ends with Pentecost; God's Word is not interested in any other events. Even biblical events are only meaningful in the eyes of faith. Christians do not claim that historians can find proof of the resurrection or the Pentecost event because those things are only true through faith. We do not expect everybody to believe them. The dichotomy between realms, which is already in the biblical witness, is also present today. Both concern for the shape of culture and concern for the believing community's faithfulness matter to preachers and rulers. But careful theology keeps the realms apart. World history is only a frame for the work of God's Word. The Word does not move world history as it does in Catholicism or Puritanism. It rather is concerned for its distinctiveness from the world, for leading people to turn away in authentic faith from preoccupation with the realm of law toward the realm of gospel.

The dispensationalist option. One original option that developed a century and a half ago is dispensationalism, which maintains that God cares about history, including the rise and fall of empires, but that there are several such histories and that the movement from one to the other is where God intervenes. These several histories are called "dispensations," "arrangements," or "the outworking of God's purposes." When God placed Adam and Eve in the garden, God told them the rules and conditions of relationship. Adam and Eve did not keep the rules, so God started again and told people the conditions and purpose for relationship with God outside the garden. Once again, they did not keep the commandments, so God sent the flood. Then God started again with Noah. Each time God graciously intervened to establish a relationship with people, but each time people failed; so God started again.

This is an original and, in a sense, profound way to affirm the meaningfulness of history's movement. God moves from one economy to another. The church's mission relates significantly to this because what happens in history triggers the movement from one dispensation to the next. The church hastens the end (2 Pet 3:12). When the gospel has been preached to all the nations, then the end will come (Mt 24:14). That means the threshold between the present age and the next one depends on whether the church gets its work done. This does not mean concern for the details of secular history, such as different forms of democracy or different forms of Marxism. But Christians are at work in Western culture, and dispensationalism is especially concerned with the structure of European government as the place where the end-time political forces will arise and with the state of Israel. So there are major elements of secular history that have real theological meaning.

The secular option. There is not only one secular view, but we will try to describe it as if we were able to get hold of something that has been going in our wider culture since the Renaissance, the Enlightenment and subsequent nineteenth-century developments such as Darwinism, Marxism and historicism as a cultural discipline. Many people in the modern period would say that secular history is the only history we know. There is no other realm than the secular. Religion is not insignificant, because religion is an observable phenomenon of secular history. It involves money, takes up time and demands intellectual work. It is an accessory to or a parasite on the historical process, or it might even be its motor. Religion as a human phenomenon has real historical meaning, but it has meaning only because it makes people behave differently in the world. It has no meaning in itself—when it talks about the Trinity for example.

In this view, secular history is the only history there is, and we know it is going somewhere; it is progress. Philosophically and historically, there is only one history. It would have been meaningful two thousand years ago to talk about Chinese, South Asian or West African history and ignore Europe, but today these histories have merged. The one that came from the Near East by way of Western imperialism has swallowed up the others, not by destroying them but by interrelating with them and giving them direction. Even the largest national unity in the world—Chinese culture—says it is Marxist, and Marxism is a Western post-Jewish vision of history.

The notion of historical progress entails two things that logically support each other. First, we are better off than we used to be, so when we look at how things have been going we say that is progress. We have more food, better transportation and more medicine. We decide that this is good, meaning that it is in line with the way history is moving. It is an argument against something to say, "You are against the times," or "You are out of date." It may even be an argument against something to say, "You are ahead of your time." But that can also be a compliment, as when Roland Bainton said the Anabaptists were three hundred years ahead of their time. People often take sides on a present issue by saying, "Historians a century from now will say that . . . " or, "after the event we will know that . . . " That is, they trust that the direction in which history is moving is itself revelatory, is itself a criterion of good. A strict logician, stepping back and looking at that, would say those two assumptions cancel each other out. If we affirm one of them, the other one becomes meaningless. If we affirm them both, we are stuck in a circular argument: we cannot at the same time say the way things are going to go is good and ask for a criterion of goodness, and that we have looked at the way things are going and said that is good on the basis of some other criteria.

This secular vision of progress is most like the Puritan or theocratic view in its sense of progress, the meaningfulness of historical experience and the directional quality or the finality in historical experience. Yet secularists do not think we need the superstructure anymore. In the Protestant Reformation, especially in the Calvinist form, Christians had to proclaim that they knew God was actively at work and that they must push history to make it move toward God. But the Christians becoming secular discovered in the nineteenth century that they could drop God and the same sense of purposiveness would work anyway. The central symbols of that were Darwin in one sense and Marx in another. Secular philosophers saw that history's purposiveness—the fact that it moved forward rather than degenerating or spinning cyclically—was the nature of things. The word *evolution* as a cultural slogan was the explanation that nature has it within itself, and therefore history growing on top of nature has within itself, the ability to go forward. It can become more competitive, more adaptive, more productive and more powerful. We can drop the Puritan God and history would be just as meaningful.

That kind of cultural vision pushed many churches to strongly affirm history as where God is working. Hence, the slogan "God is at work in the world; let's join him," was fitting in terms of the evolution of culture and modern Western thought in the 1960s.

The social gospel option. The social gospel also reinforced church acceptance of "God at work in the world." Walter Rauschenbusch, the German Baptist evangelist Pietist who coined the phrase "the social gospel," preached that we ought to help make the world a place where it is possible to be converted, where it is possible for people to find the freedom, wholeness, time and bodily repose to be able to decide whether to be Christian. Rauschenbusch saw that as a genuine struggle. But the later popularized social gospel took up the optimism of evolutionary secularism and the pragmatism of American politics and seemed to say something different: "We are optimistic, things are getting better and better, the human person is basically an adequate animal, and all we need to do is to improve our tools and techniques and the direction of history will be assured."[2]

WORLD HISTORY AND THE CHURCH

The church received a mixture of the specifically modern strand of positive thought about history and the older Magisterial Reformation's affirmation of the secular. The modern strand came to the church from the nineteenth century secular vision of historical events as being in themselves good, self-sustaining, self-authenticating and self-propelling. This modern view is a new form of what Luther and Calvin said in different ways: the realm of history is important. These two strands of thought, the new one and the old one, coincide in this respect and thereby give people a chance to connect their traditional preaching to the current debate about the relationship of God and history.

---

[2]This secular optimism has received many critical responses. The point now is to try to understand the strength of this position and not its obvious limits.

The positive view of history in these two strands can lead to saying that the course of world history is more important in God's purposes than what the church does—church in the narrow sense of the organization, the members and what they do together. God's real purposes for the world are the development of democracy so that people can have dignity in their relationships to each other and to sources of power, the development of technologies so that people can communicate with each other and be housed and fed, the development of health services so that people can stay alive and well, and the development of global unity where we know and care about each other. God cares about the church as a way to get these things done, not about the church for its own sake. The church is an assembly of servants who were the first to know about God's purpose for the world and by proclaiming it, got it rolling. This approach is neither unconcerned for the church nor negative about it, but is modest about the visible church as a sociological reality.

In this approach, the course of world history toward global cultural unity was an echo of the mission of the church. That is to say, if it had not been for the Christian mission, we would not have one world. The missionaries first thought about the rest of the world as people; the businessmen followed. The Christian faith first affirmed that God cares for the rest of the world; cultures followed. This unified world history was also, however, a presupposition or tool of the mission. That is, the modern missionary enterprise was only possible because the boats and colonial administrators were there. Before that, the missionary enterprise consisted in a few people begging their way around the world, which did not make one world. The unity of the world was not only a product of the mission, it was also a presupposition of the mission.

World history then became a rival of Christian mission, in that once the unification happened world history became independent—the adolescent left home and did not need the home anymore. The unity of world history became autonomous in relation to mission because of the degree to which the Western Christian message had succeeded.

If world history is an echo, a presupposition and a rival of the Christian mission, then we must be able to say that God cares about history. We can no longer use the old dualistic forms that strongly separate God and world, the spiritual and the material. With the same kind of divine intervention in mind that we find in the creation story, we must look at the providence story, the history story, and say the same thing. God has worked, and God says it is good. So we praise God for it and to the modest extent we can, we tag along helping God with it and blessing it.

Biblical faith as secularization. An affirmation that became current in the late 1960s was that biblical faith by nature is a secularizing or a historicizing witness. The word *historicize* points to concern for the sequence of events. The word *secularize* points to concern for looking away from the cultic, the ritual and the mystical toward the visible.

How was biblical faith a secularizing witness? In this view the basic difference between paganism and biblical faith was that pagan religion sanctifies and celebrates what is. The layman's term for that is *ontocracy* or the *ontocratic* which means that what is, is that which rules. People in primitive cultures celebrated the shape of nature: the trees, waterfalls and storms. They saw divinity in nature and adapted to it. They tried to manipulate it with magic or to fit in by figuring out its rhythms. Worship was designed to integrate humanity and nature so that nature would be friendly to humans. In more organized societies—agricultural societies, for instance—the seasons and fertility were important. In Caananite religion, Baal was the divinity of the field and the flock. Agricultural religion meshed people with the most regular and reliable things there are, such as the circulation of the stars and the seasons. In more highly developed pagan cultures, people celebrated the empire. The emperor supported the priesthood, whose main business was to say that God had put the emperor in place. Religion dramatized, celebrated, reinforced and saw God in what is. That is *ontocracy* on all its different levels.

Biblical faith brought movement in various ways. For one thing it included moral demands that did not just say, "What is, is good." They said, "What is, is a sin. Do not do that. This is God's will." The covenant's moral demands intervened and interfered with "what is," in the direction of change.

Another element of biblical faith was that a new Hebrew community arose that was not identical with nature but that God called to move and to change as a pilgrim people. This community differed from the givenness of the previous human communities not only because of different ethnic background, but because their God told them to do things and go places. This biblical faith debunked idolatry and its related ritual. This community saw past the celebration of the Baalim or of Marduk, of the trees and the waterfalls and began to ask about what made the religious system work. They saw that the priestly caste had financial interests in keeping things as they were.

One characteristic that all of these pagan religions shared was the conviction that there was a religious realm distinct from the historical: the realm of the taboo or the realm of cult. In English *cult* connotes the secret or the strange. But its Latin root means concern for worship rituals. That is, the cult does not build a community, change things, concern itself with ethics or produce things that meet human needs. The cult may have an element of mystery or focus on the mystical or the priesthood, but it does not have to. By contrast, biblical faith looked away from the cultic, the ritual and the dogmatic toward work, family, telling the truth, feeding the poor, getting food from the soil—in general to ordinary life rather than to a specific religious domain.

Unfortunately, this secularizing impact of biblical faith, which operated from Abraham to the third century, was halted when the church was merged with the religiosity of the times. In order for the church to take over Rome, it merged with Rome. It took over the cult of the dead and the local deities, the use of Easter eggs and Christmas trees, and it honored the emperor—the sacred emperor—in order to affirm culture. But the effect was a backward-looking affirmation rather than something forward looking. It was religious rather than secular, picking up Greek or Germanic religious elements and projecting the idea of an aesthetic sacral world unity.

Those who argued that biblical faith had a secularizing witness pointed out that God was not to be bottled up in religiosity for long. In the modern age—Renaissance, Reformation and Enlightenment—God broke free again. This modern breaking free of God's concern for the secular partly took an antireligious form because the Enlightenment thinkers were against the kind of Christianity that had allied itself with what they considered an irrational religious worldview. But their new humanism, which claimed that humanity is basically good, was in its essence Christian and political, according to those who emphasized the secularizing impact of the Bible. They claimed human goodness is biblical both in its origins—we can trace it back to the Bible—and in its substance—it says the same thing the Bible says. But because of the unfortunate alliance of medieval Christianity with conservative religiosity, this modern humanism thinks it is anti-Christian. So the argument goes: we should affirm secular humanism because what it says about humanity is right.

As some people tell it, the story from Abraham to Moses, through the prophets to Jesus was progressive desacralization, humanization and moving out of the realm of the secret, the mystical and the cultic into the realm of the ethical and communitarian. One sample of this is the concept of *deus ex machina,* which is a label used in theater when the omnipotent God intervenes in a plot near the end to make things come out right. That view of God's intervention is one of the leftovers of the prebiblical worldview that was still around in the Middle Ages. For instance, in the Middle Ages people would pray with great faith for rain or for a plague to go away because they thought of God as an omnipotent person who, if asked fervently enough, would change things. Those who emphasize the Bible's secularizing role say that modern people know better. We may for sentimental reasons maintain the old forms, but when we look on the map and see that there is no humidity and that the pressure is such that there cannot be rain, we will not pray for it. If we do, we will pray for rain a couple days away because we do not really believe God intervenes to change weather. Humans are in charge of the world. That is the ultimate outworking of secularization, which is the long-range echo of the biblical faith.

Given the view that biblical faith is secularizing, what is the church's mission? Its mission is not to propagate an ancient, medieval or Western worldview. What the Bible did with the worldviews that it encountered was to accept that culture's framework but hollow it out from the inside. It used the language of the time in order to proclaim God's sovereignty over it. In the same way, that is what we are supposed to do: claim as the work of God the humanization of the world that has now become possible, put it into effect and celebrate it.

The idea that biblical faith is inherently secularizing has many strengths, as its advocates argue. First, it makes us less apologetic about the age of empire than some of us have been. There has been an anticolonial or antimissionary thrust that warned us not to threaten the solidity of Confucian, Buddhist or Hindu culture with a Western message because it interferes with the authenticity of religious response. It warned our missionaries to get over their Westernness when they meet others around the world. Ever since Arendt van Leeuwen wrote about biblical faith as secularization, those who shared his view have had a response to this concern: we no longer have to be ashamed of being Western, because the gospel produces modernity. Thus modernity is part of our mission. We do not try to shelter people of another culture from either the impact of God's one world history or modernity's secularizing effect. We do not need to be ashamed of the West's power, because that is indirectly God's power. This kind of theology will be happy about what happened in China because Marxism can modernize China better than Confucianism ever would have. And modernizing China is good for people. One of the strengths of this position—if you are on its side—is that it makes the Western missionary less apologetic about being Western and less embarrassed about the fact that one's cultural impact coincides with the cultural impact of capitalism and Marxism.

Another strength is that this message makes people less fearful and more hopeful. Hope here is not a vague emotional hopefulness, but about making concrete affirmations about history. We can say the world is moving toward democratization; the common person is going to have more of a say; the poor are rising up and will no longer let themselves be trampled upon. Those are the signs of God at work, which the advocates of this view want to contribute to and celebrate.

Yet another strength is that there are biblical references for this desacralizing thrust and concern for how people behave as over against how they pray.

Finally, it could be argued that this view is a corrective for church-centeredness in the clericalist sense that priests ought to give everybody orders, or in the sense that some Catholic development has called "triumphalist," a confidence that God's purposes in history are for the church to become more and more respected, organized and efficient.

What are the limits of this approach? One limit is that the other faiths have also produced aggressive and productive civilizations, such as in China or India. Moreover, the phenomenon of religious thinkers seeing through sacral dualism to an active and culturally positive vision of humanity has happened in other religions as well. It is not only the product of Western Christianity. There is also the possibility that much of the West's strength was fortuitous, that is, it was the result of a particular climate in Germany. The barbarians were on the edge of the Christian empire, which made them work hard to produce an effective culture so that they could take over the live elements of the Roman tradition and make a new cultural thrust. Or maybe what made Western culture effective were the Greek and Roman elements and not the Christian injection the Roman culture got later. To say that it is precisely the Hebraic thrust that secularizes is to short circuit cultural history.

A second general critique focuses on this vision's view of history as progress, which is naive in its optimism and one-sided in considering as evolution only those things that are good. It does not take equally into calculation the other side of the picture: that there are more people starving to death today than ever in world history; that technology feeds into the hands of a new degree of militarism, police states and destruction; and that there are phenomena of social degeneration and decomposition in the most advanced societies that makes one doubt whether they are advanced. Moreover, progress is not necessarily good if we are using up our air. Insights about pollution and the finiteness of the planet were not around when this optimism developed. To see history as being one forward-looking line assumes that we are part of a comfortable Western culture. From Europe or North America it makes sense to see all history pointing up to where we sit atop. We should be aware that this is a selective way to view history; viewed from the bottom side, history has a different shape.

Although the biblical worldview sees history as meaningful movement, at every point there are two possible ways to move, and at every point some people make the wrong decision. Besides *Heilsgeschichte,* there is apostasy; besides progress, failing and falling. This makes the picture more complicated.

Salvation history is world history. My response to the question of the relation of God and history would begin with the affirmation that not all world history is salvation history. We cannot look at the course of events in the whole world and simply say that is what God is doing. Yet all salvation history is world history, that is, there are not two realms—a realm where salvation history happens and another realm. But there *are* two commitments: those places where God's work is discernible because of the context of faith and other events where God's purpose and activity are not discernible.

In the community of faith, faithful deeds are both salvation history and world history because there is no distinction between the two. Faithful deeds are real mission and real progress. *Mission* is the salvation-history word; *progress* is the world-history word. But that progress and mission include conflict and suffering. We do not move world history forward only, usually or normatively by pushing it from the top with coercive power. But deeds of faithfulness, including suffering, do move history forward. We do not work with a fundamental dichotomy between two kinds of history, but rather between the two stances from which history can be discerned, evaluated and engaged.

Outside of faith a person can see any pattern he or she wants in world history. One can see progress and also degeneration depending on what index one takes to measure it and depending on how a person relates to the particular things he or she is measuring. Usually a group or a person taking sides regarding a pattern will appeal to his or her faith commitment whatever that is—ideology, self-righteousness—to illuminate the ups and downs, and that is no surprise.

The people who affirm that God works in world history are right in one sense. There is no other world in which God works. But the world in which God works is a world of struggle, alternatives and decisions. Consequently, history's place in God's mission in the world cannot be read off the surface of the events apart from the commitment of faith. In that sense, the secularizers are naive. They are incorrect in thinking they can simply look at history and see what happened without bringing some kind of faith or ideology to bear.

We must relate to world history, but not world history in general. Rather we relate to particular events about which we can say that was a step forward or that was a step backward. Particular events have to be evaluated, and how they are evaluated depends on one's view of the church. What does, for instance, the age of empire mean? That age was present in different ways from the time of Constantine until this century. Was that good or bad? The line of thought which began with Eusebius, continued through Augustine and remained dominant in Western Catholic thought and in most Western Protestant thought said that was good. God's truth was using the power of culture, including the Christian statesman, to propagate itself around the world. Another category of people—the monastic movement, the underground churches of the late Middle Ages, and then the Radical Reformation—said that linking the church with empire was a serious misconception or deformation of the church's message. A more shaded, careful alternative is in Max Warren's *Caesar the Beloved Enemy.* Warren maintained that though God used the empire to spread the church, it spread the church in a questionable way. It not only spread the church, it also spread medicine, education and economic development. Those things are good for people, but this process has its built-in dangers.

What would be another alternative, careful like Warren's, but perhaps more critical than his? In the New Testament the civil order, when seen as coercive power, was rebellion against God; this was the biblical vision of the state all the way back to Babylon. But God used that rebellion in the wider providential governing of events. So empire, as coercive power, was basically negative. It abused power. To link that power with the Christian message deforms the Christian message.

Furthermore, empire is provincial, which is paradoxical since empire always tries to be worldwide. But what it tries to be worldwide about is the pattern and power of a particular place in Europe. It does not affirm that all kinds of people belong in the same community. It says that all kinds of people belong *under* a certain Western cultural mode. Moreover, empire does not simply spread the church but also turns people away because of its foreignness and coerciveness. At the same time one points to the churches in these places, we must also ask who was driven away, who was offended or what distortion has come into the nature of those churches through being linked with empire.

But empire can be used for good and has been used for good, despite itself and beyond itself. It has produced a world consciousness, an awareness of the rest of the globe, which is a good thing despite the fact that it came into being on the back of world dominion. The empire, in fact, provided the basis for the later critique of its abuses by educating people, providing medical services and fostering an economic base for independent development, thereby provoking the colonized peoples into self-respect, which they might not have developed if there had not been the same sequence of oppression and response. So we can recognize and be grateful for the benefits of the age of empire without agreeing that this was the only way to achieve these benefits or defending empire when it weakens.

Yet while we affirm the long-range positive dimensions to the Westernization of the world, we are aware also that we have abused resources, misallocating wealth drawn from the rest of the world. Often those resources are not developed or used with a view to help the people of each place as much as possible. They are rather developed with a view to world markets, markets that manipulate prices so resources are sucked out of the poorest countries to be used in the industrialized countries. It is not for the world that the world is being developed.

Once again we say, "yes, but" or "no, but" about the course of world history. The movement is there because of the gospel, because of the biblical witness. But because it moves beyond the community of faith, some of this movement is simply destructive and even that which is positive is ambiguous in its meaning. We have to be both in favor of it and critical of it. We cannot simply join the categorical slogans about our needing to celebrate God's work in the world. We need first to discern and to critique the historical movement we see and then celebrate what we can.[3]

---

[3]In the literature this point is admitted by those who distinguish between secularization as a process and secularism as an ideology. If we make that distinction cleanly, we can approve of the use of the term *secularization* as a process, but reject the ideology that would make an *-ism* out

Salvation Is Secular

We have moved from one topic to another, talking sometimes about history, sometimes about nature and sometimes about the secular or world as if they were all the same thing. These are three different themes: nature, history and the world. But they are all the same in that they polarize something and say that it is not in the church; it is there in the world.

Rather than try unsuccessfully to clarify neat differences, we will simply have to run through some of the same thoughts again in the other forms they take by the people who like the word *secular* and use it as a corrective. Some of this will overlap with what we have said before, but the attention here is less on the development of Western culture and empire as related to mission. The discussion here focuses on the place of the church in her own world, wherever that is, and dealing not so much with events as with the structures in the world.

The kingdom of God versus the church. Johannes Christiaan Hoekendijk claims that the biblical message is kingdom-centered and that should mean downplaying the self-sufficiency or centrality of the church as the instrument and purpose of mission, which was a major focus of missionary theology until the 1950s. The church's mission was seen to be planting the church in new places. At the 1952 World Missionary Conference in Willingen, Germany, Hoekendijk argued that this should be downplayed. The church should be seen as the vehicle for proclaiming the kingdom of God. The church is responsible to point beyond itself to God's kingdom, which Christ proclaimed, which the prophets before him proclaimed and which the church should keep on proclaiming.[4]

This is a necessary corrective over against institution-centeredness, that is, over against a missionary process that was focused on how the foreigners' compound—with its schools, hospital, missionary personnel and specialized services—created the church as a new community. The proclamation of the church must be broader than that, much more God-centered and also less centered on getting individuals into the

---

of *secular,* thinking we can find a solution there. It is all right when *secularization* happens, but we should not think we will get much guidance or salvation from *secularism.*

[4]For an overview of this meeting and Hoekendijk's contribution, see Andersen, "Further Toward a Theology of Mission," in *The Theology of the Christian Mission,* ed. Gerald Anderson (New York: McGraw-Hill, 1961), pp. 300-313.

church, because that is a different focus of concern than the sovereignty of God and the proclamation of God's honor.

What do we focus on when, instead of looking at the church, we look at the kingdom? First, we distinguish between possession and promise.[5] The church's mission is not to share what she has but to proclaim a promise. The church is people who gather around that promise. But they are not holding and then sharing something that is their own possession. They are rather sharing a hope. They are looking forward and inviting other people to look forward to something not realized yet, but in which we trust and toward which we live.

Second, we should care the most not about cult or worship, not about the hierarchy or church order and not about spreading dogma, but about ordinary life. Christ was prophet and priest, but more than that he was king. What is needed in the rest of the world is the proclamation that in ordinary life, there is a new kingdom, a new way of listening to orders, a new way of obeying, a new quality of community.

One more way to describe this difference is to say that the witness of the church is not God's instrument to do what God wants done in the world, but rather a sign of the coming kingdom. If we think of communication as an instrument, then we will believe that we must transmit from our home culture to the foreign culture all of the content of Christian faith that will make a difference. How are they going to know it if we do not tell them? The kingdom-oriented view claims that witness is much more a sign than it is a pipeline of communication. It points to something. It makes people aware of something. But what happens to them is a product of their faith and response to the proclamation. It is not that we have exported through a pipeline what we know needs to happen so that we can manipulate events. The fact that we are preaching *is* a sign to the world. This language is strong in the New Testament, especially in John's Gospel. Jesus' presence is perceived not as communicating a certain amount of information; what is meaningful is who he *is*. Jesus' deeds are meaningful apart from words about them. Similarly, the church or mission effort as a sign of the kingdom is meaningful and is

---

[5]Hans Margull, *Hope in Action: The Church's Task in the World* (Philadelphia: Muhlenberg Press, 1962).

projected as an alternative to the church as an instrument.

This whole shift in mood, for which we can take Hoekendijk as a symbol, expresses itself by the use it makes of two biblical concepts in particular. This movement revitalizes *laos* or people, which we discussed earlier, but in the sense that the church remains a people even when scattered. They proclaim the kingdom by their presence wherever they are. Second, it makes use of the concept of place or house.

The New Testament church met in different homes, where people not only lived but also did their work. The house was not simply a dwelling in the modern sense, a place from which people commute to everything else we do. Until modern times the house was also where a tentmaker made his tents and the carpenter used his tools. For example, the church met in the house of Aquila and Priscilla, who were tentmakers. It was not a building like the medieval church to which everybody went and, when nobody went, was empty. The church met where somebody was at home.

That would mean that we could well conceive of New Testament mission as going to the houses where people were at home and where they worked. Today people function socially not by having customers come into their homes to buy tents and otherwise making the house the place for most social relations, but by going out to the office, the factory, the shopping center or the school. Those places, for us, are the *oikos*, the place the gospel has to enter. It is there the church has to go because those places function like the house did in the New Testament.

The enclave mentality of the church. This thrust of secularizing the gospel was a corrective. It arose from the conviction that past practices were inadequate. What were these inadequacies? The one that was argued the most evidently and openly was that the church, especially in the non-Western missionary context, had chosen to be limited to a ghetto.[6] Instead of being at home in southern Asian society, the church made new subcultures or enclaves in which to be safer but also to be less involved in wider society. In the Near East this was designated by the

---

[6]The word *ghetto* is one younger churches use sometimes for themselves. It is the wrong word, however, because historically the Jews did not choose to live in ghettos; Christians forced them to live there. They got out as soon as they could in the early modern period. So *ghetto* is the wrong word, but the point still stands.

Turkish word *millet*, which was taken over by the British administration in the interwar and is still used in the various Arabic and Jewish countries of the Middle East. It refers to a subcultural group which has not only its own ethnic ties, but even its own law courts, marriage law, way of dealing with heredity and rules about how to finance the church. The same thing happened in India with the caste system, which made a slot or special subcommunity for everybody. When missionary Christianity came into such contexts, how could it avoid being put in the same box? The new movement would be just another one of the subcommunities that are expected to live side-by-side and not bother each other. If our point is that the church is missionary, then we want to bother each other, and we cannot accept the enclave ethos of the subcommunity. That enclave mentality is the one thing the Hoekendijk movement corrects.

The narrowness of its agenda. A second inadequacy of past missionary practice that the kingdom of God movement addressed was not the church's limitation to a ghetto or millet, but the narrowness of its agenda. The movement saw mission as being concerned for private morality, not for public ethics, of being concerned for doctrinal finesse or liturgical propriety and leaving aside the wider questions of how a social order evolves, of educational politics, of political economy or of public health.

The problem of proselytism. The third problem with missionary practice was *proselytism*, which is the word for being overly concerned for getting a maximum number of converts without being sure they have freely made that decision. With an emphasis on getting converts, missionaries can also feel defeated about those individuals who are not brought into the organization. This kind of mission takes the question of getting people into the church so seriously that they don't focus on the message. Looking for members instead of proclaiming God's Word is what it means to proclaim the church instead of the kingdom.

More affirmative ways to state the concern about proclaiming the kingdom. One way is to claim that this approach is based on the classical doctrine of incarnation. God came to work among people in human form in Christ. We must make this message take on flesh again and again, and that means something broader than focusing on the church. That means assuming all the dimensions of the life of the people wherever we go.

Another slogan that fits here is that of service, *diakonia*. Christians are to help people where they hurt and meet their needs. To be a servant means to do what a master wants, that is, to accept the standards of relevance of those one serves. A servant does not go to his or her master and say, "You told me to do this, but this is not what you really need. You really need something else. So I will do something else." You might do that if you are a neighbor or a father, but not if you are a servant. If you are a servant, you do what you are told. So if people in the culture in which we are ministering think they need schools, then we should not claim that what they really need is piety or joining the church. We do not give orders; we do what they want, using our tools of technology and education.

Another way to make the same argument is to refer to the doctrine of providence. God is in control of the world, which means that God is in control of more than the church. When we proclaim Christ's lordship, we proclaim something that is already there, bringing it to life. That is why we have the right to proclaim it. It is not some foreign fact that we bring to foreign places. It is the truth of their situation, which we help them unveil.

Strengths and limitations of the secularization of the gospel message. What are we to think about the secularization approach from the perspective of the Bible and history, which we have already analyzed? I think we need to affirm some validity to this thrust as a corrective. It is one way to reaffirm that the gospel has a social character and is not merely focused on individual piety and conversion. It is a way to be reminded not to measure the integrity of our effort by the impact of our institutions and not to seek affirmation or justification by their effectiveness at building their own new culture in some foreign land. Moreover, it is a valid corrective to admit that God uses forces beyond our control. There is something to our message that does not depend on what we can achieve but points beyond ourselves; it is a sign and hope of a quality and power of sovereignty that is much more than what is presently at work in the church.

We turn now to the limits of or possible confusion underlying this theological approach. When we say that the kingdom has meaning beyond the church, are we going to say that everything beyond the church is good? Is everything that secularizes, everything that moves out from under the tutelage of religious institutions a good development? Don't we rather need to distinguish between what is good and what is rebellious? Is the fact that the church is relinquishing questionable control over some areas of life always progress, or is it only progress if the control was unworthy or maintained by the wrong kind of power?

A deeper way of responding to the whole corrective thrust is that it did not start from scratch. It did not start from the New Testament as a whole or from a larger biblical view. It rather took one theme that provided leverage to criticize something the corrective movement thought had gone wrong. But that reaction skewed the discussion by taking the wrong kind of church or the wrong kind of missionary experience and standing it on its head. It took a church in which sacred and secular were two different options, in which not peoplehood but the liturgy and not obedience but doctrine was the center and said, "Now, that was wrong; we will stand it on its head." Instead of starting from scratch and asking how the missionary effort went wrong in failing to find an integral perspective from which to move forward, it took a skewed situation and tried to skew it the other way, which is a way of being subject to that which one critiques.

Another peculiarity of this corrective thrust is that it did not take its critique to the heart of the theology of the church. It said it was adding this concern for secular reality to an understanding of the church that was essentially right. The center of church life was still the liturgy, for instance. True, the centrality of ritual was not enough; the church needed to add strongly this secular element and make it our theme. But liturgy still remained central in a way that Hoekendijk and others did not explain. It seemed as if they lost their nerve and said they did not really want to produce an alternative but only a corrective. They would affirm all the things that the church previously had been relativizing. This secularizing theme, therefore, was not a whole new approach. It could not stand on its own feet. It provoked a reaction and assisted in critiquing contemporary missionary agenda, but it did not add something fundamental that would take us beyond the agenda we had before.

One more slogan came to be used in the same discussion, and that is the theme "comprehensive approach." The term is not used in English much, but it has become a technical term in Dutch mission principles. The Dutch have specific schools for the science of missions. Being eclectic in their use of language, the Dutch picked up the phrase "a comprehensive approach" and made it a concept in missionary philosophy. This phrase responded to what we were talking about earlier as a dualism of realms, but it related to institutions rather than to realms. This phrase suggests that the missionary institution should take responsibility for every dimension of need in a particular place. Instead of being selective and saying we will only preach or instead of focusing selectively on certain institutions—for instance, schools—there will rather be an effort to meet every dimension of need encountered. God cares for every dimension of our being. Jesus cared for every dimension of the people he met. Humanity is a unity. The kingdom of God is a society. The slogans are all the same we have heard before, but the outworking is different: the missionary structure coming into a culture should take a total inventory of needs in order to recognize the wholeness of the human person and community.

Did that mean we try to control that culture? Did it mean we use political power? Of course it did. This approach made the most sense in the colonial context, where the church could collaborate with the colonial economic power structure in getting needed things done. In this approach the church had a quasi-state function in developing culture: around the compound everything would happen. It is an interesting coincidence that the position derived from this theology of the wholeness of the human person wound up being more old-fashioned, more power-centered and more colonial than the ones it critiqued. By taking responsibility for more dimensions of life, it was less critical of its own power position. Thus, some of these things ran side by side and used the same slogans but actually came out on the other side of the question.

16

SALVATION IS
FOR THE WORLD

One more subsection of the world culture themes is the slogan "responsible society." This phrase did not originate in the missionary world, though it found a great echo there. The phrase was originally coined by the Life and Work Movement, which was one of several strands of interchurch activity that gathered together in Amsterdam to form the World Council of Churches in 1948. At this initial 1948 meeting the World Council studied together what vision the churches should have for the wider society, especially after the great trauma of the Second World War. It was the beginning of the collapse of empire, so the overseas churches began to have ideas of nation-building. The slogan that gained currency at this meeting was "responsible society." But what did a *responsible society* mean?

In the original 1948 study papers, this concept meant taking a mediating position between extremes. On the one hand there were the capitalist nations, and capitalism risked being unjust because of social discrimination. On the other hand there were the socialist nations, which ran the risk of limiting freedom. Another polarity the slogan meant to mediate was democracy and dictatorship. Democracy, by letting everybody have a say, ran the risk of demoralizing a society with pluralism and paralysis. Participants in the WCC study blamed democracy for the rise of Hitler: that is, he stepped into a power vacuum because democracy did not work. On the other hand, there was extreme authority, of which the Nazi regime and other Eastern Europe dictatorships were examples. On the more abstract level of ethical theory was the polarity between rules, which were too rigid, and flexibility that was so flexible as to be arbitrary and unreliable. The phrase "responsible society" was meant as a mediating slogan to describe some livable options between those concerns. It intentionally had several meanings.

What did it mean to say that a society is responsible, as opposed to saying that the people within it are responsible? It meant that being responsible characterizes all of society's relationships. Those who have authority are under God, unlike the fascists who claimed total authority on their own. But it also meant that individual Christians and the church are concerned for broader social life, as over against the "irresponsibility" of Pietism. Further, the various institutions within society should be responsible or accountable to one another: they have to explain themselves and justify their actions. No agency within society should be autonomous. There should be a network of giving and receiving accountability. Agencies are accountable to God, to the citizens and to other nations.

Furthermore, there should be numerous nongovernmental institutions in a healthy society. There should be volunteer organizations and nonstate organizations, including the churches, doing as much as possible. A strong emphasis in the 1948 documents was on the importance of nongovernmental functions in the social order to keep it healthy and to keep the network of accountability pluralistic and lively. If there were many organizations doing many things in society, there would be no one boss and no one social organism; this would keep the state modest.

The documents were intentionally pluralistic about what it meant where they said *responsible*. The phrase did not mean merely that the authorities are responsible to citizens. It did not mean only that individuals were responsible to be involved. It did not mean only that we admit accountability before God. It meant all of those things together.

The study papers were also ambivalent, although less consciously, about whether the standards of our responsibility are Christian, or in what sense they are Christian. We are Christian. But do we try to run a Christian country? Since most churches represented at the World

Council had a Constantinian background, this ambiguity was built into the discussion. There was always a merging of what is possible for all of society with what is Christian. Some accepted the idea that Christian standards are for everyone—our Lord is the Lord of all—without ever stopping to think that not everybody confesses that lordship.

Others affirmed that Christian standards apply to everybody because Christian standards are not specifically Christian, but natural. What it means to do the good or to be fair are in the nature of things. As the literature developed, this idea of natural law became stronger and stronger. "Man is a being whose nature is to be responsible" is a statement within the documents. What it means to be human is to be a person who is not artificially called to account but who, in his or her very being, is in a relationship of needing to give account. That is what it means to be human. They were unfolding that sense of responsibility when they said that a society should be a responsible society.

Intrinsically that slogan did not say much to the missionary situation. The vision statement was not drawn up for that purpose. It was drawn up by a study group to help the church see how it could exist in a modern Western world after disestablishment at the end of the Second World War.[1]

A second slogan in ecumenical use, "rapid social change," developed in the 1950s when the younger churches in newly independent nations found themselves unprepared for the rapid social change that arose out of Westernization and industrialization. This technical term came into ecumenical language in order to avoid saying *underdeveloped* any longer, since that term implied an elite perspective. So everyone said "rapid social change" but meant the same thing. The younger churches accused the previous missionary generation of not preparing them to be responsible in their young nation. They said the missionaries had not done this because the missionaries were Pietists or because the missionaries had preached a too peaceable and apolitical gospel. This was an interesting impression since most of the missionaries had been neither Pietists nor pacifists. In any case, the churches had not been formed or mobilized to play their part in the life of a young nation.

---

[1]Reinhold Niebuhr, incidentally, was one of the main drafters of these papers.

Suddenly, as these nations became independent one-by-one in the late 1940s and 1950s, the Christians found themselves being social leaders far out of proportion to their numbers in many societies. This was partly because they had been to Western schools, partly because of their moral qualities and reliability, and partly because of their awareness of the West. In response, the World Council of Churches mobilized an ambitious study program about rapid social change under the slogan "responsible society," which brought it great visibility and resonance.

Another line of development of concern for Christian social responsibility stemmed from the breakdown of the moral confidence of Europe. Many people have referred to the First World War as a refutation of the simple confidence some liberal Christians had that the world was getting better and better. Some churches in the 1920s came out of that breakdown still optimistic, but the more dramatic and more destructive Second World War led to more sobriety and to concern about the fault and place of Christians in these events. In most European countries there were Christian political parties, usually called Christian Democrats. Was that a good way for Christians to be socially responsible? What would be the alternative? This was another area in which there was awareness of the inadequacies of old answers and openness to new ones.

THE SYNTHESIS OF RAPID SOCIAL CHANGE AND CHRISTENDOM SELF-DOUBT

The overseas study related to rapid social change and the European awareness of the breakdown of the old model of the church/world relationship flow together in a resulting synthesis I will try to describe.

The primary claim of this synthesis, found largely in the World Council of Churches but which reaches well beyond, is that the first service of the church to humanity is political. *Political* here had to do with the social order because the social order is where humans have to be human, and if the social order is inhumane a person cannot be fully human. The synthesis claimed that the present social order does not permit us to be truly human, and that is why we have to change it. It is fitting that it should be our Christian commitment to change it, because the whole political concern for humankind is socially stated: "the people of God" and "the kingdom of God." If the unworthy social order keeps us from being human, then it should be the church's business to change that, which means getting involved in politics and its foremost instrument, the state. Therefore, the argument went, the course of history as administered by the civil order is the concern of the church, and not only indirectly. The dismantling of oppression is itself the church's concern because it is our business to make the world worthy of humanity.

In a sense, this synthesis simply updated Constantinian social philosophy: "It is our concern that the conditions of our existence as they are structured from the top be restructured from the top. We do so by setting social goals and then implementing them through the power structure. This is our responsibility: to get power and to restructure power." Not everybody spelled it out that way, but that was the general thrust of the assumptions behind the debate.

CHRISTENDOM ASSUMPTIONS THAT DO NOT APPLY IN MISSION

Yet this view of responsibility, which was derived from Christendom, was extended to the whole world, even where Christians were a minority under, most often, authoritarian non-Christian governments. In these situations the assumptions that made sense in the Middle Ages within Christendom no longer held. For example, in the Middle Ages it made sense to think that there is a universal moral law. Everybody in Europe thought the same thing about morality: there was a universal human nature and everyone had the same moral reflexes. However, the larger the world became and the more honest the recognition of the variety of societies in it, the less possible it was for people to assume there was a universal moral law. Cultures are so different that it became harder and harder to claim that there was any common moral insight or any common definition of human nature. Missionaries could still affirm that their own definition was the right one, but they could not assume, as medieval Christians could, that all sane people think the same way.

Another element of Christendom that people tended to assume could be taken for granted around the world but cannot be was the idea that people in public office have a service mentality. There are some people in public office who have that mentality, but not necessarily in the same proportions in different parts of the world. That mentality itself is partly a Western product deriving from the Puritan ethic.

This vision of responsibility also assumed considerable power in the hands of nonstate structures such as free universities, church hospitals, voluntary associations and private foundations. We have in our culture large depositories of power that pluralize the total social mix and make it possible for many decisions to be made that are not administered from a central power. There are many cultures that have much less of that plurality or in fact deny permission for nonstate structures to work.

Another assumption of Western Christendom that does not apply in all parts of the world is the presence of a large, literate elite who are able to criticize, share authority and participate in decentralized decisions. Those people are simply not there in many places.

A further assumption of Western Christendom that does not apply in the rest of the world is the fact that to some extent even non-Christians in Western society today admit to some degree the tutelage of the church. Even though for at least 150 years the majority of North Americans have not been churchgoers, the President of the United States always has had to be a churchgoer. Even though many people in the States would insist that they do not have any obligation to religious authorities, most of them did not insist until the 1970s on doing away with public prayers and religion in schools. Western society at large accepts a certain moral authority on the part of the church. This does not apply in the rest of the world where Christians are minorities.

It is strange that this responsible society language that made sense—even though it could be debated—in the Western world from which it came was widely propagated around the world through the World Council of Churches as the way to help majority world Christians know what they ought to be doing in their own societies. The Western church set before these younger Christians an ideal that was no longer practical in the West and was even less practical in parts of the world where Christian resources were spread much thinner and their ability to change the social order was much more limited.

THE CONTENT OF THE RESPONSIBLE SOCIETY ETHIC

What about the content of this ethic? If we say that what we want is a responsible society and our Western standards of responsibility are making it possible for humanity to realize its potential, what does that mean in terms of theory of knowledge or of revelation? It means that we will not get much social ethical information from the Bible or from early church history because that situation of Christianity was pre-Constantinian. It was a church that was not yet "responsible," given Christendom standards. The word *responsible*, as we have seen, has many meanings, and one of them is the opposite of *irresponsible*. To be responsible means we Christians take over society. We do not let somebody else do it. In the language of Reinhold Niebuhr, *irresponsible* comes to be the main insult. This view admits that it is our duty to be in charge of the direction of society, but what we ought to do does not come from Jesus or the Sermon on the Mount. That source is so far from the problems of running a nation that we have to get our guidance from somewhere else.

If we tell Christians in a given culture that they are responsible for the welfare of their society, most of the decisions they will have to make will be technical decisions having to do with banking, interest rates, organizing medical services and civil engineering. All of those are technical problems. Christian faith will motivate their action, but when it comes to knowing what to do, what is needed are experts who know about banking or engineering.

The standard pattern of the discernment process for many World Council conferences and study papers was to send the theologians into one room to write a preamble and then to ask "responsible" lay people to write the main documents (because they were the ones who really knew what they were talking about). The lay people who knew the field would say what Christians ought to do based on standards from economics and engineering, and then some theologians would say why Christians should care about social responsibility. The assumption was that Christ speaks to our motives but not to our standards for social involvement. The nature of our social involvement would be dictated by the existing structures. There is no such thing as a Christian rate of interest any more than there is a Christian mathematics or a Christian nuclear physics. So, they proceeded to get the experts to tell us what to do and the theologians to tell us we are able and responsible to do it because of our faith. This meant that specific Christian standards, such as those having to do with giving money away or renouncing violence, were not fit standards for the society which it is our business as Christians to want to build.

If it is said that way, and I don't think this analysis is unfair, then this entire responsible society movement is new language for saying something that the old Pietism had said. The old Pietism said that first you get your heart right and then you go out and do what is called for in the order of creation. If you are a prince, then be a loving and responsible prince. If you are a merchant, then be a loving and responsible merchant. The standards for what to do come not from one's new heart but from the structures of society.

More than has been admitted, the responsible society language and literature in world missionary circles were, in their shape, a new Pietism in service of a new power elite. I do not mean the dimension of Pietism that called for cultivating religious experience and having prayer meetings, but rather its ethic. Pietist ethics said that faith gives a person a motive, a concern or a duty, but what a person should actually do would be dictated by the surrounding culture and power structure. The responsible society movement condemned the old Pietism because it served the wrong power elite, the old one rather than the new one. But it retained the rationale for being a Christian power elite, whereas a more radical biblical ethic would ask whether any power elite could be God's major instrument for making a society human. The biblical elements of servanthood and lordship and of the church itself being a new society were not thinkable in the responsible society framework.

That gap is all the more striking if one goes back and looks at the literature. In the 1948 documents, the specific articles in which "the responsible society" appeared as a slogan had a major section on the "church as a model community." This section spoke about servanthood and also about how the church ought to pioneer new ways of making decisions. Here the document assumed that the church was a distinct body, a different kind of structure than the other social power structures. That was not developed in the later literature, even though it would have been especially fitting in a situation where the church had little power and where the model-like character of the church would have had special visibility due to the small number of Christians.

After debating with this literature, my conclusion is to agree with its complaint about the social inadequacy of earlier missionary social ethics and the wrongness of withdrawal or irresponsibility as a church attitude, but to be dubious about the leap into the standard patterns of defining the meaning of social responsibility. That is, I am dubious about the idea that Christians have to plunge in and help create a more humane society in terms of democracy, social welfare and the other ordinary moral standards that Western society has told us to develop.

THE SEARCH FOR A COMMON LANGUAGE

One of the themes in our larger discussion, which was identified briefly when I asked what standards might apply when we are working in a society that is mostly non-Christian, is a call for common ethical language. Those who advocate this direction say that we cannot ask non-Christians to use the language of Christian ethics because they are not Christian and because they probably have an uncomplimentary vision of Christian ethics on the basis of some negative experience with people from the West who claim to be Christian. Therefore we have to look for some other common ground.

They say we need a common human ethical language. That means we need to back out of distinctly Christian ethical language in order to get a vision of human society that is not denominational or sectarian. It assumes that backing out of one's particular identity will make one more open or broad. This concern to find a common language is reinforced by anticolonialist reflexes, cultural anthropology and other social sciences that tell us how every language is relative to a given culture. Therefore we need secular or nonreligious language in order to talk about our visions for a good society.

What would that common language be? Where would we go to get it? The literature of people who try to start with their own Christian orientation and drop it in favor of something else suggests there are two main paths, and neither of them works very well. One is the idea of secularity, which we already examined. But what is a secular human being? If you try to find a definition, you might discover that it is a post-Christian Westerner. The idea of secularization is a Western experience. It comes from the withdrawing of the religious dimension from the vision of humanity that dominated in Western society. If in other parts of the world secularization happens, it is a result of the impact of the West. It is not a base that all human beings had in common before we learned about one another.

The other path is relativism: your standards are for you, and hers are for her. The point is that nobody's standards have any weight. The only thing we can be sure of is that relativism is an imperialistic stance because it tells everybody they are wrong. Relativism is a corrective for absolutism, but it cannot really tell us what to do next. So we do not get anywhere looking for a common human ethical language by backing out of particular Christian identity.

Another path would be to affirm the particular identity of each ethical position but to correct it in the direction of tolerance and mutual recognition. This is not to say that all positions are equal. Rather it is to say that this mutual recognition position can most clearly explain why it tolerates others, affirms their rights and works toward living together in ways that respect the particularity of all the various people that are present. It does this not by boiling them down to a common denominator, but by affirming them as they are. Not all positions are equally right, but they are all worthy of respect.

Most of the value systems in the world are not tolerant. Christendom Christianity has never been tolerant. Islam does not believe in tolerance. Secular nationalism does not believe in tolerance. But New Testament Christianity—believers church Christianity—by definition is committed to being tolerant. That does not mean that those who accepted it always lived up to that commitment, but the vision was there. As long as Christ is Lord, he is at the same time the Lamb. He is not a sovereign but a servant in the implementation of his desire for all people.

SALVATION IS PERSONAL

One further theme and debate that touches on the responsible society emphasis in mission is the place of Christian social involvement and

God's work in the world relative to personal decision for Christ. Just what is the meaning of salvation and to what extent is it personal or corporate?[2]

One of the striking things is that although this mission-related debate started in the 1970s by focusing only on this question, it is clear that it was actually a global set of debates about all kinds of questions: about the dominance of North Atlantic culture; about the place of the missionary professional; about divergent attitudes toward different forms of socialism; about biblical authority. The debate was much bigger and messier than simply saying that certain people believe in personal salvation and other people do not, or that these people believe that social action is valid in itself and those people believe it derives only from a personal encounter with Christ. Describing the debate in terms of some people being for personal salvation and others putting it lower on the list is a deceptive formulation. But it is always there in the mission literature.

The Division of World Mission and Evangelism within the World Council of Churches met in 1974 in Bangkok, Thailand, about "Salvation Today." The preparatory materials for that meeting asked what salvation means and sought to answer that question by asking people what they needed. A large body of documents reported what people wanted. Some were hungry and wanted food. Some were lonely and wanted company. People defined all kinds of human fulfillment they felt were missing. The discussion at Bangkok was to be about how those definitions were the same thing as the salvation about which the gospel speaks. But that is a different question than they started with, which was what the Bible says it means to be "whole."

A foundational question lay beneath the strong emphasis on "salvation as historical" that we reviewed earlier, beneath the debates about "social responsibility" above, and it shaped the WCC discussion about salvation: What is God doing in the world and how should we respond to it?

In "The Church's Response to What God is Doing," David Stowe suggested that there are two ways to proceed in making the affirmation that God is doing something. We can start by assuming that we have some

---

[2][The remainder of this chapter was constructed from brief lectures in 1973 and 1976 and from Yoder's much longer responses to students' questions. Therefore this material was more heavily edited than other parts of the book. —Ed.]

notion of who God is and what God would want us to do, and then go out and find where that is happening. For instance, we might say God wants liberation. Then we look around the world to see where that is happening. God wants people to be fed. We find where that is happening and support it, affirm it, celebrate it and share in it.[3]

The other logical option is to believe that it is God's nature to work in the world, but not to claim to know ahead of time what God wants to do. We then go out and see what is happening and say, "Well, that is it." We recognize God's work not by prior criteria but by discerning what is happening in the world.

This was the approach that was fostered in the preparatory booklet for Bangkok, "Salvation Today in Contemporary Experience," which was a collection of excerpts from all kinds of literature—poetry, diaries, political accounts and fragments of novels and short stories. If salvation is something that when we have it, we are grateful for it, and when we do not have it we feel lost, then we can go around and see where somebody says he feels lost or ask what she feels is missing. Where someone feels wholeness, we can ask about the shape of that wholeness. That is what this booklet did. It tried to start without a definition of wholeness or lostness and went around asking people, "What is lostness as you are experiencing it? What do you testify to be the wholeness that you have found? What makes you happy?" German theologian Peter Beyerhaus described one critique of this approach this way: "the ecumenical idea of 'contextuality' dissolves the concept of salvation into a number of widely disparate experiences. There is no clear recognition of the one basic reality of salvation that transcends all its specific expressions and consequences."[4] That is, salvation is definable; it is distinguishable from consequences, from things God has not yet done—like concluding the redemption of the world—and from the widely disparate ways individuals experience it.

The Bangkok approach to salvation was particularly troubling to

---

[3][David Stowe, "The Church's Response to What God is Doing," in *Protestant Crosscurrents in Mission*, ed. Norman Horner (Nashville: Abingdon, 1968), pp. 139-77. —Ed.]

[4][Peter Beyerhaus, "The Theology of Salvation in Bangkok," *Christianity Today*, March 30, 1973, p. 17. Beyerhaus was describing a critique of Jürgen Moltmann's presentation. —Ed.]

evangelicals, especially the place of personal experience and conversion. This is the way the National Association of Evangelicals (NAE) spokesmen probably most often focused the issue. Is there really a call to individuals to respond with a personal decision for which conversion is the traditional proper name? Should the focus of Christian mission be on an evangelical experience?

The polarity came to be structured in a more visible way as organized opposition developed to the ecumenical study process in which responsibility and secularity were the dominant themes. The old form of this organized opposition, which is still very alive, is the North American evangelical movement of which *Christianity Today* is the most prominent voice. The movement had several cultural bases. The denominations that as a whole opposed the WCC emphases on responsibility and secularity were one base. Many, but not all of them, were involved in the NAE. Strikingly, some of the more historic ones—the Missouri Synod Lutherans, the Christian Reformed and the Southern Baptists—were not active in the NAE. Second, there were some major denominations of the mainstream traditions that were conservative and critical toward this kind of movement. Third, many individuals and some local congregations within the denominations that participated in the organized conciliar movement were unhappy about this understanding of salvation.

An article in *Christianity Today*, "Salvation Is Not the Same Today," captured the evangelical concern.[5] It said that there was a position on salvation that was once settled and correct and was now being attacked. It referred to the current historical mood, claiming the WCC was moving the landmarks. Evangelicals at the time referred to this way of speaking about salvation as a departure, a selling out, even a betrayal. They claimed that there was a classic model of what it means to be the faithful missionary church, that this model was clear and was being practiced and was now being set aside or undermined by certain ecumenical missionary agencies in larger denominations, who justified that unfaithfulness in terms of secularity, service, the autonomy of the local church or other considerations.

---

[5]Donald Hoke, "Salvation Is Not the Same Today, " *Christianity Today*, February 2, 1973, pp. 37-38.

The evangelical call to individual renewal was also a call to return back to the Bible, back to the historic position, the defense and confirmation of the faith. One clearly gets the impression, as an observer seeking to be somewhat objective about this whole process, that there were underlying social and psychological issues. But our concern ought to go beyond that observation to ask something more basic, more theological.

However, we should ask first not about the meaning of conversion or whether salvation is the same today as in the past, but rather what it means theologically to affirm the missionary past as one's guide. This points us to some confusion about what that past was. Appealing to the missionary past as a guide seems to assume the missionary movement had been correct, established, ratified and official or accepted, so that one could say, "The historic missionary position of the Christian church is the one we are reaching back to." If you read the story of the historic missionary movement, it was a minority movement most of the time. It was divisive in its relation to orthodox theological education and church organization. Most of the time it was divided within itself in its strategies and convictions about how to proceed and especially about how to relate to the established churches, which generally did not support it. The intellectual and structural authorities in the home churches usually looked down on it. On a factual level, there is something dubious about appealing to the historic missionary position of Western Christianity as an authority, as if that past had been official somewhat like the way the Augsburg Confession was official.

A further question is whether it was indeed the case that there was a new problem, a redefinition of salvation that was being imposed on the missionary movement from the West in such a way as to undercut the meaning of mission? Or was that a misinterpretation of the issue? The response of some of the people from the two-thirds world at Bangkok was, "Do not bring us your Western problems. You Western people have a hang-up about the relationship of conversion and ethics, or the relationship of present salvation and future salvation, but we do not. So stay home and solve your problems back there. Then you can tell us if you have anything to say."

The real question raised by the people back home was, "Is there one way to define salvation—in transcultural, universal, objective terms—and are all other experiences of wholeness or lostness distinct from that? Or is it the other way around: wholeness and lostness are what humans know them to be when they encounter them, so we should not try to look for a central definition of salvation?" Those who would argue for this latter approach would say that we should not look for one definition of what it means to be saved because it would be stated in terms of somebody's particular culture, for instance, in some German Pietist or North American Baptist language. They would say instead that we should be contextual. In that case we would ask what it means to experience salvation in contemporary experience. If for somebody salvation is a break away from the oppressiveness of false traditional religion to a sense of authenticity, honesty and doubts about traditional theology, perhaps that is salvation for that person. If someone says, "I found a loving community," "I found independence from an oppressive father image" or "I found a call into a movement that demanded my total devotion in the service of my neighbor," that would be salvation as they experienced it.

The WCC meetings did not assume that all contemporary experiences of salvation were self-authenticating. At their meetings, including Bangkok, there were always serious inductive Bible studies. But the passages selected for Bangkok were all about liberation. There were no passages about how to live in the exile, how to bear the cross or how to be a minority community. All the biblical passages from the Old Testament to the New were about liberation and the wonderful city God is going to set up for us.

But this did not mean that individual salvation was completely overlooked. Jürgen Moltmann, for instance, tried to bridge the gap between the evangelical concept of a predominately personal and eschatological salvation and the ecumenical concept with its this-worldly emphasis. He said, "Salvation is the peace of the people of Vietnam, independence in Angola, justice and reconciliation in Northern Ireland and release from the captivity of power in the North-Atlantic community, or personal conversion in the release of a submerged society into hope, or of new lifestyles amidst corporate self-interest and lovelessness."[6] All those different things were the meaning of salvation. That is, Moltmann claimed not to eliminate the personal but to relate it to the social. This view would probably have been true of the rest the people contributing to the WCC process.

The overall emphasis, however, was not on the personal level, and the study process did not seek to balance the two. A good summary of the issue from an evangelical perspective was that of Harold Lindsell, who was editor of *Christianity Today* at the time:[7]

> Bible Study Group II seemed to get a little closer to the truth [which, of course, means his position] in its statement that "salvation can only be conceived as liberation from sin." But the statement goes on to say: "it is necessary, however, to state clearly what sin means and to name without fear its present forms, especially its social and political forms." [Why especially its social and political forms? So there is a bias that way. But only a bias, that is, when you say "especially" you also mean that the individual forms would be taken into account.] Nowhere was sin or liberation from it clearly defined in the biblical sense. Sin is the lack of conformity to the will of God [well, nobody at Bangkok would have disagreed with that]. While sin may be manifested in corporate ways, responsibility always lies at the doors of individuals. Society as such cannot commit adultery, for instance; individual sinners do this.[8]

That last sentence is key. But what does it prove? For Lindsell, the meaningfulness of the statement "that is a sin" is that an individual can be called to account for it. He or she can repent of it or refuse to repent of it—and then is guilty. *Responsibility* is once again a key word but this time with an individual focus: "I am responsible, I have sinned, I confess my sin, I repent." This individual experiential focus is certainly biblical. But does it have as well all of the dimensions of peoplehood and the wider social realism of the biblical view, which includes the context of personal sins?

The relative emphases on individual and corporate salvation have im-

---

[6][Beyerhaus, "The Theology of Salvation in Bangkok," p. 17. —Ed.]
[7][Lindsell was editor of *Christianity Today* from 1968 to 1978. —Ed.]
[8][Harold Lindsell, "Dateline: Bangkok," *Christianity Today,* March 30, 1973, p. 9. —Ed.]

plications for mission. Where should we begin in talking with others about salvation? For example, if we are trying to talk with someone from the non-Christian world who cares about social agenda, would that mean that we should not talk individualistically about salvation? How would we talk to that person about salvation if we do not accept his agenda? Would we say, "Well, of course, we will talk about social justice too, but we will first have to talk about Jesus, or we will first have to talk about personal sin"? Or would we say, "I will talk with the person about social justice, but then we will discover that we have to talk about Jesus before we are done, or that we have to talk about personal selfishness and personal repentance before we are done"? Those would be two different ways; a third would be that it is enough simply to talk about social justice.

One question is whether we would accept the other person's theme at all. We could say, "Yes, that is a good subject, and I will be able to talk with you about that but only later. First, we have to talk about the heart, about personal experience. Or first, we need to have a biblical basis, that is, talk about Jesus and Abraham." Or, we could accept their theme. If we were talking to a Marxist, for example, we might say, "Well, I will start talking with you about the problems of the economy.[9] But I warn you that we will discover before we are done that there is something wrong with peoples' personalities, devotion or their hearts. They are selfish. That is why Marxism will never work. We will never get a humane society because Marxist bureaucrats are just as sinful as the rest of us. And therefore what is really needed is a change in the heart." Or we could say, "Yes, I will accept your agenda, but you are going to find out that there are deep problems about the nature of truth, and you will finally have to come around to figuring out where Marx got his concern for a humane society. You will have to go back to some kind of historical source of respect for persons. And that will bring you back to the biblical criterion again."

There would be others who would say that someone's theme is simply wrong. It is wrong because it is put to us by anti-Christian forces, and we

---

[9]There are, of course, as many kinds of Marxists as there are Christians. It might be that we would meet an existentialistic Marxist who would share about his new heart right away, so then we would have to talk about the historical Jesus instead of whether we have a new heart free from guilt. Or you we might meet a Freudian Marxist. If she is already a liberated personality—she has no guilt or she has been forgiven—then we have to discuss the Sermon on the Mount.

must call people to be converted from that agenda. We understand the theme, and we will not stop talking with them. But we cannot really accept it as a basis for discussion, because it is the wrong question. It might come from an atheist stream in Western culture or from elsewhere, but we will solve the problems of a humane society better precisely by not accepting that theme and its terms.

We could also say that for the time being it is enough to talk about accepting the non-Christian as a fellow human and accepting his concerns as our concerns for now. In this case we would not ask about the difference between the individual and the social, but about the difference between our view and his view of a humane society.

Wherever the conversation begins, the personal and the social belong together. The striking thing in the ecumenical-evangelical debate related to Bangkok was that the people who talked about keeping the personal and the social together in one bag—the people who were running that meeting—apparently failed to convince their critics that that is what they were doing. The evangelicals also wanted to hold the two together, but they wanted to be clear about the distinctions within the unity in order to deal with both of them honestly.

The "Salvation Today" document was saying the opposite: if salvation is all one bag, then we do not have to keep talking about the personal and the corporate all the time. That is the meaning of a bag. Wherever we pick it up, we have the whole thing. So we do not always need to make a point that there are two parts. Of course there are two parts. There are also sixteen parts, if we slice it in two often enough. But if we say salvation is a unity, then we should not have to always take the parts apart. If somebody asks, "How can we have a humane society?" and we get hold of that, we have the whole gospel. If someone else asks, "What do I do with my sense of guilt?" and we truly pick that up, we have the whole gospel. If somebody says, "Hallelujah! I found a community that accepts me," and we pick that up, we have the whole gospel. That is what the WCC booklet "Salvation Today" tried to do. It took all kinds of good and bad experiences and identified them as lostness and salvation.

This view requires a certain openness and trust, even regarding what the "real agenda" in the conversation is. If one knows ahead of time that the real agenda is always the four spiritual laws or is always participation in the liturgical life of the church, then any other discussion will be just a shield or preamble to get at that real thing. But we could also say, "Because I know we will ultimately get to everything, I don't need to know ahead of time in what sequence we will deal with what. So I will simply start with that neighbor. What is his or her problem? What agenda do we have in common? What do we want to do together in the world?" And we will trust that all items will come out in the proper order. Personal conversion might be the last thing to arise or it might come up third. We will not know ahead of time at what point something that separates us will call the other to accept our faith or will call us to accept their faith. Does it help or hinder to know ahead of time where that will be, so that we are always behind the scenes steering toward that? Should we rather say, "I trust that there is a decision process going on here somewhere, and I will throw myself into the conversation, trusting that it will show up"?

Taking Lindsell's side now, it was the people who organized the Bangkok meeting who avoided having to call others to decision by selling out to them. If they met a Marxist; they would sell out to him. If they met an atheist; they would sell out to him. If they met a women's liberationist; they would sell out to her. Whatever the other's agenda is, they would say, "God bless you. That is a wonderful agenda. Can we talk about it?" That approach avoids the call for decision, because there is no judgment and no gospel message.

A BELIEVERS CHURCH RESPONSE

I see increasingly in this kind of debate a replay of the way the Pietist centuries have determined the options. The options are either that you bless Christendom or that you critique it by seeking personal authenticity. And neither of those options includes that of the believers church. The two options have structures, and their independent agencies continue to develop as time goes on, but the definition of the Christian mission is not the building up of the church as a new people in which there is both the dimension of social identification—visible, structured decision-making, responsibility, economics and so forth—and the responsibility of every individual to become part of this group by his or her own decision. Absent in the debate is confession of the unfaithfulness of the church—looking more critically at the past than either party does—and the dimension of the believing community. The believers church as a historical type is an option that does not get into this debate. It would be a third alternative that might avoid the debate or transcend it. But that, coming from me, is a prejudiced statement.

A Pietist, if he or she accepts the believers church as a theological model, not just as a historical organization, would be committed to a new social style, not simply to insistence on the authenticity of personal experience. Official Pietism says the outward structure of the church is immaterial, whereas the believers church says outward structure is an indispensable part of the faithfulness of the community. If someone from a dominion tradition would join the community, part of their commitment would have to be servanthood as an alternative to trying to run the world. People could come from various backgrounds and there would be correctives for these tendencies.

We cannot say that the believers church as expressed in particular denominations has been "right." But I think we can say that there is a total biblical witness that would help with the get-with-it-in-the-world thrust. It says, "Yes, but." That is, it says that in our being with it in the world we have criteria for discernment, rather than joining the stream and baptizing whatever goes on. The teachings of Jesus provide some criteria in relation to both social experience and inward experience. What matters is if they issue in discipleship and peoplehood.

Simply saying, "Join whatever is going on in the world; it must be good because somebody is experiencing it as salvation," is not critical enough. From a believers church perspective it cannot be adequately critical, because it does not have a people to be a base for the critique, to provide the discerning "Yes, but." The evangelical alternative that says salvation is not the same as what goes on in the world, for "salvation is always the other inward thing," is also not critical enough. It is not as concerned about history as the Bible is. Present in the believers church are both the elements of a people in the world and of decision and inwardness—at the point of membership and at the point of the ongoing openness to admonition.

The believers church would also be dissatisfied with superficial understandings of conversion, whether group conversion or individual conversion. It would make more of the Christian community's newness. It would not polarize on right-wing or left-wing social action. It would rather see social presence as the outworking of the believing community. It would be as critical, if not more so, of colonialism than the recent ecumenical discussion, but that would not mean it would be systematically revolutionary. It would be as independent from current trends in mission as the critics of ecumenical trends would want to be—but for different reasons.

17

MESSAGE AND MEDIUM

Presence

Is there a limit to the instruments—the medium and the methods—that can be used to spread the gospel? Are there some methods or tools that are fundamentally wrong, or is it a message that can be carried on almost any vehicle? This question came to the surface when we were talking about church growth. The question in chapter fifteen was whether there might be some ways of getting new members that would be counterproductive because they would confuse the meaning of membership or the meaning of conversion, and therefore the growth would not be genuine. Now we are asking that question more generally. Are there some ways to communicate the Christian message that cannot possibly communicate the *Christian* message because of their very structure?

One example might be the Crusades. To link holy violence with the propagation of the faith is a contradiction in terms or a contradiction in the message's very structure, if it is the case that the gospel means the repudiation of holy violence. Whatever one thinks the content of the gospel message is or includes, certain missionary methods that deny that particular content would seem to be excluded. If somebody's conviction about the nature of the church is that membership is for believers, then baptizing people in great numbers by marching them through a river, as Clovis did with his army in the fifth century, or baptizing a whole African tribe with a fire hose—something that Karl Barth once referred to as a parody—would seem to be a contradiction in terms.

Whether or not those things ever happened, they are good illustrations of the point.

If our concern is for the validity of the response, then the use of conditioning techniques—about which we can be more conscious since Pavlov—is also questionable. That is, at what point does consciously manipulating an individual's response by use of techniques that we know produce certain responses become questionable? That depends on how much we care and in what form we care about the authenticity of and freedom from coercion in the decision.

There might be other words or symbols that have meanings we cannot possibly use to say what we want to say in a given context. For instance, in Christian language and experience we have some sense of the positive meaning of the cross. But to a Muslim the cross is the military symbol of violent Europe. The crusade was a war carried on under the banner of the cross. It is not a simple thing to say we know what the cross means. Symbols mean what they mean to whom they mean it. We cannot go to the Muslim world with the proper biblical evangelical meaning of the cross and think we are communicating that meaning; for them the cross has taken on another meaning. If we would fail to adjust, we would be communicating the wrong thing.

That is the simplest, most sweeping form of inappropriate content and vehicle. There are some things we cannot possibly say through some words or instruments because they communicate the opposite of what we mean.

Another set of questions would be whether we should be careful or critical about skewing the message but not in such a sweeping way, that is, saying something that is not false but also is not enough or is not on center, something not incorrect but out of proportion. For instance, if it is the case that Christian faith involves commitment to a process of ongoing relationship and growth after conversion, then what does it mean if a message is propagated in such a form that the convert does not have a teacher or a context for growth after decision? The whole message was not communicated if it was not a call to enter into a community of growth, mutual support and further teaching. Or to say it another way, what if the message is a call to enter into a community, a fellowship, and yet the convert is reached and won—one by one—and stands alone? What if the message is that God takes every individual seriously and that each person should believe that he or she is personally the object of God's concern, but the only way the listener is evangelized is in a mass? All of these are possible ways in which a message, which in its verbal content is perfectly adequate, can be skewed by the context in which it is being communicated.

LIMITS OF THE MASS MEDIA

One context that has this kind of limit is the mass media. What happens to a message when it is propagated by a messenger who is present not physically but through a voice, a video or a written document? One limit is that the person who responds to a mass media message responds alone sitting in front of a receiver or reading a pamphlet or a tract. Neither the experience nor the communication produces a link to the Christian community. It may be possible to move from that point to discovering a local community. Information about the church may be included in follow-up correspondence with the broadcaster or it may be included in the counsel given by the broadcaster. But the experience of community does not happen through the communication medium itself.

There are other limits to what can be said by means of the mass media, although this is just a sample of the kind of critical approach we should bring to all vehicles of communication. A second limit to mass media is that these tools of communication multiply the power of especially gifted people and not of ordinary people. If a teacher, a speaker or a preacher is communicating with a local congregation, he competes within that congregation for the attention of the listener only with other communicators in that same area. But once the mass media have entered people's homes, the competition for attention is with the best people in the profession in terms of the capacities and gifts that contribute to effectiveness. Many more people are able to hear and encounter whatever is impressive about the ministry of a greatly gifted person who is technically well supported by the media. But the number of such gifted people who can be encountered in this way is by the very same definition fewer and fewer. That is, there are more people who will not be heard because those who are highly gifted are heard more.

Further, while listeners experience these gifted communicators as powerful, they seldom encounter them in a personal sense, because the more widely the outgoing communication takes place, the less likelihood that the communicator—an editorial writer of a great journal or a television show speaker—will carry on any conversation with a responder. Although that could happen, how often do such people try to develop a personal communication with the constituency? More than one Mennonite broadcast has tried this in the past, but it is not typical of the way the media works to expand the power of the gifted person.

Another limitation of the media is that objectively there are some things we can do and some things we cannot do. Communication specialists talk about the distinction between *presentation* and *communication*. Communication is when there is enough back-and-forth between the parties that we end up with an understanding in common. By various means—and they do not always have to be talk-back—there is some testing of whether what got across is really what was intended. An alternative, according to communication theory, is what they call *presentation*, which just says we make an idea accessible. We do not find out how people perceive it. We do not check whether they believe it. Rather we make a public aware of the existence of an idea, option or orientation. This is what theater does. It does not claim to get a response. It dramatizes something. It states something.

Another way communications specialists speak about the modest contribution of the larger media is to say that they do not carry on a conversation but they create a climate for discussion elsewhere, and in that sense validly make a contribution. Through the media we can help construct a background to public opinion or expand the common awareness of a whole society, on the basis of which then other kinds of communication can take channels that might not have been possible previously.

The media have the additional limitation that they must hold the listener. The listener does not have to stay for half an hour. A person does not really have to stay in church either, but it is easier to turn off a radio or television at home. That implies that there are some things the listener does not want to hear. Tuning out may involve physically turning off the radio or television or may involve diverting attention in another way. Martin Marty wrote a book, *The Improper Opinion,* focusing on the phenomena that the media assume because of the conversational context of the society at large.[1] That means there are some things we cannot say, or we can say them but nobody will listen. For example, if a person is working in a market economy, he or she cannot say something the same way that someone would say it in a socialist society. The need to reach the listener, therefore, puts limits on what can be said. That is a different set of limits from the ones talked about before which are simply built into the fact that a person is distant from the listener or has many different listeners at once.

The more we care about some particular element of the communication, the more questions we have to ask about the authenticity of the communication technique. One example that I have never had occasion to hear discussed seriously on the part of the people who care is the understanding of public prayer in the mass media. In the past Christians have believed that when a community gathers and somebody prays, that prayer is, in a meaningful sense, the expression of that community's mind and in some sense God hears that. What does it mean when it is someone on a video who prays? There may be a community watching, but the speaker is not present. Is the listener praying? Is God hearing? The more we care about the authenticity of what is behind the portrayal, the more we have to wonder what is going on. Something is going on; there may be authentic decisions or genuine events in response to the video. But how, when and how often do they take place? To what limits are they subject? Do they represent a meaningful community process?

This reference to the mass media and its limitations is meant to open up the field for the two topics of presence and servanthood. The concern about communication asks us to consider the link between the channel and the content. But we should not think that the concern for that link comes only from criticism of the media or disapproval of certain techniques. The question is wider, and we might be able to speak affirmatively also about how the form of the message fits its content.

---

[1][Martin Marty, *The Improper Opinion: Mass Media and the Christian Faith* (Philadelphia: Westminster Press, 1961).]

PRESENCE

In part the question of presence is an effort to unfold the concept of incarnation. What does it mean for the way we communicate our message to take seriously the fact that when God wanted to communicate with us, God had to come among us? That is the message of the first words of Hebrews, "Long ago God spoke to our ancestors in many and various ways by the prophets, but in these last days he has spoken to us by a Son" (Heb 1:1-2; cf. Jn 1 and Col 1). What is the ongoing equivalent in the church's life of God coming among us? What does it mean that instead of sending us messengers, God is with us?

There is a whole body of mission literature and argument that uses the word *presence* for its slogan. What does this word mean? Negatively it may mean do not push for individual conversions because they may be inauthentic. Conversion may be foreign. It may be the response of a listener to something that by definition is not understandable because it is alien to that culture. Therefore it must be a wrong response, even if it is sincere, because a person cannot respond except wrongly to something he or she does not understand. *Presence* may mean negation of conversion and church growth, because some critics feel that conversion and church growth extend some of Pietism's practices that critics believe to be wrong.

But what does the word presence mean affirmatively? It emphasizes the importance of identifying with a place. The first thing the missionary messenger must do is compensate for foreignness by being there. What matters the most is not to stop off and offer the Christian message, but to affirm that place as a place where the missionary wants to belong, as a place where he or she is convinced that in God's purposes it is possible to be who one is and to be there. One must become a neighbor, a participant in the social process taking responsibility for ongoing involvement in that community. The act and decision to be there and stay there—*identification*—is itself the message. Of course, once God was among us in Jesus, God did things and said things, but first of all God became one of us. The becoming one of us is not only the prerequisite of the message, it is part of the message. It is the heart of the message. Without it, the talk and the deeds could have been done by somebody else.

In between the simple affirmation that being present is the primary message and the simple negations of foreignness and alienness, there is a search for the authenticity of the form in which the message is spelled out, spoken, dramatized and exemplified. The message that Scottish Presbyterians brought to West Africa was very often a Scottish message. If they had identified more, it would have been less Scottish and more African, and that would have been better. Only by deep and long identification with a place can one know how to state the message in local terms. We have to be there. We have to know the language, the people, their style and their reflexes so that what we communicate is not simply a Scottish Presbyterian prejudice against Pietism, for instance, but it is a new way of speaking, a new way of implementing concern for the cultural appropriateness of the message in the form that it is heard.

What is the foreignness that presence is concerned to deny? First, it is the cultural foreignness of a message that is formulated elsewhere. Second, it includes the sociological form of a priest or preacher who originated in a situation different from the leaders in the new younger church.[2] The priest who does not have to earn his living, who does not have to take care of a family and who has the privilege of a special education, is foreign. However, if he were to identify with their situation, if he were to be present, they would understand what he is saying. This is the kind of thought that lies behind the worker-priest movement in Europe.

Third, presence seeks to deny the political foreignness of being linked to a power structure. If the missionary person or even more if the missionary agency is visibly marked by the character of colonial presence, then that power status will say something about the message, something the presence approach to mission would want to deny.

Moreover, lying behind all of the cultural, sociological and political foreignness, there is the inadequacy of words—apart from incarnation—to say what needs to be said.

What can presence say better? Since we are now making the case for "being there" as the message, what is it that being there can say better?

---

[2]This may apply to the priest or preacher even in the homeland because their particular place in society is so different from ordinary church members that they are not sure he is really with them with his promises or his demands.

One thing that being there can communicate better is dramatizing repentance for the sins of the West. Repentance, after all, is part of the Christian message. The missionary can repent of the sins of the West even though he or she did not commit those sins. The missionary need not be an imperialist or a racist. He or she need not be fixing the price of coffee on the world market to repent of the sins of the West. While in a verbal or formal way, such repentance is not quite honest or authentic, yet as a participant in the culture from which he or she comes, bearing its passport and skin, the missionary is identified with the sins of the West. It may be the person is more to blame for them than he or she admits. Claiming one should not be blamed, even for something one is not responsible for directly, is not much of a posture from which to communicate forgiveness. To dramatize one's presence in the mission setting, to identify there, is partly meaningful as a renunciation or even a denunciation of one's foreign identity. It is not that the foreign identity is in all things wrong or improper, but taking one's distance from it may permit or symbolize the renunciation of self-righteousness, the recognition of limits and the denunciation of uncritical solidarity with the identity that the home culture has in the minds of the people to whom one goes.

Another affirmative value stated negatively is the disavowing of religiousness. This is illustrated by Catholic worker-priests. The sacred person, the priest, is put into a slot that in traditional societies is respected but not very powerful or relevant. In modern secular societies, that slot no longer may be respected and is even more irrelevant. The priest in a communist society—say, in a French industrial town in the suburbs of Paris—may still be respected by the non-Christians but for something he represents that is distant and certainly not something that would have any claim on the lives of people. For that priest to move into an apartment in the factory housing or to get a job mining or in the factories like anybody else would be to pull the gospel out of that special sacred slot into which established culture, and especially secularized post-established culture, have put it. It is a new way of affirming relevance, because the priest now lives in our world.

There are some additional considerations in the Catholic traditions in favor of missionary presence. One is the meaning of sacrament. There are

Catholic missionary monasteries that make the point that what they are doing in a pagan or Muslim country is mission because they are sacramentally present. What matters is to be there with the monks celebrating the mass. It is not their business whether any Muslims ever want to be baptized. Their presence is that they are there offering the sacrament—first of all the monks' sacrament of orders and then the sacrament of the mass. That means something. God is doing something in that country because these sacraments are there; they are God's presence already. It is God's business whether this will ever issue in church growth. Whether they should take sides in politics might be an important question if it were a situation of national uprising. But the point is the same. What God wants done first is for worship to be going on there, moving toward glorification of God in the territory. Social transformation and converting people, especially making them become members of European religion, will happen sometime, but they do not think it is their business to say when.

Catholic eschatology is not one of imminent expectation but of the long view. If we are Catholic we can afford to take a long view. In the long view there have been rises and falls in the church's visible success in faithfulness and mission. There were times when there seemed to be success and it turned out to have been hollow. There were other times when there seemed to be failure and persecution, and it turned out that there was still vitality. It is not for us to reckon these things; we know that God will conquer and that God will take up into that fulfillment our ministry of presence. We do not have to figure out when or how soon this will happen. In fact, one of the things that God uses for divine purposes is our patience, which means our willingness to take the long view. In that Catholic framework, it is possible to be satisfied with presence as the center, maybe even the major factor, of the missionary ministry.

In the Protestant context it can be argued that this phenomenon of missionary presence is effective, even if on the surface of things something else is going on. If the missionary has been preaching or if the missionary agency has been carrying on a program of ministries, schools and medical services, and then those years of effort are crowned by people responding and a church being formed, is it because they were preaching or because they were there and cared? Did they win people because they were offering all those services, or was it because they were being there and caring about them? Partly that is an impossible question to answer. But to recognize it as a question is already a step forward from thinking that it was obviously preaching that won the people. Perhaps what won the people was simply staying there. There are anecdotes from certain heroic epochs in missionary history where a mission center would labor for a generation with no visible results and then all of a sudden there would be a shift and significant response. Was it that suddenly a new preacher came with less of a foreign accent? Was it finally that some strategic person in the host society changed his mind? Or might it have been that it took that long for the mission to prove that it was going to stay, and it was the commitment to stay that really won the people? Was it the depth of the identification that finally got past the threshold of credibility?

One more dimension of the possible strength of presence as a conscious self-understanding is the concept of reverse pressure. If we are concerned for tangible, measurable, affirmative response, that concern will put a bind on relationships. It will tend to make us impatient and feel threatened. It will tend to make us sales people, and it will be perceivable that we want people to respond in a certain way. The hard sell, or any kind of sell in certain circumstances, produces resistance. It might be that precisely the patient renunciation of any selling concept, any caring deeply about immediate response or any dependence on response in order to feel affirmed would undercut certain resistances. Maybe this approach would be the ultimate testimony of confidence in the product, the gospel message: "I do not have to try to win you if I am really sure of the truth of what I am saying. Maybe my needing to win you and my need for your affirmative response communicates to you that I am not really sure of my message. Perhaps if I were more sure, I could be more authentic as your neighbor, more present. Maybe that kind of presence would communicate a confidence in the message that my salesmanship does not."

MENNONITE PRESENCE
There are two places—which are, significantly, both in the Muslim world—where Mennonite agencies have worked in a way that does not

immediately reflect high strategic priorities of church growth. Their approach has drawn from the concept of presence: "it is better to be there than not; it is better to be there in low profile than not to be there at all."

In the case of Algeria the work began as a service project subsequent to an earthquake in 1954. That was before the liberation movement in the country was strong. The liberation movement was not present at all in the part of the country where the earthquake was, but as the movement spread, people in the area had to have some attitude toward that issue. In the eight years following the earthquake everything changed. The French Catholic and Protestant population withdrew to France, and Algeria became an independent Muslim country with a history of Christianity being the colonial religion. What was a Mennonite agency that represented the religion of people who had come, taken over the country and been pushed out, still doing there?

Meanwhile, the initiative for the work had been shared jointly by Mennonite Central Committee (MCC), which was a relief organization, and the Elkhart Mission Board. A small community of believers—some European, some American, some Berber and some Arab—had grown from their work; however, the missionary personnel had concentrated their efforts on self-supporting ministries such as school teaching and agricultural development rather than on pastoral work. This is not an ideal case to test the model of missionary presence due to the element of postwar relief and rehabilitation. There were other countries, of course, where a relief program had not resulted in a missionary presence. The Mennonite group in Algeria at least did not come into being through aggressive missionary techniques such as were being used by other Western Protestant agencies.

The Eastern Mennonite Board in Somalia is a still more striking case in that they decided, in response to a government condition, that in order to stay and administer schools they would teach Islam in the Mennonite schools. Agreeing to have an Islamic teacher in the Somali Mennonite schools teaching Islam was more than presence. That was working with the enemy. Or was it? That degree of identification with that place and that culture takes some explaining. It also adds a positive dimension in its affirmative interpretation of another faith; this is an issue we will return to later in the book.

For our immediate focus on missionary presence, neither of these cases tests only the presence question. One overlaps with service, and the other overlaps with letting the dominant religion work within mission institutions. Both of those factors make our examination of missionary presence harder.

From a believers church perspective, we might say that the ministry of presence might be even more important if part of the message is the reality of community. In this case the message is not only something about God that a person ought to know or something about conversion that he or she ought to experience but something about the privilege of being part of a peoplehood. Those receiving the message need to know that this is not just any community, but a nonviolent, power-renouncing, cross-bearing, serving peoplehood. If that is the message, then there is yet another set of arguments that count against the self-conscious use of instruments to push the message harder and that count in favor of missionary presence as part of the message itself.

18

MESSAGE AND MEDIUM

Servanthood

One of the sources of servanthood language as a way to describe the status of the missionary witness is the apostle Paul's language. He often used servanthood language in the "we" passages where there is a peculiar mixture of meanings of *we*. In one sense he was talking specifically about himself, saying things that were uniquely true of himself. But when he said these things using *we*, he always hinted at some applicability of what he said to others as well. One place where servanthood language is especially self-evident is his apology or self-interpretation in 2 Corinthians 3–4: "Such is the confidence that we have through Christ toward God. Not that we are competent of ourselves to claim anything as coming from us; our competence is from God, who has made us competent to be ministers of a new covenant" (2 Cor 3:4-6). After then talking about the difference between the two covenants, Paul said:

> Therefore, since it is by God's mercy that we are engaged in this ministry [servanthood], we do not lose heart. We have renounced the shameful things that one hides; we refuse to practice cunning or to falsify God's word; but by the open statement of the truth we commend ourselves to the conscience of everyone in the sight of God. And even if our gospel is veiled, it is veiled to those who are perishing. In their case the god of this world has blinded the minds of the unbelievers, to keep them from seeing the light of the gospel of the glory of Christ, who is the image of God. For

we do not proclaim ourselves; we proclaim Jesus Christ as Lord and ourselves as your slaves for Jesus' sake. (2 Cor 4:1-5)

Paul, being the servant of the Corinthians for Jesus' sake, is in a backhanded way part of the proclamation. What he preached is not himself
but Jesus Christ as Lord, and therefore he, standing in relation as a
servant to the Corinthians, is part of his message.

The theme of servanthood and service involves a mixture of what
could be clearly distinguished—two different levels of the meaning of
the word *service*. On the one hand, some of the material deals with specific services to be rendered by the missionary agency to specific categories of persons with needs: schools, hospitals, agricultural development, feeding programs in case of famine, and other services. On the
other hand, there is a deeper or more abstract discussion of the sense in
which the Christian or the missionary is a servant and his or her motivation for service. These two do not have to coincide, but they certainly
overlap and intermingle.

Throughout mission history there has been a service dimension, not
only on the level of personal motivation and mood, but also on the level
of institutionalized functions to meet people's specific needs. This goes
back to the origins of Pietism, which in its European base partly formed
fellowships to share spiritual experiences but also formed institutions
such as children's homes, orphanages, old people's homes and poor-
houses. The immediate sense of responsibility for the most elementary
kinds of suffering was always part of the Pietist ethic. This has also characterized Mennonite missionary experience. The oldest North American
Mennonite missionary efforts in India by both of the conferences that
now make up Mennonite Church U.S.A. began with famine relief. In
numerous other places, what became a program relating to the Mission
Board began with disaster relief or postwar relief efforts under the Mennonite Central Committee. Given these developments, service activity
in the missionary cause should be looked at and interpreted.

THE PRIORITY OF CHURCH GROWTH
How should we interpret this missionary service? One obvious way is to

say that these service activities are wholly and properly subordinate to the one primary goal of winning people to church membership. We cannot simply arrive and evangelize people, because they will not listen; we have to meet their needs in order to get their attention, in order to have a reason to be present or in order to demonstrate love of neighbor. There are many good reasons to do service while still saying that its only ultimate value is that it contributes to the evangelistic cause of the missionary enterprise.

The effect of this justification, which is sometimes an affirmative justification and other times a limiting critique, raises serious questions. There is the question of the sincerity of the whole relationship. If the service being offered has an ulterior motive, it is being explicitly used as bait. The effect is also to put the evaluation and long-range motivation of many such efforts under a shadow.

The church growth movement is quite critical of most missionary institutional services because they do not make churches grow as much as had been hoped. One missionary executive actually did a cost-benefit analysis. He analyzed the statistics of several missionary agencies, how much money they spent in different types of missionary activity and how much church growth occurred. He found out that souls were much more expensive when they were reached through hospitals than when they were reached through evangelists. This suggested mission agencies should use their money where the souls are most available and where money or personnel will reach the farthest in terms of yield. This debate, however, is not quite a pure debate because it has been mixed up with the issue of whether the church should control service institutions. Many of the people who say we should not have church-controlled missionary hospitals and schools still want to have schools and hospitals. They want somebody other than the church to structure them, and they want them to be in another relationship to the host culture. But they would still favor Christians working there, and they would still want those needs to be met. The debate is not as clean as it first seems.

The more serious limit is that the concern for measurable results in growth of church membership may denature the service dimension of mission. Can it be genuine service if what we are trying to do is make somebody else an object of our control? If we are concerned with receiving gratitude from those to whom we give a gift, then is it really a gift?

Another problem with the approach that says service is valid only for the sake of church growth is that it presupposes a body-soul dichotomy in the personality both of the service agency personnel and of the persons being served, which is not realistic or biblical.

One of the marginal quibbles related to the place of service in evangelism is how to interpret Matthew 25, the parable of the judgment in which the sheep and the goats will be separated on the basis of how they dealt with "one of the least of these." This is often interpreted as a specific mandate to help the poor and the needy either as contributing in the long run to their eternal welfare or simply as a mandate to be concerned for their physical well-being. Mennonite discussions about relief and service motivation usually interpret this text the second way. Unfortunately for that usage, the passage is actually talking about service to "one of the least of these," which in the early church context where Matthew was written certainly meant service to Christians who were hungry or in prison. The people who rendered the service, it says, are the nations, and they did not know they were rendering the service. According to the most careful commentators, the text affirms some relationship between God's purposes and those non-Christian people who took care of persecuted Christians in the early church. But a Christian serving a hungry person *knows* he or she is serving them and is doing it out of a motivation of love. Therefore Matthew 25 does not provide motivation for Christians to give to organizations like Mennonite Central Committee. In fact, as soon as we appeal to this passage as a description of Christian relief services, we are tempted to become self-righteous. Unlike the non-Christians who did not know that they were doing good, we know what we are doing when we do good. That does not mean it is wrong to have some kind of awareness of doing good. Often a spontaneously loving person will do good without self-consciously thinking much about the fact.

THE SEPARATE PRIORITIES OF SERVICE AND EVANGELISM

The second approach to the same set of questions is to say that we have two mandates. They are both ministry. They are both necessary and obligatory, but they are each independent of the other. We should affirm both but keep them apart. One is religious ministry; the other is social. One is proclamation; the other is service. One is focused on membership; the other is not. Both service and evangelism should be done, and each will be done best if they are kept apart. This seems to have some advantages compared to the first view in that it affirms the integrity of service for the sake of those who are in need.

But it has some weaknesses too. One is that this approach dichotomizes the giver and the receiver by saying we must keep the functions of evangelism and service apart. If we are in school or in the hospital, the missionary will be concerned for learning or healing. Those who are served do not have to believe the missionary's religion, and the missionary does not have to tell others about Christian faith, because this is a service relationship. They would not mind if others would come to church on Sunday, where it would be possible to have a mission relationship. This dichotomy is dubious because there are significant links between evangelism and service in motivation and in the integrity of personality of both participants in the relationship.

Another shortcoming of this simple duality is that it does not give guidance on the level of strategic thinking about the relative accent that should be placed on these two kinds of activity. If we have so many thousand dollars or so many persons available, how should the money be spent and how should the personnel actually use their time? It takes more dollars to support the work of a medical doctor than the work of a Bible teacher. Should we invest the same amount of money in both kinds of work? How should time be allocated? How does the emphasis vary between rich countries and poor countries or old countries and new countries? We do not get guidance on these questions by saying, "Evangelism and service are both good—but keep them apart."

This approach does not provide guidance either regarding questions of how to structure service. Assuming that service is a good thing, how shall it be managed? Shall the church run it or shall it be turned over to the host society or the local government as rapidly as possible? Perhaps service should not even begin until the host society has a way to structure it and we go work for them? What is the authority of the missionary in this process? There are many such procedural subareas to which this statement "do them both but keep them apart" does not provide answers.

THE PRIORITY OF SERVICE

Still another option is to say that only the service dimension is justifiable. We only have a right to go to a distant country and interfere with the society there if we are doing them some good. It is all right if we take along our faith. People will sometimes ask what brings us there and what we believe. We should be free to share that; but we must place a priority on service, because that is our only real excuse for being in that place. If evangelism or church growth were the priority, it would be cultural imperialism.

This position has a long history in the Reformed and Lutheran doctrine of vocation and is also present in some contemporary ecumenical discussion about missionary methods. It can also be found in more evangelical contexts with reference to countries where Christians are not permitted to go as missionaries. Missionaries may still go using a secular vocation as the basis for being present and awaiting the initiative of local neighbors before explicitly sharing something about faith.

Again, there are limits to this approach. It assumes that taking a service project or skill to another part of the world is a less partisan intervention or is less culturally imperialistic than going there with a religious message. But that is not self-evident. If we observe what a service agency does to the local society, it may be highly useful and wanted, it may not be wanted by the leaders of that culture but be very useful or it may be wanted but not useful. In any case it is an intervention into the politics, economy and the cultural development of that place. More often than expected, it has negative side effects or even negative direct effects.[1] For instance, it is possible for a school in an underdeveloped

---

[1]The so-called Green Revolution in South Asia meant they could produce three or four times as much wheat on the same ground as they did before, but that did not mean South Asians had a healthier society. As long as we made traditional assumptions about development—the more people who know how to use commercial fertilizer the better—we could have a good conscience about service. The deeper set of questions about whether service does any good would likely be more of an embarrassment to the people who say service is the only excuse for being there than

culture to have the effect of piping out of that local culture the brightest people because they become qualified for things they cannot do back home. Urbanization and the international brain drain can result from missionary schools if the level on which they provide specialized training does not foster reintegration into the host culture. The same kind of thing could be said about other kinds of services.

Another limit of this approach is that the decision not to be vocal about one's faith motivation, although immediately preferable to compulsively talking about or imposing one's language and agenda, may itself speak as a denial of faith. Silence may say something it does not mean to say. It may make the service person seem more secular, less motivated or less concerned than he or she is. If we are explicit about faith only when we are with other Christians or when those who receive our service ask why we are there, that amounts to saying that Jesus, the Spirit and the community of faith are not there, although they are.

SERVANTHOOD AS PRESENCE

Beyond these three standard answers, each with its shortcomings, I suggest that it throws more light on the question to move from the level of service agencies, service institutions and especially mission-managed service agencies to the other part of the question, that of servanthood. That is, the stance of the minister is perhaps more important and basic or should be looked at first because it may throw more light on the meaning of servanthood ministry than looking first at what he or she does.

Instead of prioritizing our help with schooling, healing or food, I suggest that we start with Paul's language that because we are proclaiming Christ our proclamation includes that we are servants to others for his sake. We would be saying, "We are here to be at your disposal. We are here for your sake because of Jesus." Maybe this would throw light on the procedural questions as well, and even if it does not, it is the right place to start. It may overcome the dichotomy of body and soul in the giver or in the receiver of the aid by affirming the wholeness of personality at both ends of the relationship. That we are another's servant for

---

it would be to those who would say servanthood presence is the reason to be there.

Christ's sake keeps us from distinguishing between our faith and our vocational ministry; it keeps us from distinguishing between our physical need and other needs.

What if we said that while being a servant is not the whole message, it is integrally the message? It is not a buildup to the message as in "I will be your servant for a while so you will listen to me." Nor is it an epilogue to the message as in "We have fellowship so now we help another." It is the message "We are here for your sake." Similar to our earlier point that the message of the church was the *being* of the church, that the church itself is the message of reconciliation, so here I am suggesting that being a servant is much more than a way to get the job done, a way to get some other message across or a way to get a foot in the door to preach the gospel. Being a servant is what we are and why we are. It is one of the ways that Jesus interpreted his presence, most dramatically at the Lord's Supper. He said, "I am among you as one who serves," which does not refer to the actual washing of feet but to servitude as the alternative to lordship (Lk 22:25-27).

Might it not be that the gift we give someone is precisely our lack of concern for his or her gratitude? That is, if we want gratitude, it is not really a gift. Perhaps the witness to our recognition of the integrity of the person to whom we speak is precisely at the point of our deeply internalizing the relationship and our renouncing the cultural and technical superiority which accompanies our ability to meet their needs. Maybe grace is experienced precisely in gratuitousness. That would mean there is no other reason to feed those who are hungry than that they are hungry. It is not that we are going to get somewhere by feeding them. It is not that we are going to produce a reaction. It is not even that we are going to feel good about it. It is simply that they are hungry, and we are their servants.

This leads us back to a deeper root of the presence theme. Where a history of domination needs to be disavowed, where the identification of Christianity with imperial power or even with ethnicity has been made—such as the French in North Africa essentially presenting Jesus as a Frenchman—then the fact that one's presence does not pressure others may be the only way to communicate servanthood.[2] Just as Paul renounced cunning and made no case for the integrity of his message except that he kept on saying the truth, there may be something about the renunciation of goal-relatedness in missionary ministry that itself is a prerequisite of the message's authenticity. That is, identification or presence as slogans might be linked with renunciation of pressure or not needing to push faith or culture on others, rather than with silence or refusal to speak.

There is a Benedictine settlement in Toumliline, Morocco, that happened to be founded at the time the liberation movement began. The Benedictines had trouble being between the camps of the French occupation and nationalism. But that was not intrinsic to their presence there. They also ran a school, an orphanage and a dispensary as part of their servanthood, but they did not let those things define their mission. A few paragraphs from the conclusion of a book about the monastery illustrate this:

> What if the Moroccans suddenly decided that the good done by the monks was outweighed by the other considerations? Dom Denis's answer to this is simple: "Ce m'est égal." If the Moroccans ever decide to suppress the Cours, or shut down the orphanage or take away the dispensary, he says, "It's all the same to me." He regards the services of the monks as fruits of their essentially contemplative life of worship and prayer. If its interior life is in good health, he says, then all of the exterior work could be pruned away without damaging the monastery.[3]

The text then goes on:

> Moved as newly ordained priests, it seemed to us that we were exercising

---

[2]What pressure means has to be discerned sensitively in the situation. Every culture is different. There are cultural contexts in which the very fact that one is a guest puts pressure on hosts to do what they think you want because their culture makes much of hospitality or pleasing the stranger. There are other places where the danger of illegitimate pressure would be primarily through financial or other benefits made available. [The statement about Jesus as a Frenchman refers to the French Christians who controlled Algeria from 1830 to 1962 as a colonial power that only withdrew from Algeria because of strong Algerian resistance movements. French Christianity would have been a major barrier because it was intertwined with colonial power rather than servanthood. —Ed.]

[3][Peter Beach and William Dunphy, *Benedictine and Moor: A Christian Adventure in Moslem Morocco* (New York: Holt, 1960), pp. 202-3. —Ed.]

for the first time the baptismal power of redeeming and saving souls with our Lord. We were here primarily for that reason. Here where a people lives apparently outside of the Redemption, our task is to place them in contact with it. And even if this people, faithful to the Koran, is invincibly ignorant of this "good news," and if the pressure of their surroundings renders them effectively unconvertible, they remain capable of receiving the effects of the death and resurrection of Christ. They remain open to grace and able to lead their lives as children of God.

We understood from that moment that the principal and most efficacious means of acting in conformity with our responsibilities as Christians was the Mass. Thus, even before we had become acquainted with any of our neighbors, invisible but intimate ties bound us to them. How could we have considered them as strangers? A living mystery united us to them within a supernatural kinship.[4]

The monks were clearly aware that being there was first of all their message. As the monk who wrote the book put it:

This hidden work of redemption was completed by a more visible one. The monks lived under the eyes of the Moslem workmen with whom they worked to transform the original buildings into a monastery. We quickly realized that our actions, especially our collective actions as a Benedictine community, had value. If they recalled to Christians the sense of their life, they taught Moslems the meaning of the Church. A young man told me, "I had believed that all Christians were bad. I see now that there are some good ones."[5]

Renouncing pressure and accepting the fact that the people were "effectively unconvertible" was the way to dismantle the identification of Catholicism in former French colonies with a colonial power and to identify instead with the presence of a fellowship.

There is a strong theological root of presence, identification and servanthood in some of the deepest theological themes. Was God any less busy saving the world during the first twenty-seven years of Jesus' life when Jesus was not doing anything that got reported? The acceptance of a context and its limits, the affirmation of "what is" as the place God

---

[4][Dom Denis Martin, quoted in ibid., p. 203; pp. 204-5. —Ed.]
[5][Dom Denis Martin, quoted in ibid., p. 205. —Ed.]

wants people to be served and saved—these are some of the broader ways of making the case for servanthood and for the genuineness of response to the gospel. A genuine response is driven only by the Holy Spirit and not by gratitude, invitations, bribes or the shame of being told that your background is not as acceptable as what we are offering you. In a sense this whole emphasis on presence is one further spelling out of the meaning of believers baptism. Concern that the decision be a genuine one means not putting any pressure on the deciding person other than the opening of a new option.

Renunciation of pressure and power is not just apologizing for Constantine, Charles de Gaulle or King George. Renunciation of pressure and power is not just clearing up misunderstandings. Renunciation of pressure and power is part of the message. It is the meaning of the call to genuine conversion. Even if there were no imperialism to live down, the message would still be the cross. The originality of what Jesus brought was not so much that he taught new ideas about God as that he took the position of the cross. To be servants, to be concerned for the authenticity of the other party's response and therefore to withhold the pressures one might bring to bear as a technically qualified person meeting real needs is itself part of the very invitation.

SHORTCOMINGS OF SERVANTHOOD

One shortcoming of this servanthood theme is the lack of place for what in past missionary motivation was a sense of urgency, of caring about the destiny of all of those persons who do not know Christ. Can we lower the pressure we put on those people? Can we recognize, as the Moroccan Benedictines did, that a population is objectively unconvertible and still care infinitely about them, their relation to God and their liberation through Christ?

From a Protestant perspective, this is a sacramental idea of presence—thinking that because there are baptized bodies, monks praying and the Mass being celebrated, there is really something physically different about that terrain. This is something that Catholics consistently can believe and Protestants cannot in the strict sense. Yet there is some historical truth to it even for Protestants. Lutherans still pilgrimage to

Wartburg although it is four hundred and fifty years since Martin Luther made that ink stain on the wall by throwing his ink bottle at the devil. Places do have meaning because of what happened there, even apart from a Catholic concept of sacrament. But this aspect of presence is challengeable.

Also challengeable is an eschatological patience. Catholicism in its missionary vision assumes we have time. Evil is ultimately self-defeating. Truth is ultimately victorious. We can afford to wait; if we do not win out this time, we can in a few centuries. That eschatological patience is challengeable both biblically and historically. Historical development appears to be going down rather than up in many ways. It is not the case that institutionalized historic Christianity is bound to win out in the end or in any form we know.

Moreover, what about the biblical mandate to talk even when it is not fitting, "in season and out of season" (2 Tim 4:2 ESV)? Isn't a prophet precisely somebody who talks when it is not welcome, who has a message that does not depend on whether people are going to accept it? This particular critique calls for some obvious footnoting. The prophets in the Old Testament story, the powerful preachers in the New Testament context and Jesus himself were in a world where their language was completely known. They were not seen as representative of some distant power. Their message was unwelcome, but they assumed that there was such a thing as prophecy and that the prophet was responsible to speak for God things people did not expect to hear. These were part of the biblical culture. When he spoke to Israel in the name of Yahweh, the prophet was not bringing something foreign or putting pressure on that culture it had not requested.

Another criticism is that if we live for a generation only with the idea of being present, we lose our critical edge; we are no longer clear about the points at which there is something wrong with the situation. Jacques Ellul, who gets most of the credit for popularizing the term *presence* in his book *The Presence of the Kingdom*, wrote a follow-up titled *The False Presence of the Kingdom*, in which he objects to the misuse that was made of the concept of presence. Ellul says that by affirming only presence and not talking about biblical content or moral standards one runs the risk of affirming things as they are. It is possible to use this language of presence and identification to say in effect, things are all right in the world. The world is not really lost. We just want to be among you.

Ellul refers to some of the phrases that have come to be current in this connection, such as "the lordship of Christ."

> The starting point for the logical construct is the lordship of Jesus Christ. Jesus Christ has conquered the world. He has stripped thrones, powers, and dominions of their pretensions and of their autonomy. He is now and in actuality the Lord of the world and of history.
>
> That is all quite right and basic, but there is drawn from it a set of conclusions which are altogether wrong. It is assumed that the works performed by man in this world have henceforth become works that are valid, saved, and expressive of the will of the Lord. . . .
>
> The Christian can only pronounce the great "Yes" of God over these works. He can only attest the good will of God, affirm that these works are a fulfillment and will become part of the Kingdom of God. . . .
>
> Thus human actions are positive actions and the Christian should take part in them, not as a last resort, not as in an absurd and meaningless world, but on the contrary, in a world which is positive. . . . Therefore it is not for the Christian to "Christianize" the actions and works of secular man.[6]

Ellul argues that the lordship of Christ in biblical thought does not mean the world has been made completely new yet. It does not mean that all human action out there is good. It does not mean that the structures of society have been fundamentally changed yet so as to be usable in the kingdom. The Fall is still with us.

It could be suggested in response to several of these shortcomings that it would be helpful for missionary presence in the world to be the presence not only of individuals who ask, "Am I going to be present or not?" but of a congregation, which has more equipment for asking how they are going to be present. Are they going to do this or that with the time they have? What is the process of evaluating various ways of being present? To say this last point another way: silence can be false when there was an invitation to speak or when there was a truth needing to

---

[6]Jacques Ellul, *False Presence of the Kingdom* (New York: Seabury Press, 1972), pp. 13-14.

be said. Just being there and identifying can relativize or even deny loyalty to Jesus. There will be times when the only honest way to be present is to take sides against something. This is easier when there is a congregation.

Presence must not be boiled down to the old doctrine of vocation—"I find my spot in society and do that well." Christians cannot be present everywhere. There are some places where there is no such thing as a Christian vocation, although we could debate the best examples of that, whether it is the Army, Madison Avenue, Honeywell Corporation or a Mennonite rural community. But at least there is such a thing as a place where we should not be. In that context, identification and silent presence are false witness.

Mennonite Silent Presence

The Western Mennonite church comes out of a long period of quietism. In the first part of the twentieth century—longer only in the Netherlands— Mennonites were drawn into missionary activity. We are now aware of and concerned for the world beyond our membership. We feel responsible in terms of stewardship and vocation. In these ways we have caught up with what the mainstream Protestant denominations were doing by way of world missions. We have begun to do what they were doing a few decades ago. But now, coming partly from the mainstream, is a counterthrust saying maybe mission should not have been so organized or institutional. Maybe missionaries should not have brought so much Western machinery along. This is partly a critique from people in the younger churches. It stems partly from biblical insight about how being the church is prior to doing the mission. It may be, negatively speaking, loss of nerve or, affirmatively, insight into servanthood. Questions about missionary activism have come to us from the same Protestant mainstream from which a few generations ago we picked up missionary activism. Does this mean that the old quietism was right after all? If not, what is the difference?

I think there are differences. There were some special weaknesses in the Mennonite silent presence. One was a kind of self-righteousness: "The reason I do not need to talk much is that I witness by my life.

People can see how good I am. So I do not need to tell them how good I am." Usually when one asks what it is that people can see, the answer is that someone refused a cigarette or some other visible virtue. The whole question of what it is that we witness to becomes problematic when the group that is silent is promoting the righteousness of its own cultural shape.

But more fundamentally, that historic Mennonite presence did not cross borders. It crossed political borders in migration, but often did not cross ethnic frontiers. In fact, it often built new walls by migration in ethnic groups from places where the neighbors talked the same language into new countries where the neighbors did not talk the same language. These communities, according to some witnesses, were not always deeply loving communities either. The case for presence as the way of being the church in mission does not relate much to the Mennonite experience of just being in a place.

We still need to ask, as we consider missionary presence, whether there may be times when activism is an escape from being the church back home. One of the examples that has been argued most visibly was to ask how it could happen that a white Southern Baptist who would not want to have a black person in his church in Georgia in the 1930s could have a profound spiritual motivation for going to Africa to be in churches with black people. There may have been times when activism was itself an escape from the challenge to be the church at home. However, that does not mean that staying home until our churches have solved their problems, or especially staying home the way Mennonites stayed home in their quiet faithfulness, is an adequate alternative to going and serving.

We have identified in our study at least three concepts of presence. One is the concept that places priority on identification: "You are not present unless you are like us. You do not have a right to be different until you are like us first." That is the one I emphasized. Another meaning is presence in an administrative or communication structure that has a tentacle in that place. A third meaning, which is linked to Jesus' call to servanthood, is Christian presence as demonstrating what is different from the world. The challenge Christians bring must include their being a body there rather than offering only a message, political center or doctrinal scheme. Presence offers critique but it is not a matter of going around denouncing evils. Rather, it is presenting the alternative that Christian faith represents in that new place.

19

THEOLOGY OF RELIGIONS

Particularity and Universalism

The general topic of the remaining chapters—Christian theology of religions—has elicited a bulk of literature and a number of subthemes worthy of much more attention than we can give them. As we will observe along the way, we cannot talk about other religions in general without doing violence to the fact that they are all different, not only different in that they give different answers to the same questions, but even different in their estimates as to what questions matter. It is not the case that there are a given number of major world religions and that we can describe them all in parallel columns.

Another difficulty in getting hold of this territory is that the usual approaches are inadequate. The simple answers that were convincing in another age are felt to be even more inadequate by people trying to study the matter further. One of the reasons is that when different faiths seem to be in conflict or to collide, the usual way to carry on a conversation almost by definition cannot work. If a person asks how his or her faith is truer than another person's, or vice versa, how would we test that? The paradox of the conversation is that there is no way to test it. I cannot use my faith to test yours, and you cannot use your faith to test mine.

What often happens is that in a given culture there is a set of wider assumptions and both sides try to appeal to them. But that means that the wider set of assumptions has become the absolute, and it needs accreditation just as much as the religious assumptions. Our choices seem to be to find grounds for accreditation that are not based on those faiths and that have only the weight of their own culture behind them or else to consciously accept circular thinking and say that from the Christian point of view the Christian faith is the best faith, which is true but is not a very profound statement.

One example would be the Christian apologetics of late antiquity—the age of Justin Martyr and Tertullian—in which the tendency was to argue that since the most intelligent philosophy around was Neo-Platonism, Christianity was the best Neo-Platonism available. They appealed beyond Christianity to some wider cultural philosophy and said Christianity was the best example of it. Christianity had the highest view of the ideal nature of God. It had the noblest moral vision. It had the purest understanding of revelation. Around the turn of the twentieth century, the arguments comparing faiths would often say that Christianity makes for democracy, humanization, a higher view of woman, hard work and other good things. But why are the good things in the wider culture criteria for determining which religion is better? They had not proved that; they assumed it.

In this chapter, I will not plow through the random answers to that fundamentally unmanageable question, but I will try to clarify the themes in the debate, perhaps get past some short-circuited assumptions that do not hold, and then ask about the relevance of a specifically Radical Reformation theological perspective. For instance, does it make a difference with regard to the relationship of Christianity to the other faiths to have a concept of the church that assumes believers baptism rather than one that tries to sweep everybody in? Does it make a difference for this question to have an opinion on the church-state relationship and on coercion in matters of faith? Does it make a difference for this question to say that in the Middle Ages we needed a Radical Reformation rather than simply an incremental clarification of the nature of the church? As we consider the relationship of Christianity to other faiths, would a Radical Reformation understanding of Christianity handle these questions any differently than a Constantinian understanding of Christianity?

OUTSIDE THE CHURCH THERE IS NO SALVATION

It was Cyprian in third-century North Africa who first stated the phrase "outside the church there is no salvation." What does that mean? What questions does it raise? One question is what church we are talking about. Are we talking about the organized Roman Catholic communion or the unity of all true believers? Cyprian meant the organized Roman Catholic communion, and he meant that statement to exclude some people who thought they were Christians but were not according to him, namely bishops who had lapsed in faith during persecution.

What kind of statement is the phrase, "outside the church there is no salvation"? Is it an affirmation so that after we have heard it we know more than we knew before? Or is it a tautology? Logicians distinguish between analytical and synthetic judgments. Is this an analytical statement that tells us what we mean when we talk about church, namely, that realm which is identified as the realm of salvation? Or is it a synthetic judgment that relates the concepts of church and salvation, which were not related before? Still another way to ask about the same question is whether the statement is historical or metaphysical. That is, is there no salvation outside the church because salvation is something we can only hear about through people? Or is there no salvation outside the church because the metaphysical meaning of salvation is something that is under the priest's or bishop's control?

There was a clear answer to these questions in the Constantinian age. The church in question was an organization. It was the sacramental society of the Roman Catholic communion with its visible structure and rules. It was that body outside of which there is no salvation. That sacramental society had the backing of a particular empire—the Roman Empire—and its position in the middle of the world. Furthermore this church identified its stance with dogma, with one coherent system of truth that had to be affirmed. It was not simply that people had to be in relationship to the priest under a bishop under a pope, but they had to have the right ideas. In fact, faith came to mean more the truths people believed than their fellowship with the communion, although both were necessary. By definition it follows from these observations that this church outside of which there is no salvation excludes other

Christians—the Eastern Orthodox, the Donatists, the Arians or the Persians—which makes the fellowship of salvation much narrower than the total Christian movement.

From this perspective the missionary mandate is to make the Roman Catholic communion available to the rest of the world. This includes all the doctrines, stated in Latin, as well as the sacramental fellowship, prescribed in the Roman form, and some kind of cultural relationship to the empire. Although Christians could conceivably be one in faith without joining the Roman Empire, at least people had to agree that Rome was the center of the world.

This is one side of a polar debate about missions, which links salvation to a specific form. But the same issue, not highly different in shape, is also involved in discussions by and around the Protestant evangelical world. The Protestant views, of course, would not identify a given communion, but they would identify a given message and perhaps a given experience in response to the message as necessary.

UNIVERSALISM

At the other extreme of the polar debate about missions is what might be called "the new universalism." It is new in relation to the older Catholic form of universalism we just described, which links the message of the church and its salvation specifically with a given communion. The new universalism would seem to deny the necessity of a link with the message of the church at all. This universalism claims that all people can be and perhaps even will be saved apart from Christ or the church, and it challenges the more exclusive or particular kinds of claims about the necessity of the message of Christ for salvation.

The first main observation about universalism as a strand of thought is that the historic forms of universalism are the result of a high Christology. They do not come from having a low view of Jesus and therefore a low view of his importance for the world's salvation. They rather come, quite the opposite, from having a high view of Jesus' saving work, seeing it as reaching beyond the borders of the visible church.

Thus statements that suggest such a view is heretical are simplistic. For instance, the Wheaton Declaration states that, "During the first nineteen centuries of the history of the Church, any teaching suggesting that all men ultimately would be redeemed was vigorously rejected as heretical. In our day, universalism is rapidly coming into the mainstream of teaching acceptable to some leading Protestant and Roman Catholic theologians. Many prominent church leaders increasingly champion this viewpoint. . . . The teaching of universalism, which we reject, states that, because Christ died for all, He will sovereignly and out of love bring all men to salvation."[7]

This statement is fairer than many previous statements. But when they state that "any teaching suggesting that all men ultimately would be redeemed was vigorously rejected as heretical," it is true only if they mean that every time there was such a teaching somebody was against it. But the ordinary reader would take this as a proven historical fact that never before during the nineteen centuries of Christian history were there any significant numbers of Christians who believed that "all men ultimately would be redeemed," and that all the creeds and councils were against it. But that is plainly false. It was not condemned by major creeds or councils, and it is by no means the case that it is a new idea arising from a low view of Jesus or high view of non-Christian religions. That kind of affirmation has been in the church at least since Irenaeus, who said, "The Word was ever present to the human race until the day when He united Himself with His creature, and was made flesh."[8] Irenaeus means that the *Logos*, the second person of the Trinity, by his very nature did not begin to be only at the point of incarnation and therefore the world was not without the revelatory presence of God before or beside—that is, outside the realm of—the Christian impact on history.[9]

---

[7]["The Wheaton Declaration," in *The Church's Worldwide Mission: An Analysis of the Current State of Evangelical Missions, and a Strategy for Future Activity*, ed. Harold Lindsell (Waco, TX: Word Books, 1966), p. 223. —Ed.]

[8][Irenaeus, *Against Heresies*, 3.16.6. —Ed.]

[9]St. Leo the Great said that "The incarnation of the Word produced its effects not only after but also before its realization in time, and the mystery of man's salvation was never, in any age of antiquity, at a standstill. . . . From the foundations of the world he ordained one and the same cause of salvation for all. For the grace of God, whereby the whole body of the saints is ever justified, was augmented by the birth of Christ, but it did not begin then." In other words, through Jesus we confess as incarnation the divine nature and purpose and even function (because *logos* is a function, it is the function of speaking) that is eternal. Then you cannot say a priori that people who have not seen the incarnation have not been reached by the *Logos*, by the

Ireneaus's language also picks up biblical language about the *summing up* of all things in Christ. The English *summing up* is a translation for the words we have, for instance, in Ephesians 1:9: "it is made known to us in all wisdom and insight the mystery of his will according to his purpose which he set forth in Christ as a plan for the fullness of time to unite all things in him."[10] *Unite* is a weak word for *anakephalaiōsasthai*, which means to bring everything together under one head, to sum up or to restore. This describes God's saving purpose for the universe in Christ. Sometimes it is said looking forward; sometimes it is said looking backward. But in each case the phrases say that the saving meaning of Christ reaches beyond the body of Jesus in his earthly ministry and beyond the visible church. Therefore we must affirm God's ultimate capacity and purpose to save all people.

In the Reformation period, the Anabaptist Hans Denck said something like this, as did other sectarian individuals. Universalism became much more widespread in the high age of German Pietism. In North America, the Universalist denomination originated as a branch of Pietism, though the denomination has since changed its character and merged with the Unitarians. In Mennonite experience, universalism is responsible for the only Mennonite division that had a doctrinal basis, namely, the origins of the Stuckey Amish in Illinois in the last century, a group that eventually became part of the Mennonite General Conference and then Mennonite Church USA. Karl Barth also held a view something like universalism. These figures and groups are different, but they all stand in the stream we have been describing. If God is all-powerful, and if God wills the salvation of all persons, and if it is the nature of grace to melt the sinner's resistance, then how can we possibly say that certain people are unsavable? That is the logic of it; it is that simple and pious. Biblical language, a set of texts and affirmations, point in this direction that God is all-powerful, that God's purposes cannot ultimately be resisted and that God's purpose is to save all people.

Word of God. That is said looking back in terms of traditional trinitarian thought. ["St. Leo the Great: The Universal Sacrament of Salvation," in *Catholicism: A Study of Dogma in Relation to the Corporate Destiny of Mankind*, ed. Henri de Lubac (London: Burns and Oates, 1958), p. 266. —Ed.]

[10][Eph 1:8-10 ESV. —Ed.]

Different Degrees of Universalism

There are differing degrees in the way people state what it is that they affirm about the possibility of salvation for people outside the church. I once tried to categorize them and came up with five different degrees.

First, the most broad—universalism in the most proper sense of the term—affirms the ultimately possible or certain salvation of all people, and sometimes even of angels, devils and all creation. This view goes back to Origen.

A second form of universalism says that all people may be and potentially are saved, but they do not all know it, so they are not truly saved yet. The difference between potentiality and actuality is clearly visible and that is what it means to be lost. The missionary task is to inform people of what is already true: that they are saved in Jesus. But what does it mean to be saved and not know it? What does *know* mean in this context? Can a person be eternally in a state of being saved and not know it, and, if so, how is that different from being lost? That has not been spelled out. This universalism is reflected in a widespread body of preaching and writing.

For the third we could use the apparently contradictory heading "partial universalism," which affirms the possible salvation of people beyond the church but not of all people. There are several sub-possibilities here. One of them might be an outworking of an affirmative attitude toward some other religion. A person might have observed in Buddhism a concept of grace or in Islam a concept of submission to the holy will of a perfectly righteous and omnipotent God, and he or she might say that those concepts are the equivalent of saving faith for that context. That person cannot deny that somebody who is a genuinely, wholly committed and devoted believer in that context is responding to ultimate reality in a saving way. But they do not say that about everybody. They only say it, for example, about true Buddhists who trust in grace. Second, it may be possible to affirm God's saving attitude toward people who are truly sincere in responding to whatever it is that they know; here someone could point to the biblical examples of Naaman, the people of Ninevah and the Canaanite woman.[11] Finally, the Old Testament vision of the Gentiles coming to Jerusalem to learn the law and go back to live in peace (Is 2 and Mic 4) does not say they will become Jews and bring their sacrifices to the temple. There seems to be around the fringes of the Old Testament vision a concept of a saving relationship to God's righteousness that is not the same as joining Israel.

Another even less sweeping statement might be called "quasi-universalism," which does not really affirm the salvation of other persons or cultures but negates the negation. This view says that on the basis of what we know about God in Christ, we cannot identify any realm where Christ's victory does not apply. We do not have any basis for either affirming or denying the salvation of people we do not know or of people in places who have never heard the message. We do not deny the reality of sin or rebellion, but neither can we, if Christ is confessed as Lord, affirm that rebellion can be permanent and ultimate and can forever resist the loving pressure of a gracious God. This kind of position is most often taken on grounds that are christological, that is, on the basis of what we have learned about God in Jesus, not simply on the basis of God's omnipotence: "if God is God he must conquer every pocket of resistance." If God is the God of Jesus, of graciousness, of forgiveness of sinners, then that is the most significant thing we can say about God. What business do we have after that thinking that God is interested in rejecting people? This view is, I suggest, the mainstream of what is called universalism, from Irenaeus to Karl Barth. It has a certain biblical basis and has been around a long time. It has been rejected also—but then, almost everything else in church history has been rejected by somebody as well.

---

[11]For example, conservative North American Protestant Bernard Ramm wrote, "The operation of God's grace may well be wider than the knowledge of the gospel just as the grace of the God of the Old Testament was wider than Israel. Certainly in Melchisadec we have a man who was not in the stream of covenantal history who was nevertheless a priest of the most high God and the type of the royal priesthood of Jesus Christ. There is the leper, Naaman, who was cleansed by the prophet and Jesus said this happened to a Syrian and not to any leper in Israel (Lk 4:27). Furthermore there is the story of the great repentance of Nineveh, a pagan city, yet for which God had great compassion (Jn 4:11). Jesus found more faith in the centurion than among any of the covenantal people (Mt 8:10). He also found remarkable faith in a woman of Canaan who would not depart until Christ had healed her daughter (Mt 15:21-28). Such incidents ought to teach us that there is a wideness to God's mercy so that faith will be found in the most unexpected quarters." See Bernard Ramm, "Will All Men Be Finally Saved?" *Eternity*, August 1964, p. 25.

These first four options represent an old universalism that is still alive and present in church life. I have the impression in the debate about universalism that the people who are against what they call universalism tend to move toward the top of the scale I have so far outlined in defining what they are against, rejecting the simple affirmation that everybody is saved. Yet the people who affirm universalism tend to be lower on the scale of definitions. They are simply saying that they cannot believe there is no opening outside the church for some kind of genuine reconciliation to God's purposes for someone whose response to grace is real in the terms in which he or she encounters it.

We should observe especially that this whole stream is not based on a high view of other religions or a low view of Christianity or of Jesus. It is a doctrinal debate within Christianity. It might undermine missions for some people. It might also support missions for other people because if we really believe that all people are savable, we are more likely to go tell them about it than if we believe that most of them are not. That is the mainstream of the thrust for universalism in Western Christian history.[12] Its implications for mission are not clear cut.

There is another strong stream of universalism, a fifth type that rejects provincialism and looks for a broader concept of God than the Christian God. This position holds that it is impossible to believe that with the number of Christians in the world decreasing, a God who wants to save all people should have limited himself to such a feeble instrument. This is the kind of position one sees ex-fundamentalists or liberal Catholics holding most firmly. They have a concept of a narrow, exclusive faith—one they once held or saw a community holding—and are now apologizing for that kind of narrowness. They see the particularity of Christ as linked with European Christendom, and since we have grown beyond the cultural provincialism of Europe, they do not want to impose the particularity of Christ on people in other places. I

---

[12]There is more complexity here that would have to be worked at if we wanted to debate universalism for its own sake. There would be the Catholic idea of purgatory in which the unsaved get saved. There would be the Adventist or Jehovah's Witness thinking in the direction of the annihilation of those who are not saved. But our point for now is to observe that the affirmative view is one that has an ancient history. It is derived from a high view of the centrality of the work of Christ rather than from a high view of the pagan religions or of human dignity.

would tend to share the doubts of evangelical critics at this point regarding this stream. Denying Christ's centrality in every sense may be a sellout. But it is understandable because it apologizes for something that needed to be critiqued. It overcompensates for the way in which Western Christendom had become the cultural religion of the European tail end of the Asian continent.

MEDIATING VIEWS

Between the "no salvation outside the church" theme and these two kinds of universalism—the loss of nerve kind (#5) and the high Christology kind (#1–4)—there are some efforts to mediate: to say a little of one but not sacrifice all of the other; to observe some possibility of grace beyond the church without selling out the church's identity in mission.

An interpretation of Romans 2. One mediating view would say that faith is a kind of response, and we know the shape of that response. We can identify its shape where it is happening even apart from Jesus. One debatable example is the affirmation of Romans chapter 2 about the Gentiles outside of the law.

> All who have sinned apart from the law will also perish apart from the law, and all who have sinned under the law will be judged by the law. For it is not the hearers of the law who are righteous in God's sight, but the doers of the law who will be justified. When Gentiles, who do not possess the law, do instinctively what the law requires, these, though not having the law, are a law to themselves. They show that what the law requires is written on their hearts, to which their own conscience also bears witness; and their conflicting thoughts will accuse or perhaps excuse them on the day when, according to my gospel, God, through Jesus Christ, will judge the secret thoughts of all. (Rom 2:12-16)

It can be affirmed on the basis of that text that there is enough knowledge of God's purpose for humanity in the Gentile that he or she not only can usually be condemned by it, but conceivably might be justified by it as well. This is not the place to debate the text. There are other interpretations of that passage which would declare it irrelevant for this purpose. But this mediating reading is the majority reading of that text.

Anonymous Christians. Another form that mediates between particularity and universalism is found in Karl Rahner and his followers who often use the phrase "anonymous Christian." An anonymous Christian is a believer who responds to God's grace, which means that the person confesses that the world is fundamentally a structure of grace to which one may respond in trust. A person says yes to creation because she believes it is on her side. Superficially that is neither easy nor automatic. Creation looks threatening, and so most people do not respond to the universe around them by assuming that it is an expression of grace that can be trusted. But some people do so. Rahner might say that the *Logos* is behind the cosmos and that it is revealed in Jesus. But if someone responds to the universe as if it were grace and accepted that grace without knowing Jesus' name, the response is still the same. Neither she nor others know she is Christian, but the response is the functional equivalent of Christian faith. It has the shape of the act of believing. What God asks for in God's saving work is such faith, not certain information about Jesus, Abraham or the pope. God asks for a response to the universe as if there were grace behind it. For some people the phrase "anonymous Christian" almost means universalism. But in Rahner's own argument it only means that there may be some people from other religions or with no religion who respond to a gracious universe.[13]

So far we have not looked at other faiths. But what about Hinduism or Buddhism as a religion? Is it possible to affirm that the cosmic Christ, or the Logos, or the Spirit of God is working in other faiths as well? The most affirmative possibility is to say that the true Spirit of the true God works in more than one form. There is in that other faith saving truth with its own authenticity and adequacy, which we affirm without needing to test it. We simply affirm that God's Spirit is universally present. That is a real pluralism—the vision of many paths

---

[13]John Vernon Taylor said something very similar in a tale about an African woman finding grace in a secular experience of interacting with a prison guard. The *logos* revealed in Jesus is the backbone of the cosmos. What happened in Jesus is the way things always happen, which means the reason a secular experience of faith is saving is that what happened in Jesus is the way it always happens, the true pattern wherever it emerges from the tissue of history. See John Taylor, "Christian Motivation in Dialogue," in *Face to Face: Essays on Inter-Faith Dialogue* (London: The Highway Press, 1971), pp. 6, 14.

leading up various sides of the same mountain, but the mountain only has one peak.

A second affirmation says there is truth in the other faith but that we only know how to affirm the truth when we find and recognize it. We do not say that everything those from other faiths believe is true; we say that they will believe some truths that we will recognize and share with them. This position goes all the way back to the ancient Christian apologists who talked about the *logos spermatikos*, the seed-like word or the Word present in the form of seed in all people and therefore also in other religions. We have to sift the other faith to find in it some things we can affirm and other things we cannot.

Another still basically affirmative position is to speak of other faiths as "preparation." The faith of the New Testament community was planted in the soil of the Old Testament. Judaism is thus a preparation for Christianity. Christianity claims to fulfill Judaism. In a similar way other faiths are incomplete, inadequate and look forward to something, and Christianity can fulfill that looking forward as well. This means Christians do not have to plant the Jewish foundation everywhere so that we can stand on top of it. We can stand on top of any foundation. We can take any faith and perceive its coming to fullness in Christ, and state this fulfillment in the terms provided by that culture and its faith rather than bringing in the foreign terms of the Hebrew heritage.

There is a considerable body of literature about the way in which Catholic Christianity is a fulfillment of Hinduism. There are numerous Catholic monks and priests who started as Hindu monks and priests and affirm the continuity of that conversion experience. They are not Hindu anymore, but they certainly have not become Jews. Their Catholicism has become the fulfillment of what they were already moving toward as Hindu mystics. The Christ they worship through Catholic mysticism can be described with most of the vocabulary they used as Hindu mystics and monks.

Finally, *reconception* is the word that has come to describe a way to navigate particularity and universalism. When Buddhism has to come to terms with the Christian witness, the Buddhist is a new kind of Buddhist because he has had to deal with Christ, although he thinks he is staying Buddhist. The Hindu, although he thinks he has simply taken Jesus into his pantheon with all the other thousands of divine figures, is changed because of the novelty of the meaning of Christ for his pantheon. The person's faith is a different faith now. It has been restructured by the impact of the Christian presence. We do not say that Christianity is the fulfillment of Buddhism, but we do say that a Buddhist is now following Jesus. One example of this would be Gandhi. Another would be the place of Jesus as one of the prophetic figures in certain strands of Hinduism. That does not mean the people cease to be Hindu, but Jesus has a central, dominating place in their piety and experience.

What is said here about other religions can also be said about other philosophical ways of putting the world together such as the secular humanism of the Marxist or the secular humanism of the believer in education. The reconception position would point out that there too we have an outworking or unfolding of the Christian impact on the world which is related to Jesus even though people love their neighbors and give of themselves selflessly without knowing about Jesus.

DENIAL OF THE SOUL

There is one more phenomenon to be observed which does not really belong here, but it keeps coming into discussion about mission. Universalism is the wrong word for it, but it is talked about in that sense. That phenomenon is the many contemporary "secular" views of humanity that deny anyone can be lost because there is no meaning to eternal destiny. If people cannot really be saved, how can they be lost? This view says the idea of the destiny of persons beyond life or beyond the grave is mythological; it is left over from another culture. We do not know how to talk about it. What would it possibly mean to say that certain people are lost outside of Christ? It does not mean anything.

This view can result from various perspectives. It can come from one particular way of understanding biblical realism and Hebrew metaphysics. In that case the claim would be that the Western theistic Neo-Platonic vision of the soul going on when the body drops off is not biblical. The kind of saved existence that is a part of the Western cultural vision—even in secular magazines you have jokes about people sitting on clouds with harps and halos and wings—is not a biblical idea. Meta-physically it is borrowed from Neo-Platonism or from something else.

The denial of eternal destiny may also come from a modern logical analysis that says words are only meaningful when there is some referent, when we know what we are talking about. When we talk about eternal destiny, there is no such thing to which we can relate our language.

Such positions may speak of salvation, but they have a worldview that denies any meaning beyond the present. These views may be genuine cases that undercut mission, that link universalism to liberalism, humanism, modernism or any bad "ism" that an evangelical can be against. But the denial of eternal destiny is not real universalism because it does not affirm anything of the long-range destiny that entered into the earlier discussion.

To further address the question of the relationship of Christianity to other religions and to consider various issues from a free church perspective, we need to examine the concept of religion itself.

20

RADICAL REFORMATION
PERSPECTIVES ON RELIGION

Religion is, among other things, an anthropological term. In the way anthropologists make sense of their observations of cultures, Christianity is clearly one of the world religions. What does that mean? What is a religion?

Religion has a number of dimensions. It is a complex and holistic phenomenon. Among other things a religion is a body of beliefs and practices that holds together a social group. Those beliefs and practices usually focus on certain areas of our most common and basic cultural needs, such as the life cycle, coming to grips with catastrophe, helping us make sense of the world and providing legitimacy to the structures of society.

Usually religion also has some relationship to something beyond the visible world: hidden forces that can be dealt with and tapped or another world with which we can have contact by virtue of special disciplines, special techniques or special persons. Every culture, every civilization, large or small, old or young, primitive or developed has a religion in this broad sense. Christianity in Christendom is no exception.

In relation to the missionary question, it is obvious to some people that when we think about other parts of the world and other religions, Christians have to affirm that Christianity is the best religion. What does it mean to make that claim? One thing it means is that we will compete in the market and show that this religion is better than the others by gaining ground, by converting people and by winning people to the insight that our religion is better. In free-market competition, the superiority of our religion will be evident in that it will attract people by having better answers to the meaning of birth and death, of puberty and marriage, of seed time and harvest, of catastrophe, and other functions that a religion discharges. Christianity does it better.

The other way people claim Christianity is a better religion is more abstract or philosophical. We would set the religions on a scale, step back from them and then measure them against each other by the use of some broader or more objective criteria that somehow stand above them both. For instance, in the mid-twentieth century it was fashionable to argue that Christianity is better than Islam because Christianity's rejection of polygamy means that it respects women more than Islam does. Many people made similar arguments with respect to other religions in relation to slavery, infant sacrifices or binding the feet of little girls. This view compares religions by using a yardstick that is somehow beyond both of them.

The problem with that approach is that it is just a projection of one's own preference for Christianity or it grants another yardstick—modern humanism or the common denominator of the modern cosmopolitan world—unquestioned status. Why should we respect women? Why should we not tie the feet of little girls? Why should we object to having slaves? Why should we refuse to sacrifice children? This approach uses our own Christian yardstick to prove the superiority of our own position, or if it uses another cultural yardstick that is assumed to be beyond Christianity and the other faiths, then that philosophical worldview is really the superior "religion."

The idea of finding a neutral criterion by which we can measure the superiority of various religions and testify to the superiority of our own will not work. The free-market approach, which once seemed so convincing to Christians, is now less convincing because Christianity is not gaining ground in the world. If we feel good about the superiority of our religion because we are pushing back the other religions around the world, then we will not feel good if, in fact, we are not pushing them back. Today eastern religions have resurged. Islam has a new missionary vitality. Confirmation of our own superiority on the basis of the spreading of Christianity is not as convincing as it used to be.

CRITIQUE OF RELIGION

There is another approach to the whole problem and that is to say that Christianity should not properly be conceived as one of the world religions. One way or another, this claim means that we must take the phenomenon of Christianity as the religion of Christendom and say that it is not all good. We look at what Christianity did in Italian culture for fifteen hundred years and say that is not the same thing as the Christian faith or as the gospel. There are the various ways of making the point that Christianity is not a religion.

One line of thought is Karl Barth's, repeated in numerous of the moderate or conservative Protestant traditions, especially the Reformed tradition in Europe. Religion is what humans do to seek God and to affirm ourselves as God-seeking beings. It is a form of self-affirmation, self-righteousness and self-confidence. Christianity proclaims that we cannot find God, that God has come to us despite our incapacity to come to God. That is the concept of revelation. This is a completely different approach than comparing the relative effectiveness or adequacy of the ways people seek God. If the claim that we cannot find God but God has freely initiated self-revelation makes any sense, then Christianity cannot be measured on the same scale as the other forms of religious expression.

Dietrich Bonhoeffer has been quoted and become the symbol of several additional ways of saying that Christianity should not be interpreted as a religion, or at least that we no longer mind giving up the Christian faith's religious dimension. Bonhoeffer means a number of different things that we must disentangle. One is what he calls "methodism," which should not be interpreted denominationally but as pointing to a method or a discipline for producing or running through the paces of the faith. Faith is a response to a certain kind of situation or it is a certain kind of feeling. To reach someone with the gospel we must speak to the person's need, but if people are self-confident or doing something useful, religion will not affect them because they do not recognize their need. So we have to demonstrate to them through some method that they need what we have to offer. In this perspective religion exploits human weaknesses instead of affirming human dignity.

Second, Bonhoeffer noted that much of the case for religion has been that in order to figure out the world, humans need God. There are certain things we cannot explain, leaving gaps in our capacity to make sense of the world. God fills those gaps. We say the world does not make sense unless there is a mind behind it or a Creator above it. Religion is what every person needs to fill the chinks in a reasonable worldview.

A third dimension of Bonhoeffer's critique is that we compartmentalize religion, seeing it as one segment of the human personality. We all have physical, intellectual and religious needs. Religion is not the same thing as intellectual stimulation or ethics; it is some other compartment of a person's being. So, one gets more religious as he or she becomes less political, less focused on neighbors or less concerned for truth and intellectual understanding. Religion is something else to be concerned about.

A final part of Bonhoeffer's critique is that usually religion has had the effect of confirming social privileges. This could actually be two distinct points. First, some people have money and power, that is, social privileges. Second, religion brings them trust and peace and tells them that they do not have to feel guilty or anguished. They can feel happy and carefree. They can look down their noses at the people who do not have it made religiously. Religion is also selfish: "I am concerned for *my* salvation. I try to get you concerned for *your* salvation. If each of us is concerned for our own salvation, then we will all be religious."

Although much of this is the language of caricature, caricature only hurts when there is some truth to it. In any case, these are the kinds of things that Bonhoeffer points to in saying that we should understand Christian faith as not fundamentally "religious" at all. Therefore, we need to reinterpret biblical concepts nonreligiously. A nonreligious interpretation of biblical concepts is one of the standard Bonhoeffer slogans. It means taking the Bible's message and restating it so that it does not fall under all those criticisms that I lined up above.

Still another thrust against conceiving of Christian faith as a religion has been the theological impact of biblical realism. Biblical realism as a

twentieth-century school of thought is concerned to be faithful in letting
the Bible speak in its own terms, rather than forcing the Bible to speak
in our terms by insisting that it use our language and respond to our
questions. We should find the preoccupation of a biblical writer and
receive that message rather than take our question to the Bible seeking
an answer. When we listen to the Bible on its own terms, we discover
that the message of the kingdom of God is less like a religion than it is
like a people. Christian faith is in that sense comparable to Judaism and
Islam in that it cares more about the public order and the righteousness
of people's relations in their peoplehood than it cares about the life cycle,
surviving a catastrophe and other typical concerns of religion. Judaism,
Christianity and Islam, although they have a religious dimension in the
cultural anthropological sense, are really ethical or political movements
according to the biblical witness. That is the meaning of talk about God
as king in the Old Testament, the kingdom of God in the New Testament
and Jesus as the Messiah. Religion is not even the best cultural-
anthropological category into which to put Christianity. We should
speak of it as an ethical renewal movement or a new cultural thrust.

The next criticism of Christianity as a religion we should link with the
book *Honest to God* or the whole current of contemporary apologetics.
These are popular books written for people who think that Christianity
is committed to a worldview that is no longer believable, a worldview
that says things about a God who is up in the sky and in a way that
nobody can take seriously, since we have satellites and have gone to the
moon. Christianity is linked with an outmoded worldview.

There would be more strands saying that the Christian faith is not a
religion like other religions, but they are similar enough in their variety
that we have to say there is an element of faddishness here. It is not
clear what we are left with if we say Christianity is not a religion. What
is it then? One of these approaches would say that it is an ethical
movement, but others suggest something else. Moreover, one of the
striking things in this discussion is that although from many different
perspectives they challenge the assumption that Christianity is one of
the religions, all of the critics still maintain the special religious func-
tionary. None of them gets back to the New Testament's originality at

that point. Thus we should not be overwhelmed by this fad.

But a point has been made. Just as there are many ways in which biblical faith is not comparable to other faiths, so there are many ways in which each of the other non-Christian faiths is not comparable to all the others. A Hindu would have to say that Hinduism is not comparable to Islam, Buddhism or Christianity. All of those others are similar, but Hinduism is different. A Buddhist or animist would have to say something similar. From within the perspective of each religion, our way is unique and the others are all similar.

THE RADICAL REFORMATION ON RELIGION

Is there anything distinctive that comes into this picture if we try to look at religion specifically from a Radical Reformation or believers church perspective?

Uniqueness of the Christian witness. There is something about the Radical Reformation claims that we should go back to the Bible in a critical way, that we should critique what has become of Christianity and that we should understand Jesus as a teacher or master whom we follow as disciples that fits with the biblical realism thrust. That thrust said the uniqueness of the Christian witness is not a philosophical uniqueness but a historical uniqueness in that there was only one Jesus. That does not sound especially profound, but maybe that is the point. A historical event's uniqueness is a category of reality that is perhaps deeper than a philosophical category or a feeling category. If history itself is reality, then the uniqueness of something is its historical uniqueness. We simply say there is no other example of that thing.

When we say, "outside the church there is no salvation," that is a tautology in the good sense. It is not a new piece of information; it is a description of reality. There is no relationship to the Jesus story without being related to the people who tell the Jesus story. It is not a profound statement, but it is a solid statement. Salvation is being part of the people who follow Jesus. The uniqueness of salvation for the people who follow Jesus is that there is only one Jesus. Therefore, there can only be one people following Jesus, even though that people can be mixed up and split. We do not have a theory of uniqueness in terms of a normative worldview, experience, visceral communion or social posture—although all of those things have their place. The uniqueness is that there is only one Christian movement in the sense of going back to Jesus. The movement that makes the point of going back to Jesus is the most authentic Christian movement, as over against the movements that make a point of leaving Jesus behind or moving on from Jesus.

The uniqueness Christians talk about is not a uniqueness we prove in terms of higher or more general categories but is simply the fact that there is only one story like this one. Other stories have validity to the extent that they share similarity to the Jesus story. The St. Francis story, the Michael Sattler story and the Martin Luther story all have some value in that they are something like the Jesus story, and they can point us to the Jesus story. Jeremiah, Paul and many other people are of value as models because they point us to Jesus' story.

This goes beyond the suggestion that if we read the Gospel of John with the right mindset we are more likely to be persuaded that story is the way to convince others of the power of the gospel; sometimes argument is a way to convince and sometimes lifestyle is a way to convince. What we are trying to convince people *about* is a story. It is not only that story is a more convincing method. The story is also the content. There may be some people for whom storytelling will not be convincing, but that this man Jesus did these things and that it was on our behalf is still the message's content.

Apostasy. The second point where the Radical Reformation contributes to the discussion about religion is in its concept of apostasy. The Reformers' conviction that something had gone radically wrong in medieval Italy should make other radical reformers more able to retract, dismantle and move past the claims that Christendom as a "religion" has been making. We should be freer to critique or even to abandon some of the ways in which Christianity became a religion. One of the obvious examples of this is infant baptism.[1] Supporters of religion

---

[1][Yoder here uses the example of infant baptism only in relation to "religion." It is not an attempt to engage the theological bases for or against infant baptism, which would involve much more sophisticated and sensitive argumentation. See John H. Yoder, "Adjusting to the Changing Shape of the Debate on Infant Baptism" *Oecumennisme* (Amsterdam: Algemene Doopsgezinde Society, 1989), pp. 201-14. —Ed.]

might say, "If Christianity is to be a good religion, we will have to celebrate the phenomenon of childbirth. Every religion does it. That is what Christianity had to do to become a religion." If we have a reforming view of the church that is not afraid to label apostasy, we can identify that thinking as selling out to the wrong concept of how a religion operates.

Christianity as a cultural process has been wrong about many significant things: Christian empire, Christian crusade, Christian social conservativism and Christian antifeminism. The concept of apostasy frees us to use the critical impact of the Bible and the challenge of the encounter with modern humanity to set aside, dismantle or redefine those mistakes that have been made in Christianity's name. Naming apostasy also frees us from saying that Christianity as a total cultural phenomenon over the centuries has been better than other religions. It might be the case that in certain cultural contexts some other religion was better than Christianity in the form in which it came to that place, because the Christianity that was brought was so deformed and so different from Jesus.

One good example would be Buddhism in Vietnam. It can be argued that Buddhism was more humane than the Roman Catholic establishment in South Vietnam, which was the only form of Christianity there until a couple generations ago. Catholic Christianity held considerable power in that situation. Buddhism—with its nonviolence and its rootedness in the acceptance of nature, with its integration into village life and its independence of the colonial presence—was a more humane religion in South Vietnam than French, Roman Catholic, imperial Christianity.

How do we test that? We test it by Jesus. If our tradition has a concept of denouncing apostasy, we would be free to denounce that imperial Christianity. That does not mean we would say Buddhism is an adequate expression of Christian faith. But it means that we do not have to say we are always better than religion X. If the way Jesus has been represented has been fundamentally unfaithful at certain points, then perhaps religion X is better.

Another example that I have referred to often is the Algerian who said that Jesus is French, which was right in his experience. The Jesus he had heard about was a French colonialist. If that is the Jesus he had heard about, then we have to talk about somebody else. To get to the true Jesus we have to dismantle some things.

Nonreligious faiths. Another observation that is fitting to make from the Radical Reformation perspective is that it might well be that in a specific context the main counterclaim on the loyalties of people would not be a religion in the traditional sense but some other faith or movement. For instance, it might be that in Eastern Europe or Soviet Russia it is more important to challenge Marxism than it is to challenge an Orthodox Church that aligns itself with the state. If we are less sure that Christianity is a religion, then what we might expect to encounter— the main clash, the main challenge or the main open door—would not be at the point of religion but at the point of something else. It might be the construction of an intellectual world in the university context or the construction of an economic world in the Marxist context, and we would have to talk about Jesus, discipleship, love of neighbor and suffering servanthood as an alternative to those constructions of reality. We would not ask first the religion questions.

Another implication of a Radical Reformation approach would be that we would not be bothered by much of the modern Western attack on religion, be it by the anthropologists, the *Honest to God* religious modernists or the atheists and agnostics. We would not worry about defending the traditional Christian worldview against that kind of unbelief, not because we agree with the unbelief, but because the Christian religion it rejects is not what we affirm.

For a while George Buttrick was a university preacher at Harvard and often students would come to him thinking they had a great challenge. They would announce, "I am an atheist. I do not believe in God." His normal response was, "Tell me who the God is you do not believe in. I probably do not either." Often what one thinks is a radical critique of the tradition is a radical critique of something that is not the tradition. Maybe we can agree with the critique or maybe we can say it is irrelevant. We would be freer to take that stance if the Radical Reformation revision of the apostasy of the West were worked more deeply into our own reflexes.

"Functional equivalent of faith." What about the possibility that there might be a nonreligious equivalent of Christian faith? I earlier quoted Max Warren in referring to Karl Rahner's phrase "the functional equivalent of faith." Faith affirms that there is a God who made the universe as an outworking of God's gracious purposes toward us. That means that I respond to the universe as a structure of grace which is *for* me and which I am to trust. There is such a thing as the human side, the subjective side, even the individual side of being a believer, which can be spoken of in terms of structure or shape apart from naming the God who made that world and who presides over it. It would seem to me that with the awareness we have of the inadequacy of past Christendom systems, we cannot actively deny that there could be such a thing as a morally valid response to the universe that has the shape of Christian faith but without the name of Jesus. We cannot deny it. But neither can we affirm it except by relating it to Jesus. We might come to a post-religious agnostic and perceive in him or her a response to the world that has the shape of faith. But we can only see it if it rhymes with Jesus: "What you are doing, Jesus is the name for. We know the name and you did not. Welcome." That we could perhaps affirm, but not apart from Jesus. We cannot play with the idea of being an anonymous Christian except by naming it, and then it is not anonymous anymore. We cannot deny the response of an agnostic that fits with Jesus, but in affirming it, we baptize it.

We have not yet considered carefully enough the orientation of Christian faith to other faiths. We will turn to that aspect of theology of religions next.

21

CHRISTIANITY AND
OTHER FAITHS

One of the headings recently used in discussions about other faiths is the phrase "the finality of Christ." The word *finality* can be given quite different interpretations, all perfectly proper from a linguistic point of view, so it becomes a kind of pun. Even the way to say the sentence depends on which meaning is given. Does it mean Jesus is final in the sense of being the last word? That is, there was some kind of religious evolution or a history that had not yet reached its end up until Jesus but in Jesus has gone as far as it will go. Given this meaning, when we say "the finality of Christ" we affirm the ultimacy of the authority we receive in Jesus. That, of course, has implications for our attitude to other faiths.

But the word *final* or the word *end* has another meaning which may be almost opposite in its implications. That would be to say that Christ is the goal toward which other worlds point. Other faiths also have finality in the sense of purposiveness. If we affirm this meaning of the finality of Christ in relation to other cultures and faiths, we are saying they point to him too.

Third, *finality*, especially in other languages, can be taken to mean that history is goal-oriented. The goal-orientedness of a faith is its finality. That does not sound quite like the word's normal meaning in English, but it resonates in the other languages in which people write ecumenical papers.

Which of these meanings do we have to keep in mind when we talk about other faiths? In what sense is Jesus the ultimate authoritative end, or the end as that beyond which we do not go, or the end as that toward which we move?

CHRISTIANITY AS A RELIGION

We observed in the last chapter that Christianity has become in the anthropological sense a religion. That is, it has put together a package of responses to deal with human needs. It is the built-in tendency of any religion, anthropologically speaking, to try to serve a whole society. In fact, for many sociologists of religion the only religion they will look at is one that seeks to serve a whole society, and they ask about the religion's function in the culture as a whole. That means religion's truth claims are self-evident. It does not argue with other religions why it is right because it is the established religion of its place. It is also religion's tendency to be self-serving. There are organizations in the United States whose theme is to find many ways of telling people that it would be good for them and good for the country if they would go to the church of their choice. It does not matter which church or synagogue. Just go somewhere to be religious and it will be good for the country.[1] It is also religion's tendency, in this anthropological sense, to syncretize elements in order to satisfy all tastes within that culture.

In several of these senses biblical faith is antireligious. It rejects idols, those objects of devotion that we humans set up for ourselves. Biblical faith entered into Canaan in the early Hebrew period with a critique of culture religion, whether that was the agriculture religion of the fertility cults or the urban cultural religion of Babylon, Assyria or Egypt. It rejected the idea that every local territory, every hilltop or every neighborhood had its own local god. Although the Jewish faith, once it had settled down to be the established faith of Palestine, did have an annual religious cycle like the pagans, it gave to these annual feasts historical meanings and not simply ritual fertility meanings. That is, in the spring they did not simply celebrate planting or in the fall the harvest, but they related these cycles to the Exodus, the Passover and the wilderness wanderings. The annual cycle became a reminder of their people's history.

---

[1]One common slogan is "families that pray together stay together," as if that is the reason we ought to pray.

With time Christianity also became an established religion and worldview, especially in the medieval West. What does that have to do with the change in the quality of the relationship to other faiths and especially to syncretism or mission?

Christianity as a religion only became a problem in the modern period. In the pre-Constantinian period, it was no problem; the minority church was acutely aware that it stood over against a dominant pagan majority. The positions that Christians took in the second and third centuries included talking back to the pagans and borrowing their philosophical language and other elements of pagan culture with no question that this would jeopardize their distinctiveness. Some elements they frankly accepted. Some they accepted more critically, such as Stoic philosophical language about virtue. Some elements they brought into the Roman world from outside, namely, from Judaism—the cultural form of the synagogue and the philosophical concept of monotheism. In other aspects they did not borrow from the Jews; the place of Jesus and their attitude toward the sword were things that were uniquely their own. There was no danger of uncritical identification with any one culture or religion other than their own.

After the great shift in the fourth century when Christianity became the official religion of the Empire, the danger of syncretism and of becoming paganized or acculturated was present. However, Christians were not aware of this danger because they thought it was a victory. They thought that when the Roman authorities established the church it was a great step forward. When the Germanic tribes did the same thing later, they thought that was another great step forward. In the process they synthesized elements of the non-Christian background and the Christian background and smoothed over the tension. They did not need to think about the status of non-Christian options because they were either swallowed up and baptized into Christianity or banished as part of the non-Christian world.

The medieval revival movement and the Reformation did not really change this identification with some pre-Christian cultural patterns from Rome or from the Germanic tribes, so the German or the Swiss Reformation could be proud of being a German or a Swiss Reformation.

They maintained the medieval attitude toward the Jews and the pagans: Christianity was the cultural religion of their part of the world, and paganism was elsewhere. Mission, then, was understood as the propagation of a religion, including its civilization. Christians could not separate Jesus from their civilization. They could not separate the civilization of the Indians or the Africans from their idolatry. They saw the clash of faiths as a clash of whole cultures. The only way to do missions was to export one's whole world.

CHRISTIAN ORIENTATIONS TO OTHER RELIGIONS

This thinking has been called into question by cultural relativity, that is, by our awareness of the extent to which every culture is limited in its applicability to other places because of the way it depends on its own past. It is called into question by comparative religion, which dramatizes the integrity and coherence of other faiths through studying them more objectively and conversing with them. The Christian religion's self-assurance has been weakened by unbelief and freethinking in the West, by more tolerance in manner, by more sensitivity about not coercing belief and by the increasing awareness that the self-evidence of any faith is limited to its degree of contact with other peoples. People only think their faith is self-evident if they have seen only their own faith. With global awareness and intercultural contact, the self-assurance of Christianity as the religion of superior culture has come to be much less certain or even something for which to apologize.

Apologetics. In apologetics we claim our superiority not by taking it for granted, but by arguing it. But we argue it on the basis of our own criteria because we cannot find a wider objective marker. For instance, we might say that Christianity is better than animism because it has a higher view of God and because superstition is crude and idolatry is silly. We might claim that Christianity is better because it is more humanitarian or because of the tremendous civilization it has built.

The first reaction against this is that the argument is circular. The criteria used to prove Christianity's superiority derive from Christianity itself. Second, people in the rest of the world observe that many Westerners, whether they call themselves Christian or not, do not live up to the ideals talked about in this Christian synthesis, for instance, with regard to solidity of marriage. In African or Muslim cultures, where for a couple generations they have been told by white Christians not to have more than one wife, they found out that white men have found other ways of having more than one wife, namely, legal divorce. In many Islamic countries, to buy alcoholic beverages all one has to do is prove that one is a Christian, for Muslims do not believe in using alcohol. Increasingly such experiences challenge the adequacy of the Western synthesis.

Selective reception. Also, we increasingly fall into what anthropologists call "selective reception," that is, we observe the ideals of our faith and the vices of other faiths. We compare our best records with their worst performances. As a corrective there has been movement to more benevolent comparison, which we can observe in several forms.

One corrective is to look for compatible elements between faiths in order to communicate at points of affirmation. For instance, some point out that there is in Buddhist thought something like grace, something like trusting that if one abandons oneself to the unmerited goodness of God, there is acceptance. It cannot be the same as Christian grace because the Buddhist ultimate reality is not the same as the Christian God—there is not the same interest in a personal, willing or acting divine power. But some suggest that a Buddhist can still take a stance of trust toward whatever is ultimately real and somehow this can be saving. In Islam, there is the tremendous accent on God's sovereignty, which is a biblical theme and a point of common affirmation. The benevolent comparison approach would ask, "Why don't we start with that?" In other faiths that are more or less theologically focused, there is some kind of a Golden Rule. We could begin with common ground instead of making an issue of our differences.

Sometimes this looks like syncretism in the sense of putting together things that do not necessarily belong together. More often it is a form of idealism: if we have little units of thoughts that are somewhat similar in two different contexts, they might be the same thing or the outworking of the same idea. It is assumed that the same thought in different cultures is still the same thought. That is subject to serious question from the cultural point of view—whether even the same word or the same shape of ideas can mean the same thing in different contexts.

Learning from other faiths. Herbert Jackson has argued that Christian theology should use ways of thinking that can be borrowed from other religious cultures and that this might solve some problems that our Western context has made for us in theology.[2] It could also enable us to communicate better. For instance, it might be that in some other part of the world there is a different way of thinking, a different kind of intellectual process, that would be more helpful for certain purposes than the way we have learned to think in the West. In Greek thought, he says, when we observe variety or contradiction, we try to decide which is right and which is wrong. We assume they cannot both be right. If they are in any sense both right, we have to define the sense in which this can be possible. We do this by classifying and finding ways to avoid ever saying both "A" and "non-A" at the same time. The Eastern mind does not have that same fear. It does not assume that we have to decide who is wrong and who is right. Rather, it is possible to affirm both sides and to assume there is a wider reality that is best dealt with by affirming it all. If both sides do not appear to be reconcilable, then it is necessary to think some more about how to get them together.

This is not the place to debate that at greater depth partly because there is a certain contradiction in Westerners trying to argue logically about how Eastern thought is different at the point of logic and partly because the tools it would take to debate that would have to be extremely refined and sensitive. It is enough for our present purposes to identify this as a relatively new approach—saying that we need to learn from the cultures we are trying to converse with not simply a new language in which to state what we want to say, but a new logic that may challenge whether our logic can even handle the largest truths. Given this awareness, one can see in other faiths, especially in the Eastern faiths, not simply another place to send missionaries, but a place Western Christians could get some help in learning to think more holistically.

Preparation and fulfillment. Another of the more benevolent ways to compare Christianity and other faiths is the language of *preparation*

---

[2][Herbert Jackson, "The Forthcoming Role of the Non-Christian Religious Systems as Contributory to Christian Theology," *Occasional Bulletin, Missionary Research Library* 12, no. 3 (March 15, 1961): 7. —Ed.]

and *fulfillment*. Each religion in its own way is preparation for the Christian message. Just as Judaism is a pedestal on which Christianity comes to stand, so Christianity can fulfill Hindu expectations or the expectation of a tribal religion.

THE CATEGORY OF RELIGION

Is the category of religion in which all of these various world faiths have been put a helpful category? Are Islam, Buddhism, Shinto and the practices of a South American Indian tribe similar enough that it is helpful to say that all of them are religion? They all answer certain questions. They all make sense out of life for those people. But do they perhaps make sense in such different ways that we do more harm than good by putting them all in the same bag?

It is not simply that we have a certain set of questions and all of these different faiths answer them in different ways. They answer different questions and, in fact, have different opinions as to what the real questions are. The problem of Islam is how to know and do the will of the unique sovereign God. Buddhism is not interested in that. Buddhism is interested in a concept of enlightenment in which sovereignty, God and holiness no longer make sense. Confucianism is interested in keeping a society stable. Shinto, if it is a religion at all, is interested in making a society vigorous. Other faiths are not interested in building a society at all. So it would help—whether or not we want to debate the use of the word *religion*—to push ourselves toward a greater awareness of the differences among the many faiths by which people live.

Because of these differences, the question of how Christians should relate to or would seek to testify to different faiths has to be asked separately each time. We cannot say much in general about how to relate across the frontier of faiths. There are some faiths that have had a historic relation to the West and considerable interaction with Christians, of which Islam is the most evident case. Islam never existed apart from its relationship to Judaism and Christianity. There are other faiths that were independent of Western history and where the encounter with Judaism and Christianity has been only in the form of political colonialism.

DISPLACEMENT AND RECONCEPTION

Probably the first step that laid the groundwork for contemporary debate about mission and other religions was the so-called Hocking report. William Ernest Hocking was a North American lay churchman and professional philosopher who led a commission that developed the Laymen's Report.[3] The report recommended that our attitude toward other faiths should be much more benevolent or affirmative. It claimed that we have much to learn from other faiths not only to increase the fruitfulness of any service or witness we have to other people but to gain greater insight into dimensions of human experience and discover other models of being religious that may be helpful to us.

The Laymen's Report used the two terms *displacement* and *reconception*. Displacement referred to what missions had been doing. We brought Christianity as a new faith and it pushed aside whatever faith was there before. One faith has to push the other away.

The alternative that the Laymen's Report proposed was *reconception*. The Buddhist encounters the Christian witness and that changes the person's whole world. He has to reconceive his faith in the encounter with the witness to Jesus, but it is still his own reconception of who he is and what he believes. This is not syncretism in the sense that one accumulates side-by-side elements from two different religions and tries to mix them. It is not unbelief, in which case one would say that Jesus has nothing to contribute, was not who he said he was or was not who Christians say he was. Rather, it is a new kind of faith. It trusts the uniqueness of Christ to remodel the other cultures, to force on other cultures a reconception process, after which they cannot be the same again because Jesus truly makes them change. The person must respond to Christ by reconception.

This is better than synthesis. Syncretism generally means combining things so that from two poles a new merged or fused reality comes into being. Reconception is different from that: the two elements that come

---

[3][Hocking led the Commission of Appraisal, an independently financed group of lay people who from 1930 to 1932 visited and evaluated the mission work of six Protestant denominations in Burma, China, India and Japan. He wrote the report published as *Rethinking Missions: A Laymen's Inquiry After 100 Years* (New York: Harper & Brothers. 1932). —Ed.]

together are not simply a reaction to the other, like a thesis and antithesis that precede the synthesis. Christ is not simply the antithesis provoked by the Buddhist thesis nor is the Buddhist reality the antithesis provoked by the Christian witness. They are two genuinely different things. When they meet, a new thing arises.

Reconception is not simply an idea; it has happened. For example, when Gandhi read Tolstoy about Jesus and then created a new way of dealing with Western Christian violence, a way that was derived from Jesus, Gandhi said he was still a Hindu. He said that he was not a Christian because for him *Christian* was defined by racist white people who would not let him into church in South Africa and who ran an oppressive empire. He did not want to be a Christian. But he was following Jesus not only in technique, but in morality and to some extent in worldview, and he remodeled his Hindu heritage to make that possible. He was not a representative Hindu, although he read some Hindu scriptures and found in them what he had first found in Jesus. That might be a good illustration, although probably not the only one, of what Hocking meant by *reconception*.

The position of the Laymen's Report was not representative of what was going on in the 1930s. It was a minority position. Most missionary activity proceeded with a classical self-understanding. But the Hocking report was vocal, novel, and got attention. People who came from prestigious places in North America—university people and philosophers—wrote it, and the lay leaders who promoted it were important people. The current of questioning it set loose picked up and grew and was felt to support, although not necessarily intentionally, the other relativizing and pluralizing forces of the time.

BIBLICAL REALISM

Hendrik Kraemer, a lay missiologist from the Netherlands, wrote a response to the type of interfaith interaction represented in the Laymen's Report. Prepared for the International Missionary Conference in southern India in 1938, Kraemer's *The Christian Message in the Non-Christian World* was the first to reject the identification of Christianity as a religion.

Kramer advocated biblical realism, which rejected identification with all religions or with any religion. For Kraemer religion was a human creation in which people tried to save themselves. From this perspective the idea of religion as a dimension of human existence was not part of God's purpose for humanity but part of humanity's fallenness. When we look for security in what we do in our religions, that is part of our sin. In fact, the center of humanity's fallenness is that we try to solve the God problem with our own resources. Religion in this sense is not simply irrelevant or an inadequate category to describe Christianity; religion is to be condemned. If people engage in Christian practice to be secure and self-righteous through ritual faithfulness, that has to be rejected too. According to Kraemer that is what the Reformation was about and that is what the ongoing concern for reformation of Christianity needs to address.[4]

What then do we do about other faiths if we are not much interested in or are even critical of religion? Kraemer said that we have to study them because we need to know the framework of any audience, population or individual to whom we speak and who we are trying to reach. But we study the religion more as a cultural framework within which people think than for its content. We do not care too much about their theories about God or their interpretations of religious experience. We simply want to know more about those to whom we speak. We will be careful not to relate to the new religion with the old agenda of superiority or inferiority. We are not out to displace other religions with a better religion, nor are we out to fulfill other religions with a better religion. We are out to proclaim the grace of God in Christ, and that is not a religion. Grace is not something that people can create for themselves to provide themselves security.

We might speak of the totality of a culture as being made up of many units, concepts and elements and then say that the culture and the religion with which we are becoming acquainted affirms these things. The Christian faith, when it is made relevant to that culture, affirms some of these things and negates or ignores others. If we stand with the Christian presence in that new world, we can say that there are certain lines of

---

[4]The early Karl Barth also rejected all religion, including Christian religion, when it functions as a way for humans to hide our fallenness and to find God by our own resources.

fulfillment and other lines of discontinuity. But we can say this only after the fact, looking back. We can never come to a new culture saying we are bringing fulfillment or that our faith will represent discontinuity.

If we say with Kraemer that we are proclaiming the grace of God in Jesus and that this is not one religion beside others, this not only frees us to be respectful, loving and affirmative about the faith of other people, it also frees us to recognize the superiority of other religions at certain points. We do not try to prove that our religion is better, but only proclaim grace because we love others as persons and want to tell them about Jesus. Therefore we can affirm that some particular movement within Hinduism or Buddhism is able to nurture profound spirituality and deep mysticism through disciplines of insight much better than ordinary Christianity can. We can recognize certain human and religious qualities, powers and resources as superiorities in those faiths instead of feeling that they decrease our mandate or our message.

That means also that we do not need to discuss uniqueness. The uniqueness of the Christian message is the historic uniqueness that there is only one message like it, as we noted before. Since it is not a philosophical uniqueness, we do not have to enter that debate. If the Christian faith is not trying to be a religion among religions, claiming to be the better one, we do not need to talk about either uniqueness or displacement.

The effect of this emphasis from Kraemer and company in the late 1930s was to break through the old lines of debate. The theological and cultural conservatives in the missionary movement were happy with Kramer's criticism of Hocking's Laymen's Report and with his strong Bible-centered, Christ-centered focus. They were not happy with the idea that there would be something to criticize or disavow in Christian religion in the West as well. The people who wanted to see themselves as more liberal in terms of the method and attitudes represented in the Laymen's Report could not call Kraemer narrow, because he was widely read and had himself become an expert in Islam through his experience in Indonesia. Yet they could not understand the particularism with which he talked about Jesus. Kraemer stopped the old debate without really starting a new one. It was not quite clear what one could go on debating after this new boulder had been thrown into the pond, because the ripples ran in a different way than they had before.

FREE CHURCH AND OTHER FAITHS

Can a believers church perspective help loosen up the situation or provide a new way of debating? What does the believers church perspective do as we consider other faiths? It does something of what Kraemer was trying to do, although from another angle. Kraemer approached the problem at the level of worldviews: Christianity is not trying to be a coherent worldview; it is a proclamation of Jesus. But Kraemer did this within the state churches of Western Europe. Might we challenge the question of church and society more deeply than he did? That is, the Radical Reformation view in which we identify the state question, the power question, the membership question and the church discipline question, as Western Protestantism has not, would provide a still deeper critique of the way in which Christianity has become an establishment. What implications would that have? How would it support or perhaps modify the kind of question that Kraemer raised?

For one thing it would push us to recognize that the other culture is not as convinced, happy and monolithic in its proclaimed faith as we tend to assume. The anthropological critique that missionaries go into an African tribe and get them mixed up with new ideas assumes that they were happy before. Often the question is: if they were happy as they were, why bother them with the new faith? That assumes not only that they were happy but also that they all believed in some deep way the dominant cultural understandings, that is, they not only took them for granted, but were really living by them. If we have learned in the West to challenge the assumption that everybody is a Christian, then maybe this can free us to challenge elsewhere the assumption that everybody is whatever she or he is supposed to be there. We need to know their cultural frame to communicate in it, but we do not have to assume that it satisfies everybody who lives in that culture. We do not insult that culture by assuming that there are people within it who are not convinced by its religion or satisfied by it or totally living by it, because we know this is the case in our own cultures. We respect those who do deeply value the official culture or religion of their place, but we do not have to impose that position on people who do not. If one goes to Algeria, it is evident that this is a Muslim country. But that does not mean that every person one meets is ready to discuss Islam as a theology or is deeply devoted to and is consistently living up to the meaning of Islam as a lifestyle. It might well be that sometimes a missionary concern to respect the faith that is there would push the person with whom one speaks to more identification with the official religion than he or she actually holds.

If Protestant missionaries go into a Latin American country and assume everybody there is Catholic, they might start debating about the Virgin Mary and the pope. This is the way missionaries used to work. It might be that many of the people they meet are not that convinced about the Virgin Mary and the pope; they simply might not care very much. If missionaries start at some other point without presupposing that the people they meet are in the box of the dominate religion, that might be a freer way to proceed than to assume that all of the people of that country or culture are completely committed to it.

Another element of originality would come from the claim that the merger of Christian thought with Western pagan thought—that is, Greek or Roman traditions—was not first of all an intellectual operation. It first happened socially when the church and the world were merged. In the process, theology and philosophy were merged. In this case the first correction would not be to pull the merged thought apart and redefine Christian faith as an alternative to "religious" thought. Rather it would be to pull church and society apart, that is, to make them visibly distinct again, to find the believers church again as the place where Christian faith is operative and to trust that from that visible community we would have the ability to pull the thought packages apart. This is different from Kraemer, who believed that once Christians got their thought pattern right—according to biblical realism—the rest of the cultural and religious pattern would untangle itself. Perhaps what we really need in order to untangle these thought patterns is a visible Christian community.

22

THE MISSIONARY CHALLENGE OF NON-NON-CHRISTIAN FAITHS

We assume that we know the difference between being Christian and not being Christian. Any kind of mission presupposes that difference. Yet when we look closer the difference is not as firm and clear as we have assumed. It is possible to relativize the difference on the grounds of etiquette—we do not want to exclude anyone—or a philosophical relativism that says that the differences between faiths are relative to local culture rather than matters of truth and falsehood. But those points are questionable when made basic.

If truth is timeless and ideal in the Platonic sense, we can always disavow ultimate responsibility for the imperfect shape it takes in the world. We know that the ideal is there in God's mind or in the realm of pure ideas. If, however, truth is historical, if it is in God's nature that we meet God in history and if we encounter there God's real character, then truth can only be known the way history can be known, namely, as it is traditioned, reported and passed on. That means that etiquette or philosophical relativism are inadequate bases for a Christian response to other religions. Because of the historical nature of Christian faith, it assumes that there will be variations in the degree to which people understand truth and in the degree of faithfulness to that understanding.

Further, if truth as God reveals it and faith as humans respond to it constitute wholeness, the vehicles we have to propagate this wholeness are limited. They are organizational or doctrinal, or they are abstracted out of the wholeness of personal relationships and process. We create the possibility of having correct doctrine or correct organizational procedure without the reality of faithfulness. Those two considerations— the simple fact that truth is historical and the fact that truth must be served by vehicles that are not themselves the wholeness of faith—open the door to imperfect forms, not simply by accident or failure but by the nature of the case.

Further, if faithfulness is called to take the shape that we have called "free church" but Christendom has mostly propagated the faith, then there can be additional errors in definition, confusions as to what the message is and thereby errors in the reactions of others to Christianity. There may be people who have responded affirmatively to the message of Christendom, but that is not the same as faith in Christ. There may be other groups that have responded negatively to the message of Christendom, but they have not thereby turned down Jesus. We should expect that there will be groups calling themselves Christian who are not really Christian when measured by the call of Jesus or the New Testament witness. We should expect also that there may be other groups who do not call themselves Christian, but who may be more Christian than they know.

The phrase "the finality of Christ" means that after Jesus has been confessed as Christ and Lord, nothing can be the same again. It means also that after Jesus there can be such a thing as non-non-Christian faith, a faith that it is not Christian because it is not faithful to him, but it is not non-Christian because it is within the world that has undergone the impact of his presence and the confession of his lordship.

THE MISSIONARY CHALLENGE OF NON-NON-CHRISTIAN FAITH

One form of faith within this marginal area would be movements that consider themselves Christian but which have been seriously degenerated through identifying their Christianity with a particular culture or nation. The established church of Ethiopia which has persecuted evangelicals; the established church of Greece which supports a fascist government and persecutes the Protestants; the established church of czarist Russia; the established church of Latin America; the established church of Scandinavia; the old colony Mennonites—these are all groups who sincerely intend to be Christian but whose inclination about what it means to follow Jesus is so structured through the peculiarities of their cultures that we have to raise serious questions about their Christian presence and witness. They are profoundly tied to a class and power structure in a given society and culture; they have the backing of the political and economic rulers. They have no missionary interests. They do not affirm God's continuing creative work in their history except to maintain the past model. These groups may come to hold positions we would consider doctrinally heretical—there are things about the Ethiopian church that would be pretty far from the Bible—but they need not be. For instance, there might be aspects of the theoretical preaching in empty Scandinavian churches that are clearly biblical. But that is not the key question.

What does this social phenomenon of an established, run-down Christendom raise for a missionary faith? If we were to send missionaries to Ethiopia or Latin America, as Mennonites have done, what should be our approach to the cultural religion in those places that happen to call themselves Christian? One approach would be not to go at all because there are already Christians there. For a long time this was the attitude of many European missionary societies with regard to Latin America, which they considered already Christianized.

A second alternative would be to go because we think they need our more up-to-date, more biblical or more missionary message. But we recognize the church already there as a church and try to work within that church for renewal by getting people to read the Bible and by identifying service needs and ethical issues. This is what those churches would ask for if they accept the guests at all. Several mission agencies have tried this in Ethiopia and in the Near East among Orthodox churches. Mennonite Central Committee adopted this approach in Crete and Greece. Of course this is not a position that those established groups would take toward other churches in return. If a particular British mission recognizes the established church of Ethiopia as a sister church, the church of Ethiopia does not return the complement and recognize the Protestants of England as a true church. In fact, one of the characteristics of these established groups has been that they are highly sectarian with regard to other groups. The church of Ethiopia at this time does not even recognize other Orthodox Christian groups or Roman Catholic groups as being acceptable, to say nothing of Protestant renewal movements.

The other extreme, most fully worked out among dispensationalists and the Plymouth Brethren, is to make a positive theological virtue of being against that establishment: establishment is apostasy. Language from the book of Revelation and elsewhere can be used for that purpose. These missionaries are a minority and are likely to be under serious disadvantages or even active persecution. If their message is heard, it will not be by the existing church as a whole but by individual converts, and they will often be those who are on the margin of the common religion. The more strongly a person is convinced of this antiestablishment approach, the more it will work out to be true. It is a self-fulfilling prophecy to say that the established church is not renewable. Setting up a counterorganization directly in conflict with that tradition is the way Protestant missions have usually operated.

But we should call into question the clarity of those two missionary alternatives—working for renewal of the established church or working against it. Are they as clear as they have seemed to be to both parties? Do they need to be that clear? Do we have to accept this polarization? What would be the alternative?

First, we might note that there are degrees to which one group recognizes another Christian body as church. There may be local congregations which recognize one another fully as sister congregations. They exchange visits, membership and sacramental practices in full mutual trust. But as soon as denominational structures are added or as soon as there is a division in a group with a history behind it, the situation requires many degrees of affirmation in relation to other groups instead of absolutely yes and absolutely no.

Moreover, many Christians make a decision about a church's status by considering factors on the hierarchical level—the denominational structure, the central office, the creed or the bishop. For instance, if we believe that it is crucial to have a bishop, then we make our decision about the validity of the Greek church on the basis of its bishop. Other Christians focus more on factors at the level of the congregation or functioning fellowship. If we do not believe that episcopacy centrally defines the church, then why would we judge all the Greek Christians in every parish on the basis of the episcopal structure that we have just said is not crucial? In this perspective it is possible to label both apostasy and communion through the local criteria of love and witness to Christ, and that does not have to correspond with the judgment one makes about a structure, a tradition, a hierarchy, a synod or a creed. So the first question has to do with our understanding of *church* in relation to the clarity we think we have about a church's faithfulness.

Second, this discussion has been initiated under the assumption that we—the mission agency, the home church or denomination—are faithful. It assumed a solid base from which criteria for faithfulness could be projected toward the other party. But that solid base is not there in terms of performance. What this tends to do, which is always one of the temptations in interchurch relations, is to measure their performance by our ideals, rather than taking into account the fact that our performance does not measure up to our ideals either. For instance, some of the grounds we have used to condemn the church of Ethiopia would also be grounds for condemning some churches close to home. We make the point at home that we have to accept people as they are, to work with what we have. We have to evaluate people's response on the basis of how much they have understood. Should we not use that same criterion rather than some more demanding one when we are working around the world?

The last critical argument related to these simple alternatives is more difficult to evaluate. It has to do with what I previously called "the finality of Christ." We cannot name Jesus Christ in vain. Where he is named or confessed hypocritically, it works judgment, and we ought to say that. But when he is named in a context where the unfaithfulness was that of another age, can we really affirm that there is guilt or apostasy by heredity? Would we not have to say that if the name of Jesus is there, even confessed in ignorance, immaturity or unfaithfulness, the name is still an open door? If the appeal we make is not to

Western Pietism or Anabaptist renewal but to the Bible, would it not follow that our approach toward Christendom could never be systematically negative or affirmative but will always be an uneasy combination of affirmation and critique?

This more relativized missionary approach would simply say that if those in established religions are talking about Jesus, we can talk with them. We would not come with either prior rejection or prior affirmation of their faithfulness. We would not first send an ambassador to the bishop for an authorization to run a renewal movement in his church; it would not start with that degree of affirmation. On the other hand, we would not say that this is the land of apostasy; there has never been Christian faithfulness here and we come to bring liberation. Rather, we would say, "If you are talking about Jesus, so are we. Let's study more what it means." It might mean some crucial break with the world we are in. It might mean some revitalization of things that are already going on. But we would not have to choose between the two extremes of accepting the structures of the established religion and rejecting them.[1]

POST-CHRISTIAN FAITHS

Another category of non-non-Christian faith are the post-Christian faiths—post-Christian in the literal sense of coming after Christianity, but also in the deeper sense that they claim to incorporate the truth of Christianity in some larger truth or to improve on historic Christianity. One general category is syncretism. Though there are various independent movements in Africa, one strand claims that there must be black Christianity that adds specifically African elements, just as there has been for so long white Christianity. They do not mean simply that

---

[1]It matters to me to say that we gather around Jesus and the Bible rather than around conversion, discipleship, nonresistance, believers baptism or some of the other formal criteria. We measure whether we can meet around Jesus and the Bible. Nonresistance, believers baptism, and those other things will follow later—maybe. At least they are not the message we have to have settled before we begin.

However, the place this approach gets administratively crucial for believers church missionaries is whether we promise not to baptize people or, at some other point, whether we make a procedural commitment about mutual recognition. In these cases it would clearly make a difference whether we are committing ourselves to the adequacy of the structure that is there or simply saying we do not write it off.

we make the Christian message readable in African terms but that African culture traditionally had some authority besides Christ and often some revelatory source besides the Bible.

Yet at the same time that they add an element of identification with their own world, they see that when the white missionaries had made such identification with the world from which they came—bringing a white Jesus or the Scottish national faith—it was questionable. African Christians want cultural identification partly to have genuineness in their context, but also because they have been told by white people to identify with their own nation or whatever it takes to be indigenous.

I am not sure that a syncretistic group shuts itself off from the possibility of renewal because it has adopted extra things. It would depend on what authority they ultimately claim, whether they claim, for instance, to have a second more authoritative Messiah, a different set of revelations or an additional Bible, or whether we can meet on the basis of our common background.

The Latter Day Saints and Jehovah's Witnesses both fit under this category of syncretism as well. Christian Science, likewise, claims to adapt and correct Christianity, but in a more philosophically or speculatively oriented way.

What all of these groups want to do is restore the element of divine authority and intervention: "God really breaks into your life to change it. There is a God whose law we must keep, whose reality marks our reality, whose reality is more real than the reality of the person in the street." Those are correctives that have arisen in post-Christendom pluralism.

One approach to these groups is to say that they will run through the sect cycle just like everybody else. Groups start out being proud, distinctive and confident, but as they grow older they run into the same problems everyone else has foundered on, until finally they become more pluralistic and polite. At that point they will join the local ministerial association and want to be counted as Christians after all.

Another approach would be to ask to what extent they claim to take Jesus seriously. Sometimes they do, and sometimes they do not. That seems like a more constructive way to go about this conversation. They may quickly realize that they do not take Jesus very seriously, or the conversation might relativize their peculiar loyalty or particular theosophy and create the possibility of their recognizing other persons or groups after all.

Still another alternative would be to say that we know without talking with them that they have false doctrines, and therefore they are apostates. That is easier to say about some of those groups than about some of the established churches already mentioned. But there is some doubt about whether making a decision based on their doctrines is adequate grounds for rejecting them if they represent in some sense a renewal phenomenon that takes God's law seriously. In the same category are post-Christian positions that incorporate Jesus and the Bible in a wider sect, groups who say they are not Christian and yet recognize Christianity in their past in a backhanded way.

The oldest of these would be Islam, which came into being not as a new religion, but as a purification and correction of the Jewish-Christian tradition. Muhammad corrected Christianity and Judaism by means of rationalism regarding God's unity and spirituality. Because of this thorough and consistent rationalism about the fact that God is spirit, Muslims believe we cannot have an incarnation of God. Jesus can be a prophet like Muhammad, even greater in some senses. He can even be a messiah who will come back, but he is a man like Muhammad. He cannot be an incarnation of God. Likewise, we cannot affirm the Trinity because God is one. Rationalism served as a tool of purification.

Second, there was a renewed national identification in that the Arab people became the vehicle of this renewal movement. Within a century and a half the Arab people were spread across North Africa all the way into southern Asia and halfway across Europe into Spain, making it a worldwide movement. Islam was not sectarian, but another world culture like that of the Roman Empire, which could have just wars and crusades like the Christians. But where Islam was established worldwide, it was also tolerant. In fact, Islam was more tolerant toward people of other religious movements than Christianity was in its time. In any case, Islam was clearly a post-Christian correction.

A modern equivalent of a corrective to Western Christian culture would be secular humanism and Marxism, a subcategory of the same. It has taken also the forms of free enterprise, democratic capitalism and majority world nationalism. I suggest that in some significant sense these are all forms of the same post-Christian faith. Whether they are theistic or atheistic is not crucial. They are in favor of history, in favor of humanity, concerned about the movement of history for the sake of humanity, and therefore critique the Christian past for having failed to live up to its own purposes, which were these same humanitarian purposes. Nationality and rationality are tools of their critique, that is, the idea of an elect people to be the bearer of this new wisdom and the idea of getting rid of the superstition of the Christian ritual.

All of these post-Christian faiths—looking back from Islam through Marxism to Western free thought—are aware of Jesus. They are phenomena that arose in a world where the impact of the Hebrew story and Jesus made this world what it is. They are not pagan.

THE POWERS AND PRINCIPALITIES

Hendrikus Berkhof, in his effort to get some illumination from the apostle Paul's thinking about the powers, suggests that there are three levels of reaction to the lordship of Christ. The first level is paganism. The powers are in control of humanity, but there are so many of them that they do not run away with anything. The structures of creation are autonomous and there is not a sense of historical movement. The second level is when the powers have heard the claim that Christ is Lord and are no longer autonomous. Their sovereignty and their rebellion are broken. At this level there is some awareness that humans can be freed from bondage to the powers and can be humane. It is the church that proclaims this, but it is heard beyond the church. In the third stage, which Berkhof calls "the angry powers," the various bondages and idols of humanity talk back, rise up and reject their submissiveness and the claim that they are to serve humanity. Then we get a Hitler or any other phenomenon in which some particular cultural value or focus takes over, absolutizes itself, denies any limits and makes itself the new lord.

Berkhof rightly refers in this connection to Jesus' story about exorcism. If a devil is cast out, that person is like an empty house. The devil will roam around, come back and find it empty and bring six more colleagues. The house will be in a worse situation than it was before. There is something about the irrevocability of Jesus or covenant in salvation history that means that the world can now become worse than it ever could before. Humanity can be more vulnerable in the post-Christian situation than we would have been before because of the powers' response to the finality of Christ.[2]

POST-CHRISTIAN CONSTANTINIANISM

All of these post-Christian movements have in common that they critique Christianity's rituals and dogmas—precisely the things that we already identified as religion. They assume that they can change religion with rational critique because religion is irrational. What they keep is not personal discipleship or the local reconciling community. What they keep is the use of national power, cultural insight and civilization in order to move history in the direction of human fulfillment. Yet that shift is one Christians had made long ago, moving from personal discipleship in the reconciling community toward a form of Christianity which would use power, the elect nation, education and cultural strength to move history in the right direction. So these movements retain the Constantinian vision of how values work in history, chop off the Christian ritual and leave aside, because they had not noticed it, the believers church as an additional option. In other words, they take the framework of Constantinianism and use it for secular humanist post-Christian values instead of for Christian values. They do not ask why Christianity became Constantinian because they are Constantinian.

What do we do in the face of this much more complex shape of unbelief in our time, which is often wrong in the same place Christendom was wrong and is sometimes right at the same place that the gospel is right? One thing I suggest is willingness to confess Christendom's inadequacy even if we are not to blame for Christendom. That is, the Marxist or the modern Western atheist will not understand it if we say, "What you are criticizing is Christendom, and I am against it too. My forebears were against it four hundred and fifty years ago." This might help later,

[2][See Berkhof, *Christ and the Powers* (Scottdale, PA: Mennonite Publishing House, 1977), pp. 53-64. —Ed.]

but I suggest we need to begin with the recognition that the Christian image that the post-Christian is rebelling against was inadequate and is to blame, even if that confession is to some extent vicarious.

That should enable us to recognize the validity of the critique. Much that the Marxists, the Muslims and Western atheists say was wrong about Christian history is correct, such as the Inquisition, economic exploitation and sexism. This suggestion leads to my related suggestions that we renew the reality of the reconciled community as what is central to Christian faith and that we are clearer about abandoning control and power within the Christian context.

Moreover, it probably would be wise not to try to prove Christ's uniqueness because even if they do not know it, these groups all assume that. They are post-Christian. What we must talk about is Jesus' identity, not whether he was unique or whether he was ontologically what the old creeds say. We should talk about what he said and did, and we should make it visible. Most of these people have never heard that the center of what we believe about Jesus is neither a new Gnosticism, which has secret ideas about his metaphysical composition, nor his role in a tribal culture linked to Rome, Geneva or Witmarsum. What is important about Jesus is the life he called people into and the relationship to the Father that he made possible, which is a basis for some of the same critique of what happened in Christendom that the post-Christian focuses on.

Maybe that kind of approach toward post-Christian persons would enable us to find some blend of love and limits in mutual recognition. We do not have to be threatened by their systems of thought. We see how they are derived from a Christianity that lost its way. We see they have made the same mistakes that Constantine did, the same mistakes we already made. We do not have to be convinced about the intellectual power of Marxism or of Islam as a set of answers in order to have great respect for that system and culture as the clothing of the person we are trying to love.

23

JUDAISM AS A
NON-NON-CHRISTIAN FAITH

Mainstream Christianity since the second century has been outspokenly anti-Jewish.[1] The form in which this anti-Jewish bias first appeared was the supersession theory, according to which Christians have replaced the Jews as the people holding the right understanding of the Old Testament and carrying forward its holy history. Already within the apostolic writings an argument had begun about how properly to understand the Hebrew Scriptures and the fulfillment of their hopes. However, when that material was written, the debate on that subject took place within Judaism according to the rules for Jewish debate. Since the early years of the second century, the claim of Gentile Christians to be the valid heirs of the faith of Abraham was no longer part of the Jewish debate as in the first century but rather had become an anti-Jewish argument.

Beginning in the fourth century, the anti-Jewish bias of Gentile Christianity was correlated with the political ostracism of the Jews. Once the entire Western world had been Christianized from the top,

---

[1] [The 1973 recording of the class lecture was so badly damaged that it was impossible to transcribe it. Fortunately, Yoder had a transcription made of that lecture in 1981. It is available in the MCUSA archives at Goshen, Indiana. See "Judaism—Non-Non-Christian," The John Howard Yoder Collection, Hist. Mss. 1–48, Box 136, Mennonite Church USA Archives, Goshen, IN. Yoder explained that "the following material was part of the lecture content of the course 'The Theology of the Christian World Mission,' offered several times between 1964 and 1973 at AMBS. It is written down as a base for critical dialog in view of the fact that the course will no longer run." However, he also taught the course in 1976 and in 1983. —Ed.]

there were no more pagans within the *oikoumenē*. The remaining Jews within "Christian society" took over the role of the "infidel." Frequently this expressed itself in persecution or expulsion from particular places. When the rejection was somewhat milder, it still forced Jews into a separate ghetto culture. In rarer circumstances a ruler afforded special privileges to some Jews, in compensation for their special loyalty. Generally speaking, Christendom did not deal with Jews as fairly as Islam did a few centuries later.

Frequently the rejection was more than ostracism or banishment, and it moved to aggressive persecution. Sometimes the intent was the physical destruction of Jews. In other less brutal times and places, it was the end of their identity as Jews, that is, they were forced to convert to Christianity. When they were tolerated, it was for special reasons, such as the financial services that some late medieval bankers rendered to the princely houses of Europe.

Undergirding this anti-Jewish cultural bias was a strong theology of the infidel Jew. This theology held that the Jew was not, like any other non-Christian, an honest adherent of some other faith or no faith: the Jewish person was positively the infidel, the negator of proper belief. The formal reproach of "deicide" brought together in a powerful way a number of theses or assumptions:

- a specific historical reconstruction of the way the execution of Jesus took place, with "the Jews" functioning as the accusers and affirming their desire of taking responsibility for Jesus' death

- a specific naive understanding of the deity of Jesus Christ, so that it could be claimed that in letting the man Jesus go to his death, those who brought about that decision could also be killing God

- the still further questionable assumption that people can be held guilty of the sins of their distant forebears

Behind these specific accusations were a host of anti-Jewish attitudes found in the wider culture, such as legends about the wandering Jew, the Jew as a cheating merchant or usurer and Jews as a threat to the peace of society. When, with theological modernity, this kind of complaint was no longer credible, more sophisticated theology developed to shore up the bulwark. This theology saw Jesus as specifically opposing Jewish tradition in his attitude to the law or in specific moral teachings such as his rejection of violence or of divorce. It saw the apostle Paul as even more eminently rejecting Judaism; Paul seemed to reject the law in a far more logical and sweeping way than Jesus had and developed with regard to Jesus a "high Christology," which must have seemed blasphemous to the Jew.

As a result of the generally negative attitude of Western Christianity toward Jewish identity, there has been an abiding ambiguity in the face of the question whether "mission" should be addressed to Jews. One segment of Protestantism has been especially preoccupied with studying Jewish culture and addressing the Christian witness to Jews. Usually this preoccupation was rooted in pietistic or chiliastic convictions that gave to the conversion of Jews a special place in the end-time scheme. More often, however, the larger Christian church bodies ignored Jewry as potentially the target of the missionary message. Since the church prototypically thought of missions as "going overseas," it did not seem to apply to the Jews who were at home in Europe. Jews were not considered "pagan" as were the people elsewhere to whom missionaries would go to bring knowledge of the only true God. Since Jews were informed of the Christian tradition and had rejected it, they were considered to be refractory "infidels," a less promising "target audience" than genuine pagans would be.

In recent generations a number of new cultural currents have thrown a different kind of light on the question of witness to Jews. Because the Enlightenment had boiled Christianity down to the truth value of its various statements about human nature, the existence of God and the nature of the morally good, and it thought of the name of Jesus and the content of the Christian faith as simply one expression of those more general truths, it became possible to consider Jewish moral monotheism as one more religious variety. It was comparable to Protestantism and Catholicism that also, in order to be evaluated philosophically, were boiled down to moral monotheism. Especially in those theologically more liberal traditions where the classical formulations of Christological confession were not considered important or perhaps even not credible, nothing stood in the way of treating Judaism as one more Christian denomination. Nothing stood in the way, that is, from the Christian side. Traditional and Orthodox Jewry had their own good reasons for not wanting to accept this compliment. Some strands of Reform Judaism however, especially before 1948, could feel relatively at home with their newfound acceptance as one more variant, in fact the oldest and quietest, of "Judeo-Christian tradition."

The most prominent Protestant exponent of this view in his age was Reinhold Niebuhr, who explicitly opposed the thesis that Christian faith has anything to offer to the Jew. This disavowal was enormously reinforced by the strong reasons Christians in the West have for embarrassment about and disavowal of modern anti-Semitism.

An utterly different Philo-Judaic orientation was the eschatological tradition of John Nelson Darby. For him the Jews have a permanent priority as a people possessing the promises of God, in no way superseded by Christianity. All of the promises made to Israel by the ancient Hebrew prophets are still to be fulfilled in favor of the Jews who live among us today and who will be alive when those promises are fulfilled. Contrary to both the anti-Jewish and liberal post-Enlightenment views, Darby was strongly committed to evangelizing Jews, since their conversion has a place in the divine scheme quite distinct from that of Gentiles. At a certain point the church—meaning the Gentiles—will be removed from the scene. The Jewish people, returned to their homeland, will then be won to faith in Jesus as the Messiah by the few believing Jews left over from the previous dispensation. Then the main line of prophetic fulfillment will resume: re-establishment of the throne of David and the fulfillment of the promises of world sovereignty that were interrupted in the first century when Jesus was not accepted as king.

This special evaluation of the place of Judaism correlates with the personal and social predilections of the small number of Jewish individuals who have been converted in response to such a message. These individuals tend to prefer to maintain some Jewish identity rather than be swallowed up in ordinary, predominantly Gentile Western churches, therefore special missions to Jews of "Hebrew Christian" fellowships are more satisfactory to them. They tend to reconstitute a messianic Jewish fellowship in which Gentiles, while not excluded, would hardly be expected, thus bringing into being "from the other side" the kind of separation between Jews and Gentiles that was the subject of Paul's explicit objection in Galatians 2.

A third form of renewed respect for Judaism has arisen in European Protestantism as a result of the combination of neo-Reformation theology, represented by Barth and Bonhoeffer, and the experience of the Holocaust. Especially in the Netherlands, but significantly as well in France, Switzerland and Germany, the confession of the sin of Christendom against the Jews correlates with a theological renewal of respect for their distinctive mission in salvation history. From this new biblical perspective, as well as from the liberal one of Niebuhr, some have come to reject the notion of any explicit Christian proclamation to Jews.

This latter development is the most profound of the three. It arises from biblical and theological renewal rather than from the dilution of Christian specificity or from an esoteric eschatology. The first thesis is that the election of Israel is irrevocable. Not even rebellion against the gracious call of God can subtract that privilege from the elect. In fact, once the fulfillment of the meaning of the election of Israel has come in Christ, the ongoing existence of Jewry is only possible because of their refusal to accept that fulfillment. Only in revolt against the meaning of election does Judaism exist and thereby becomes the most dramatically paradoxical sign that the grace of God persists in maintaining the identity of the elect even as the elect rejects it. That very survival of unbelief is a sign of the grace in whose fulfillment Jews refuse to believe.

Christians could not make these theological statements about the identity of unbelieving Israel if it were not for the historical fact of the survival of Judaism in the West. Is this historical fact itself theologically important? We can say, at least, that it prevents our forgetting the call and the election of Israel. There is clearly mystery in the survival of the Jews, as no other people has survived without common territory, common authorities or common language. There is also a mystery in the sense of scandal in how the various host cultures sought the destruction of the Jews who lived among them. The facticity of survival and scandal reinforces the theological confession of election.

This line of thought has gained the most momentum since the 1960s when this lecture material was first prepared. It has found several vehicles within European Protestantism, with the World Council of Churches, in various Christian research agencies in the Holy Land and more recently in the writing of a growing number of revisionist Christian theologians. Some of these explicitly recognize the Jews as a sister communion within the biblical faith, to the point of disavowing any invitation to recognition of Jesus as Christ. Others, without drawing specific negative conclusions, focus their concern so strongly on matters of atonement, Christian guilt and the special suffering of Jewish minorities that the idea of an evangelistic message to Jews seems extraneous.

Thus far our task has been descriptive. There are varieties of attitudes seeking in numerous ways to reverse the anti-Jewish bias of mainstream Christianity. They are all still minority positions. Most of the rest of Christendom—whether Eastern Orthodox, Western Catholic or Protestant—if not explicitly anti-Jewish, would in their missionary concerns pay no specific attention to Jewish identity. In effect they neglect the Jews as a people to be told about the Messiah and thereby remain unable to counter anti-Semitism with any effectiveness.

We might seek to reopen the issue at a point where the Radical Reformation and the New Testament coincide, namely, in seeing the reconciliation of peoples as having more importance in defining the nature of the church and her message than is usually recognized. In the New Testament this meant that the gospel proclamation was inseparable from the reconciling of Jew and Greek. The truth of the claim that the Messiah had come was inseparable from the new community in which two kinds of people were one. The form of the same concern in the sixteenth century was the rejection of coercion, of the backing of particular churches by particular state governments and of the imposition within every country or province of one theologically monolithic religious culture. These two commitments may provide the leverage with which we can return to our question in the hope of finding deeper understanding. Rather than starting by regretting the repressive fruits of Christendom's anti-Semitism, let us begin where the argument began.

Jesus was not anti-Jewish. What he did with the law was, in his own words, to fulfill it, not to set it aside. He sought to increase its bindingness, its wholeness and fullness and depth. At some points he differed with some of his rabbinical colleagues on exactly how the provisions of the law were to be obeyed, but his difference from others on those matters was well within the parameters of tolerable diversity within the Judaism of the time and within the diversity Judaism today can tolerate. The same is no less true of the nonviolence or nonresistance of Jesus: if Jesus was the fulfillment of the law and the imitation of the suffering servant, nonviolence was his path. That they should be nonviolent was the same conclusion that other Jews had drawn from their defeat in the first Jewish-Roman War (66–73 C.E.) and was the view with which Johanan ben Zakkai opposed the Zealot general Menahem a generation later. The newness that Matthew reports Jesus as proclaiming in the Sermon on the Mount (Mt 5) is fulfillment: it is not even supersessionism, to say nothing of rejection.

Paul likewise was nothing if not Jewish. The reason he went to the Gentiles to proclaim the coming of the Messiah was that as a Jew he believed this was what had to happen in the Messianic age. Nobody but a Jew could meaningfully believe that the Messiah had come. Any Jew who would believe the Messiah had come would believe that this would open a new epoch for the nations to know the name and the law of God. What Paul did in this respect, including his solutions to the detailed problems of building communities in Corinth facing dietary and calendar conflicts, was very similar to the solutions which had been found to the same problems during the previous two centuries of Jewish proselytism under the leadership of the great missionary Rabbi Hillel. The work of Paul in Gentile cities always started with the synagogue. When that synagogue community was divided because some accepted and some rejected his message, the "believing Messianic" portion resulting from that division still operated like a synagogue.[2]

Not only was this affirmation of Jewish identity the center of the mission of Jesus in the first generation and of Paul in the second: the

---

[2]Both "Jesus" and "Paul" in the above summaries are named as symbols. We cannot know all of the details of the biography or the thoughts of either of these men: what we have to speak of is the record and the interpretation of their impact as we have it in the apostolic writings.

social fences remained down between church and synagogue for two or three more generations. The early Christian or Messianic Jewish communities remained basically Jewish in language and style even in the Hellenistic cities. It was only well into the second century that Gentile minorities started to take the church away from the Jews, thereby moving one step toward the creation of a provincial Christianity. Hellenistic culture at that time was widespread around the Mediterranean basin and thought of itself as "the whole world" (Lk 2:4), but in terms of world culture it was already a serious narrowing of the faith community when it came to be identified with that culture, its language and its wisdom. The "fall of the church," which Anabaptists have been talking about since the late middle ages and which they usually located in the fourth century because of the importance of Constantine and his sword, really began in the second century.

The apologists who reconceived the Christian message so as to make it credible to non-Jewish culture—whether to philosophers or religious people, practical or powerful people—detached the message of Jesus from its Jewish roots and transposed it into an ahistorical moral monotheism with no particular peoplehood and no defenses against acculturation. With the loss of its Jewish roots, the church lost

- a vision of the whole globe as under God with all nations, even those beyond the Roman Empire, as having their place and needing to hear the message

- the understanding of Torah as grace and as privilege, not as entrance requirements or a basis for recompense

- a readiness to live in the diaspora style of the suffering servant

These very elements were the ones the Radical Reformation reached back to recover. When the radical reformers—whether the Waldenses or the Czech Brethren or the Anabaptists—reached back, they were finding in the New Testament those things the church through acculturation had lost. As a matter of fact, they were also "reaching sideways" to the continuing presence of Jews in their midst.

I have told this story as it is usually experienced and told—as a story within Christian consciousness. We should, however, not dodge the challenge of seeing the same story from the Jewish side.

The calling of Israel was always to be a mouthpiece for the proclamation of the lordship of Yahweh. Beginning with the break-up of the state structures in the land of Israel, this had already begun to include inviting significant numbers of people of non-Jewish birth into the fellowship and lifestyle of the covenant. In terms of social structure, what Jesus did was simply more of the same: the communities that confessed in him the coming of the Messianic age were simply more free and aggressive in doing in the Gentile cities what the synagogues had already been doing.

For something like eighty years after Pentecost the synagogues were not closed to Messianic believers and the "churches"—that is, the Messianic synagogues—did not break communion with Judaism. When the year 70 C.E. sealed the abandonment of visions of national restoration, Johanan ben Zakkai firmed up the nonviolence of the remaining rabbinic leadership and their acceptance of diaspora as a base of Jewish identity. This was an affirmation that, as far as ethical substance is concerned, led Jewish people to act in exactly the same way as the Christians of the same period. There are those who believe that one reason the synagogues rejected Christians was that the Christians had refused to share in the defense of Jerusalem, given their pacifism. Ben Zakkai also rejected the Zealot battle and withdrew from it. At whatever point the further separation between Jews and the early church took place, the Jews at this time were not fighting for Jerusalem either. The only possible exception to this statement would be if we thought that most of the Jews were together with Bar Kochba after 130 C.E., but most of them were not. It may be that Rabbi Akiba thought, or thought for a time, that Bar Kochba might be a (or the) messianic liberator, but this is not clear, not permanent and not representative.

Thus the move of Judaism whereby it was able to survive the loss of the Temple and the loss of such approximation to a Jewish "state" as the Sanhedrin represented, went toward, not away from, an acceptance of the diaspora situation in Hellenistic and Babylonian society. It was not in itself a denial of mission.

Some time, about a century later, the Mishna backed away from this continuing missionary openness, becoming less missionary because the Christians were more so. We cannot really be sure what was cause and what was effect in this shift. But writers began increasingly to refer to messianic and nonmessianic Jews as "Christians" and "Jews." Once it was sure that intervisitation between these two groups was being discouraged by the Jewish authorities, as was first recorded solidly in the Mishna, Jews began to make sense out of the difference by building up further theological background. They said that the reason for this rejection is that the Christians affirmed that "Jesus was God" and that "the Jews" could not accept this. However, that is a construction after the fact. It does not deal with the fact that all of the "high christology" statements about Jesus which we find in the New Testament were made by radically monotheistic Jews and were not, when made, seen to be in any sense polytheistic or idolatrous. Further, we do not have any record that Jews in the first century rejected such formulations, whether made by messianic Jews or by anyone else.

Whenever and why ever it happened, Judaism slowed down and stopped its missionary openness before the onset of serious persecution by Christians. Persecution of Jews by Gentiles was endemic to the ancient Roman world. It may be that "Christians" progressively differentiated themselves from Jews in order not to suffer that persecution and thereby indirectly diverted the anger of Gentiles toward the nonmessianic Jews. Yet this in itself would not explain the Jews' abandonment of missionary openness. Actually, it could have had the opposite effect. Jews no less than "Christians" could argue that they had no secrets, that their God was for everybody and that their law was reasonable, as many of their thinkers were, in fact, arguing.

In any case, Judaism turns out to be an ethnic enclave that is much less missionary than before, if not at some points actually committed to a near rejection of the accession of the Gentiles to membership in the community. The abandonment of the missionary perspective on the part of Judaism is a backhanded adjustment, not to the Gentile world in general, but to Christianity. With time we have to say that the fact that Judaism is nonmissionary is a product of Christian history or a part of Christian history. For Jews to be nonmissionary means that they have been "Christianized," that is, they have accepted their role within a context where telling the Gentiles about the God of Abraham is a function that has been preempted by the "Christians." Pressures are such that "Jews" are willing to leave it that way.

If the first stage of the "Christianization of Judaism" was the abandonment by Jews of their missionary thrust, the last stages of that "Christianization" are to be observed in their acceptance within the Western world of assimilation or pluralism. In modern America, Protestants, Catholic and Jews are the three kinds of equally legitimate theism, equally entitled to claim to represent the common "Judeo-Christian heritage." In some circumstances this has led Jews to a degree of theological and cultural assimilation, so that Reform Judaism becomes socially much like Protestantism.

If this full adjustment to pluralism was the rounding out of the Christianization of Judaism, the development of Zionism was its culmination. Zionism is a nationalistic movement that supports, in Palestine, a Jewish state after the model of the states of the West. It defines Jews in such a way that most of them may be unbelieving and unobservant. In the pluralistic West the Jews are a "church," with the increasing abandonment of the claim to represent a normative lifestyle; in the state of Israel Judaism is a nation but no longer a believing community. Once the state has been created, the separate existence of a Jewish ethnic body is no longer needed as the base for religion. In the historic depth sense of the word, to be born in the state of Israel makes one less a Jew than to be born in a ghetto. Of course this is exacerbated by the fact the state of Israel was formed in such a way that it needs to tolerate other non-Jewish population groups in its midst. Committed Judaism, that is, a discernible people thoroughly and sacrificially ready to order their lives around their convictions as to what constitutes the substance of Torah, is a minority sect in Israel just as is Christianity.

We set aside the kind of study that would need to be done at considerable depth if we had stayed in the realm of intellectual history. Jewish culture and philosophy have not only interacted with Christian and post-Christian models in the last centuries but have borrowed extensively from them, and with no apology. Feuerbach, Kant and probably Kierkegaard could be echoed in reformulations of Jewish thought. The most adequate continuing advocacy of the moral philosophy of Immanuel Kant may well be the Jew Herman Cohen. The best interpreter of the thought of Reinhold Niebuhr in mid-century America was the Jew Will Herberg. In the case of Cohen there was no sense of betrayal or acculturation involved in this interaction.

As we asked with regard to the other faith communities we had talked about earlier, we should ask with regard to Judaism whether this discovery of its Christian character or any other element of our awareness of its tragic history should lead to distinctive conclusions as to how Christian witness should be represented and formulated. I would conclude with the following suggestions:

1. As was the case in relation to the Muslim world and colonial missionary work, *the Christian witness needs to be repentant.* With regard to Judaism the reasons for repentance are especially numerous and dramatic. It applies not only to the pogrom and the forced conversions of Jews in medieval and modern Western history, and not only to the Christian roots of the Holocaust, but also to the more gentle kind of coercion involved when toleration itself is a pressure toward accommodation.

2. *What Christians must talk about is Jesus Christ not Christianity* as religion or culture. We should not focus on dogma about Christ in the forms in which it has come to offend Jewish monotheism. What we preach with regard to the Jews in particular is not that they are rejected, although they have the same freedom as anyone else to reject the call of God. Rather, the message is that the messianic promise is directed in a historically special way to them. As is the case with regard to other specimens of "other religions," we should not assume that all the people who are part of a religious culture have a deep faith in the particular theology that is typical in that culture. As we should not assume that all Danes are Lutheran by conviction, we should not assume that all Algerians are Muslim, or all Israelis convinced Jews. Not all North American Jews are convinced of Jewish theology and piety. The arguments against "bothering people" who are "happy in

their own faith" should not in most cases apply in such a way to keep the Christian witness from being addressed to most people.

3. *Judaism is not just one more case of "another religion."* It is exceptionally representative of some issues and crucially different in others.

   • Judaism represents, in a unique way, the indispensable Old Testament that saves the church from syncretism. This could be followed up at greater length; it is treated in numerous studies including one by Emil Brunner.

   • Judaism in relation to Christianity is particularly representative of the wall between Jews and Gentiles spoken of in Ephesians 2 and 3.

   • Judaism is the special focus of the apostasy that took place in the third century when Christianity began moving toward ethnocentrism and racism. Thus the issue of Judaism as a potential audience for the witness to Jesus must retain at least a symbolic if not a quantitative or chronological priority.

4. *An anti-Jewish or non-Jewish Christianity is always ready to sell out to some other pagan god.* In Hellenism it was ready to sell out to speculative theology. Usually it is ready to sell out to political provincialism believing that God chose some other nation to represent God's holy will in the world. Sometimes it sells out to emotional religiosity, which separates the intensity of the faith from its impact on life. In some renewal experiences it sells out to antinomianism.

5. When the Christian takes a pro-Jewish commitment in light of the arguments indicated above, this commitment *should be addressed predominantly to the memory and the dignity of historic Judaism through the centuries* and to the story of Jewry in the recent European experience rather than being focused on the Westernized population and administration of the state of Israel, as if the latter were somehow the best incarnation of Jewish identity.

Afterword

AS YOU GO

As You Go *was not originally part of the theology of mission lectures.*[1] *However, Yoder asked his students to read this pamphlet as part of their course work. It is a more carefully developed statement of his idea of "migration evangelism" than the oral lectures provide and has been out of print for many years. This material does not serve as a summary chapter for the entire book, but we think it is a fitting and important addition.*

Herald Press (Scottdale, PA) first published this pamphlet in 1961 when Yoder was serving as assistant to the foreign missions secretary of the Mennonite Board of Missions and Charities (MBM) from a base in Europe. In preparing the manuscript for current publication, we decided to lightly edit it and remove the original foreword by J. D. Graber, who had served as general secretary of MBM beginning in 1944. —Ed.

AS YOU GO
The Old Mission in a New Day

THE CHANGED SITUATION IN WORLD MISSIONS

Fifty years ago it would have been pointless to ask what is meant by the term *missionary* or why the missionary exists. Obviously, a missionary was a person sent and supported financially by an organized church group in Western Europe or North America. He or she went to some other part of the world to proclaim the gospel and to establish Christian fellowships in non-Christian societies. The "homeland" was assumed to

---

[1]John Howard Yoder, *As You Go: The Old Mission in a New Day*, Focal Pamphlet No. 5 (Scottdale, PA: Mennonite Publishing House, 1961).

be a Christian nation, and the Christian message brought to the other people of the world was considered to be a contribution of great value to other societies and of eternal worth to individuals.

Now the world scene has changed. No longer is it self-evident that the homeland is a Christian nation. Some serious Christian thinkers even challenge the desirability of taking to other nations and cultures the religious heritage of Western Christianity. In this discussion we are most interested in those changes that affect the form and method of missionary endeavor, especially in distant places, where primary responsibilities for supporting it cannot be borne by local congregations founding churches in their own neighborhood.

One basic aspect of this change has been the political one. Fifty years ago missionary work was carried on under the friendly supervision of colonial administrators representing Western European countries in Asia, Africa or the Pacific Islands. This was assumed to be a good thing. This relationship often guaranteed to the missionary a degree of protection, freedom of movement and sometimes financial assistance for medical or educational enterprises. Today the number of nations in Asia, Africa and the Pacific Islands still subject to European administration has dwindled rapidly. We may safely assume that the colonial age has come to an end as far as direct political supervision is concerned. Opinions differ as to whether the missionary should welcome or regret this development. In any case he or she can no longer depend on the security and support that missionaries once possessed because they represented the Western world.

Another basic change has taken place on the cultural level. Fifty years ago any North American of above-average ability and initiative knew more about mechanics, health, reading and writing and had more of the tools of civilization than the immense majority of the people in Africa, Asia or Latin America. In some places—China and India, for instance—there were highly educated or highly wealthy people, but they were few. Today the time is fast passing, or completely gone, even in the least developed countries, when the Westerner can be an all-around amateur and still hold a significant cultural advantage over other peoples. The rest of the world is fast developing experts in engineering, medicine, education and government, as well as in church leadership. Beside them, the Western Jack-of-all-trades is no longer useful, respected and needed as was once the case.

Rapidly developing younger countries still do need the services of specialists; some of them are still willing to have such specialists come to them from the West—to fill certain technical needs for which they do not yet have sufficiently numerous trained personnel of their own. Engineers, educators and agricultural advisers, for instance, are still in great demand.

In the Christian churches the situation is much like that we have noted in the cultural realm. Fifty or one hundred years ago, Western missionaries could find, in almost any part of the world, great expanses of territory and masses of population completely untouched by the Christian gospel. The missionary was indispensable if the Christian message was to reach these peoples. One did not need to be highly educated or a gifted theologian or evangelist; one could still represent the essential elements of the gospel in such a way that at least some people might be touched by the Holy Spirit and the church planted.

Today this too has changed. In most parts of the world to which missionaries have access, the church of Christ is present, even though often pitifully small and quite imperfect. Many tribal peoples are unreached as yet, but they represent a small minority of the earth's population and reaching them is a task for specialists. In most major cultures and peoples of the world the church is present and should no longer be under the direct leadership of Western missionaries.

As in the cultural realm, this does not mean that no one desires additional Western assistance. But as in that realm, the assistance others need and desire is that of specialists. Increasingly, national leadership must take over bringing the gospel to one's neighbors and building the church through pastoral and local teaching ministries. What continues to be needed is the aid of trained experts in theology, new techniques of evangelism, urban problems, special pastoral services, interchurch statesmanship and services of the church to the larger society. Nearly all the younger churches are highly desirous of continuing to receive this kind of assistance from the West.

All these developments taken together mean that the "missionary" in the traditional sense of the word, that is, a person financially supported and sent to another part of the world to witness to the gospel, will increasingly need to have exceptional gifts and advanced training for a particular work. No longer can mission agencies in the West send average individuals and persons with all-around training, or simply decide to send people with spiritual gifts, irrespective of the needs and desires of the churches they go to serve. Thus many mission agencies are making extended theological or other technical training a prerequisite for all missionary personnel. Other mission agencies, which do not have formal standards of this kind, more strongly encourage their candidates for missionary appointment to seek such training.

Still other factors at work in North America make this effect even more marked. In a day when few special ministries within the home churches called for gifted persons, individuals with a strong sense of evangelistic responsibility would naturally find their calling in foreign mission. Today there are many more tasks where qualified and consecrated persons are needed and wanted in the churches at home, in their institutions and in their local evangelistic endeavors. Likewise, commerce and industry exert a greater attraction on many young people making their vocational choices than in years past.

To this we must add still another factor. The cost of sending and supporting overseas missionaries is steadily rising, as both costs and living standards in the countries to which they go constantly climb. Rising population density increases prices of staple foods in many areas as these foods become more and more scarce. The coming of modern industries or the competition of military establishments raises the cost of local labor. As living standards of cultural leaders in an overseas country rise, the missionary must attempt to maintain a comparable level.

Rising costs of missionary support and rising educational and technical qualifications for competent missionaries combine to reduce the relative number of missionaries whom Christian groups can send and support full time in foreign countries. In proportion to the total resources of a given group of Christian people, fewer will be qualified. Of those qualified, more will be needed in other occupations. Those who are qualified and available will cost more to send and support. The number of persons who can be sent as missionaries in the traditional sense will therefore tend to decrease proportionately.

This development does not necessarily mean that we will be seeing an immediate decline in the number of missionaries. Even though the cost of supporting a missionary rises, the amount of missionary giving may rise more rapidly. Even though the number of persons qualified for missionary service decreases, the proportion of those people who actually commit themselves to missionary vocations may increase if they are better informed about the needs and more effectively challenged to make their vocational choices in the light of Christian faith. One extremely significant recent development—worth a pamphlet in its own right—is the participation of non-Western churches in missionary sending, with Japanese going to Brazil or India, Indonesians to the Pacific islands, and Brazilians to Angola. There are already over two hundred such missionaries and fraternal workers serving outside their own homelands, thus correcting the mistaken impression that "missions" are only a phase of the expansion of the West. Thus the effects of a changing missionary situation may, for several reasons, not be felt immediately by all churches in a decrease of missionary program. We, however, should not permit this to hide the serious and fundamental nature of the changes nor the urgency of being prepared to adjust to them.

CHURCH EXPANSION THROUGH THE CENTURIES

Our discussion thus far has made it seem quite clear that, because of changes taking place in our world and our new understandings of missionary methods, there will be proportionately fewer possibilities for using the services of missionaries supported financially in foreign countries by specialized church agencies. This seems to be a certain fact. But how then can we reconcile with this fact our understanding of the missionary duty of the Christian church and of every Christian? Should we resign ourselves to present trends because of which Christians are every year a smaller fraction of the total world population, falling further and further behind the goal of bringing Christ to all peoples? Has sending missionaries become so costly, and is the task of the missionary so difficult, that we should allow the gospel witness to become the concern only of a small elite of specially gifted experts?

Before we conclude that there is no other solution to this problem, we should take a look at the whole sweep of Christian history. The kind of missionary of which we have been thinking has actually not been the predominant pattern, and, by and large, not the most effective pattern for spreading the Christian message across the centuries and across the face of the earth. What we call the "foreign missionary movement" is a relatively recent phenomenon in the history of the church, beginning about 1800 and corresponding in a peculiar way to the particular cultural and political situation it met. Hundreds gave themselves heroically in this great movement, and myriad stories are told of effective devotion to the Christian cause. Yet it would be wrong to limit our thinking about the future of missions to one particular concept of Christian witness that developed in the great "missionary century."

Throughout the history of God's people, the gospel has been brought to new parts of the world primarily by migration of financially independent Christians. In Acts the faith spread from Jerusalem to Samaria, from Samaria to Antioch, and from there to Cyprus before the churches at Jerusalem and Antioch gave any thought to organizing to propagate their message. Christians were dispersed, sometimes because of commercial or family interests, more often because of persecution. Where they went, they took their faith with them, and new Christian cells were planted.

Even the so-called missionary voyages of the apostle Paul are no exception to this rule. Wherever Paul went, he began with the circle of faithful Jews and God-fearing Gentiles who gathered in the synagogue. These Jews had been dispersed, once again for personal and commercial reasons as well as by a degree of persecution. Thus they were to be found in every major city of the eastern Roman Empire. Since Paul believed that the Christian church is a continuation of Israel, he was able to come to each of these synagogues as to a potential church, already planted in the city by the migration of God's people. Paul did not do what the modern missionary movement did—enter a country where no one confessed faith in the true God. He completed and nurtured the faith of the scattered faithful worshipers of God wherever he found them already gathered.

Let us observe just one example from the early days of the church. When the apostle Paul reached Corinth, paying his own way with his tentmaking trade, he went into partnership with another Jewish tentmaker, a refugee from Rome named Aquila. We are not told just when and how Aquila became a Christian, but we do know that when Paul left Corinth for Jerusalem Aquila and his wife, Priscilla, went along. We are not told that they moved to find a place where there was a greater demand for tents—this move may well have been the first step in their lives as Christian disciples. Paul left them behind when his boat stopped at Ephesus, and they were the ones who corrected the theology of the brilliant Apollos and introduced him to the church at Corinth. Later we find them back at Rome, with a congregation meeting in their home.

If we were to study in detail the history of the spread of Christianity through the Roman Empire following the age of the apostles, the lesson would once again be much the same. By the end of the second century Tertullian could boast that Christianity was represented in Britain, beyond the confines of the Roman Empire. In a similar way churches developed on the eastern borders of the Roman Empire, and later served as bridges for bearing the gospel all the way to India and China. This church growth was not a matter of organized missions. Christians, often serving as artisans or merchants, following the ordinary lines of travel and commerce, established themselves farther and farther from their original homes, taking their faith with them and making an economic contribution to the society into which they moved. In many other cases, Christians moved about independent of their own will, as slaves or servants in the households of the wealthy. Already in the New Testament we read that there were Christians, probably servants, in "Caesar's household." This kind of spreading was much healthier spiritually than the later growth of churches by mass baptisms when it was Caesar himself who felt authorized to propagate the faith by means of his political authority.

The place of "ministers" in this expansion was definitely a secondary one. Teachers and bishops were called to the frontier areas when there were already sufficient Christians there to have need of their services in teaching and in organizing common worship. Still later, when the Germanic tribes of Western Europe were also progressively brought within hearing of the gospel, this work was not done by specialized preaching ministers sent from a distance. Instead, colonies of monks supported themselves as they went and involved themselves in the economic and cultural life of their people. Although monasticism in some respects represents a deformed Christian witness, in many other respects it is an example of a healthy form of evangelization by colonization. It is more comparable to colonization than to what we have been calling "missions." In the Christianization of northern Europe there was also a distressingly large imperialistic element, with the "conversion" of certain tribes and areas of the countryside being largely a political event. The connection of missions with colonialism is not a modern phenomenon. Yet if those nations finally became Christian in more than name, we still owe it more to the missionary monks who moved to live among them than to the princes who bargained to have them baptized.

On the American frontier the church again was built by migration. Seeking a better place to make a living, Christians from Europe and from the eastern seaboard moved west. When established, they called ministers to serve them. There was no "missionary work" (among the whites) in the sense of preaching to pagan multitudes among whom there were no Christians present. The great revivals and the patient ministry of thousands of circuit riders and part-time ministers were effective in bringing the gospel to pioneer America, not because of the quality of the ministers alone but because of the universal presence of Christians who had migrated to the frontiers.

Those Christian fellowships which are growing the most rapidly today are still those that count most on the initiative of self-starting, self-supporting witnesses, even for major responsibilities of leadership in organized congregations. The basic reason for this is not the financial savings of not needing to support many ministers. It is rather because it is spiritually more valid and healthier to cast responsibility on every Christian, giving opportunities to persons without ministerial training and status to exercise leadership and to take initiative in witnessing on their own.

The effectiveness of this approach has not been limited to Christian missions. The expansion of Islam into Africa south of the Sahara and into Indonesia has been much more effective than attempts of Christian missions to enter these same countries, and has taken place in a similarly unofficial way. Islam has spread into these areas without missionary organizations and without political domination. Faithful Muslims travel, making their way and making themselves useful as merchants and artisans, settling amidst villages of primitive religious traditions. They bring with them their very visible and very conscientiously practiced forms of faithfulness—the prayer periods, the abstinence from eating pork and the annual fast. They may intermarry with the villagers. If they do, it is taken for granted that the wife, and perhaps even the in-laws, accept their faith. Within a generation it is possible for this "colony" to invite from some center of Muslim education a teacher who will instruct the children of the village in the Qur'an and proclaim publicly the times of prayer. The professional religious leader comes only when there is a community for him to serve. In this way, rather than through political conquest, Islam is continuing to grow, especially in the two parts of the world mentioned where it has not placed barriers in its own way by earlier political imperialism.

PUTTING TWO AND TWO TOGETHER

Thus far we have made two fundamental observations. One is that the great foreign missionary movement of the last two centuries has been a unique phenomenon, called forth by a situation in political and cultural history that was also unique. It must draw to a close, whether its task has been completed or not, with the end of the colonial age. The achievement of this great movement has been to plant Christian fellowships in almost every part of the world. This achievement probably could not have come about in any other way, but in our age Christians can no longer seek to continue or complete it only by using the same methods. Yet the closing of the colonial era leaves the missionary imperative just as clear and as urgent as before. In fact, the rising population of the world and the degeneration of political and social order give the missionary task still greater urgency.

Our second fundamental observation was that through most of the history of the Christian church, the geographical and numerical expansion of Christianity was not the result of separately organized, centrally administered and externally financed missionary specialists. It came through normal, often unplanned, usually self-supporting movements of Christians who took their living faith with them as they moved with their sources of livelihood.

As we continue to wrestle with the assignment of obeying the unchanging missionary imperative in a changing world, it would seem most logical to ask whether the church can grow today in a conscious and carefully coordinated way, using the method that has been most effective down through the centuries rather than that of the foreign missionary movement. For want of a more striking and poetic name let us speak for the present of "migration evangelism." Let us attempt to envisage what such an approach might involve.

Migration evangelism would mean that numbers of Christians from the Western, white, Protestant world would move into parts of the world dominated by other cultures, peoples and religions. These migrants would need to go in sufficient numbers that they might help one another to establish their policies and meet their needs as a group in their new homeland, yet not in sufficient numbers to create a cultural island of their own.

These migrant missionaries would support themselves financially by providing professional and technical services needed in the countries to which they go. The major needs in many cases would be in the areas of education and modern mechanical and electronic techniques—refrigeration, communications and transportation. In some cases more highly specialized services in agricultural methods, social work or the like would be needed. They would identify themselves with the people they serve and to whom they have chosen to witness. Presumably, they would work toward acquiring the nationality of that country. They would plan to raise their children there and live on the level permitted by their own earnings. The "religious" impact of these people would be made primarily by their work and witness as lay Christians in the normal contacts of daily life. They would be served by supported religious personnel only if they were able to call and support such persons from their own resources.

There should be no idea of a colony, taking with it a Western, Germanic or Anglo-Saxon culture which the local people would then be invited to join. The purpose of migration evangelism would not be for Christians, or for representatives of one denomination, to save their life as a group, identifiable by a particular language, a particular set of family names or particular cultural patterns. Rather they would expect to lose their identity and perhaps even their names in the birth of first-generation Christian fellowships or in the revitalization of existing fellowships in the lands to which they go.

While avoiding the creation of a cultural island which would permanently identify them as a foreign body, such persons would want to be of sufficient number and to maintain sufficiently close relationships in the early years to assist one another in making cultural adjustments and to constitute from the very beginning an organized and functioning Christian fellowship. Should they go into a part of the world where the local educational and medical facilities are seriously inadequate, they might band together to provide certain of these facilities. They would not, however, provide for themselves alone the schools and hospitals which they might establish; they would be open on the same conditions to their neighbors.

THE ECONOMIC CONTRIBUTION OF MIGRATION

We should understand clearly that serving the needs of people's bodies or of their society and bearing the proclamation of the Christian gospel are not alternatives between which Christians can choose. Even though some individuals may be called to concentrate on one aspect or the other, the imperative for every Christian is to concern him- or herself with all the needs of the neighbor. Thus far we have discussed primarily considerations of effectiveness in evangelism, in the narrower and more specific sense of this term. Let us now turn our attention to the fact that there are also very significant considerations of material need which would also favor this approach.

It should not be necessary here to document in detail the fact that most of the world is becoming poorer and poorer. A certain rate of industrial and agricultural expansion is required if a country is to break even in its ability to feed, clothe, house and transport its growing population.

Western countries, being well above this minimum rate, are becoming richer and richer; others, even those like India and Nigeria that are well-governed and that lay careful plans, are in danger of losing ground, while most of the Asian and African countries are falling behind rapidly.

Thus far the only methods for dealing with this problem have been either massive donations of relief aid, given in the form of goods or money, or investment of great amounts of capital for expansion of basic industries. Major investments may be effective in the long run, but in the short run they actually disrupt still further the society in which a steel mill or a mine is planted. In any case, they require resources beyond what any Christian group can contribute. The direct relief approach—as distinguished from disaster relief, which is quite another matter—is being seen with increasing clarity to have a bad psychological effect where aid is given to people in chronic need. Considerable attention is being given now, especially in Protestant and secular circles, to some sort of birth control as a way of avoiding overpopulation. Entirely apart from the moral issue that is involved here for many Christians, there is good reason to doubt whether this campaign is either politically or anthropologically realistic. In any case Christians cannot count on it to make a significant change in world hunger in the short term.

Actually the only kind of help that will still be really useful and effective is the actual going of people who place their skills at the disposal of the needy. The increase in hygiene, literacy and productivity that can only come in the form of technically qualified persons is in the long run the only way to fight hunger.

One standard that any Christian should use in deciding on an occupation is the need for his or her services in various possible professions and places. Even apart from the Christian obligation to witness to one's faith, any serious person should give attention to whether the work being done is the largest contribution he or she can make to society's needs.

In view of world hunger, almost anyone who is technically qualified in a useful profession is more needed elsewhere than in the West. Whether a person is a mechanic, refrigerator serviceman, accountant, dietitian, merchant or (especially) teacher, social worker or engineer, his or her services are more urgently needed elsewhere than in northern

Indiana, eastern Pennsylvania, the Shenandoah Valley, Kansas City or Los Angeles. Not everyone has the flexibility, imagination, training or freedom to respond to this call. The person who does have these qualifications is technically capable of making a significant contribution. If someone truly believes in trying to serve where most needed, that person should ask seriously whether that is where he or she now is.

THE CULTURAL CONTRIBUTION OF MIGRATION EVANGELISM

The Christian's primary responsibility to bear witness to the gospel does not prevent most Christians from considering further the cultural contributions they can make to the larger human community. Likewise, an investigation of the possibilities of migration as a possibly more effective way of spreading the gospel calls for some consideration of the cultural significance of such an undertaking. Would such an approach mean that Christians would thereby lose their chance to make an effective social contribution because they would find themselves a small minority and representatives of an unpopular race in other parts of the world?

Insofar as we can learn from history in realms such as this, it is clear that the most significant social and cultural contributions have usually been made by minority groups. This is not the place to document in detail such a claim, but several obvious examples may well be cited.

In the political realm it is most obvious that the major characteristics of a civilization are the contributions made by minority groups. We speak of the Roman Empire as representing one of the great epochs of Western cultural history. Within this empire only a tiny minority of the population was Roman; in fact, few people spoke Latin at all. It was the organizational and cultural genius of this minority, coupled with, but not completely dependent on, their political and military force, that enabled them to set the tone of Western civilization for hundreds of years.

We are accustomed to speaking of the Germanic invasions of Western Europe after the end of the Roman Empire as if great masses of people had moved westward into Germany, France and northern Italy. In reality, what happened was once again primarily the movement of a relatively small elite group, with a major body of the population remaining from the earlier Gallic or Roman stock. The Germanic elements were the cultural leaders, often in spite of actual political weakness, adding a new element to the heritage of Rome.

By no means is the significance of the cultural contribution of a minority limited to minorities that have political domination. In fact, it is very often the case that a minority social group is made more effective in their cultural contribution by virtue of the fact that they have no political responsibility. This may be said of Quakers in England or of Mennonites in the Netherlands. Because the routine tasks in government and the state church were closed to them, enterprising Quakers and Mennonites were driven into the cultural frontiers, which in the seventeenth and eighteenth centuries were commerce and manufacturing. In these areas they made a contribution out of all proportion to their numbers.

Most commercial leadership in the societies of Southeast Asia and Indonesia has been provided by migrants from China. Similarly, Indians have in recent centuries given economic leadership to the cultural centers along the east coast of Africa. This is actually not too different from the financial and commercial specialization of the Jews in Europe and to some extent in North America. Although this contribution has sometimes been held against them, it is actually a demonstration of their exceptional creativity as a minority group. The very fact that a group is a minority means it is guided away from those functions in the nonproductive maintenance of society that the majority seeks to control. Today, similarly, Arab traders are moving southward across central Africa. We have already noted the effectiveness of this movement as a way of spreading Islam. It is effective only because it also brings a higher standard of living as these migrants make available the services of a merchant or the skills of a tinsmith, cobbler or other simple artisans.

In most cases, minorities have made an exceptional cultural contribution in what might be called "social techniques"—common morality, work attitudes, family stability and ways of getting along together. In only a few cases was the new contribution an actual economic technique, such as a new way of tilling the land, of irrigating or weaving. A minority can actually make a stronger cultural contribution, at least from the short view, when the techniques it provides are of immediate economic significance. Education—more specifically education in mechanical, electrical and medical fields—is so strategic and in such short supply that it justifies additional persons entering even an overpopulated region, if the capacities they possess are in great demand. In many countries undergoing rapid economic and social change, this would be the case for most of the technical professions. When persons with these wanted technical capacities are at the same time Christians with peculiarly Christian convictions about family life, honesty, industry, and friendly relations between neighbors and between ethnic groups, this should make their cultural contribution still greater.

The significance of these economic and cultural considerations would be especially great in those countries that seriously limit the movement of missionary personnel. For many countries, not only former colonies like India but also places like Australia or the Soviet Union, it would be easier to enter as an immigrant intending to identify with the economy and culture of that nation than as a missionary envoy. Christians with trades and skills plentifully represented in the West, but severely needed in the younger nations, would be making a much greater relative economic contribution through the same amount of work in their new home than in the old. This would make it quite likely that, far from having difficulty in entering new places, such persons would really be wanted by government and by economic and social leaders there.

THE WITNESS VALUE OF THE PRESENCE OF THE CHURCH

One of the most fundamental objections to the foreign missionary movement by its critics, both Christian and non-Christian, has been that it was a tool of cultural and even political imperialism. Certainly this accusation has been exaggerated unfairly and uncharitably in many quarters. Yet the problem to which the criticism points remains.

However well-intended, and however seriously a foreign missionary attempts to overcome every barrier to fellowship and communication, he or she does not cease to appear to be the emissary of a foreign culture. He or she may maintain social ties with the commercial and even political or military representatives of the "homeland." The missionary represents the economy, the culture and sometimes even the politics of the part of the world from which he or she comes.

It has thus been extremely difficult, even in more recent years when the problem has been more visible, to avoid giving the impression that the Christian church is one of the various ways in which Western culture seeks to impose itself on the rest of the world. As a result, missions have sometimes called forth an "indigenous" reaction that is just as artificial and as unhealthy as foreign domination. Members and sometimes even leaders of younger churches make the difference between themselves and the missionary a major spiritual issue. They call for independence and attempt to remove the traces of fraternal relationships with Western churches, as if this would make their church genuinely their own. In so doing, they simply mirror the mistake that had been made before them, attempting in their turn to tie their church to their own culture as Westerners had done.

A further dimension of this spiritual handicap of the missionary's status is that the missionary retains a legal and psychological footing in the "home" country. After a term of service, the home to which the missionary goes to rest, and where he or she maintains nationality and a safe-deposit vault, is somewhere else. When the missionary returns "home," he or she hopes to come again to the "field" to serve the same church. This is, however, never sure, since the missionary's return may be decided against by an agency in the homeland or may be delayed for the sake of family considerations. As a result, even individuals most clearly devoted to and spiritually identified with the people they serve find their fellowship occasionally being called into question by a long absence from their field of service.

The pattern of migration evangelism, though by no means solving these problems completely, would do much to neutralize their harmful effects. The fact that a Christian community exists and the life of this community is ordered by the gospel is itself a witness. Certainly one significant shortcoming of traditional missionary methods has been the missionary's preaching and serving as a solitary individual, who for at least a number of years does not belong to a local fellowship in which basic Christian understandings of spiritual unity and mutual concern could be worked out. When in the past the missionary has made up for this aloneness by maintaining an attachment to a foreign culture—to the diplomatic or commercial or military people from his or her home country—this has stood in the way of witness. The missionary has had no channel for relationships with other Christians of background like his or her own where a Christian social group could be observed in action by the surrounding society. As a result, when a national Christian fellowship comes into being, it has only the example of the single missionary administrator to follow, with no clear example of an already existing Christian fellowship.

This consideration is still more significant if we keep in mind that the validity of missionary witness will be increasingly related to the clarity of the church's stand on social and ethical issues. If there is but one missionary in the village, it is not clear how much of his or her love and concern for social welfare is missionary technique, and how much is spiritual concern in its own right. If there are numerous immigrant families, most of them self-supporting, then not only their life together but also their criticism and constructive example to the society around them will be without ulterior motive and therefore more believable.

One major unsolved problem of all missionary methods is how to integrate Christian faith into the culture to which it is brought, without loss of true Christian character. Alongside failures resulting from efforts to keep churches Western, there have also been experiences of too complete assimilation of local cultural and religious traditions. The result has been an indigenous Christian movement progressing rapidly, but losing something of its Christian character in adopting pagan attitudes or practices. This excessive "indigenization" is, of course, not something for which the persons who carry it to extremes are to blame. They are simply reacting to the excessive Westernization of Christianity as it was brought to them. Nevertheless, we would hope that the presence of a number of Christians who really throw in their lot with the people they serve might be a healthy corrective to the danger of mass movements returning to paganism. At the same time, having made a permanent commitment to their new homeland would release such people from much of the temptation to reproduce the church "back home" in the new context.

Missions have always provided certain social services, and presumably should continue to do so according to need. If such services—

especially schools and hospitals—are provided by an immigrant group meeting both their own needs and those of the community around them, this could avoid the frequent impression that educational or medical help has been doled out at arm's length. Here the service rendered to others would be the same as the immigrant group is providing for itself. That the immigrant group provides for all who need it the same educational or medical facility that it uses for its own personal needs will be the strongest testimony of their integration into the adopted culture and of their desire to make a contribution to that culture.

A significant drawback of traditional missionary methods has always been the unnatural position of financially supported ministerial workers in contrast to the rest of the population. A coordinated immigrant group supporting the services of a specialized minister would make his position much less open to question than if he were financially supported without a group of Christians to serve. The missionary's evangelistic outreach would be a part of the life of the church in the most wholesome way, avoiding the unhealthy pattern of simply subsidizing "native evangelists" with no congregational connection.

THIS MEANS YOU

An unintended, but nevertheless unavoidable, result of the foreign missionary movement has been the feeling of many conscientious church people that the "missionary call" is a special experience or a special status reserved for a very few people. In spite of constant efforts of missionaries to argue, as they sincerely believe, that Christians who remain at home can and should also be witnesses wherever they are, this sincere repetition of an obvious truth is still insufficient to offset the effects of the missionary's special title, mobility and secure livelihood.

We have already spoken of the fact that ministerial leadership within a group of migrants would stand in a much more healthy relationship to the surrounding community. What interests us now is the awareness that the migration method could once again make unmistakably clear to the "home church" that every Christian, whatever his or her gifts, should be making vocational choices in the light of missionary obligations. This means you.

One reason only exceptional persons have served as missionaries in the past has been the very real element of danger and sacrifice involved in such service. As long as missionary work was a special performance of special people, this element of sacrifice, perhaps partly compensated for by values of education, prestige and adventure, could be considered as simply one part of the special calling. If, however, we are suggesting that every Christian should consider him- or herself a missionary, the element of sacrifice calls for more careful analysis.

In all past thought about missions, it has been assumed that the missionary was basically committing his or her life to the cause of the gospel. Furloughs and other arrangements for the missionary's convenience and welfare were understood not as ways of avoiding the necessity to make real sacrifices, but rather as ways of increasing effectiveness. If it should now be the case that careful study tells us migration is the best approach to evangelism in other cultures, the fact that this would involve a real sacrifice should therefore not be an argument against it. The missionary is by definition someone who is ready for whatever sacrifice is involved in carrying the gospel in the most effective way. But according to the gospel this basic readiness to sacrifice should be characteristic of every Christian and not the specialty of certain peculiarly consecrated persons.

It is good that here, as in other callings, a degree of sacrifice should remain as part of the decision to dedicate one's life to any Christian vocation. This will help avoid burdening the migrant group with mere fellow travelers who do not share the basic motivation. "Colonization," or the movement of persons from rural areas to the city, has not made a major contribution to the cause of churches when the motives of the "colonists" have been mixed. Thus there need be no embarrassment about the very real sacrifices involved, especially with reference to family ties and the ease of making a livelihood, for those who would migrate for the gospel.

Yet let us not overly dramatize the suffering and loss that might be involved in following such a call. It is no longer the case, as it was a century ago, that those going outside the Western world greatly risk exposure to disease and the possibility that they will not receive necessary medical or surgical assistance. With transportation now available and the spread of medical education, whatever the remaining shortcomings, medical help for urgent needs is within a few hours of any point on the globe. Likewise, there are more ways of arranging for educational needs to be met. Especially if the migration work could be undertaken in a carefully planned way, with a number of persons involved going to one general area, this group presumably would also be able to take care of some of their children's basic educational needs if they were in a culture where schools were not adequate. Thus it is not necessarily the case that such migration would mean depriving one's children of a decent education.

In past years it has been possible to assume that the moral education of young persons was best provided by enabling them to grow up in North America. There is increasing reason to doubt that this is the case today. The rates of juvenile crime and the prevalence of unwholesome literature and entertainment are greater menaces in North America than anywhere else in the world. If one wishes to train one's child to respect the dignity of work, to realize that Christian faith requires a personal commitment that distinguishes the Christian from the world, and to have ideals of etiquette and careful concern for other persons, there is considerable reason to doubt that helping a child to spend his or her teen years in North America is the best way to serve that young person.

Being in a minority group anywhere in the world imposes a special burden on a young person. However, being a member of a minority group because of his or her parents' evangelistic concern and desire to be of use where they are needed would be a spiritually appropriate kind of minority status for a young person. It would help the young man or woman understand and live with this status more than being a member of a self-conscious denominational minority in a Protestant society would. It would also be more appropriate to the real spiritual calling of Christians than being a member of a Christian majority in a church-dominated culture. Thus the general assumption that migration as a missionary method would necessarily involve injustice to one's children probably does not hold.

FOREIGN MISSIONS AT YOUR DOORSTEP

We have been thinking of distant lands because, for many, the barriers of space, color and culture seem basic to the Christian missionary understanding. Certain areas of Western Europe or North America would, however, be especially fitting for a similar pattern of missionary approach. We are not thinking here of the normal expansion of Christian congregations within similar cultures and language areas by the gradual moving about of their members. Within the broad sweep of North American society, from the small rural town to suburbia, this kind of church growth should be considered as normal and basic. "Fringe areas" exist within our North American society, however, where barriers of culture, language and human need go beyond the limits of "normal" social mobility. Some fringe areas involve relatively small numbers of people—such as Native American, Chinese or *nisei*[2] quarters of some cities. Others are just as populous as some of the younger nations in Africa. No white American Protestant would normally, in the course of ordinary social mobility, find him or herself moving into the colored or Spanish-speaking part of his or her own metropolitan area. To go there, stay there, belong there and make a meaningful contribution would call for just as profound Christian commitment and just as much cultural and linguistic understanding as to go halfway around the world. The day of "city missions" is over if by that term we refer to well-to-do persons from across the tracks temporarily entering an underprivileged quarter to "hold services." The mission of Christians to the city is therefore all the more urgent.

TO SUM UP

The conclusion to this study can be written only by the reader. The writer can survey, on the grounds of common sense, history and spiritual principles, the challenge of a new (or rediscovered) and potentially more effective method of witnessing. Only the reader can decide whether and how the challenge is to be met.

For some, perhaps a brief experience as an exchange student or in

---

[2][Japanese term for second-generation immigrants. —Ed.]

voluntary service may provide the first occasion to develop acquaintance with distant places, persons and needs. Others may find openings in overseas activities related to the American economy. It is reported that nearly two million Americans are now overseas. Although about half of these persons are presumably related to some church in North America, those who actually consider their overseas work a method of Christian witnessing is very small. Many are, of course, engaged in military, diplomatic or commercial enterprises that render difficult or impossible their effectively reaching the hearts of nationals. There might, however, still be within the overseas operations of such American agencies, especially those engaged in developing the resources of other countries (plantations, mines and factories), opportunities to render a really useful service while getting acquainted with possibilities for settling there.

A greater area of need is the realm of public services in the younger nations; teachers in public school, medical and public health experts, agricultural extension agents and the like are needed in unlimited numbers. Persons with Western training not only are welcome in such services, but generally can earn a decent living as part of the economy of the young nation while working side by side with nationals. This kind of opening will probably turn out in many cases to be the most promising because the Christian who takes one of these badly needed service assignments competes the least with nationals and because his relationship to the public services of the younger nation frees him or her from the reproach of serving a foreign power and culture.

In a few places of the world there are still geographical frontiers, undeveloped areas needing to be brought into agricultural or mineral production. Opportunities for migration for such purposes as these could be found in Australia, the Soviet Union and parts of Latin America. In still other cases, like Barnabas of old returning to Cyprus, Christians may return to places they knew earlier. From among all these possibilities and others, only the committed Christian seeking with Spirit-driven conviction can choose the place and the method to which he or she is called. The aid of farsighted mission and church agencies will be needed if the migration is to relate effectively to both existing young churches and untouched areas. Patience and impatience will be needed in equal proportions—also careful study and blind faith.

But let us not conclude that the major problem of the "migrant missionary" would be finding a place to go. The real challenge is to be the kind of person worth being there. In our conformist culture, how many of us are qualified to adjust imaginatively and lovingly to new neighbors whose habits, values and standards are surprisingly, even disgustingly different? In our individualist society, how many of us have had experiences that trained us to live, work and solve trying problems in close quarters with others and in spiritual unity with fellow Christians to whom we are bound, for better or for worse? In our efficient, materialistic culture, how many of us have learned to take time for one another and to do without the luxuries that our advertisers call necessary? And above all, in our "Christianized" culture where "religion" is considered a good thing, how many of us see clearly and can communicate what there is in our faith that would survive without the props of social approval? Might it be that the reason we have left evangelism to supported specialists is that our own faith is not of export quality? The grind of hard work and loneliness, misunderstanding and insecurity, will polish diamonds but wear away clay.

This is no calling for the lover of adventure or comfort, or for those who want to "do good" while "finding themselves." Yet for those who seek first the kingdom of God and its righteousness, whose concern for the least among us constrains them to seek not security but service, the promise that "all these things shall be added" will once again not have been in vain.

APPENDIX

While this book provides the most comprehensive and integrated presentation of Yoder's thought about the church and mission, the following bibliography lists other primary sources—both published and unpublished—that are most directly related to his theology of mission. It might be argued that almost all of Yoder's thought is related to his understanding of the church and its mission; we have selected items that focus specifically on mission and evangelism and some that address interfaith and ecumenical relations. We have included *Body Politics* since Yoder's theology of mission includes the way in which the church embodies the gospel witness "before the watching world."

The online John Howard Yoder Digital Library pilot project hosted in Elkhart County, Indiana, contains more than thirty unpublished or hard-to-secure items. More will continue to be added as possible. The library can be accessed at http://replica.palni.edu/cdm/landingpage/collection/p15705coll18.

Church-Related Publications

"After Foreign Mission—What?" *Christianity Today*. March 30, 1962, pp. 12-13.

"Clarifying the Gospel." *Builder*. August 1973, pp. 2-7. Available online in the John Howard Yoder Digital Library pilot project.

Four articles based on Yoder's experience in Algeria were published in *Gospel Herald*, a Mennonite church publication: "Islam's Special Challenge to Christian Mission." December 31, 1957, pp. 1142-43. "Islam's Challenge to Mennonites." February 4, 1958, pp. 110-11. "Our First Three Years in Algeria."

February 18, 1958, pp. 158-60. "Missions and Material Aid in Algeria." April 1, 1958, pp. 306-7.

"The Missionary Church." *Gospel Herald*, January 8, 1963, pp. 38, 42.

"The Place of the Peace Message in Missions" appeared in two installments in *Gospel Herald*, December 27, 1960, pp. 1108-9, and January 3, 1961, pp. 14-15, 19-20.

"The Theology of the Church's Mission." *Mennonite Life* 21 (January 1966): 30-33. Journal available free online: http://tools.bethelks.edu/mennonitelife/pre2000/1966jan.pdf.

UNPUBLISHED PAPERS AND PRESENTATIONS

"Anabaptist Understandings of the Nature and Mission of the Church, with Implications for Contemporary Mennonite Church Organization." Unpublished presentation for the Consultation of Nature and Mission of Mennonite Church. April 10-11, 1967, Pittsburgh, PA. Anabaptist Mennonite Biblical Seminary (AMBS) General Papers, Elkhart, IN.

"The Believers' Church in Mission: Systematic/Polemic Perspectives." Unpublished presentation at the Conference on the Concept of the Believer's Church, Louisville, KY, June 1967. Mennonite Historical Library, Goshen, IN.

"Concepts of Evangelism in Current Debate." Unpublished presentation at Associated Mennonite Biblical Seminaries, Goshen, IN, February 13, 1967. Mennonite Historical Library, Goshen, IN.

"Confessing Jesus in Mission." Unofficial English translation by Alle Hoekma of a Dutch article for the journal *Wereld en Zending* [*World and Mission*] 24 (1996). Available online in the John Howard Yoder Digital Library pilot project. [This is a significant piece, written near the end of Yoder's life. —Ed.]

"Creativity in Missionary Personnel Administration." Unpublished paper for the Overseas Personnel Committees Consultation, Mennonite Board of Missions and Charities, September 24, 1969. AMBS Library General Papers, Elkhart, IN.

"Explorations of the Issue of Evangelism in Contemporary Debate." Unpublished memorandum on Mennonite Board of Missions and Charities stationary, September 2, 1968. AMBS Library General Papers, Elkhart, IN.

"Friends Interested in Feminism and in Missions." Unpublished memorandum dated December 31, 1980. Available online in the John Howard Yoder Digital Library pilot project.

"The Homogeneous Unit Concept in Ethical Perspective." Unpublished paper for a consultation held in Pasadena, California, May 31–June 2, 1977.

Available online in the John Howard Yoder Digital Library pilot project.

"Outline Commentary on Matthew 28:16ff and Acts 1:8." Unpublished paper in AMBS Library General Papers, 1965.

"Power and Powerlessness in Mission." Audio address at the World Mission Institute, at Lutheran School of Theology at Chicago, 1982. Available online in the John Howard Yoder Digital Library pilot project.

"The Third World and Christian Mission." Unpublished paper presented at the Theological Conference of the International Federation of Free Evangelical Churches at North Park Seminary, Chicago, IL, September 3, 1971. Available online in the John Howard Yoder Digital Library pilot project.

"Understanding of Salvation in the Believers' Church Perspective." Address to seminar "Biblical Foundations for Evangelism," Associated Mennonite Biblical Seminaries, Elkhart, IN, January 1972. Available online in the John Howard Yoder Digital Library pilot project.

JOURNAL ARTICLES AND ESSAYS IN BOOKS

"Church Growth Issues in Theological Perspective." In *The Challenge of Church Growth: A Symposium*, edited by Wilbert R. Shenk, pp. 25-47. Elkhart, IN: Institute of Mennonite Studies, 1973.

"The Contemporary Evangelical Revival and the Peace Churches." In *Mission and the Peace Witness: The Gospel and Christian Discipleship*, edited by Robert L. Ramseyer, pp. 68-103. Scottdale, PA: Herald Press, 1979.

"Discerning the Kingdom of God in the Struggles of the World." *International Review of Mission* 68, no. 272 (1979): 366-72.

"Discipleship as a Missionary Strategy." In *Radical Christian Discipleship*, edited by John Nugent, Andy Alexis-Baker and Branson Parler, pp. 163-70. Harrisonburg, VA: Herald Press, 2012. First published in *The Christian Ministry*, January–March 1955, pp. 26-31.

"Evangelization Is the Test of Our Ethical Vocation." *International Review of Mission* 72, no. 288 (1983): 610.

"The Experiential Etiology of Evangelical Dualism." *Missiology: An International Review* 11, no. 4 (October 1983): 449-59.

"Glory in a Tent." In *He Came Preaching Peace*, pp. 69-88. Scottdale, PA, and Waterloo, ON: Herald Press, 2004. First published 1985.

"Peace as Proclamation." In *Radical Christian Discipleship*, edited by John Nugent, Andy Alexis-Baker and Branson Parler, pp. 157-62. Harrisonburg, VA: Herald Press, 2012.

"Reformation and Missions: A Literature Survey." In *Anabaptism and Mission*, pp. 40-50. Scottdale, PA, and Waterloo, ON: Herald Press, 1984.

"The Social Shape of the Gospel." In *Exploring Church Growth*, edited by Wilbert R. Shenk, pp. 277-84. Grand Rapids: Eerdmans, 1983.

Books and Pamphlets Containing Related Material

Body Politics: Five Practices of the Christian Community Before the Watching World. Scottdale, PA: Herald Press, 2001.

The Ecumenical Movement and the Faithful Church. Scottdale, PA: Mennonite Publishing House, 1958. Republished in *Radical Ecumenicity*, edited by John Nugent, 2010.

The Jewish-Christian Schism Revisited. Edited by Michael Cartwright and Peter Ochs. Grand Rapids: Eerdmans, 2003.

The Royal Priesthood. Edited by Michael G. Cartwright. Grand Rapids: Eerdmans, 1994. This collection of essays and presentations drew on Yoder's work from 1959–1983. Essays of particular relevance include:

    "The Disavowal of Constantine: An Alternative Perspective on Interfaith Dialogue," pp. 242-61.

    "The Imperative of Christian Unity," pp. 289-99.

    A series of early essays: "The Otherness of the Church," "A People in the World," "Let the Church Be the Church," "Christ, the Light of the World" and "Christ, the Hope of the World," pp. 53-101 and 168-218.

Subject Index

Abraham
   costly pilgrimage of, 223-24
   faith of, 57
   God's calling to, 49
   Israel's identity built around, 52
   as layman, 247
   as prototypical believer, 129
   relevance for mission, 223-24
acculturation, 393, 397
African Indigenous Churches (AICs), 224-26
Algeria, 320
Anabaptist
   attitudes toward churches that formerly
      persecuted them, 190
   first Protestant missionaries, 157
   fundamental correction to Christendom,
      180
   genuine conversion, 162
   H. Richard Niebuhr's characterization of,
      157-59
   infant baptism, 76
   nationalism, 155
   separated church from world, 252
   twin temptations of, 179
   type of free church, 148
   See also free church
apologetics, 41, 339, 356, 365-66, 393
apostasy
   denies mission, 191
   is historical, 189-90
   is local and temporal, 191
   means being fundamentally unfaithful,
      186-87
   Radical Reformation view of, 358-60
   says whether a church is usable in
      mission, 191-92
apostle, 65, 236, 240, 358-59
Athens, 139-42
atonement, 72-74
Augustine, 182
Bangkok, 299-300, 302-4, 306
baptism
   church membership and, 39, 149
   doesn't celebrate childbirth, 358-59
   group decision, 260-62
   infant, 46, 63, 76, 201
   is a commitment to process, 256-57
   requires a decision, 259-60, 262

believers church, 148. *See also* free church
Benedictines, 330-32
biblical realism, 266, 355, 370-73
binding and loosing, 236-37
Buddhism, 359, 366, 368
catechism, 35, 39, 41-42, 195, 218
Catholicism, 151, 268, 317-18, 333, 340-41,
   349-50, 359. *See also* Benedictines;
   Toumliline, Morocco
centripetal mission, 54, 63, 67, 84, 118. *See also*
   ingathering
Christendom
   Anabaptists can recreate, 253-54
   apostasy of, 177-78
   assumptions that do not apply in mission,
      293-94
   compared to free church, 149-54
   defined, 145-47
   Magisterial Reformation hardens, 178-79
   Pietism and, 208
   Radical Reformation critique of, 208,
      251-52
   responses to not the same as faith or
      rejection, 376
   sheds light on gospel, 219
Christian uniqueness, 357-58
Christian World Mission, 145, 386
church
   ambivalent status of new congregations,
      173-74
   discipline, 206-8, 261
   enclave mentality, 284-85
   esse, bene esse, plene esse, 183-84
   expansion, 403-7
   growth, 221, 237, 254-57, 263-64, 323-25
   marks of, 182-89, 191-92. *See also notae
      ecclesiae*
   membership, 149, 260
   minority status, 218-19
   as mission, 88-89, 115-18, 124-25
   model community, 296-97
   mutual recognition, 188
   new song in Revelation, 123-24
   no salvation outside of the, 340-41, 357
   North American, 154-56
   "not church," 186
   place in the world, 136
   prior to individuals, 105

in Radical Reformation, 159-60
relation to the state, 46-47, 151-56, 159-60, 176, 252
structure in mission, 194-96
unfaithfulness of, 308
unity, 202-6, 208
war and, 159
clergy, 229, 241
colonialism, 145, 168-69, 180-81, 238-39, 265-66
conciliar movement, 175, 204-6
conquest, 53n7
Constantinianism, 177-78, 384-85
conversion
individual, 156, 252, 255-56
must be localized, 262-63
no models for, 110
not manipulated, 108-9
Paul's, 91-93, 97-105
Pietism and, 37-38
theologians must have, 166-67
Cornelius, 77-78, 85-87, 96
covenant, 57
culture, 45-46, 157-59, 211-27
decision, 259-63
denominational identity
ethnic markers, 203
foreign church's, 197-98
hinder missions, 203
missions can create a new, 201
Pietist acceptance of, 196
using marks of the church, 187
world confessionalism assumes, 198-99
World Council of Churches and, 205
devolution, 195-96
Diaspora, 58, 113, 117, 125
disciples' church, 148. See also free church
dispensationalism, 269-70
Division of World Mission and Evangelism, 299
Donatists, 182
dualism, 267-69
ecumenical movement, 146, 185-86, 188, 193, 203-5, 426
Elijah and Elisha, 64-65, 71
empire, 151, 168, 265-66, 280-81
end times, 127
evangelism, 109-10. See also migration evangelism
evangelist, 236, 240
evolution, 271-72
finality of Christ, 362-63, 376, 379, 384

foreign missions, 42-43, 76-77, 114, 178, 198, 229, 399, 402, 419, 423
foreignness, 211-12, 217-18, 238, 244-45, 248, 260, 281, 315-16
free church
creates pluralism, 213-14, 261
critiques of mission of, 252-56
is not individualistic, 259
model is biblical and normative, 176-77
recognizes church plants more easily, 208-9
terminology, 146-47
See also Anabaptist
functional equivalents, 221, 263, 361
Gentiles in Jewish history, 107-8
God
"at work in the world," 266-67
in nature, 60-61
nature of, 130-31, 136
sovereignty of, 57, 124
gospel, essentials of, 214-17
Great Commission, 75-80, 113-14, 119, 237
group decisions, 254, 257-58, 261
Hellenist Jewish Christians, 81-86
heresy, 191. See also apostasy
Hinduism, 144, 348-50, 357, 370, 372
historical faith, 55
holy pagans, 55
Holy Spirit
impetus for mission, 77-78, 80, 83-84, 87-89, 209-10
leads response to gospel, 332
Niebuhrian view of, 135-38
trusting for order, 209
universally present, 348-49
work of the, 137-38
See also Trinity
homogeneous cultural unit, 255, 263
horizontal withdrawal, 242
host culture, 213, 373-74
house churches, 283-84
idolatry, 50, 56, 140-42, 215-16, 222, 363
incarnation, 131-44, 285-86, 315-16
indigenous
becoming, 196, 199, 216, 381
culture, 212-13, 217
individualism, 258-59, 262
ingathering, 74, 78, 125-26, 345. See also centripetal mission
integration, 243
intentional accommodation, 220-27
International Missionary Council (IMC),

47-48, 133, 204
intertestamental missions, 58-59
Irenaeus, 342-43
Jesus, name of, 218
John the Baptist, 63
Jonah, 54, 67
kingdom of God, 282-85
language, 120-22, 297-98
law, 94
Laymen's Report, 369-70, 372
lifestyle as witness, 117-18
liturgy, 41
Logos, 120, 342
love of Christ, 98-100
Lutheran theology, 162, 165
Lystra, 111-14, 139
mass media, 312-14
Melchizedek, 55, 121
Mennonite silent presence, 335-37
message and medium, 110-11
migration evangelism, 113-14, 156, 237-39, 263,
336, 404-6, 409-13, 417-18, 420
ministry
missionary is first example of, 246
multiplicity of, 228-32, 234-36
no missionary ministry, 126
universality of, 241
mission
affirming and critiquing culture, 213-20
Christendom and, 152-53, 177-78
Christocentric, 138-42
church-centeredness, 133
denominational competition and, 203-4
free church, 152-53
nature of God and, 129-44
Pietism and, 37
prior to theology, 96-97
salvation and, 92
as sign of the kingdom, 283-84
societies and, 37
theocentric, 138-42
Trinity and, 129-44
See also foreign missions
mission agencies, 195-96, 200-220, 233
mission societies, 172, 200-201, 241
missionary marks of the church, 187-89
missionary orders, 151, 237
missionary personnel, 282, 320, 402, 413
church membership and, 234
does not represent reconciliation, 234
economic support, 234, 249-50, 402-3
as minister, 240

as model, 246-50
no biblical, 235-37
outreach and, 202
presupposes world unity, 273
professional, 201, 233-35
role in local church, 199-200
self-supporting laypeople, 232-33
specialized, 197, 203, 234, 402
status, 197, 241-44
violence and, 310-11
monogamy, 225-27. *See also* polygamy
monotheism, 51
Muhammad, 143-44, 382
mutual recognition, 209
mystery, 93
National Council of Churches, 133
nonconformity, 116
nonethnic Jews, 52-53
nonresistance, 46-47, 380, 392
nonviolence, 359, 392, 394
notae ecclesiae, 182-89. *See also* church, marks
of
ontocracy, 274
ordination, 194
pagans, 203, 216, 318, 363-65, 383, 387-88, 398
peace, 33, 47, 50-51, 54, 62, 71, 77, 126, 303, 345,
355, 387, 425
Pentecost, 73, 80-81, 86, 98-99
people's church, 147. *See also* Christendom
personal decision, 46, 208, 257, 299, 301
personal salvation, 298-307
persuasion, 98, 109-10
Pietism
active in the world, 174-75
church model, 156-57
conversion and, 37-38
denominational identity and, 196
irresponsible, 290
laity and, 231-32
moralism and, 38, 169-70
view of war, 175
piety, personal, 162-63, 170-71, 208
polemics, 41-42, 50, 174-75, 267
polygamy, 220n1, 225-27, 353
post-Christian faiths, 380-83
prayer, 314
presence, 315-20
primitivism, 178
principalities and powers, 95, 128, 222-24,
383-84
proclamation, 109-10, 126-28, 282-83, 323, 328
professional missionary, 232-34

progress, 270-71, 277-79, 287
providence, 57, 135, 274, 286
provincialism, 219
Radical Reformation. *See* Anabaptist
rapid social change, 291-92
reconciliation, 95, 191
relevance, 222-27
religion
    category of, 368
    Christianity as, 363-65
    critique of, 354-57
    encounter between different religions,
        349-50, 369-70
    as preparation for the gospel, 367-68
religious experience, 103, 166-67, 170, 296, 371
renewal movements, 161, 165, 258, 380, 382
renunciation, 105-7, 110, 317, 330
responsible society, 289-92, 295-97
sacraments, 317-18
secularization, 270-72, 274-79, 286-88
selective reception, 366
sending of the Twelve, 65-66
service, 164, 286, 325-27
social ethics, 174, 193, 253, 297
social gospel, 272
Somalia, 320-21
soul, 350-51
state church, 147. *See also* Christendom
Stephen, 82-84, 95
suffering, 105, 115-16
suffering servant, 51, 62, 69-71

synagogues, 363-64, 392-94, 404
syncretism, 223, 228, 369-70, 380-81, 398
temple cleansing, 67
theism, 135, 138-42
theocracy, 176, 268, 271
theologians, 36-39, 153
theology, 35-36, 39, 41-42
Toumliline, Morocco, 330-32
translation, 220
Trinity, 131-38, 143-44, 220
triumphalism, 277-78
universalism, 38, 341-47
unknown god, 139-42
vocation, 230-31, 235, 327
voluntarism, 219-20
WCC Commission on World Mission and
    Evangelism, 48
Wheaton Declaration, 341-42
Willingen (1952), 47, 133, 282
withdrawal and return, 242
withdrawal upwards, 242
withdrawal without return, 243
world confessionalism, 196, 198-99
world history, 272-81
World Mission and Evangelism, 266, 299
worldview
    converted, 97
    irrational religious, 276
    new, 99, 101
Zionism, 396

Name Index

Allen, Roland, 207-9, 250
Augustine of Canterbury, 220-21
Bainton, Roland, 271
Barth, Karl, 343, 345, 354
ben Zakkai, Johanan, 394
Berkhof, Hendrikus, 383-84
Beyerhaus, Peter, 300
Blauw, Johannes, 54, 72-73, 124
Bonhoeffer, Dietrich, 354-55, 390
Buttrick, George, 360
Caird, George, 65
Carey, William, 76, 124, 203-4
Congar, Yves, 229
Cullman, Oscar, 68
Cyprian of Carthage, 340
Darby, John Nelson, 389
Denck, Hans, 343
Ellul, Jacques, 333-34
Forsyth, Peter Taylor, 129-30
Gandhi, 370
Gill, Theodore, 133-34
Gregory (pope), 220-21
Hocking, William Ernest, 369
Hoekendijk, Johannes, 36-37, 282-87
Irenaeus, 342-43
Jeremias, Joachim, 64
Kraemer, Hendrik, 229-30, 370-73

Lindsell, Harold, 304-7
Luther, Martin, 151
McGavran, Donald, 207, 254-55
Melanchthon, Philipp, 154
Moltmann, Jürgen, 303-4
Neil, Stephen, 188
Newbigin, Lesslie, 184
Niebuhr, H. Richard, 134, 136, 157-59
Niebuhr, Reinhold, 295, 389
Rahner, Karl, 361
Rauschenbusch, Walter, 272
Richardson, Alan, 66
Roels, Edward, 103
Rowley, Harold, 51, 54
Schweitzer, Albert, 66
Simons, Menno, 188-89
Smith, C. Stanley, 138, 141
Stowe, David, 299-300
't Hooft, Visser, 184
Taylor, Vincent, 66
Troeltsch, Ernst, 157
Van Leeuwen, Arendt, 267, 277
Warren, Max, 49, 280, 361
Weber, Max, 148
Webster, Douglas, 235
Zwingli, Ulrich, 153

Scripture Index

Genesis
1–11, *57*
2:24, *227*
14:17-24, *55*

Exodus
12:38, *52*
18, *55*

Numbers
11:4-6, *53*
22–24, *58*
23:8-9, *58*

Nehemiah
13:3, *52*

Psalms
46, *50*
67:3-4, *51*

Isaiah
2:1-4, *50, 54,*
    345
10, *57*
18:7, *50*
42:1-4, *51, 62,*
    69-70
42:6, *93*
45, *57*
49, *51, 62, 69*
49:6, *72, 79*
50:4-9, *51*
52:13–53:12, *51-52*
53:11, *73*
56:7, *67*
61:2, *64*
62:11, *70*

Jeremiah
3:17, *50*
16:19, *50*
42:11-12, *57*

Ezekiel
28:25-26, *50*

Micah
4:1-4, *50, 54,*
    345

Zechariah
8:20-23, *50*
9:9, *70*

Malachi
1:11-12, *55*

Matthew
8:11-12, *67*
10:5-6, *65, 69*
10:14, *65*
12:15, *70*
12:18-21, *70*
15:21-28, *67*
15:24, *65*
21:5, *70*
24:3-14, *68-69*
24:13-14, *127*
24:14, *270*
25, *325*
28:18-20, *74,*
    76-77, 119

Mark
1:8, *78*
6:6-13, *65*
6:11, *65*
7:25-30, *67*
10:42-45, *70-71*
11:17, *67*

Luke
1–2, *62*
2:29-32, *62*
2:32, *93*
2:34, *62*
4:14-30, *64*
4:24-27, *71*
4:25-27, *64-65*
9:1-6, *65*
9:5, *65*
10:10-11, *65*
11:29-32, *67*
13:29, *67*
22:25-27, *329*
24:46-49, *77*

John
1:11, *64*
1:19, *118*
3:16, *119*
4:1-3, *66*
4:35-38, *68*
10:16, *67, 120*
11:50, *68*
11:52, *68*
12:20-23, *68*
16:7-8, *119*
17:9, *74*
17:14, *74*
17:20, *74*
17:20-26, *120*
17:21, *119*
17:22-23, *74*
20:21-23, *77,*
    119-20
20:31, *118*
21:24, *118-19*

Acts
1:8, *77, 84*
2, *80-81*
2:16-21, *79*
2:39, *79*
3:25, *79*
6, *81-83*
6:7, *80-81*
6:9, *82*
6–7, *73*
7, *82*
7–11, *83-86*
7:49, *84*
7:60, *83*
8:1-3, *84*
9:15, *92*
10–11, *85*
10:42-43, *78-79*
11:15-18, *78*
11:19-21, *85*
11:25-27, *85*
13:44-47, *72, 79*
13:47, *93*
14:7, *112*
14:8-10, *112*
14:15-17, *112*
15, *77, 85-87*
15:5, *81, 85*
15:7-11, *96*
17:9, *74*
17:14, *74*

17:15-34, *59-60*
17:16-34, *139-42*
17:20, *74*
17:22-24, *74*
18:5-6, *92-93*
22:15-17, *92*
26:4-5, *91*
28:24-28, *93*

Romans
1:5, *93*
2:12-16, *347*
9–11, *72*
11:1, *91*
11:13, *93*
12, *126, 231, 235*
15:25-26, *107*

1 Corinthians
8, *215-16*
9:3-12, *107*
9:20-22, *106*
9:27, *106-7*
12, *126, 231, 235*
14:18, *104-5*
16:1-4, *107*

2 Corinthians
3:4-6, *322*
4:1-5, *322-23*
5:11-15, *97-100*
5:16, *97, 100-102*
5:17, *101, 108*
5:18-21, *102*
8–9, *107*
10:14-16, *93*
12:2, *105*

Galatians
1:13-14, *91*
1:15-16, *93*
2:7, *85*
2:10, *107*
2:11-14, *85*

Ephesians
1:8-10, *343*
2–3, *108, 111, 203*
2:10, *94*
2:14-15, *94*

3:1, *93*
3:1-12, *93*
3:3, *94*
3:10, *128*
4, *231, 235*
4:1, *126*
4:2-3, *126*
4:13, *126*

Philippians
1:12-18, *104*
3:4-5, *91*

Colossians
1:23, *93*
1:26, *93*

2 Timothy
4:5, *236*

Hebrews
1:1-2, *315*
6:4, *121*
12:17, *121*
12:22-23, *122*

1 Peter
1:1, *117*
2:9-10, *115-18*
2:11-12, *118*
2:15, *117*
3:12, *270*
3:13-18, *116*
3:15, *117*

2 Peter
3:11-12, *127*

1 John
1:1-2, *119*
2:15, *119*
5:19, *119*

Revelation
4:8, *122*
4:9-11, *122-23*
5:3-5, *123*
5:8-9, *123*
5:12, *124*